Finding Answers in
Science and Technology

Finding Answers in Science and Technology

Alice Lefler Primack

VNR VAN NOSTRAND REINHOLD COMPANY
NEW YORK   CINCINNATI   TORONTO   LONDON   MELBOURNE

Manufactured in the United States of America

Published by Van Nostrand Reinhold Company Inc.
135 West 50th Street
New York, New York 10020

Van Nostrand Reinhold Company Limited
Molly Millars Lane
Wokingham, Berkshire RG11 2PY, England

Van Nostrand Reinhold
480 Latrobe Street
Melbourne, Victoria 3000, Australia

Macmillan of Canada
Division of Gage Publishing Limited
164 Commander Boulevard
Agincourt, Ontario M1S 3C7, Canada

15 14 13 12 11 10 9 8 7 6 5 4 3 2 1

Library of Congress Cataloging in Publication Data

Primack, Alice Lefler.
Finding answers in science and technology.

Includes index.
1. Science—Library resources—Handbooks, manuals,
etc. 2. Technology—Library resources—Handbooks,
manuals, etc. 3. Libraries—United States—Handbooks,
manuals, etc. I. Title.
Z7401.P86 1983   [Q158.5]   507   82-20082
ISBN 0-442-28227-3

To Bob, without whom I wouldn't have done it,
and to Eric, Mary-Anne, and Glenn, in spite of
whom I did it,
for all scientists and potential scientists—
we need you!

"All that mankind has done, thought, gained
or been—it is lying, as in magic preservation,
in the pages of books."

Thomas Carlyle
1795–1881

"The literature is a tool just as surely as is a
spectrograph or a microscope."

"A tool is as good as its user."

Winifred Sewell

Preface

This book is intended for use by "hobby" scientists, advanced high school, junior college, and undergraduate college students, and the teachers and librarians helping these users. It provides an introduction to the libraries and literature of science and how to find information, is a reference guide to specific titles, and could serve as a basic text for a course in scientific or technical literature, for science or library science students.

The first chapters deal with the different kinds of information available in science, where to find quick information, strategies for searching in depth, and information on the use of libraries and on general reference works in science. There follow separate chapters for each area covered, for example, astronomy, chemistry, and engineering. A list of large scientific and technical libraries in the United States completes the book. This is not a bibliography, but rather the informal essay form is designed to encourage the reader to read clear through, or at least through chapters of interest, to become familiar with what information is available, even if that information is not immediately wanted.

Specific materials included are those that are appropriate for the users mentioned above, are generally current and in print, and are available to the public. Emphasis is on U.S. materials. Many items included are geared toward or may be used by students, but only those also suitable for non-student users have been included. Inclusion of how-to books has been severely limited. It is generally easy to find those books in a library or bookstore. Also books expressing a particular point of view have been largely eliminated. Special attention has been given to "hobby" areas, such as plants and gardening, bird watching, stargazing, and electronics.

The book is arranged basically by the Library of Congress classification categories for ease in browsing and finding sources in most scientific libraries. Dewey Decimal Classification numbers are also mentioned, since this is the other most common system of classifying books in U.S. libraries. Subject headings that would be useful in searching in any library or bibliography or reference list are given.

The book assumes some knowledge of the subject being dealt with as to basic terminology. If the user does not have this knowledge, the dictionaries and encyclopedias listed in each subject section will provide it.

This book will help you to answer the questions:

What is this subject all about?
What kinds of information are available?
What are the facts in this subject?
What research led to and backs up these facts or these findings?
What is happening currently in this subject?

Suppose you have been a backyard bird watcher for years and now you want to learn the names of those birds, the different sounds they make and how they make them, why different birds appear at different seasons, how to attract more birds, and other types of information that will come up or occur to you as you begin to find out answers to these questions. Or suppose you are interested in adding an alternative form of energy, such as solar, to your home. Instead of relying on salesmen and sales brochures, you want to get background facts for yourself and check what the current research has found. This book will provide you with alternative strategies for finding these answers, descriptions and bibliographic information for specific books and other materials to consult, and sources for these materials.

First read the chapter on search strategies to get ideas on how to find the answers you want. Then use the chapter on general science sources and then specific chapters if you want more information. For most categories, sources described in the subject chapters will supplement the more general sources, so that the general sources should be used first and then the more specific. In some categories, for example, lists of theses, no additional sources will be given in the subject chapters.

If you want the answer to a very specific question, such as a word meaning, consult this guide or a librarian for a specific quick reference tool. Such tools are described in a special section of the chapter on general science and each subject chapter.

Suppose you are a student just entering a scientific field, or not in a scientific field but taking some courses in science. The importance of knowing the literature available and how to use it cannot be stressed too heavily; in fact, such knowledge can make the difference between success and failure in your studies and future work. In this case the most helpful approach is to read the book clear through, skimming those areas you are not interested in now.

The appendix, listing large scientific and technical library collections in the United States, will give you ideas of where you might go to get materials or from where they might be borrowed through your local library.

A couple of notes on the use of the book: (1) In the arrangement of information, subjects were given preference over types of materials. Thus general bibliographies will be described under the heading bibliographies within any given chapter, but bibliographies of very specific topics will be included with other literature on that topic. (2) Many materials are listed as open entries; that is, the date of the first volume or edition is given followed by a dash and a space. These are items that are published over and over, even if irregularly, and the chances are good that a new edition will be published during the useful lifetime of this book. For these items you would almost invariably want to use the most recent volume or edition published.

The most important ingredient of finding answers in science and technology is to let your childlike curiosity loose to search, follow leads, double back. This book will help you to find your answers smoothly, efficiently, and completely. Have fun!

Alice Lefler Primack

Acknowledgments

Many people have helped with this book directly or indirectly, and to all of them I wish to say thank you. In particular I want to mention those who helped with references for particular areas or read my roughly completed chapters and made suggestions in their various areas of expertise: Helenjane Armstrong, Anita Battiste, Tex Browning, Carol Drum, Heinrich Eichhorn, Barry Hartigan, Tony Harvell, Peggy Hsu, Ann King, and Roger Krumm.

Thanks go also to Celia Schoeneman, who typed most of the manuscript.

And a special thank-you to my parents, who provided the background that enabled me to do this sort of thing, and to my family, who ate lots of McDonald's the last month.

Contents

Finding Answers in Science and Technology

1
Finding the Answers

SEARCH STRATEGY

When you want to find information, the information desired is generally one of two types: the answer to a very specific question, for example, a word meaning, or a broader type of information, for example, how solar energy works and how it could be used in your home. When you want the answer to a very specific question, you may have the tools to find the answer at hand, perhaps a dictionary, almanac, or handbook. Or you could consult this guide or a librarian to learn of an appropriate quick reference tool. These materials are described later in this chapter and in each subject chapter. The answer to this kind of question can usually be found in just a few minutes using the right tools.

Finding answers to a broader type of question involves more steps. If starting from scratch on a question in science or technology, what you generally want to find out is:

What is this subject all about?
What kinds of information are available?
What are the facts in this subject?
What research led to and backs up these findings or this knowledge?
What is happening currently in this subject?

You begin at the beginning, and each question follows the one before in logical sequence. Now you may already know the answers to some of these questions, and so enter the sequence at that point. And you may find out all you care to know before you finish the sequence and so stop there. Most of this book is designed to help you find the answers to these questions.

Using a definite strategy for finding scientific and technical information makes finding the information easier and much more accurate. Strategy discussed in this book is oriented toward using a library, or libraries, as the base of your search. Briefly, the steps are as follows:

Find out: What is this subject all about?

1. Familiarize yourself with the subject in general by reading introductory books and encyclopedias.
2. Decide whether or not you want to search for further information yourself. If not, choose an alternative. If so, proceed to step 3.
3. Define your goals.
4. Ask a reference librarian for help.

Find out: What kinds of information are available?

5. Look in the card catalog.
6. Use bibliographic materials: guides to the literature, bibliographies, catalogs, reviews of the literature, and indexing and abstracting services.

Find out: What are the facts in this subject?

7. Use secondary literature materials: books, periodicals that interpret and comment on developments, and reviews of progress.

Find out: What research led to and backs up these findings or this knowledge?

8. Use primary literature materials: research reports, conference proceedings, periodicals reporting original work, patents, standards, and theses and dissertations.

Find out: What is happening currently in this subject?

9. If you wish to keep up with current developments, use a selective dissemination of information (SDI) service or current awareness tools, read current journals, and attend conferences.

It is important to follow these steps in an orderly fashion, and to keep accurate records of what you have done. If you, say, jump into using an indexing and abstracting service right away, you may do more work than is needed, as some or all of the information may have been collected into a readily available book. Also, if you haven't listed subject terms, you may search willy-nilly through several indexes under one term, only to find that that does not produce the answer and you have to go back to those sources again and again to search under other terms.

These steps will be discussed here in more detail. Books or other materials mentioned, unless used just as an example, will be described in detail in the chapters that follow, and these descriptions may be found by consulting the index of this book. In each chapter, the literature sources described will generally follow the order in which they would be used in the searching procedure discussed in this chapter.

WHAT IS THIS SUBJECT ALL ABOUT?

The first step is to familiarize yourself with the subject in general by reading in an encyclopedia. Start with a general one, such as the *World Book Encyclopedia* (Chicago, Field, 1917–   ) in its latest edition, and then proceed to more specialized encyclopedias, such as the *McGraw-Hill Encyclopedia of Science and Technology*. You might also read an introductory book you know of, or that you find by browsing in a library or bookstore, or that someone tells you of. Sometimes several articles on a subject are collected in one volume providing an introduction to the field with several different approaches of different authors.

You now need to decide whether or not you want to search for further information yourself. If not, you may wish to choose an alternative. You might ask someone. A recent study of physicists in the United States found that the time used in personal communication for information was more than twice that used for all other ways of obtaining information. President Woodrow Wilson is reported to have said, "I would never read a book if it were possible to talk half an hour with the man who wrote it." The problem is that the "man who wrote the book" is seldom available to us. Also most people have accurate up-to-date information only in very narrow areas. Information obtained this way may be incomplete or inaccurate. You might take a course in a school, college, or community education program. There are information services: those sponsored by the U.S. government are usually free of charge, some manufacturers or industrial research laboratories will provide information, and there are commercial information sources.

The Library of Congress has prepared a guide entitled *Science Information Resources* (New York, Science Associates/International, 1980). The second volume of this two-volume set is on information services. There are guides to information available from organizations, government agencies, and information services.

Research Centers Directory (Detroit, Mich., Gale, 1, 1960–   ) is issued periodically, with the 7th edition published in 1982. This directory of nonprofit and university-related organizations is arranged in sixteen broad subject areas, for example, engineering and technology, with centers listed alphabetically within each subject section. There are indexes by subject, institution, and research center name. The address and the phone number of each center are given, as well as information on research activities and fields of the center, publications, and services. Many of these centers will provide information for the public, and many publish informative pamphlets. This volume is kept up to date by *New Research Centers,* issued between editions. *Industrial Research Laboratories of the United States* (New York, Bowker, 1, 1960–   ) is issued irregularly, the 17th edition in 1982. Arrangement is alphabetical by the name of the corporation, with indexes by place (state and city), staff names, and subjects of research activities. The address of the laboratory is given, and other information includes the laboratory's chief research activities.

The National Referral Center in the Library of Congress has a subject-indexed file of organizations that are information resources. These resources include professional societies, university research places, federal and state agencies, industrial research laboratories, museums, and individual subject experts, as well as libraries and indexing and abstracting services. The center refers patrons to sources of information. Anyone may write or call the National Referral Center, Library of Congress, Washington, D.C. 20540; phone (202) 287–5670. Their services are free of charge.

The *Directory of Fee-Based Information Services* by Kelly Warnken (Woodstock, N.Y., Information Alternative, 1978) lists commercial information services. Arrangement is alphabetical by states in the United States, with a separate section for Canada, and then alphabetical by names of services within each state. For each service, address, phone number, and key individuals are listed, together with hours, rates, services offered, and areas of specialization. Indexing is by names of people or institutions mentioned in the directory, and subjects covered.

A network of fee-based information centers that provide services at a nominal fee for people working in business, industry, and government is provided by the United States National Aeronautics and Space Administration (NASA). There are nine such centers across the United States, each serving a geographical area. Additional staff members are located in many cities, so that a user can talk directly with one of these field representatives. If you come to them with a question, the centers will do a computerized literature search on your topic and provide you with abstracts or the documents themselves. They can also provide a current awareness service to keep you knowledgeable in a certain area. These centers are listed in the appendix of this book.

If you decide you do want to search for the information yourself, the next step is to define your goals. Do you want all the information there is on the subject or just enough to answer your question, or a little more? Of course, any of these decisions can change at any time. Do you want recent information? historical information? both? What time frame do you have: when do you need results? how much time are you willing to spend searching? Are you willing to spend some money, for example, to buy books, pay for photocopies of articles through interlibrary loan, pay for a computerized literature search? Do you want to keep current in the subject in the future?

It is helpful to jot down subject headings and terms to be searched. Start with subject headings as mentioned throughout this book. As you search, note any new terms not on the list. In making and using this list of subject terms, remember to think of synonyms. Sometimes the same subject will be listed under different synonymous terms in different bibliographies and indexes. Also be careful about specificity of terms. If you are finding articles too broad, be more specific; if you are finding little or nothing, perhaps you need a broader term. Usage of terms changes over the years, so keep alert and always be adding to or refining your list of possible subject terms.

Next ask a reference librarian to help you. You'll probably begin with the library most convenient to you, but you may want to get to a large university or other large or specialized library as listed in the appendix of this book or in a directory of libraries.

Three directories of libraries are helpful here, each issued periodically, and each covering libraries in the United States and Canada. *Subject Collections* by Lee Ash (New York, Bowker, 1, 1958–) is issued every few years as a guide to special collections and subject emphases in academic, public, and special libraries. Arrangement is alphabetical by the topic of the collection and then by state and city in which the collection is located. Information given for each library is address of the library and information about the collection, including number of volumes, publications if any, and notes on scope and type of materials. Some subject heads are very specific, for example, energy economics; some general, for example, engineering.

The *Directory of Special Libraries and Information Centers* (Detroit, Mich., Gale, 1, 1963–) is in two sections to provide approach by name of library or geographic location. The first section is arranged alphabetically by name of U.S. and Canadian libraries. Information given includes address and phone number, and information on the collection, such as subjects covered and number of volumes. Appendixes list networks and consortia, libraries for the blind and physically handicapped, patent depository libraries, and federal information centers. The second section is a geographic index that is alphabetical by state and city and tells the address of the library. A supplement called *New Special Libraries* keeps the list up to date between editions.

The *Subject Directory of Special Libraries and Information Centers* (Detroit, Mich., Gale, 1, 1963–) provides subject access to the libraries listed in the above *Directory of Special Libraries and Information Centers.* It is divided into several volumes by subject area, and each subject volume is subdivided by subject, then arranged alphabetically by names of the libraries. The sections of the science and technology volume include agriculture libraries, energy libraries, environment/conservation libraries, and general science and technology libraries. The listing for each library includes address and phone, number of volumes and periodical subscriptions, services, and other brief information.

WHAT KINDS OF INFORMATION ARE AVAILABLE?

Perhaps people you have talked with have suggested sources in the literature that you will want to look up now. Look in the card catalog at the library under the subject terms you have listed to find books on the subject. If these terms do not appear in the catalog or do not seem sufficient, check the Library of Congress list, *Subject Headings* (Washington, D.C., U.S. Library of Congress, 9th edition 1980), to find the correct subject headings. This two-volume set lists all subject headings in use by the Library of Congress, and gives cross-references from other terms and lists of related subject headings. If the library you are using does not use Library of Congress subject headings, the librarian will tell you where to find a similar listing for the kind of subject headings used in that library.

According to the Information Industries Association, there are about 500,000 books published per year internationally, plus 250,000 technical reports, 200,000 dissertations, and 250,000 periodicals. This gives you some idea of the huge store of information waiting for your use, and also suggests that some effort will be needed to sort through it to find what you want. The figures above include materials on all subjects.

Written records are especially important in the sciences. A study by the Association of Special Libraries and Information Bureaus (ASLIB) in Great Britain notes that "when we come to look at the sources from which chemists seek data, it is notable that published sources are more important than personal ones—to a much greater extent than is usually found in information use surveys."

Luckily there are many sources to help you sort through the literature. You will want to use as many of them as available and appropriate. As you do, keep a careful list of the sources used. Make lists of items you want to find. Follow leads.

Many subjects have guides to the literature written about them, as this book you are reading is a guide to the literature of science and technology. A guide to the literature is an overview of the kinds of printed materials there are on that subject, and lists some specific books and other materials. It usually includes information on library use in general, how to get started finding information, and special features of reference works in the field and how to make best use of them. It is a good idea to leaf through such a guide first to see what kinds of information are available, and then to read through it or read and use sections specific to the information you are looking for.

Bibliographies are lists of printed materials. A bibliography may list all kinds of materials on a subject: books, periodical articles, reports, and so forth. Strictly speaking, indexing and abstracting services for periodical articles are bibliographies, as are lists of dissertations, for example, *Dissertation Abstracts International,* and patents, for example, *U.S. Patent Gazette.* A bibliography may be a list of new books, for example, *New Technical Books* put out by the New York Public Library. Or it may be a basic list such as the *McGraw-Hill Basic Bibliography of Science and Technology,* or a reader's guide such as the *AAAS Science Book List.* It may be exhaustive, for example, *Books in Print.*

Catalogs of holdings of libraries are usually a reproduction in book form of the catalog cards of an excellent specialized library. These usually comprise several volumes, and may be in order by subject heading or alphabetical by author or title. These are useful in two ways: as a bibliography of most materials that are published in the specialization of the library, and as a list of what you could find or borrow at that library (but here you must keep in mind that although the list was correct as of a certain date, library holdings change).

Reviews of the literature are written in narrative form and usually discuss briefly the current developments in a subject, say in the past year, and mention books and periodical articles that report these developments.

Indexing and abstracting services are usually published as a separate publication, for example, *Applied Science and Technology Index,* but may be a feature in a regular journal, for example, *Journal of the Science of Food and Agriculture.* They are published periodically, and list references by subject. Most cover just periodical articles, but some also cover books, reports, theses, and proceedings. Some also provide an abstract of the material, telling very briefly what it is about and perhaps its conclusions or findings. The abstract may be descriptive, to enable the user to decide whether to obtain the article or publication, or it may inform the user by summarizing the article;

seldom does it evaluate the article. Sometimes the abstract is written by the author of the article; more often by information specialists. There are about 2,000 indexing and abstracting services worldwide for science and technology. Many of these indexes are now produced with the aid of computers, but most still use trained specialists to input subject headings. Key-word indexes may be produced mechanically, using, for example, each word in the title except articles as a subject heading. The indexes and abstracts are usually printed out in conventional form, but they may also be available on the computer. Some are available only on the computer; others may be in card form or microform. When searching these indexes, be sure to copy the entire citation. To locate a journal article you usually need the journal title, volume, date or issue number, and pages; the author and title of the article are helpful. If abbreviations are used, consult the list in the source you are using to see what the abbreviation means. Record the source, including page number where the citation was found in case you need to refer back to it. This is also helpful if your library is borrowing the item on interlibrary loan. Search under each of the subject terms you have prepared. You may also want to follow up leads provided by cross-references and "see also" references in the index. If you are using a computerized index, a list of terms, called a thesarus, is usually provided to help you choose the best subject terms for your search.

WHAT ARE THE FACTS IN THIS SUBJECT?

The bibliographic materials discussed above are sometimes referred to as tertiary literature, the literature used to find other literature. There are generally two types of literature to be found, sometimes called secondary literature and primary literature. Secondary literature is compiled from the primary literature sources. It includes books, periodicals that interpret and comment on developments, reviews of progress, and reference books such as encyclopedias, dictionaries, handbooks, and tables. Primary literature is new knowledge, and includes research reports, conference proceedings, periodicals reporting original work, patents, standards, theses and dissertations, and such nonpublished items as laboratory notebooks and personal correspondence.

The secondary literature sources generally answer our question

"What are the facts?" Books are of three types: a treatise attempts to cover a whole subject field; a monograph is on a narrowly defined topic; and a textbook aims to develop understanding rather than impart information at a precise level. A variation of textbooks is how-to-do-it books.

Periodicals have been found to be the most frequently used sources of information for scientists and technologists. Published weekly, monthly, quarterly, or some variation of these, periodicals may be called magazines, journals, serials, transactions, proceedings, or bulletins. Scientists may read general science journals, such as *Scientific American,* to keep up with general developments. Journals are also a medium for scientists to establish themselves as authorities in a subject area, and a way for scientists to let their findings be known. They may contain correspondence columns, book reviews, editorials, and society news. Periodicals may originate from learned or professional societies or academic bodies, for example, National Academy of Sciences *Proceedings* or American Mathematical Society *Bulletin;* from government agencies, for example, U.S. National Bureau of Standards *Journal of Research;* from independent research agencies, for example, *Battelle Technical Review;* or from commercial publishers, for example, *Popular Mechanics.* Periodicals are generally more up to date than books, but there are problems of too many periodicals and of the long lag time between submission of an article and its publication.

A special type of periodical publication is a review of progress in a subject. This is generally a critical summary of developments, and it may appear as one article in a regular journal or separately, often annually. Examples are *Advances in Nuclear Science and Technology, Annual Review of Physical Chemistry, Progress in Materials Science,* and *Viewpoints in Biology.*

Reference books, which are a form of secondary literature, will be discussed later as quick reference sources.

WHAT RESEARCH LED TO AND BACKS UP THESE FINDINGS OR THIS KNOWLEDGE?

After you have read about the subject in the secondary sources that report and interpret it, you may want to read the original information in the primary literature. Original research may be reported in journal articles, but some research results are not appropriate for this format, and are reported in research reports, conference proceedings, patents, standards, and theses.

The U.S. government produces much of the world's report literature. This is usually in the form of individual paper-bound booklets of a few to hundreds of pages. Most of these reports are also available in microform, usually microfiche. They report research, findings, and conclusions, with references. This is research that has been funded by the government and carried out in universities, laboratories, and research establishments all over the United States. These reports are available for use in depository and other collections scattered through the United States, and copies are also available for purchase.

Individual states in the United States, similarly, produce documents of research especially applicable to those states. Also most foreign governments publish research reports, as do international agencies such as the World Meteorological Organization, International Atomic Energy Agency, and Food and Agriculture Organization.

Many indexing and abstracting services include research reports, both government and nongovernment. The government reports are also listed in separate bibliographies or indexes usually published by the government of origin.

Conference proceedings consist of papers presented at meetings of learned societies, or in the case of working conferences of experts in a field the proceedings may be a transcript of discussions held at the meeting. This is often the first method of reporting new research, before any journal articles are written about it. These may be published separately in book form, either by the sponsoring organization or by a commercial publisher, or as part of a journal, for example, the *Annals of the New York Academy of Sciences.*

Patents are the official records of inventions, as registered by the country of origin. Some information in patents is not available elsewhere, as it may be that no article is published about a patented item. Many patents include a discussion of the theoretical basis of the invention. There are two parts to a patent: disclosure, which describes what has been discovered and why it is important, and claim, which tells what the inventor patents as his legal right. In the United States, patents are granted only to individuals. Some subject journals include notes of new patents. Patent information is especially important in the field of chemistry, and *Chemical Abstracts* indexes patents of all countries, using a special notation of "P" in its indexes to indicate a patent. Several other indexing and abstracting services include patents, but they are not identified as such in the index. Some indexing and abstracting services index patents only, for example, *Polymer Science and Technology Patents*. All U.S. patents are listed and briefly described and indexed in the United States Patent Office *Offical Gazette: Patents,* issued weekly with annual indexes. United Kingdom patents are listed in the United Kingdom Patent Office *Official Journal.*

Standards are issued by many different bodies in the United States, including government agencies, professional organizations, and technical societies. The standards set down the ideal characteristics or specifications of the materials or product, or how testing of new materials should be carried out for uniform results. Some U.S. agencies that put out standards are Underwriters' Laboratories, National Electrical Manufacturers Association, and American Society for Testing and Materials. These standards are either published separately as one or more pages or gathered together into books of standards. The American Society for Testing and Materials standards, for example, are published in approximately fifty volumes yearly, containing all of that society's standards, test methods, classifications, definitions, and practices currently in effect. According to the foreword, the American Society for Testing and Materials is a scientific and technical organization founded in 1898 to develop standards on "characteristics and performance of materials, products, systems, and services; and the preservation of related knowledge." Many standards from different sources are approved by the American National Standards Institute (ANSI) and then assigned an ANSI number and included in its collection of standards. The United States National Bureau of Standards is the other major organization involved with standards in the United States. It was established in 1901 with the purpose of strengthening and advancing science and technology in the United States and facilitating applications of science and technology for the public benefit. The bureau conducts research, and it provides the basis for the physical measurement system, provides scientific and technological services for industry and government, and promotes public safety through technical services. There are three laboratories where work is performed: National Measurement Laboratory, National Engineering Laboratory, and Institute for Computer Sciences and Technology. The bureau puts out several publications, including the *Journal of Research,* Section A physics and chemistry, Section B mathematics and mathematical physics, and Section C engineering and instrumentation. Other countries, of course, also have standards.

Theses and dissertations, which are usually required at universities for advanced degrees, are reports of the original research projects that were done to meet degree requirements. A thesis is the report required for the master's degree; a dissertation for the doctor of philosophy. In practice, both are often called theses. The thesis reports an original research project, with findings. An extensive bibliography is included. Theses are usually not published, but are typewritten and usually bound like a book, and are kept permanently at the university of origin. Information from theses is often published later in journals or books.

WHAT IS HAPPENING CURRENTLY IN THIS SUBJECT?

Current awareness services are a special form of indexing and abstracting services. These are usually published as a journal, monthly or even twice a month or weekly, listing articles in the latest issues of selected journals. Articles listed may be arranged in broad subject groups, for example, *Current Papers in Physics,* or by means of a key-word index of titles, for example, *Chemical Titles.* Some consist of complete tables of contents of selected journals, for example, *Current Contents.* Only brief bibliographic information is given so that you can locate the article. Many of these services include a list of authors' work affiliations and addresses, and you may also be able to order a photocopy of any article listed, for a fee. The main advantage of this type of service is its currency. Because there is no elaborate indexing, for example, by subject terms, and no abstracting, and because the number of journals covered is relatively small and carefully selected, there is little lag between publication of the journal and notice of articles from it in the current awareness services. Indeed the services may obtain advance copies of journals or at least of their contents lists, and be completely current or ahead of the journals.

Another way of keeping current is through a selective dissemination of information service. In this, the patron provides the service with an "information profile" describing in detail what information he wants, listing subject terms. As new information is published on these subjects, the service informs the patron of this fact. Some services provide bibliographic information only; some provide copies of the articles or reports. Many of these services are computerized. This service may be available through one's place of work or may be purchased.

Reading each issue of selected journals is another way to remain current. As noted earlier, some scientists regularly read a general science journal, such as *Scientific American, Science,* or the briefer *Science News,* to keep up with general developments in a wide range of scientific fields. Many journals have a special section mentioning or reviewing new books. For example, *Nature,* a journal published weekly, in the last issue of each month contains a section on recent scientific and technical books that lists more than one hundred new books. Careful choice of the journals to be read is important, and regular reading of the journal is the key to keeping current.

Attending conferences is another way of staying informed. New developments are discussed, and papers are read. Often this is the first reporting of original research.

FINDING ANSWERS TO VERY SPECIFIC QUESTIONS

The answers to very specific questions, for example, a word meaning, are best found in a quick reference tool such as a dictionary or encyclopedia, handbook, directory, or biographical source.

Everyone knows what a dictionary is like, but not everyone may know that there are special dictionaries for scientific terms, and even for just a specific scientific subject. An extensive scientific dictionary is the *McGraw-Hill Dictionary of Scientific and Technical Terms,* the 1974 edition of which contained definitions of an amazing total of 100,000 words. Arrangement of a dictionary is alphabetical by term to be defined, and information may be given on pronunciation, syllables, definition, foreign equivalents, word origin, and synonyms, perhaps with a diagram, graph, or table. Some dictionaries give meanings of symbols or of abbreviations and acronyms. Some give word equivalents in foreign languages for English words or in English for foreign words. Especially in botany, dictionaries may define by botanical description. An encyclopedia is also usually alphabetical by term, and encyclopedias and dictionaries often overlap in name and function. The purpose of an encyclopedia is to make available a whole body of knowledge in a concise and easily accessible form. The encyclopedia defines and explains. Some scientific encyclopedias are for general readers, for example, the multivolume *McGraw-Hill Encyclopedia of Science and Technology,* and some are very specialized for subject specialists, for example, the multivolume *Kirk-Othmer Encyclopedia of Chemical Technology.* Usually references or bibliographies are included with articles. Often articles are written by subject specialists, with the name of the specialist added at the end of the article; these are called signed articles. Tables, graphs, diagrams, and photographs are used extensively.

A handbook is a compilation of miscellaneous information in convenient form. It is almost always one volume, and gives straightforward factual information. Many handbooks are composed mostly or completely of tables, for example, the *CRC Handbook of Chemistry and Physics.* The handbook is usually organized in such a way that for some kinds of information you can just turn to the section you want. There is usually a detailed index.

Directories are basically lists of names and addresses arranged to meet specific needs, for example, alphabetical, by geographic region, or by subject. Trade or industrial directories may be lists of manufacturers or buyer's guides. *Thomas Register,* for example, is made up of several volumes, some of which are arranged alphabetically by product and list U.S. manufacturers arranged in a geographic order, whereas other volumes are arranged alphabetically by name of manufacturer and give address and what is manufactured. Directories of individual scientists may be by subject area, for example, *Who's Who in Engineering,* or membership directories of organizations, or a list of consultants. Directories of scientific and technical organizations may be alphabetical lists, or arranged by geographical location, or by purpose, for example, *Medical and Health Information Directory.* Information given is usually address and phone number and may include purpose or publications.

Biographical information on some scientists is easy to come by, but there is no published information about most scientists because most sources deal only with those who are renowned. Information on important figures is repeated over and over. There are some collections of longer biographies, for example, *Great Chemists* by E. Farber. Directories of society membership and such may be the only source of information on some scientists, and would generally give only address and work affiliation. Some biographical dictionaries give brief information about many scientists, for example, *American Men and Women of Science*. Journals sometimes have biographical notes about authors of articles in the journal, and may also have biographical articles. Obituaries are another source of information and may appear in a regular column in a scientific journal or as a special article, or may be located in a newspaper if you know the date of death and place where the person lived, or if he or she was sufficiently famous for widespread notice.

GETTING THE MATERIALS

One way of getting the materials you want is to purchase them. Books may be available in or through a bookstore, or you may order them directly from the publisher. Books currently in print will be listed in one of the listings such as *Books in Print*. Be sure to use a current edition. The price of the book will be given, and the address of the publisher. Scientific books are expensive, averaging $35 each in 1982.

Almost all materials are available from libraries. Library use is discussed below, followed by information about locating some specialized kinds of materials such as government documents.

LIBRARY USE

The first thing to do when you enter a library you haven't used before is to walk around to see how the library is organized. Where is the card catalog? Where is the reference desk? Where is the circulation desk? Where are the book stacks? Where are the journals? You may want to ask these locations at an information desk.

Visit the reference desk and tell the librarian what information you are looking for or what project you are working on. Ask for suggestions of how to get started.

The catalog is the key to the library collections. This catalog is usually made up of 3-inch by 5-inch cards and is called a card catalog. Some alternate forms are printed book catalogs, punched cards, microfilm, and computer-readable tapes or discs. There are at least two cards made for each book: one filed alphabetically by the author of the book, and one by the subject. Usually there are other cards for a book: one filed by the title of the book, and others by other subjects, and series if any. If the book was prepared under direct sponsorship of a society or other organization, there may be a card for the book filed under the name of the society. For journals there are cards filed by the title of the journal, possibly the author if a society, and by the subject of the journal as a whole, but not by author, title, or subject of articles in the journal.

Several identical cards are made for each book, and then subjects, titles, and so forth are added at the top. The subject cards have headings in red or all capital letters. Cards are filed alphabetically by what is on the top line, beginning with the first word (unless an article) and proceeding word by word. "See" references refer from terms not used; "see also" references refer to related terms. Cards may be filed all in one alphabetical order by authors, titles, and subjects, an arrangement that is called a dictionary catalog. Or the catalog may be divided into an author and title section and a separate subject section. There is another part of the catalog, called the shelf list, that may be available for public use or may be for staff use only. The shelf list is arranged in order by call number.

The description of the book on the catalog cards includes the author, title, place of publication, publisher, date of publication, number of pages, and notes. The notes might indicate that there is a bibliography, or an index, or other features of the book. For a journal the notes may tell in what indexing and abstracting services it is indexed. The tracing in the lower part of the card lists added entries and subject headings. Figure 1-1 is an example of a typical catalog card with the types of information on the card labeled. In this case, the card shown would file by author, Wilson, and there would be a subject card under PASCAL (COMPUTER PROGRAM LANGUAGE), and additional cards under the joint author's name, Addyman, and the title.

You should be careful to note special separate sections of the card catalog. For example, theses and dissertations may be in a separate file, or there may be specialized collections, for example, subject or memorial collections. Government documents may not be listed at all but may be in a separate collection.

In the upper left corner of the card the call number of the book is printed. The book is located on the shelves according to this classifica-

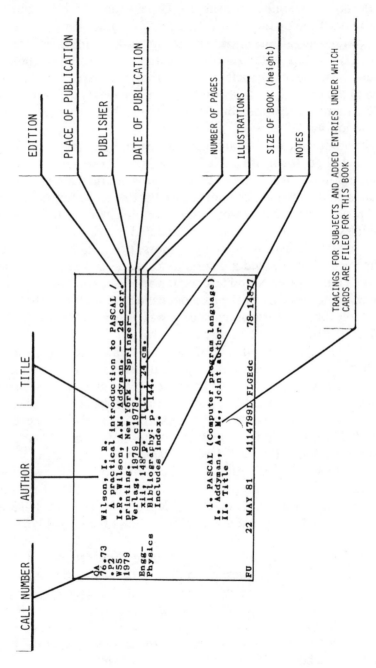

Fig. 1-1. Sample catalog card

tion number. Most of the classification schemes arrange the books in order by subject groups and with related subjects close by. The most common schemes are the Dewey Decimal Classification and the Library of Congress classification. Some libraries will have more than one classification scheme owing to changes over the years or special collections. Be sure to copy the entire call number of books you want to find, even it is "looks funny."

The Dewey Decimal Classification has ten main subject classes, of which the 500 class for pure sciences and the 600 class for technology or applied sciences are of most interest here. Each of these classes is divided into ten subclasses. The divisions of the 500 class and 600 class are as follows:

500 Pure Sciences
   510 Mathematics
   520 Astronomy &
       allied sciences
   530 Physics
   540 Chemistry & allied
       sciences
   550 Sciences of earth &
       other worlds
   560 Paleontology
   570 Life sciences
   580 Botanical sciences
   590 Zoological
       sciences

600 Technology (Applied sciences)
   610 Medical sciences
   620 Engineering & allied sciences
   630 Agriculture & related
   640 Domestic arts & sciences
   650 Managerial services
   660 Chemical & related technologies
   670 Manufactures
   680 Miscellaneous manufactures
   690 Buildings

Each of these is divided into ten more subclasses, and then decimals are used to subdivide further, for example, 595.1, 595.12. This subject class number is the top line of the call number. The second line serves to arrange the books within each subject alphabetically by author. The author's initial appears first and then "cutter" numbers to arrange books alphabetically within those with the same initial. Other lines may give the date or copy number. Here is an example of a call number in the Dewey Decimal Classification:

016.5
M147

The Library of Congress classification has twenty-one major classes, represented by letters. Five letters were not used, to allow for development of additional classes. Classes of most importance here are Q for science, R for medicine, S for agriculture, and T for technology. A second letter is added to the major class letters for subdivisions, as follows:

Q	Science	T	Technology
QA	Mathematics	TA	Engineering
QB	Astronomy	TC	Hydraulic Engineering
QC	Physics	TD	Environmental Technology
QD	Chemistry	TE	Highway Engineering
QE	Geology	TF	Railroad Engineering
QH	Natural History	TG	Bridge Engineering
QK	Botany	TH	Building Construction
QL	Zoology	TJ	Mechanical Engineering
QM	Human Anatomy	TK	Electrical Engineering, Electronics
QP	Physiology		
QR	Microbiology	TL	Motor Vehicles, Aeronautics, Astronautics
		TN	Mining Engineering, Metallurgy
		TP	Chemical Technology
		TR	Photography
		TS	Manufacturers
		TT	Handicrafts
		TX	Home Economics

Further subdivisions are done with numbers 1 to 9999 on the second line of the call number. The cutter number on the next line is like that for the Dewey Decimal Classification and consists of the author's initial and numbers that put books in alphabetical order by author. Other lines, if any, may be year of publication or copy number. Here is an example of a call number in Library of Congress classification:

Q
192
.A17
1975

The books are arranged on the shelves by call number. The order goes from left to right, top to bottom of each section. The top shelf of the next section begins where the bottom shelf of the previous section left off. Use the top line of the call number first, then the second line, and so forth. If the library owns just one copy of the book, there will not be a copy number, but if more copies, the copy number will appear alone on the bottom line. Do not confuse a number such as B5c2 on another line with a copy number.

So in the Dewey Decimal Classification, books are arranged first by numbers on the top line:

610   611   620   651

Numbers after the decimal point, if any, are treated as decimals:

610.3   610.37   610.5   610.8

Then go to the second line for all those with the same top line, and treat the number as a decimal:

| 611 | 611 | 611 | 611 |
| B22 | C37 | C375 | C42 |

In the Library of Congress system, books are arranged first by letters:

Q   QA   QC   QD

and then, in the second line, numbers:

| TK | TK | TK | TK |
| 141 | 163 | 6213 | 7804 |

The next line is a decimal:

TK	TK	TK	TK
141	141	141	141
.D461	.D68	.G38	.H736

Watch for special notations for special collections in the library you are using, for example, "B" for biographies; "Q" or "oversize" or "folio" for large volumes which won't fit on the shelf; "atlas"; "R" or "REF" for reference.

Journals may be shelved by call number right in with the books. Or they may be shelved in a different arrangement, for example, by call number but in a separate section, alphabetically by title, with current issues in a separate section, or with a group of years in a separate section, such as volumes before 1950 in a storage area.

INTERLIBRARY LOAN

Interlibrary loan is one of the most important services your library can provide, but it is often not publicized. Do not overlook this service. If your library does not own the book or other materials you need, it can probably borrow them from a library that does, through interlibrary loan. Public libraries usually work through the state library of the state they are in. College and university libraries usually have their own interlibrary loan services. Research laboratories and other such agencies that have a library or librarian often provide this service. Anyone may go to his or her library and request an item this way. You must go through your library; items cannot be loaned directly to an individual. Books may be borrowed free of charge. Journal articles will be photocopied rather than loaned, and there is usually a service charge plus a small charge per page for the photocopying. Theses that are not otherwise available may be photocopied by the university where the thesis was done.

Libraries have sources to tell them where materials may be found in other libraries. State libraries use a network system that is computerized and lists books, journals, and any other cataloged materials in cooperating libraries. An example of this is the Ohio College Library Consortium, abbreviated OCLC, which is based in Ohio but has cooperating libraries all over the United States. This network record tells what libraries own the material, and the library may be able to send an electronic message right in the system in order to borrow the book, or may send a form in the mail requesting the book. Some libraries have a referral service, so if one library does not have the book available, the request is automatically forwarded to another library. Another network is that set up by the National Library of Medicine. This network consists of regional libraries that provide back-up services for medical libraries in the area.

GOVERNMENT DOCUMENT DEPOSITORIES
AND OTHER SOURCES OF DOCUMENTS

There is a system of depository libraries throughout the United States where U.S. government publications are made available to users. There are two kinds of depositories, regional and selective. Regional depositories generally serve one state, and they automatically receive one copy of each government publication available. These publications must be kept forever in the regional depositories. Selective depositories select the material they wish to receive by subject categories, for example, all documents on forestry. These libraries may discard documents after five years. Selective depositories exist in several libraries in each state.

A list of the regional depository libraries appears in the appendix of this book. These libraries are not sales outlets. Documents may be used at the library. You may contact the regional depository yourself, or ask your local library to contact it to locate specific publications.

The United States Government Printing Office, through the Superintendent of Documents, sells these U.S. government documents at cost plus a percentage markup. The cost is not much lower than that of commercially produced materials. Some of these materials are sold in United States Government Printing Office Book Stores. These book stores stock some items and can obtain others. Also some commercial bookstores carry government documents. Documents may be ordered from the Superintendent of Documents, U.S. Government Printing Office, Washington, D.C. 20402, if for sale. Other documents are distributed by the issuing office, to which you may write.

The National Technical Information Service, abbreviated NTIS, is a central source for public sale of government-sponsored research, development, and engineering reports and other analyses by federal agencies and their contractors and grantees. These documents may be ordered from NTIS, U.S. Department of Commerce, Springfield, Va. 22161, or by phone, (703)-487-4650.

The state library is usually the coordinating agency for state publications. Publications may be borrowed through your library, or you may contact the issuing agency for availability. There may be a local office for distribution of some publications, such as an agricultural extension agent.

Canadian government publications may be purchased by ordering from the Publishing Centre, Hull, Quebec KLA 0S9, and are also available from some private outlets. Canadian provincial publications are sold by the individual provincial governments.

Government documents from Great Britain may be purchased in the United States from either of two outlets called Pendragon. In the eastern United States use Pendragon House of Connecticut, Inc., 185 Willow Street Mystic, Conn. 06455. In the western United States use Pendragon House, Inc., 2898 Joseph Avenue, Campbell, Calif. 95008.

International documents may be obtained through an exclusive U.S. distributor: Unipub, Inc., P. O. Box 433, New York, N.Y. 10016.

PATENTS

A complete collection of U.S. patents is available in the United States Patent Office, Arlington, Va. Some other libraries, scattered through the United States, have extensive patent collections. Copies of U.S. patents may be purchased for a low price, thirty cents per page in 1982, from the United States Patent and Trademark Office, Washington, D.C. 20231. This office also makes available copies of most foreign patents.

The first January issue of *Chemical Abstracts* each year has a section on "procurement of patents" that tells where to obtain patents from all countries.

There are commercial firms that do patent searches for a fee, and some of them also sell compilations of patent information on specific topics taken from searches they have done for customers. There is generally an abstract of each patent.

STANDARDS

Standards are available in some libraries. Standards included in the collection of the American National Standards Institute may be ordered from the American National Standards Institute Sales Department, 1430 Broadway, New York, N.Y. 10018. Information on standards of the United States National Bureau of Standards may be obtained from the bureau, Washington, D.C. 20234. Standards of other organizations may be located by writing the organization. A sales outlet for standards from most organizations is National Standards Association, 5161 River Road, Bethesda, Md. 20816 (phone 800-638-8084). Industry standards are available on subscription basis in microform from Information Handling Services, Englewood, Colo. 80150.

THESES AND DISSERTATIONS

Theses and dissertations are available for use at the university at which they were done. In the United States, different universities have different rules as to whether or not they loan theses and dissertations done at the university, but most do not loan recent ones.

If another library has purchased the thesis or dissertation, it may be available for loan from that library. Most dissertations are photocopied or copied onto microfilm by a commercial company called University Microfilms, in Ann Arbor, Michigan. These copies are available for purchase from University Microfilms, P. O. Box 1346, Ann Arbor, Mich. 48106. There is a flat rate charged, in 1982 about $20 for full-size photocopies and $8 for microfilm. Some foreign theses are also available through University Microfilms.

Theses not available elsewhere may be photocopied by the university at which they were done.

TRANSLATIONS

The National Translations Center at the Johns Crerar Library in Chicago gives information on where to locate translations, and provides photocopies of the translations in its collection. This center is a cooperative nonprofit service that concentrates on translations in science and technology, including medicine. It collects both published and unpublished translations into English. The center publishes a *Translations Register,* monthly with semiannual cumulations, listing translations available. Older translations are listed in the center's publication *Consolidated Index of Translations into English* covering 1953-66. These listings give bibliographic information and tell where to order translations. You may also write to the center to see if a translation is available: National Translations Center, John Crerar Library, 35 W. 33d Street, Chicago, Ill. 60616.

2
Computer Searching

One method of searching for information is to use a computer. This is a relatively new method, rather glamorized in many minds because of its newness and because most of us do not really understand the process and are rather in awe of the machinery used. Using a computer to help find existing information may or may not save time and energy, and may be more expensive or less expensive than other methods, depending on many factors. Computer searching is discussed in a separate chapter here in order to help you decide whether or not to use this method, and if you do decide to use it, to have a general idea of how to go about it and what to expect.

There are some uses for which computers have proved to be far superior to other methods. Examples are cases where accuracy and time saving are of great importance in performing routine operations, such as doing mathematical or statistical manipulations of data, or controlling telephone lines or traffic lights. These are not the kinds of uses we are concerned with here. This chapter is concerned with using computers to find existing bibliographic information that has been stored in the computer.

A data base is a collection of information, which may be printed or written on sheets of paper, in microform (for example, microfilm), or on magnetic tape or disk pack. The printed form may, of course, be read directly as you are reading this book, the microform may be read with a microform reader which magnifies it, and the magnetic tape or disk pack may be read with a computer. In common usage, a data base means a collection of information for computer use. This may also be called a machine-readable file.

Some examples of data bases are files of actual data, such as economic and financial information, corporate earnings, information on manufacturing, chemical properties, news articles, laws, survey data and statistics, or records of students enrolled in a school. This information is stored in the computer and updated frequently: weekly or monthly or even daily. These are examples of nonbibliographic data bases.

Another type of data base, called a bibliographic data base, is made up of references to the data. Examples of this are the catalog of holdings in a library, or an index of articles in journals. As with nonbibliographic data bases, this information is stored in the computer and updated frequently.

Information retrieval is the process of finding the information that has been stored in the computer. In its broader sense, information retrieval means finding any information, such as finding a fact in a textbook to answer a question, finding an answer from a table, or searching the literature to find a document or to provide citations to documents on a particular subject; but in its common use the term means finding the information by using a computer. Information retrieval from a bibliographic data base is called computerized literature searching.

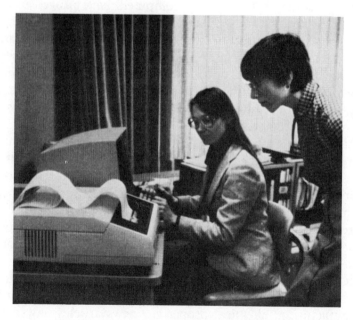

Fig. 2-1. Computer terminal with screen and printer

A terminal is used by a person to gain access to the computer. The terminal is a typewriter-like keyboard, with a display screen like a TV screen, or a printer. The user can read what the computer "says" on the screen or on paper that comes from the printer. If the terminal has a screen, there is usually an attached printer so that information displayed on the screen may be printed to keep if wanted.

There are telecommunications networks designed to handle the transfer of information from one computer to another. Telephone lines may also be used; one can dial directly on regular telephone lines with the receiver connected to the computer. Telephone rates, though, are usually more expensive than the telecommunications network rates designed to provide these connections for computers. The telecommunication networks use land lines, microwaves, and communications satellites.

Successful use of computer searching does not require a knowledge of computers or of programming. It is even possible to do these searches yourself without such knowledge. There are manuals written to explain how to use the computer, the program tells the user when something was done incorrectly, and there are people available to answer questions either at the place where the search is being done or by telephone to the place where the user is getting the data base. However, knowledge of computers and programming is helpful, and practice is essential for using the computer efficiently. Computerized literature searching is quite different from searching printed indexes, and many obstacles may be overcome by good help from a trained and experienced searcher.

Suppose you want to have a literature search performed by computer. You would probably go to a library or agency that provides this service, and be interviewed by a librarian or other search specialist as to just what you hope to get from the search. There would be a form to be completed detailing this information. The interviewer would need to know the purpose of the search, for example, for research for designing a new product. Most of the interview would be concerned with describing the information you want. Correct subject terms to describe the information wanted are very important. The computer can only search what you tell it to—no more, no less—and cannot free-associate the way a human does when looking at a printed index. A thesarus of terms will be used to help choose the correct terminology. Interrelationships between subject terms are important; for

NASA—FLORIDA

STAC

STATE TECHNOLOGY APPLICATIONS CENTER

Area Contract:_____

Job Number:_____

Name:_____ Date:_____

Position or Title:_____ Work Phone:_____

Company Name:_____

Address:_____

1. If you were to write a paper on this topic, what would you entitle it?

   _____

2. Please write a full description, in sentence form, of the subject to be searched. Be specific, define terms which have special meaning. Include names or descriptive terms for specific items, ideas, processes, methods, or techniques if relevant to your topic. Add a list to your narrative of any synonyms, closely related terms, or alternate spellings.

   _____

   _____

   _____

   _____

   _____

   _____

   _____

   _____

   _____

   _____

3. Are there any authors you know of whose work is of special interest to you in this field? Complete names, if known, are helpful.

   _____

   _____

   _____

4. Please list the complete citations (references) of two or three of the most useful articles, books, etc., on your topic, if known.

   _____

   _____

   _____

Fig. 2-2. Sample of form required for requesting a computerized literature search

5. Which of the following statements best characterizes the type of search you want done?

_____ A few good references (around 10)

_____ A working bibliography of 25 to 50 citations.

_____ A more comprehensive search which could run between 75 to 150 citations, including possible fringe information.

RESTRICTIONS OR LIMITATIONS (Optional)

6. Language: _____English Only   _____ Any language   _____Other (specify)_____

7. Dates (i.e. nothing before 1975): _____

8. Geographic (i.e. only interested in research done in the United States):

_____

9. Other restrictions or limitations (these may be used to narrow the search if too many citations are found in the database):

_____

_____

INFORMATION NEEDED

10. Check all applicable blanks which most accurately describe the ultimate purpose of the search results:

_____ Research project	_____ Dissertation (Doctoral)
_____ Grant proposal	_____ Bibliography for publication
_____ Market study	_____ Personal bibliography
_____ Product design	_____ Patent search
_____ Manufacturing process	_____ System evaluation
_____ Thesis (Master's)	_____ Other: _____

11. Financial limitations:_____
    (Please keep in mind we will try to keep costs to a minimum regardless of your answer to this question.)

Fig. 2-2. (continued)

example, you may want information on "x" only when "y" is present and "z" is absent. It would help if you knew the names of some authors who have written about this topic because the searcher might be able to find immediately one of these items and see what subjects it was listed under, and then there would likely be other items of interest under the same subject terms. You'll need to be very specific about restrictions on the search: dates to be covered, language, price you will be willing to pay, how soon needed, and approximately how many references you want.

If this were to be an on-line search, the searcher might begin the search immediately following the interview, with you available to

File No.	DATABASE (Supplier)	Online Connect Time Rate $/Hour	Offline Print Rate Per Full Record
	SCIENCE		
110	AGRICOLA 1970–1978 (U.S.D.A. Technical Information Systems)	$35	10¢
10	AGRICOLA 1979–present (U.S.D.A. Technical Information Systems)	35	10
55	BIOSIS PREVIEWS 1969–1976 (Biosciences Information Service)	58	15
5	BIOSIS PREVIEWS 1977–present (Biosciences Information Service)	58	15
2	CA SEARCH 1967–1971 (American Chemical Society)	64	20
3	CA SEARCH 1972–1976 (American Chemical Society)	64	20
104	CA SEARCH 1977–1979 (American Chemical Society)	64	20
4	CA SEARCH 1980–1981 (American Chemical Society)	64	20
311	CA SEARCH 1982–present (American Chemical Society)	64	20
174	CHEMICAL REGULATIONS AND GUIDELINES SYSTEM (U.S. Interagency Regulatory Liaison Group; CRC Systems, Inc.)	70	90
31	CHEMNAME™ (Chemical Abstracts Service, DIALOG Information Retrieval Service)	130	20
30	CHEMSEARCH™ (Chemical Abstracts Service, DIALOG Information Retrieval Service)	130	20
328	CHEMSIS™ 1967–1971 (Chemical Abstracts Service, DIALOG Information Retrieval Service)	130	20
131	CHEMSIS™ 1972–1976 (Chemical Abstracts Service, DIALOG Information Retrieval Service)	130	20
130	CHEMSIS™ 1977–present (Chemical Abstracts Service, DIALOG Information Retrieval Service)	130	20
50	CAB ABSTRACTS (Commonwealth Agricultural Bureaux)	50	30
172	EXCERPTA MEDICA 1974–1979 (Excerpta Medica)	70	20
72	EXCERPTA MEDICA 1980–present (Excerpta Medica)	70	20
73	EXCERPTA MEDICA IN PROCESS (Excerpta Medica)	70	20
58	GEOARCHIVE (Geosystems)	70	20
89	GEOREF (American Geological Society)	70	20
151	HEALTH PLANNING AND ADMINISTRATION (U.S. National Library of Medicine)	35	15
12	INSPEC 1969–1976 (Institution of Electrical Engineers)	75	25
13	INSPEC 1977–present (Institution of Electrical Engineers)	75	25
76	LIFE SCIENCES COLLECTION (Cambridge Scientific Abstracts)	45	15
152	MEDLINE 1966–1974 (U.S. National Library of Medicine)	35	15
153	MEDLINE 1975–1979 (U.S. National Library of Medicine)	35	15
154	MEDLINE 1980–present (U.S. National Library of Medicine)	35	15
29	METEOROLOGICAL AND GEOASTROPHYSICAL ABSTRACTS (American Meteorological Society and NOAA)	95	15
204	ONTAP™ CA SEARCH (American Chemical Society)	15	na
231	ONTAP™ CHEMNAME (American Chemical Society)	15	na
188	★ SCISEARCH® 1965–1969 (Institute for Scientific Information) subscriber	65	15
188	★ SCISEARCH® 1965–1969 (Institute for Scientific Information) nonsubscriber	165	15
187	★ SCISEARCH® 1970–1973 (Institute for Scientific Information) subscriber	65	15
187	★ SCISEARCH® 1970–1973 (Institute for Scientific Information) nonsubscriber	165	25
186	SCISEARCH® 1974–1977 (Institute for Scientific Information) subscriber	65	15
186	SCISEARCH® 1974–1977 (Institute for Scientific Information) nonsubscriber	165	25
94	SCISEARCH® 1978–1980 (Institute for Scientific Information) subscriber	65	15
94	SCISEARCH® 1978–1980 (Institute for Scientific Information) nonsubscriber	165	25
34	SCISEARCH® 1981–present (Institute for Scientific Information) subscriber	65	15
34	SCISEARCH® 1981–present (Institute for Scientific Information) nonsubscriber	$165	25¢
62	SPIN (American Institute of Physics)	35	10
52	TSCA INITIAL INVENTORY (Environmental Protection Agency, DIALOG Information Retrieval Service)	45	15

★Forthcoming database

Fig. 2–3. List of data bases in science and technology available through DIALOG vendor

File No.	DATABASE (Supplier)	Online Connect Time Rate $/Hour	Offline Print Rate Per Full Record
	APPLIED SCIENCE & TECHNOLOGY		
45	APTIC (Air Pollution Tech. Info. Ctr. & the Franklin Institute)	47	20
44	AQUATIC SCIENCE & FISHERIES ABSTRACTS (NOAA/Cambridge Scientific Abstracts)	62	20
112	AQUACULTURE (NOAA)	35	15
116	AQUALINE (Water Research Centre)	35	30
96	BHRA FLUID ENGINEERING (British Hydromechanics Research Association)	65	15
23	CLAIMS™/CHEM 1950–1962 (IFI/Plenum Data Company)	95	15
220	CLAIMS™/CITATION –prior to 1947 (IFI/Plenum Data Company)	95	$50.00
221	CLAIMS™/CITATION 1947–1970 (IFI/Plenum Data Company)	95	$50.00
222	CLAIMS™/CITATION 1971–present (IFI/Plenum Data Company)	95	$50.00
124	CLAIMS™/CLASS (IFI/Plenum Data Company)	95	10¢
223	CLAIMS™/UNITERM 1950–1962 (IFI/Plenum Data Company)	300	15
224	CLAIMS™/UNITERM 1963–1970 (IFI/Plenum Data Company)	300	15
225	CLAIMS™/UNITERM 1979–present (IFI/Plenum Data Company)	300	15
24	CLAIMS™/U.S. PATENTS 1963–1970 (IFI/Plenum Data Company)	95	15
25	CLAIMS™/U.S. PATENTS ABSTRACTS 1971–present (IFI/Plenum Data Company)	95	50
125	CLAIMS™/U.S. PATENT ABSTRACTS WEEKLY (IFI/Plenum Data Company)	95	50
8	COMPENDEX (Engineering Information, Inc.)	80	30
60	CRIS/USDA (USDA)	35	10
103	DOE ENERGY (U.S. Dept. of Energy)	35	15
69	ENERGYLINE⁵ (Environment Information Center, Inc.)	78	15
169	ENERGYNET (Environment Information Center, Inc.)	90	50
40	ENVIROLINE⁵ (Environment Information Center, Inc.)	78	15
68	ENVIRONMENTAL BIBLIOGRAPHY (Environmental Studies Institute)	60	15
51	FOOD SCIENCE AND TECHNOLOGY ABS. (Intl. Food Info. Service)	65	15
79	FOODS ADLIBRA (Komp Information Services)	55	10
123	INPADOC (International Patent Documentation Center)	95	20
74	INTERNATIONAL PHARMACEUTICAL ABS. (Am. Soc. of Hospital Pharmacists)	50	15
232	★ INTERNATIONAL SOFTWARE DIRECTORY (Imprint Editions)	60	15
53	IRIS (U.S. Environmental Protection Agency Information Project)	35	10
14	ISMEC (Cambridge Scientific Abstracts)	73	20
32	METADEX (American Society for Metals)	80	15
233	★ MICROCOMPUTER INDEX™ (Microcomputer Information Services)	45	15
118	★ NONFERROUS METALS ABSTRACTS (British Non-Ferrous Metals Technology Center)	45	20
6	NTIS (National Technical Info. Service, U.S. Dept. of Commerce)	40	10
28	OCEANIC ABSTRACTS (Cambridge Scientific Abstracts)	73	20
48	PIRA (Research Assoc. for Paper & Board, Printing & Packaging Indus.)	55	15
41	POLLUTION ABSTRACTS (Cambridge Scientific Abstracts)	73	20
95	RAPRA ABSTRACTS (Rubber and Plastics Research Association of Great Britain)	$65	15¢
113	STANDARDS & SPECIFICATIONS 1950–present (National Standards Association, Inc.)	65	25
115	SURFACE COATINGS ABSTRACTS (Paint Research Association of Great Britain)	65	15
63	TRIS (U.S. Department of Transportation and Transportation Research Board)	40	10
117	WATER RESOURCES ABSTRACTS (U.S. Dept. of the Interior)	45	15
99	WELDASEARCH (The Welding Institute)	65	15
33	WORLD ALUMINUM ABSTRACTS (American Society for Metals)	50	10
67	WORLD TEXTILES (Shirley Institute)	55	10

★Forthcoming database

Fig. 2–3. (continued)

File Data:

	File 110	File 10
Inclusive Dates	1970–1978	1979 to the present
Update Frequency:	Closed file	Monthly (approximately 10,000 records per month)
File Size:	1,140,000 records	275,000 Records, June 1981

Sample Question: (420086)

Provide client with all available information on the use of landscaping to achieve energy conservation.

Search Strategy:

Concept I	Concept II	Concept III
Landscape	Climate	Urban
Trees	Microclimate	City
Vegetation	Temperature	Residential
Shade	Wind	Architect
Plants	Radiation	Street
	Ventilation	House
		Home
		Dwelling

Sample Search Results:

823892   275.29 G29L   ID No: 74–9028996
Residential landscape design: Climate control. Trees.
Williams, T G Jr
Georgia, University, Cooperative Extension Service
Leafl Coop Ext Serv Univ Ga Coll Agric   169, 5 p.   Oct 1973
275.29 G29L
Search: 19731000
Source: EXT   Doc Type: ARTICLE
Cat Codes: 4055

1449589   99.9 S013   ID No: 78–9093864
The role of urban forests in reducing urban energy consumption. Vegetation, city climate.
Herrington, L P
Proc Soc Am For   p. 60–66. Ref.   1977
99.9 SO13
Search: 19770000
Source: OTHER US   Doc Type: ARTICLE
Cat Codes: 3505

7675543   79064323   Holding Library: AGL
Energy conservation in the rural home: Landscaping to cut fuel costs (Windbreaks).
Pullman, The Service
E.M. Washington State University. Cooperative Extension Service. Jan 1979. (4405), Jan 1979. 4 p. ill.
NAL: 275.29 W27MI
Languages: ENGLISH
Sponsoring Agency: U.S. Energy Research and Development Administration
Contract No: EC–77–6–01–5097
15 ref
Subfile: EXT (STATE EXTEN. SERVICE):
Document Type: ARTICLE
Section Headings: HORTICULTURAL CROPS, CULTURE (4055); SILVICULTURE (3515)

Fig. 2–4. Sample computerized literature search

answer any questions that come up as to relationships between search concepts, and so forth. However, the search would probably be done later, especially if the results were to be printed off-line, and the results would be sent to you or you would be notified to pick them up.

Computerized information retrieval services have been available since about 1970. This use of computers started in the sixties with efforts to make keeping up with the information explosion easier. Computers are used to speed up indexing, and for compiling and printing indexes. The bibliographic data are recorded on magnetic tape, and the computer is used to compile the indexes and to phototypeset the information for publication. The magnetic tapes used to generate the indexes are often duplicated and may be sold to vendors who use them for computer searching. The U.S. government was usually the sponsor of the early efforts at computer information retrieval, and usually provided the money. By 1982, there were several hundred computerized bibliographic data bases available commercially.

Computerized services will never replace traditional library services, but will be used increasingly to support those services. They are most used for business and economics and science and technology information. In 1980 the number of libraries and information centers in the United States using computerized literature searching was estimated to be 4,000 to 5,000. Use of computers may make possible information services where none was available. For example, a business, a research laboratory, or an industry that has no library or a very minimal library may by purchasing a computer have access to hundreds of bibliographic data bases and may also purchase the documents themselves as needed, through a document delivery service connected with the data base.

A library that wants to do computerized literature searching may get access to the data bases in various ways. It may buy access to a data bank directly from its publisher or lease it from the publisher. This is much more expensive than buying a printed index. Another possibility is to be part of a regional information network in which libraries band together and have a central place to provide these services. A third option is to contract directly with commercial vendors.

The largest commercial vendors of information for computer literature searching are Lockheed Information Systems, a division of Lockheed Missile and Space Company, Palo Alto, California, and Systems Development Copropration, Santa Monica, California.

Lockheed offers a service known as DIALOG, and the Systems Development Corporation service is called ORBIT. Another major vendor is BRS, Bibliographic Retrieval Services, Latham, New York. Each vendor has access to many data bases. The vendor will have exclusive access to some of the data bases, and will carry some that are also carried by other vendors. Rates charged by the vendors for searching vary, depending on the royalties required by the data base producers.

Usually the same bibliographic indexes are available in printed book form and on the computer. This is so because the computer is used to compile and print the indexes, and the resulting tapes are sold for computer searching. The tapes for computerized searching may differ in some ways from the printed form, such as having more subject headings for each item being indexed or more up-to-date citations added between printings of the index. Basically only the format is different: printed or on tape.

Usually only bibliographic citations and possibly abstracts are available through the computer. Finding the documents cited is often a problem. If the search is done at a large library, the documents may be available there. However, one study showed that only 27% of DIALOG patrons obtained the documents cited through the library where the search was done. Most of the documents would be available from some library, obtainable through loans between libraries. Sometimes the computer data base is backed up by the documents, available either in microform or through interlibrary loan or from a commercial firm. For example, all documents indexed in *Government Reports Announcements* are available on microfiche or microfilm for sale by the National Technical Information Service. The National Library of Medicine in Washington, D.C. owns most of the documents cited in its computer service MEDLINE, and these items may be used there or borrowed on interlibrary loan. University Microfilms is a commercial firm that sells reprints of articles. It is possible to have a store of the documents themselves hooked up with the computer bibliography so that they are automatically delivered with the bibliography. An example of this is SCISEARCH.

An on-line search is one in which the user is in direct communication with the data base, and the data base replys to questions by the user. The system is interactive. An off-line search is one in which there is no interaction between searcher and data base other than the initial request from the searcher. The printed results are produced in-house at the vendor's location, not at the searcher's terminal. On-line searches are immediate; off-line searches may require several days or longer before results are received.

If the library does not have a terminal, it can send to a center that performs searches and have off-line searches done in this way. On-line searches are preferable because they can be done in a more exacting way through the interaction between searcher and data base. The search may be done on-line but then printed out off-line with the resulting printout sent to the user. The advantage of this is cost. Printing on-line involves the connect-time hourly user rate which can be expensive. Off-line printing allows for lower charges in connect-time, and your money can be directed toward the full searchable record on paper of better quality, increased legibility, and format in flat sheets which are easier to read than the paper roll. However, if the search has produced only a few citations, and especially if only brief bibliographic information is wanted and not an abstract, then printing on-line may be no more expensive and has the advantage of being immediate.

Individuals with home computers may have access to data bases, through the vendors, to do their own searching, and someday it may be common to do this.

There are advantages and disadvantages of computerized literature searching. The advantages generally rated most highly by users are convenience, thoroughness, and the fact that the list of references is printed out. More specifically, advantages are:

1. Speed: The search is done in considerably less time than that required for the same search manually.
2. Currency: Since many printed indexes are produced from computer tapes, the tapes would be updated before the printing. Information on computers is usually available several months or issues before its printed equivalent.
3. Depth of search: More subject headings may be available, and more data bases may be available on the computer than in any given library. Computers are ideal for handling requests that have several variables, or identifying very new research that has no satisfactory terminology in thesauri.

4. Printout of citation: The printing-out avoids the work of having to copy and possible errors in copying.
5. Ease of duplication and exchange of data bases.
6. Convenience: The user need not be in a library so long as he has access to a computer terminal and telephone or telecommunications network lines.

Disadvantages are:

1. Most libraries or search services charge a fee, so that expense to the user is a factor.
2. Most data bases do not go back very far in years; often citations are only available for items published since 1970.
3. The user usually needs the help of a librarian or trained searcher.
4. The user must define his needs very well; the searcher may not be able to correct for errors in defining the subject as well as in manual searching, especially with using off-line searching.
5. Indexing quality of the data bases varies; subject terms that seem perfect for a search may not get the desired results, and then the user may have to do another search. This is due to differences in vocabulary, key words, and synonyms.
6. Editorial policy varies; because putting items on magnetic tape is relatively cheap, some items are included that are not really very good.
7. Unless the searcher is well-trained and experienced, the search is likely not to be good, and to be costly as well.

The cost angle of computer searching is really difficult to assess. Although most libraries charge a fee to the user, the library may actually save money if staff time and expense of buying printed indexes are considered. Another dilemma posed as computer searching becomes more common is that libraries may drop subscriptions to the printed indexes, and then they will no longer be available for those who want to use them, or indeed they may even cease publication.

A helpful spin-off of computerized literature searching is selective dissemination of information, abbreviated SDI. In this, the user submits a list of his information needs or interests, called a profile, and receives periodic notice of new publications in those areas. This may be on-line if the user has access to a terminal, but is usually off-line so that the user receives the listing in the mail periodically, with no further work from him than submitting the profile. This service may be contracted for through a commercial service, or is sometimes offered at one's place of work.

Online Bibliographic Databases: An International Directory by James L. Hall (Detroit, Mich., Gale, 1981) is a directory of 189 on-line bibliographic data bases available internationally. Arrangement is alphabetical by the name or acronym of the data base, and information given is name and address of the supplier and vendors, brief description of subject areas covered, on-line file details, and charges to users. The appendix lists vendors' addresses. There is an index of names, acronyms, and some subject terms.

The *Directory of Online Databases* (Santa Monica, Calif., Cuadra, 1979–   ) is published yearly with supplements as needed to keep it up to date. Arrangement is alphabetical by the name of the data base, and for each there is a description as to type of data base, subject, producer, on-line service, content, coverage, and updating. Both bibliographic and nonbibliographic databases are included. Indexes to data bases are by subject, producer, on-line service, and name. There is also an index to telecommunicatons networks by on-line service.

Computer-Readable Data Bases: A Directory and Data Sourcebook (Washington, D.C., American Society for Information Science, 1979–   ) is edited by Martha E. Williams and others, published every two years. Included data bases are in computer-readable form, publicly available, and used for bibliographic information retrieval or available through the major vendors of information retrieval systems. Arrangement is alphabetical by name of data base, and for each base listed information given includes basic information, availability and charges, subject matter and scope, services offered, and user aids available. There are indexes by subject, producer, processor, and name or synonym names of the data base. The *Directory of Online Information Resources* (Kensington, Md., Capitol Systems Group, 9th edition 1982) is a guide to selected on-line data bases, both bibliographic and nonbibliographic. Only data bases that are publicly available from a user's own terminal or from a terminal in a library are included. Arrangement is alphabetical by name of data base, and information given includes subject content, the printed index to which it corresponds, the organization that prepares it, dates covered, file size and content, vendor, and cost. Indexing is by subject and vendor, and there is a list of addresses of producers and vendors.

There are several books on computer searching and how to do it. Three of the most useful are *Introduction to Automated Literature Searching* by Elizabeth P. Hartner (New York, Dekker, 1981), the *Library and Information Manager's Guide to Online Services* by Ryan E. Hoover and others (White Plains, N.Y., Knowledge Industry, 1980), and *Basics of Online Searching* by Charles T. Meadow and Pauline Cochrane (New York, Wiley, 1981).

3
General Science

INTRODUCTORY MATERIALS

The popular science writer Issac Asimov provides an introduction to the study of science in *Asimov's Guide to Science* (New York, Basic, revised edition 1972). Physical and biological sciences are included in two volumes. Chapters cover various topics, for example, "What is Science?," the reactor, the molecule, microorganisms, and the mind. All is written so that it is understandable to the lay person. There are indexes by name and subject. Also by Isaac Amimov is *The Beginning and the End* (Garden City, N.Y., Doubleday, 1977), a collection of his essays reprinted from various sources. The essays are grouped in three sections: the past, the present, and the future. Included are such interesting titles as "The Democracy of Learning," "Man and Computer," and "America—A.D. 2176." *What is This Thing Called Science?* by A. F. Chalmers (St. Lucia, Queensland, University of Queensland, 1976) is intended to be an elementary introduction to modern views of the nature of science. A bibliography is included, and there is an index.

Butter Side Up: The Delights of Science by Magnus Pyke (New York, Sterling, 1977) is made up of snippets of about 200 to 400 words on many different topics. The reading is fun, with such interest-catching titles as "Popeye and the can of spinach," "chocolate must be brown," and "rain behind the ears." There is an index. Edi Lanners's *Secrets of 123 Old-Time Science Tricks and Experiments* (Blue Ridge Summit, Pa., TAB, 1980) describes experiments using ordinary household items. Experiments have such intriguing names as "Columbus's up-dated egg," "pigs in clover," "water into wine," and "the man in the bottle," and cover concepts of equilibrium, inertia, behavior of liquids and gases, optical and acoustical phenomena, and electrical forces. There are many illustrations. *The Invisible World: Sights Too Fast, Too Slow, Too Far, Too Small for the Naked Eye to See* (Boston, Mass., Houghton Mifflin, 1981) is a picture book with brief text. The reader is treated to spectacular photographs of such diverse subjects as drops of water being splashed in a bowl, X-rays of Egyptian mummies, and views from a spacecraft.

The Excitement and Fascination of Science (Palo Alto, Calif., Annual Reviews, 1, 1965–   ) is published irregularly and contains autobiographical essays reprinted from annual reviews of various scientific subjects published by the publisher. There is a portrait of the author of each essay, and in his essay the writer usually discusses his early years and education and his career, and reflects on his views of science. A bibliography is included in most essays. *Scientific Thought, 1900–1960: A Selective Survey* edited by Romano Harre covers main currents of scientific thought in roughly the first half of the present century. There are essays by many authors in different fields, each answering the broad question "How does science in your area since 1900 strike you?" Topics covered are logic, relativity and cosmology, matter and radiation, geophysics, chemistry, biochemistry, molecular biology, ecological genetics, hormones and transmitters, cell biophysics, viruses, and ethnology. References are included with each essay, and there are indexes by author and subject. *Harvest of a Quiet Eye* by Alan L. Mackay (London, Institute of Physics, 1977) is a collection of scientific quotations. Quotations are arranged alphabetically by names of the persons quoted, and their dates of birth and death, if dead, are included. The printed sources of the quotations are listed. There is an index by subject.

Van Nostrand's Scientific Encyclopedia (New York, Van Nostrand Reinhold, 5th edition 1976) is a large one-volume summary of scientific topics. Arrangement is alphabetical by term, with cross-references as needed. Articles are one paragraph to several pages in length, and number over 7,000. Topics included are both broad and specialized, with the articles giving an overview of broad topics and detailed information about more specialized ones. There are many illustrations. Some of the major, longer articles include a list of selected references for further study.

Comparisons by the Diagram Group (New York, St. Martin's, 1980) has a descriptive subtitle: "of distance, size, area, volume, mass, weight, density, energy, temperature, time, speed and number throughout the universe." This volume provides a visual guide; for example drawings of planets as they compare to each other in size and as they compare in size to a person, or actual-size drawings of invertebrates grouped together with a ruler. There is an index. *Life-spans, or How Long Things Last* by Frank Kendig and Richard Hutton (New York, Holt, Rinehart and Winston, 1979) gives data on human and animal life spans for about half of the book. Then it goes on to life spans of celestial bodies, oceans and rocks, plants, foods and beverages, and "products of man," which range from the pyramids and other monuments to golf balls. The appendix lists dates of birth and death for famous people.

C. Singer's *Short History of Scientific Ideas to 1900* (Oxford, Clarendon, 1959) provides an introduction to scientific thought from ancient times through the nineteenth century. There are many illustrations, and many brief biographical notes. Indexing is by names of persons. *Science Since 1500: A Short History of Mathematics, Physics, Chemistry, Biology* by Humphrey T. Pledge (London, H. M. Stationery Office, 2d edition 1966) is a survey of the history of science, with references. *Dictionary of the History of Science* edited by W. F. Bynum and others (Princeton, N.J., Princeton University Press, 1981) contains leading scientific ideas and concepts of the last five centuries of Western culture, and also has some coverage of the cultures of antiquity and the Middle Ages. Articles, by about 100 scientists, are arranged alphabetically. Biographies of some scientists are included, and there is a bibliography.

History of Technology and Invention: Progress Through the Ages edited by Maurice Daumas (New York, Crown, 1969–) is a four-volume set that provides much interesting reading. The first volume begins with a discussion of primitive societies and continues on through the medieval age; the beginnings of the modern industrial era are discussed in the second volume; and the expansion of mechanization in the third and fourth volumes. Chapters or sections are written by different authors. There are many illustrations, mostly drawings, and each volume includes a bibliography. The *Dictionary of Inventions and Discoveries* edited by Ernest F. Carter (New York, Crane, Russak, 2d edition 1976) gives brief historical information about inventions through the years. Arrangement is alphabetical by invention, for example, acetylene, aircraft, and aluminum. Each invention is listed, with brief information about it. There are "see" references from names of some inventors to their inventions.

Breakthroughs: Astonishing Advances in Your Lifetime in Medicine, Science, and Technology by Charles Panati (Boston, Mass., Houghton Mifflin, 1980) has three main sections: medicine, science, and technology. Each section is made up of several chapters, including, for example, nutrition breakthroughs, dental breakthroughs, aging breakthroughs, weather breakthroughs, and energy breakthroughs. At the end there are "notes" that contain references.

The current state of science is discussed in *Sciences Today* (New York, Arno, 1977). This is one of three volumes published at the same time on sciences, social sciences, and humanities to bring together writings of noted authorities on recent developments. It is made up of articles taken from an annual publication called *Great Ideas Today*, originally published in 1961–74. Chapters are on various aspects of science, for example, "Physical Science and Technology" by George Gamow, and "Revolution in the Earth Sciences" by Peter Wyllie. Each article contains a brief bibliography. *Scientific Enterprise, Today and Tomorrow* by Adriano Buzzati-Traverso (Paris, UNESCO, 1977) deals with science as it looked at the beginning of the last quarter of the twentieth century. The book begins with a consideration of sciences and the needs of man, and then a survey of the present status of scientific research in various disciplines, grouped into three areas: universe, matter, and life. The third part of the book illustrates how scientific enterprise is organized at national and international levels, and the fourth part summarizes problems of modern societies as they are affected by scientific or technological progress. There is a subject index. *Outlook for Science and Technology: The Next Five Years* (San Francisco, Freeman, 1982), prepared by the National Research Council, examines the frontiers of research and outlines prospects for new developments. This is done by many authors, who are subject experts. Photographs, figures, charts, and graphs are used to present data. This report complements and extends another report also prepared by subject experts: *Science and Technology: A Five-Year Outlook* (San Francisco, Freeman, 1979). This is a study of current and emerging problems of national significance in which science and technology are involved. Introductory material contains general observations on

American science and technology, and chapters deal with specific subject areas.

Subject Headings and Classification

Materials of the kinds described in this chapter will usually be found in the subject part of the card catalog under the headings listed below. These subject headings may also be used in indexing and abstracting services.

Science
   (also subdivisions of Science)
   —Abbreviations
   —Abstracts
   —Bibliography
   —Dictionaries
   —Experiments
   —History
   —Formulae
   —Methodology
   —Problems, exercises, etc.
   —Research
   —Social aspects
   —Terminology
Science and civilization
Science and ethics
Science and industry
Science and law
Science news
Scientific apparatus and instruments
Scientific libraries
Scientific literature
Scientific recreations
Scientists

Most of these materials will be found in libraries shelved in the Q class of the Library of Congress classification or in the 500 to 509 class of the Dewey Decimal Classification.

BIBLIOGRAPHIC MATERIALS

Guides to the Literature

There are several excellent guides to the literature of science and technology. Although each has unique features or orientation, they may be divided very roughly into groups of guides that are mostly discussion and guides that are mostly lists of books. The lists are of two types: those arranged primarily by type of literature, for example, bibliographies, dictionaries, and so forth, and those arranged primarily by subject area, for example, chemistry, physics. You would decide which ones to use based on which approach fits your needs best.

Science and Technology: An Introduction to the Literature by Denis Grogan (Hamden, Ct., Shoe String, 4th ed., 1982) is aimed primarily at students. It contains a general discussion of scientific literature and then has chapters discussing types of literature, for example, directories and yearbooks, indexing and abstracting services, with many examples of specific works mentioned and some of these described. There is an index. *Information Sources in Science and Technology* by C. C. Parker and R. V. Turley (Boston, Mass., Butterworths, 1975) discusses a plan of action for getting information, choosing sources of information and guides to information, literature searching, obtaining the literature, evaluating and storing information, and current awareness. Many information sources are listed, usually as examples in the context of the discussion. There is an index. *Reference Sources in Science and Technology* by C. J. Lasworth (Metuchen, N.J., Scarecrow, 1972) is divided into chapters on purpose of the search, general reference, subject headings and the card catalog, special reference works, and bibliographic forms. Each section has introductory discussion and then lists of books giving bibliographic information only, with no annotation. There are indexes by author and title.

Science and Engineering Literature: A Guide to Reference Sources by H. Robert Malinowsky and J. M. Richardson (Littleton, Colo., Libraries Unlimited, 3d edition 1980) has introductory discussion of libraries, literature searching, a list of some computer-readable bibliographic data bases, and discussion of forms of literature. Most of the book is chapters for scientific subject areas, for example, biology, chemistry. There is brief information of about one page on each subject area, and then there are lists of reference books in the field, with annotations. Items listed for each subject area are subarranged in groups by type of literature, for example, dictionaries, handbooks, and so forth. Indexing is by author, title, and subject. *Guide to Reference Material* by A. J. Walford (London, Library Association, 4th edition 1980) devotes the first volume to science and technology sources. Arrangement is in broad subject categories for each scientific area, with many subdivisions, using the Universal Decimal Classification system. Reference books are listed, plus a few that are not strictly reference when nothing else on the subject is available. An annotation for each listing tells about the book and sometimes quotes from the book or from a review. Indexing is by author and title. *Guide to Reference Books* by Eugene P. Sheehy (Chicago, American Library Association, 9th edition 1976) is arranged in sections of general reference works, humanities, and so forth, and then section E: pure and applied sciences. This section is divided by subject area and then subdivided by types of materials, for example, bibliographies, dictionaries, and so forth. Materials are listed, with annotations. Indexing is by author, title, and subject.

Brief Guide to Sources of Scientific and Technical Information by Saul Herner (Arlington, Va., Information Resources Press, 2d edition 1980) is arranged in sections by type of material: information directories and source guidance, information on ongoing research and development, current or recent research and development results, past research and development results. Materials are listed with informative annotations. Many computer data bases are included. There are also chapters on personal information files and on the relationship of scientists to information tools and an annotated list of major American libraries and research collections. There is an index. *Scientific and Technical Information Sources* by Ching-Chih Chen (Cambridge, Mass., MIT Press, 1977) is arranged in chapters by type of material. There are twenty-three such chapters, covering a wide range of materials, for example, selection tools, guides to the literature, manuals, atlases and maps, non-print materials, and data bases. Each chapter is divided into sections by subject area and lists materials with annotation and indication of reference works where more information on the book listed may be found. There is an author index. *Scientific and Technical Information Resources* by K. Subramanyam (New York, Dekker, 1981) begins with discussion of current practices and then has chapters by type of literature, for example, standards and specifications, directories, and so forth. Indexing is by author and subject.

Bibliographies

Bibliographic Index: A Cumulative Bibliography of Bibliographies (New York, Wilson, 1945–   ) lists bibliographies published separately or in books, pamphlets, or periodicals, that are fifty items or more in length. Coverage is since 1937, and the index is now published in April and August of each year with an annual cumulation in December. Arrangement is by specific subjects. Two basic bibliographies of books in science and technology are somewhat out of date but still useful. The *AAAS Science Book List: A Selected and Annotated List of Science and Mathematics Books for Secondary School Students, College Undergraduates, and Nonspecialists* (Washington, D.C., American Association for the Advancement of Science, 3d edition 1970) is arranged in subject areas by Dewey Decimal Classification. About 2,500 books are listed, with descriptive annotations. Supplements extend the coverage. The *McGraw-Hill Basic Bibliography of Science and Technology* (New York, McGraw-Hill, 1966) is designed to be used with the *McGraw-Hill Encyclopedia of Science and Technology,* employing the same subject headings as the 1966 edition of the encyclopedia. Books are listed, with a brief annotation usually one sentence in length.

Pure and Applied Science Books 1876/1982 (New York, Bowker, 1982) is a bibliography four volumes in length, listing all books in science and technology from those years. Arrangement is by subject using Library of Congress subject headings, and books are listed with bibliographic information only, no annotation. Books published or distributed in the United States are covered, both those in print and now out of print. Indexing is by author and title.

The standard source listing books currently in print in the United States is *Books in Print* (New York, Bowker, 1, 1948–   ). This listing is published annually, now in four volumes per year. Two of the volumes are arranged alphabetically by author and the other two alphabetically by title, and price is given in addition to bibliographic information. A list of publishers at the end of volume four gives addresses. For use in conjuction with this is *Subject Guide to Books in Print* (New York, Bowker, 1957–   ), also published annually, now in three volumes. Arrangement is alphabetical by subject, with books listed alphabetically by author within each subject area. Bibliographic information and price are given. There is a list of publishers and distributors at the back, with addresses. The British counterpart is *British Books in Print* (London, Whitaker, 1, 1874–), also published annually. Arrangement is alphabetical by author, title, and subject in one order. Price is included along with bibliographic information. *Canadian Books in Print* (Buffalo, N.Y., University of Toronto, 1967–) lists English-language Canadian books, by author and title. A separate volume gives the subject approach. Publication is annual.

Paperbound Books in Print (New York, Bowker, 1, 1955–) is published twice each year to list U.S. paperbacks. Arrangement is in three sections: alphabetical by title, alphabetical by author, and alphabetical by subject. Bibliographic information and price are given. *Microforms in Print* (Westport, Conn., Microform Review, 1961–) is published annually in two volumes: subject listing and author–title listing. Books, journals, newspapers, government publications, and some other materials that are published in microform are listed. Coverage is international. The subject volume is arranged in subject groups by a classification scheme; the author–title volume is in one alphabetical order. Bibliographic information and price are given. *Publishers Trade List Annual* (New York, Bowker, 1, 1873–) is published annually in several volumes. It contains lists of many kinds of materials in print in the United States: books, periodicals, prints, games, maps, cards, and microforms. These are listed in publishers' catalogs, arranged alphabetically by the name of the publisher. There are also listings of publishers by subject specialty, an index of publishers' series, and publishers' addresses.

Scientific and technical materials currently in print in the United States are grouped together in *Scientific and Technical Books and Serials in Print* (New York, Bowker, 1972–), which is published annually in one large volume with separate sections for books and for serials. The book section is arranged alphabetically by topic, for example, aeronautics, with subdivisions, and books within each topic are listed alphabetically by author, and then the same books are listed alphabetically by author and then by title, with bibliographic information and price. The serials section is arranged alphabetically by topic and then by title of journal within a topic. Information given is frequency, price, and where indexed. There is a title index. A list of publishers with addresses appears at the back. *Scientific, Engineering, and Medical Societies Publications in Print; 1980–81* compiled by James M. Kyed and James M. Matarazzo (New York, Bowker, 1981) lists print and non-print materials produced by professional societies. These catalogs are published every two years, and coverage is international. Included are books, journals, conference proceedings, specifications, standards, brochures, manuals, tapes, maps, slides, and charts. Arrangement is alphabetical by society name, and address, phone, and ordering information are given along with a list of the society's publications. *Associations' Publications in Print* (New York, Bowker, 1, 1981–) is published annually to list materials published by approximately 2,500 associations: pamphlets, journals, newsletters, bulletins, books, and other items. The main part is arranged by subject, and gives bibliographic information and price for each publication listed. Indexes are by title, association name, and publisher and distributor.

A good source for learning about new scientific and technical books is the journal *New Technical Books* (New York, New York Public Library, 1915–), published monthly. Emphasis is on the fields of physical sciences, mathematics, engineering, and industrial technology. Arrangement is by subject in broad Dewey Decimal Classification classes. New books are listed with bibliographic information, price, and annotation with a list of contents of the book. There is indexing by author and subject in each issue and cumulated yearly. *Science Books and Films* (Washington, D.C., American Association for the Advancement of Science, 1,1965–) also lists new science and technology books and science education films. Up to 1975 this was called *AAAS Science Books*. Now published five times per year, this journal lists and reviews trade and text books, films, and filmstrips. Arrangement is by subject by the Dewey Decimal Classification, and for each item listed there is a brief informative and critical review. *Technical Book Review Index* (Pittsburgh, Pa., JAAD Publishing, 1935–), until recently issued by the Special Libraries Association, is published monthly. Arrangement is in broad subject groups of pure sciences, life sciences, medicine, agriculture, bibliographic information, and price. Sources of reviews are listed for each book, and there are brief quotes from reviews. There is an annual index, by author. The British counterpart to these current listings is *Aslib Book List: A Monthly List of Recommended Scientific and Technical Books* (London, Aslib, 1935–   ), published each month. Arrangement is by subject in a classed system, and new books are listed with an annotation and evaluation and indication of expected use of the book, for example, for general readers, reference, and so forth. There are indexes by author and subject in each issue and cumulated annually.

Ulrich's International Periodicals Directory (New York, Bowker, 1, 1932–   ), now published annually, lists journals currently being published at regular intervals of more than once a year, worldwide. Arrangement is in broad fields; for example, astronomy, chemistry, physics, and periodicals within each subject are listed alphabetically by title. Full bibliographic information, price, when the journal began publication, frequency, number circulated, and where indexed is given for each journal. There is an index by title. *Irregular Serials and Annuals: An International Directory* (New York, Bowker, 1, 1967–   ), published every other year, is a companion volume that lists journals published irregularly or at intervals of one year or more. Arrangement is also by broad subject fields, and types of information given are the same as in Ulrich's, above. Both are supplemented between editions by *Ulrich's Quarterly* (New York, Bowker, 1977–   ), which lists new serials both regular and irregular, worldwide.

The Union List of Serials in Libraries of the United States and Canada (New York, Wilson, 3d edition 1965) consists of five oversize volumes listing journals that began publication before 1950, worldwide. Arrangement is alphabetical by the title of the journal, or if published by a society, by the name of the society. In addition to bibliographic information, there is a list of major libraries in the United States and Canada that own the journal. Abbreviations are used to list these libraries, and a listing at the front tells what the abbreviations stand for. This basic bibliography of journals is brought up to date by *New Serial Titles* (Washington, D.C., Library of Congress, 1953–   ), published monthly with cumulations annually and in blocks of years, for example, 1950–70. The format is the same as in the *Union List. Chemical Abstracts Source Index, 1907–79,* (Columbus, Ohio, Chemical Abstracts Service, 1980), often abbreviated CASSI, is also a union list of journals. Journals that are or have been in the past indexed by *Chemical Abstracts* are listed in alphabetical order, and because the coverage of journals in *Chemical Abstracts* is so wide-ranging this is a very useful list. Full bibliographic information is given for each, as well as the date the journal began publication and the date ended if

1552 RUBBER — ABSTRACTING, BIBLIOGRAPHIES, STATISTICS

678   MY   ISSN 0035-953X
RUBBER RESEARCH INSTITUTE OF MALAYSIA.
JOURNAL. 1928. 3/yr. $18. Rubber Research
Institute of Malaysia - Pusat Penyelidikan Getah
Tanah Melayu, Box 150, Kuala Lumpur 16-03,
Malaysia. Ed. B. C. Sekhar. bibl. charts. index;
cum.index issued irreg. circ. 2,000. Indexed:
Biol.Abstr. Chem.Abstr. RAPRA.

678   UK   ISSN 0035-9548
RUBBER STATISTICAL BULLETIN. 1946. m.
£40($90) International Rubber Study Group,
Brettenham House, 5/6 Lancaster Place, London
WC2E 7ET, England. mkt. stat. circ. 1,200.

678   UK   ISSN 0035-9564
RUBBER TRENDS; a quarterly review of production,
markets, prices, etc. q. $265. Economist Intelligence
Unit Ltd, Spencer House, 27 St. James Place,
London SW1A 1NT, England. charts. stat.
cum.index. (also avail. in microform from UMI)

678   US   ISSN 0035-9572
RUBBER WORLD. 1889. m. $14. ‡ Bill
Communications, Inc., 633 Third Ave., New York,
NY 10017. Ed. David L. Schultz. adv. bk. rev. bibl,
charts, illus, mkt, stat, tr. lit. index. circ. 11,400.
(also avail. in microform from UMI; reprint service
avail. from UMI) Indexed: A.S. & T. Ind
Chem.Abstr. Eng.Ind. RAPRA.

057   US   ISSN 0036-0406
RUSSKY GOLOS/RUSSIAN VOICE. 1917. w. $9.
Russky Golos Publishing Corp., 130 E. 16th St.,
New York, NY 10003. Ed. Victor A. Yakhontoff.
adv. circ. 3,761.

SAFETY NEWSLETTER: RUBBER AND
PLASTICS SECTION. see INDUSTRIAL
HEALTH AND SAFETY

678   CN   ISSN 0008-2651
CANADA. STATISTICS CANADA.
CONSUMPTION, PRODUCTION AND
INVENTORIES OF RUBBER/
CONSOMMATION, PRODUCTION ET STOCKS
DE CAOUTCHOUC. (Catalog 33-003) (Text in
English & French) 1947. m. Can.$15($18) Statistics
Canada, Publications Distribution, Ottawa, Ont.
K1A 0V7, Canada. Indexed: RAPRA.

678 016   FR
L R C C BULLETIN BIBLIOGRAPHIQUE. 1958. m.
price not given. ‡ Laboratoire des Recherches et de
Controle du Caoutchouc, 12, rue Carves, 92120
Montrouge, France. circ. 200. (looseleaf format)
Indexed: Lib.Lit.
Formerly (to 1976): Laboratoire de Recherches et
de Controle du Caoutchouc. Bulletin de
Documentation Bibliographique (ISSN 0007-4233)

678   BL   ISSN 0025-9748
MERCADO DA BORRACHA NO BRASIL.
BOLETIM MENSUAL. 1967. m. Superintendencia
da Borracha, Avenida Almirante Barroso 81, Caixa
Postal 610, Rio de Janeiro RJ, Brazil. charts. mkt.
stat. (processed)

678 668.4 016   UK   ISSN 0033-6750
R A P R A ABSTRACTS. 1923. bi-w. £150($360);
plus £15($36) for indexes to non-members. Rubber
and Plastics Research Association of Great Britain,
Shawbury, Shrewsbury SY4 4NR, England. Eds. J.
MacLachlan, P. Cantrill. adv. bk. rev. abstr, stat.
index. circ. 2,000.

338.476 310   US
RUBBER MANUFACTURERS ASSOCIATION.
STATISTICAL REPORT. 1974. m. free. Rubber
Manufacturers Association, 1901 Pennsylvania Ave.
N.W., Washington, DC 20006. charts. stat.

500   PO   ISSN 0001-3781
ACADEMIA DAS CIENCIAS DE LISBOA.
BOLETIM. 1929. q. Academia das Ciencias de
Lisboa, Rua D. Francisco Manuel de Melo 5,
Lisbon 1, Portugal.

500   CU   ISSN 0020-3831
ACADEMIA DE CIENCIAS DE CUBA.
INSTITUTO DE DOCUMENTACION E
INFORMATION CIENTIFICA Y TECNICA.
BOLETIN.* vol.2,1964. q. price not given.
Academia de Ciencias de Cuba, Instituto de
Documentacion e Informacion Cientifica y Tecnica,
Havana, Cuba. abstr.

500   SP
ACADEMIA DE CIENCIAS EXACTAS, FISICO-
QUIMICAS Y NATURALES. REVISTA. (Text in
English, French, German and Spanish) 1916. q.
4000 ptas.($60) Academia de Ciencias Exactas,
Fisico-Quimicas y Naturales, Facultad de Ciencias,
Zaragoza, Spain. Ed. J. Casas.

500 510   VE
ACADEMIA DE CIENCIAS FISICAS
MATEMATICAS Y NATURALES. BOLETIN.
vol.35, 1975. q. free on exchange basis to qualified
personnel. Ministerio de Educacion de Venezuela,
Academia de Ciencias Fisicas Matematicas y
Naturales, Apdo. 1421, Palacio de las Academias,
Caracas 101, Venezuela. Ed. Bd. bibl. charts. illus.
Indexed: Biol.Abstr. Chem.Abstr.

500   BU   ISSN 0001-3978
ACADEMIE BULGARE DES SCIENCES.
COMPTES RENDUS. (Text in English, French,
German and Russian) 1948. m. 27.50 lv. per issue.

Fig. 3-1. Directory of current periodicals: *Ulrich's International Periodicals Directory*

ceased, and the translation version if applicable. Libraries that own the journal are then listed by an abbreviated code at the front. Over three hundred libraries in the United States and about seventy libraries in other countries are included.

Audiovisual resources for science and technology are listed in *AAAS Films in the Sciences: Reviews and Recommendations* (Washington, D.C., American Association for the Advancement of Science, 1980). This bibliography, with slightly varying titles, is issued irregularly. The 1980 edition lists and reviews about 1,000 films from all scientific subject areas, together with ordering information. Arrangement is in subject groups by the Dewey Decimal Classification, with indexes by subject and title and by film distributor. For new listings consult *Science Books and Films by AAAS,* described earlier.

Reviews of the Literature

Index to Scientific Reviews (Philadelphia, Pa., Institute for Scientific Information, 1, 1974–   ) is published twice a year with annual cumulations. Its coverage of review articles in journals and books is international, in all areas of science and technology. Included are review articles and state-of-the-art articles such as those titles beginning with "Advances in," "Review of," and so forth, and articles that contain forty or more references. Indexing is by subject in addition to author and title in a citation index.

Indexing and Abstracting Services

The *Reader's Guide to Periodical Literature* (New York, Wilson, 1900–   ) is issued monthly to index periodical articles from a wide variety of general interest magazines. Some scientific topics are included.

Similar but better for science information is *General Science Index* (New York, Wilson, 1, 1978–   ). This index is published monthly except in June and December, with quarterly and annual cumulations, to index English-language periodicals in all areas of science. Arrangement is alphabetical by subject, and journal articles are listed alphabetically by title. The name of the journal is abbreviated in the bibliographic information, and a list of abbreviations at the front tells the full title. There is a bibliography of reviews of new books at the back of each issue and annual cumulation.

Science Citation Index (Philadelphia, Pa., Institute for Scientific Information, 1, 1961–   ) is published bimonthly with annual and five-year cumulations. This index gives international coverage for the literature of science, medicine, agriculture, technology, and the behavioral sciences. Materials indexed are journals, proceedings, symposia, monographic series, and multi-author books. Arrangement is in three main sections: citation index, source index, and permuterm subject index. The idea behind this index is that if you know of an article on the subject you are interested in, then other articles in which this article is cited as a reference will be of interest also. Thus if you know of a specific reference to an article, use the citation index to find that reference listed, and then you will find a list of other articles that cited that article. If you know only an author or corporate author, use the source index to find references to articles by that author. If you have only a subject, use the permuterm subject index, which will lead to an author, and then use the source index by author. This will give you references with which you may use the citation index.

There are numerous abstracting and indexing services that concentrate on specific fields in science or technology. Of course there is overlap among them in subject areas covered and journals indexed. Services for particular subject fields will be described in the chapters dealing with those fields. Some services are published in several sections, each covering a particular field, and all together covering all or most areas of science. An example of this is *Bulletin Signaletique* (Paris, Centre National de la Recherche Scientifique, 1, 1948–   ), which has sections that deal with almost every scientific field. Various sections, each published as a separate journal, will be described in the chapters concerned with their subject areas.

Abstracts and Indexes in Science and Technology: A Descriptive Guide by Dolores B. Owen and Marguerite M. Hanchey (Metuchen, N.J., Scarecrow, 1974) is a guide to indexing and abstracting services. Arrangement is by subject field: general, mathematics and statistics, astronomy, chemistry and physics, nuclear science and space science, earth science, engineering and technology, biological sciences, agricultural sciences, health sciences, and environment. The *Guide to the World's Abstracting and Indexing Services in Science and Technology* (Washington, D.C., National Federation of Science Abstracting and

MEN
Age differences in serum androgen levels in normal adult males. F. E. Purifoy and others. bibl il Human Biol 53:499-511 D '81

MENINGITIS
CSF/serum glucose ratio. Am Fam Physician 25:239 Ja '82
Complications of meningococcal infections. Am Fam Physician 25:258 Mr '82
Meningitis after lumbar puncture. Am Fam Physician 25:232 F '82

Therapy
Cure for childhood meningitis. M. J. Rodman. RN 45:152 Mr '82

MENSTRUATION
See also
Amenorrhea
Delayed menarche and amenorrhea in college athletes. Am Fam Physician 25:240 F '82
Menstrual cycle and protein requirements of women. D. H. Calloway and M. S. Kurzer. bibl il J Nutr 112:356-66 F '82
Morbidity, mortality and menarche. P. T. Ellison. bibl il Human Biol 53:635-43 D '81
People vs. physiology. B. Dixon. il The Sciences 22:6 My/Je '82
Secular trend of the age at menarche of Japanese girls with special regard to the secular acceleration of the age at peak high velocity. H. Hoshi and M. Kouchi. bibl il Human Biol 53: 593-8 D '81

MENTAL health
See also
Self-actualization (psychology)
Mental health policy as a field of inquiry for psychology. C. A. Kiesler. bibl Am Psychol 35:1066-80 D '80; Discussion. 37:94-6 Ja '82
Mental resiliency of Holocaust survivors. C. A. Bridgwater. Psychol Today 16:18-+ F '82
Mental stress given environmental status; court delays start at Three Mile Island. D. Dickson. il Nature 295:179 Ja 21 '82
Pets; the health benefits. J. Arehart-Treichel. il Sci N 121:220-2 Mr 27 '82

MENTAL health services
See also
Hospitals, Psychiatric
Emotionally disturbed mentally retarded people; an undeserved population. S. Reiss and others. bibl Am Psychol 37:361-7 Ap '82
Mental hospitals and alternative care; noninstitutionalization as potential public policy for mental patients. C. A. Kiesler. bibl il Am Psychol 37:349-60 Ap '82

MENTAL illness
See also
Art and mental illness
Sir Isaac Newton; mad as a hatter. W. J. Broad. bibl por Science 213:1341-2+ S 18 '81; Discussion. 214:742 N 13 '81; 215:1185-6 Mr 5 '82

MENTALLY handicapped
Emotionally disturbed mentally retarded people; an undeserved population. S. Reiss and others. bibl Am Psychol 37:361-7 Ap '82

MENTALLY ill
Lords win rights for psychiatric patients. N Sci 93:627 Mr 11 '82
Mental hospitals and alternative care; noninstitutionalization as potential public policy for mental patients. C. A. Kiesler. bibl il Am Psychol 37:349-60 Ap '82

MENTALLY ill children
Behavior problems of Indian children. Sci N 121:139 F 27 '82

MENUS
Analysis of meal census patterns for forecasting menu item demand. S. J. Chandler and others. bibl il Am Dietet Assn J 80:317-23 Ap '82
Development of on-line real-time menu management system. L. W. Hoover and others. bibl il Am Dietet Assn J 80:46-52 Ja '82
Diet for a lifetime. il Health 14:23-6 F '82

MERCAPTO compounds
Convenient method for the conversion of thiols and disulfides to the corresponding chlorides. I. W. J. Still and others. bibl il J Organ Chem 47:560-1 Ja 29 '82
On-line chemiluminescence detector for hydrogen sulfide and methyl mercaptan. S. R. Spurlin and E. S. Yeung. bibl il Anal Chem 54: 318-20 F '82

MERCAPTO group
Salt-induced conformational changes in the catalytic subunit of adenosine cyclic 3′,5′-phosphate dependent protein kinase; use for establishing a connection between one sulfhydryl group and the γ-P subsite in the ATP site of this subunit. J. S. Jiménez and others. bibl il Biochemistry 21:1623-30 Mr 30 '82

MERCURIALIS perennis. See Dog's mercury

MERCURY
See also
Plants—Mercury content
Binding of mercury(II) to poly(dA-dT) studied by proton nuclear magnetic resonance. P. R. Young and others. bibl il Biochemistry 21:62-6 Ja 5 '82
Poison under the floor N Sci 93:697 Mr 18 '82
Slope anomaly in the vapour pressure curve of Hg. S. R. Hubbard and R. G. Ross. bibl il Nature 295:682-3 F 25 '82

Isotopes
Detection of preatomization losses of mercury in the graphite tube with the tracer technique. L. Lendero and V. Krivan. bibl il Anal Chem 54:579-81 Mr '82

MERCURY chelates
Comparison of electrochemical data for reduction of mercury(II) dihalide diphosphine complexes in dichloromethane and ^{199}Hg and ^{31}P NMR data. A. M. Bond and others. bibl il Inorganic Chem 21:117-22 Ja '82

Spectra
Correlation between NMR coupling constants and molecular structure; synthesis and ^{31}P NMR measurements of [HgX₃(cis-Ph₂PCH= CHPPh₂)] and X-ray crystal structures of [HgBr₂ (cis-Ph₂PCH=CHPPh₂)], [Hg(NO₃)₂ (PPh₃)₂], and [Hg(CN)₂(PPh₃)₂] H. B. Buergi and others. bibl il Inorganic Chem 21:1246-56 Mr '82

MERCURY compounds
Electrochemistry in liquid sulfur dioxide; a new synthesis of Hg₃AsF₆ and Hg₃SbF₆. G. E. Whitwell, 2d and others. bibl il Inorganic Chem 21:1692-3 Ap '82

MERCURY poisoning
Sir Isaac Newton; mad as a hatter. W. J. Broad. bibl por Science 213:1341-2+ S 18 '81; Discussion. 214:742 N 13 '81; 215:1185-6 Mr 5 '82

MERISTEMS
Quantitative studies of the root apical meristem of Equisetum scirpoides. E. M. Gifford, Jr and E. Kurth. bibl il Am J Bot 69:464-73 Mr '82

MESENTERY
Blood supply
Diameter, wall tension, and flow in mesenteric arterioles during autoregulation. M. E. Burrows and P. C. Johnson. bibl il Am J Physiol 241:H829-37 D '81
Effects of diltiazem on smooth muscles and neuromuscular junction in the mesenteric artery. H. Suzuki and others. bibl il Am J Physiol 242:H325-36 Mr '82

MESONS
Little machine; the nuclear accelerator system PIGMI, pion generator for medical irradiation, can treat cancers with radiation without damaging healthy tissues. I. Kiefer. il SciQuest 55:26 Mr '82
Making muonium in vacuum. C. J. Batty and G. Marshall. Nature 295:457 F 11 '82
Molecular effects in pion capture in complex materials. D. F. Jackson and others. bibl il Nature 295:557-60 F 18 '82
Relativistic time dilatation of bound muons and the Lorentz invariance of charge. M. P. Silverman. bibl il Am J Phys 50:251-4 Mr '82

METABOLISM
See also
Fish—Metabolism
Plants—Metabolism
Natural products chemistry in the marine environment. W. Fenical. bibl il Science 215: 923-8 F 19 '82
Amino acids
Arginine metabolism and urea synthesis in cultured rat skeletal muscle cells. W. M. Pardridge and others. bibl il Am J Physiol 242: E87-92 F '82
Comparative study of the net metabolic benefits derived from the uptake and release of free amino acids by marine invertebrates. J. C. Ferguson. bibl il Biol Bull 162:1-17 F '82
Effect of portacaval shunt on sulfur amino acid metabolism in rats. L. E. Benjamin and R. D. Steele. bibl il Am J Physiol 241:G503-8 D '81
Effect of zinc deficiency on histidine metabolism in rats. J. M. Hu and B. Rubenstein. bibl il J Nutr 112:461-7 Mr '82
Enhancement of histidine and one-carbon metabolism in rats fed high levels of retinol. D. Fell and R. D. Steele. bibl il J Nutr 112: 474-9 Mr '82
Metabolism of L-lactate by LLC-PK₁ renal epithelia. J. M. Mullin and others. bibl il Am J Physiol 242:C41-5 Ja '82

Fig. 3-2. Index to periodical articles: *General Science Index*

Indexing Services, 1963) is a compilation of services. Arrangement is alphabetical by the title of the service, and it lists and describes them. There are indexes by country and subject. *Ulrich's International Periodicals Directory,* described earlier, lists indexing and abstracting services worldwide, by subject, as a subdivision of each subject field listing of journals. Also, with each journal listing *Ulrich's* tells which indexing and abstracting services index that journal.

SECONDARY LITERATURE MATERIALS

Encyclopedia

The *McGraw-Hill Encyclopedia of Science and Technology* (New York, McGraw-Hill, 5th edition 1982) is a very useful fifteen-volume set covering all areas of science and technology, seventy-five different fields in all. The more than 750 articles are arranged alphabetically by topic, with cross-references as needed. Articles are by various subject specialists. Most articles begin with a definition and frame of reference for the term, and then go on to a more detailed discussion. There are survey articles for an overview of each major subject area. There is a brief bibliography with most articles. Diagrams, photographs, graphs, and tables are used throughout. Indexes are of two kinds: analytical, listing specific subjects, and topical, covering broad topics with a listing of articles on aspects of the topics. A separate section in the index volume on scientific notation contains information on the metric system, conversion factors, abbreviations, and so forth. A yearbook is published each fall to keep information up to date.

Science and Society

The relationships between science and society are discussed in *Science and Technology in Society: A Cross-Disciplinary Perspective* edited by Ina Spiegel-Rosing and D. deSolla Price (London, Sage, 1977). Three main areas are covered: normative and professional contexts, social studies of science, and science policy studies. Each part has several chapters by different authors, each with a bibliography. There are indexes by subject and name. *Guide to the Culture of Science, Technology, and Medicine* edited by Paul T. Durbin (New York, Free Press, 1980) provides state-of-the-field surveys by subject specialists.

Arrangement is in four main sections: historical disciplines, philosophy, sociology, and policy studies. There are chapters by different authors in each section; for example, the historical section includes history of science, history of technology, and history of medicine, and the philosophy section includes philosophy of technology and philosophy of medicine. Each chapter includes an extensive bibliography. There is an index. *The Nature of Science* by David Knight (London, Deutsch, 1976) contains chapters on various areas of science and takes a historical approach to each. Chapters include science as a complex activity, science as explanation, science as a career, science and government, and so forth. There is a bibliography of suggested readings and an index. *Science, Technology, and Society: Needs, Challenges, and Limitations* (New York, Pergamon, 1980) is made up of papers by different authors from an International Colloquium held in Vienna, Austria in 1970 under the auspices of the United Nations. Papers discuss such topics as "science and technology for development—the turning point: certain imperatives for the future," food and agriculture, population, energy, and so forth.

History

George Sarton's *Introduction to the History of Science* (Baltimore, Md., Williams and Wilkins, 1927-48 reprinted Huntington, N.Y., Krieger, 1975) consists of three volumes in five books: volume 1 "From Homer to Omar Khayyam," volume 2 in two parts "From Rabbi Ben Ezra to Roger Bacon," and volume 3 in two parts "Science and Learning in the 14th century." Arrangement is generally chronological through the volumes. Chapters are on particular sciences, countries, and time periods, and each begins with a summary of the main events and then has information on principal people including their life and work, and on specific events, and a bibliography. In addition to chapter bibliographies there is a general bibliography. There is an index in each volume and one in volume 3 for all three volumes. A series of books called *Album of Science* (New York, Scribner, 1978-83) provide an interesting pictorial record of science in five volumes. Volumes are *Antiquity and the Middle Ages* by John E. Murdoch, *From Leonardo to Lavoisier* by I. Bernard Cohen covering the sixteenth and seventeenth centuries, *Nineteenth Century* by L. Pearce Williams, *Physical Sciences in the Twentieth Century* by C. Stewart

Gillmer, and *Biological Sciences in the Twentieth Century* by Garland Allen, the last volumes being in preparation at the time of writing this book.

Science as it has developed in the United States is the subject of *Thinkers and Tinkers: Early American Men of Science* by Silvio A. Bedini (New York, Scribner, 1975). This is an interesting overview of how the practical sciences were needed in early America and how they were used. Many illustrations are provided, including portraits and pictures of early scientific instruments. A glossary, bibliography of further readings, and an index are included. *Early American Science* edited by Brooks Hindle (New York, Science History, 1976) and *Science in America Since 1820* edited by Nathan Reingold (New York, Science History, 1976) are both collections of articles by different authors that were previously published in the journal *Isis*. Also edited by Nathan Reingold is *Science in America: A Documentary History 1900–1930* (Chicago, University of Chicago Press, 1981).

Heralds of Science prepared by the Dibner Library (New York, Neal Watson, 1980) is an illustrated catalog of rare science books. Sections include astronomy, botany, chemistry, electricity and magnetism, general science, geology, mathematics, medicine, physics, technology, and zoology. Entries are annotated. George Sarton's *Horus: A Guide to the History of Science* (Waltham, Mass., Chronica Botanica, 1952) is a bibliographic guide with introductory essays on science and tradition. There are sections for different countries, cultural groups, and fields of science. Also included are lists of journals on the history of science and lists of institutes, museums, libraries, and international congresses. *Critical Bibliography of the History of Science* (Cambridge, Mass., History of Science Society, 1, 1913–   ) appears quarterly in the journal *Isis*. Each of these long bibliographic articles lists publications in broad subject groups by a classified arrangement, and each item is annotated. There is an index by author. The first ninety of these bibliographies, 1913–65, have been cumulated in book form in two volumes as *Isis Cumulative Bibliography* edited by Magda Whitrow (London, Mansell, 1971).

Biographies

The *Dictionary of Scientific Biography* (New York, Scribner, 1970–80) is a fourteen-volume set plus supplement and index. It contains biographical essays on important deceased scientists, worldwide from antiquity to modern times. Arrangement is alphabetical by names of scientists, and after dates of birth and death, birthplace, and brief identification, there is a biography of a few paragraphs to several pages. A bibliography of works by and about each person is included with his sketch. Indexing is by subject and name. The *Concise Dictionary of Scientific Biography* (New York, Scribner, 1981) is a one-volume abridgement of the full *Dictionary of Scientific Biography*.

Asimov's Biographical Encyclopedia of Science and Technology (Garden City, N.Y., Doubleday, revised edition 1972) contains biographical information on about 1,200 scientists, worldwide from ancient times to modern. Arrangement is chronological by the time when the scientist lived, and for each there is information as to dates of birth and death, birthplace, and brief identification of subject area, and then several paragraphs to several pages of biographical information. A portrait of each is included. An alphabetical listing refers to the numbered biographical entry, and there is an index. *Scientists and Inventors* by Anthony Feldman and Peter Ford (New York, Facts on File, 1979) gives international coverage of 150 scientists and inventors. Also arranged in chronological order, this oversize volume contains biographical information for each person on a double-page spread, with several diagrams, drawings, and photographs for each, some in color, and including a portrait of the person. Dates of birth and death, a brief biographical sketch, and a description of the scientific work and achievements of each person are given. Indexing is by name and subject. The *Biographical Dictionary of Scientists* by Trevor I. Williams (New York, Wiley, 2d edition 1974) gives international coverage of people in science, medicine, technology, and mathematics. Arrangement is alphabetical by name, and information given includes birth place and date, date of death, most important fields of achievement, and a biographical sketch of several paragraphs. A few references are included with each sketch. *World Who's Who in Science* (Chicago, Marquis, 1968) gives international coverage, from antiquity to modern times. Arrangement is alphabetical, and brief biographical information is given in abbreviated form, including dates of birth and death, education, positions held, and works published. The *Biographical Encyclopedia of Scientists* (New York, Facts on File, 1981) is a two-volume set.

Modern Scientists and Engineers (New York, McGraw-Hill, 1980) is a three-volume set giving international coverage of contemporary leaders in science and engineering from the 1920s to 1978. These volumes may stand alone, but are also geared for use with the *McGraw-Hill Encyclopedia of Science and Technology,* with reference at the end of some biographies to an article in the *Encyclopedia* for background information. Arrangement is alphabetical by names of scientists, and there is a small portrait and then biographical information including information about the person's life and work and what research he carried out. These are informal essays, usually one to two pages on each person. Indexes are by field of specialization and subject and name.

Only American scientists are listed in *Who Was Who in American History—Science and Technology* (Chicago, Marquis, 1976). Included are about 10,000 people who lived from early colonial days of the United States to 1973. Arrangement is alphabetical by name of scientist, and information is brief, including dates of birth and death, family, education, positions held, and publications. *American Women of Science* by Edna Yost (Philadelphia, Pa., Lippincott, 1955) is made up of biographies of twelve American women scientists, some living and some deceased. There is a chapter devoted to each woman, and the writing is done in an interesting informal style.

The *Biographical Dictionary of American Science: The 17th Through the 19th Centuries* by Clark A. Elliott (Westport, Conn., Greenwood, 1979) contains brief biographical information on about 600 scientists. Arrangement is alphabetical, and appendices provide access by year of birth, place of birth, education, occupation, and field of interest. There is an index. This volume is designed to be a retrospective companion to the series of editions of *American Men and Women of Science,* which will be described in the section on quick reference materials, and which gives the same type of information on scientists living and active at time of publication.

Prominent Scientists by Paul A. Pelletier (New York, Neal-Schuman, 1980) is an index that provides access to biographies in collections of biographies, histories, or works that include biographical sketches. Arrangement is alphabetical by name of the scientist, and for each there is a list of biographies. A separate section, arranged alphabetically by field of work, lists names of scientists in each field.

The *Dictionary of Named Effects and Laws in Chemistry, Physics, and Mathematics* by Denis W. G. Ballentyne and D. R. Lovett (New York, Chapman and Hall, revised edition 1981) is a dictionary of effects and laws known by the name of the person who discovered them.

BECK, WILLIAM NELSON, b Chicago, Ill, Dec 16, 23; m 48; c 3. MATHEMATICS, PHYSICS. *Educ:* Dakota Wesleyan Univ, BA, 46. *Prof Exp:* Instr physics, Dakota Wesleyan Univ, 46-49; electronics engr, Aircraft Div, Globe Corp, 51-53, chief field serv eng, 53-54; assoc physicist, 54-75, EXP MGR, ARGONNE NAT LAB, 75- *Mem:* Am Nuclear Soc. *Res:* Development and evaluation of nuclear reactor fuel materials; applications of ultrasonics in the field of nondestructive testing; neutron radiography techniques for irradiated materials. *Mailing Add:* Argonne Nat Lab Bldg 310 9700 Cass Ave Argonne Il. 60439

BECK, WILLIAM SAMSON, b Reading, Pa, Nov 7, 23; m; c 4. BIOCHEMISTRY. HEMATOLOGY. *Educ:* Univ Mich, BS, 43, MD, 46. *Hon Degrees:* AM, Harvard Univ, 70. *Prof Exp:* Clin instr, Med Sch, Univ Calif, Los Angeles, 50-53, instr, 53-55, asst prof med, 55-57; asst prof, 57-69, assoc prof, 69-79, PROF MED, HARVARD UNIV, 79- *Concurrent Pos:* Fel biochem, NY Univ, 55-57; chief hemat & med sects, Atomic Energy Proj, Univ Calif, Los Angeles, 51-57; estab investr, Am Heart Asn, 55-60; tutor biochem sci, Harvard Univ, 57-; chief hemat res lab, 57-76, dir hemat res lab, Mass Gen Hosp, Boston, 57-; mem hemat study sect, NIH, 67-71; mem adv coun. Nat Inst Arthritis, Metab & Digestive Dis, 72-75. *Honors & Awards:* Wenner-Gren Prize, 55. *Mem:* AAAS; Am Chem Soc; Am Soc Biol Chem; Am Soc Clin Invest; Am Asn Cancer Res. *Res:* Vitamin B12 folic acid; nucleic acid and bacterial metabolism; enzymology; blood cell biochemistry. *Mailing Add:* 85 Arlington St Winchester MA 01890

BECKEL, CHARLES LEROY, b Philadelphia, Pa, Feb 7, 28; m 58; c 4. THEORETICAL PHYSICS. *Educ:* Univ Scranton, BS, 48; Johns Hopkins Univ, PhD(physics), 54. *Prof Exp:* Asst, Johns Hopkins Univ, 49; asst, Sch Pharm, Univ Md, 49-53; from asst prof to assoc prof physics, Georgetown Univ, 53-64; mem res staff, Inst Defense Anal, 64-66; assoc prof, 66-69, asst dean grad sch, 71-72, PROF PHYSICS, UNIV NMEX, 69- *Concurrent Pos:* Consult, Ballistics Res Lab, Aberdeen Proving Ground, Md, 55-57, Inst Defense Anal. 62-64 & 66-69, Dikewood Corp, 67-72 & 74-80, Albuquerque Urban Observ, 69-71, Los Alamos Nat Lab, 79-80, US Army Control & Disarm Agency, 81-; Fulbright lectr, Univ Peshawar, 57-58 & Cheng Kung Univ, Taiwan, 63-64; actg dir, Inst social Res & Develop, Univ NMex, 72, actg vpres res, 72-73; vis prof theoret chem, Univ Oxford, 73; phys sci officer, US Arms Control & Disarm Agency, 80-81. *Mem:* Am Phys Soc; Am Asn Physics Teachers; Sigma Xi; Int Soc Quantum Biol. *Res:* Theoretical aspects of the structure of diatomic molecules; quantum mechanics; operations research; quantum biology; study of biomolecule conformation; electric field effects on biological cells. *Mailing Add:* Dept of Physics & Astron Univ of NMex Albuquerque NM 87131

BECKEL, WILLIAM EDWIN, zoology, see previous edition

BECKENSTEIN, EDWARD, b New York, NY, Oct 21, 40. MATHEMATICAL ANALYSIS. *Educ:* Polytech Inst Brooklyn, BS, 62, MS, 64, PhD(math), 66. *Prof Exp:* From instr to asst prof math, Polytech Inst Brooklyn, 65-67; asst prof, St John's Univ, NY, 67-68; from asst prof to assoc prof, Polytech Inst Brooklyn, 68-72; assoc prof, 72-77, PROF MATH & CHMN DEPT, ST JOHN'S UNIV, NY, 77- *Res:* Abstract algebra; topology; functional analysis; theory of commutative Banach algebras. *Mailing Add:* 1714 Madison Pl Brooklyn NY 11229

BECKER, AARON JAY, b Brooklyn, NY, Apr 28, 40; m 65; c 2. PHYSICAL CHEMISTRY, HIGH TEMPERATURE CHEMISTRY. *Educ:* Brooklyn Col, BS, 61; Univ Wash, MS, 64; Ill Inst Technol, PhD(chem), 71. *Prof Exp:* Scientist chem, Ill'l Res Inst, 65-68; resident assoc, Argonne Nat Labs, 68-71; fel, McMaster Univ, 71-73; SCIENTIST CHEM, ALCOA RES LAB, 73- *Mem:* Am Chem Soc; Sigma Xi. *Res:* Production of metals from ores; fused salt chemistry; utilization of natural resources; production of chemicals from coal; electrochemistry. *Mailing Add:* Alcoa Res Labs Alcoa Center PA 15069

BECKER, ALEX, b Bialystom, Poland, July 2, 35, Can citizen; m 60; c 3. MINERAL EXPLORATION, INSTRUMENTATION. *Educ:* McGill Univ, BEng, 58, MSc, 61, PhD(physics), 64. *Prof Exp:* Res scientist geophysics, Geol Surv, Can, 65-69; prof appl geophysics, Ecole Polytech de Montreal, 69-80; dir res, Questor Surv, 80-81; PROF APPL GEOPHYSICS, UNIV CALIF, 81- *Mem:* Soc Exp Geophysics. *Res:* Airborne geophysical instrumentation; data acquisition and interpretation. *Mailing Add:* Dept Mat Sci & Mineral Eng Univ Calif Berkeley CA 84720

BECKER, BARBARA, b Chicago, Ill, Jan 10, 32. BIOCHEMISTRY. *Educ:* Marymount Col, NY, BA, 54; Cath Univ, MA, 55; Georgetown Univ, PhD(chem), 66. *Prof Exp:* Instr chem, Marymount Jr Col, Va, 55-62; instr, Marymount Manhattan Col, 65-66; ASST PROF CHEM, MARYMOUNT COL, NY, 66-, DEAN STUDENTS, 68- *Mem:* AAAS; Am Chem Soc. *Res:* Fatty acid synthesis; enzyme purification. *Mailing Add:* Dept of Chem Marymount Col Tarrytown NY 10591

BECKER, BENJAMIN, b New York, NY, Apr 22, 16; m 51; c 2. MICROBIOLOGY, BIOCHEMISTRY. *Educ:* Rutgers Univ, BS, 37, MS, 62, PhD(microbiol), 65. *Prof Exp:* Asst prof microbiol, biochem & gen biol, Hamilton Col, 65-69; assoc prof cell biol, 69-75, prof cell biol, 75-77, prof, 77-81, EMER PROF BIOL SCI, PURDUE UNIV, 81- *Mem:* Am Soc Microbiol; Am Chem Soc; Am Inst Biol Sci. *Res:* Actinomycetes; cell wall analyses; microbial transformations; asparaginase in leukemia; leprosy immunogens; new antifungal agents; antibiotics; nonspecific immunostimulaters; lures and traps for cat and dog fleas; alternatives to pesticides. *Mailing Add:* 5126 Fairfield Ave Ft Wayne IN 46807

BECKER, BERNARD ABRAHAM, b Chicago, Ill, May 7, 20; m 44; c 4.

Fig. 3-3. Current biographical information: American Men and Women of Science

Arrangement is alphabetical by the name of the effect or law as it is known, for example, Guy Lussac's law is under "g." The definition is given.

Study

Peterson's Annual Guides to Graduate and Undergraduate Study (Princeton, N.J., Peterson, 1, 1966–) is now issued annually in several volumes. The 1982 edition is in six volumes, one for undergraduate study and five for graduate study, with those of most interest here being book 3 on biological, agricultural, and health sciences, book 4 on the physical sciences, and book 5 on engineering and applied sciences. Each volume is arranged in sections by specific subject areas; for example, in engineering there are bioengineering, engineering design, and so forth. Colleges and universities are listed with brief information, and then there are two pages of detailed information from each school that submitted this information. Each volume also has a directory of schools, listing subject specialities.

The *Annual Register of Grant Support* (Chicago, Marquis, 1, 1969–) is published annually. Arrangement is in subject sections, with those of most interest here being "Sciences," "Physical Sciences," "Life Sciences," and "Technology and Industry." Under each subject section are listed grant programs of public and private foundations, government agencies, corporations, community trusts, unions, educational and professional associations, and special interest organizations. For each program listed there is a description of purpose, eligibility, funding available, number of awards, and application information. There are indexes by subject, organization, personnel, and geographic location.

Periodicals

Following is a representative sampling of periodicals.

American Scientist. New Haven, Conn., Sigma Xi, 1913– . (bi-monthly)
Bulletin of Science, Technology and Society. New York, Pergamon, 1981– . (bi-monthly)

Endeavour. New York, Pergamon, 1977– . (quarterly)
Experientia: Monthly Journal of Pure and Applied Science. Basel, Switzerland, Birkhaeuser, 1945– . (monthly)
Florida Scientist. Orlando, Fla., Florida Academy of Sciences, 1936– . (quarterly)
Focus on Sci-Tech. Pittsburgh, Pa., Carnegie Library, 1971– . (5 per year)
Impact of Science on Society. Paris, UNESCO, 1950– . (quarterly)
Iowa Science Teachers Journal. Cedar Falls, Iowa, 1963– . (3 per year)
Isis; International Review Devoted to the History of Science and its Cultural Influences. Philadelphia, Pa., History of Science Society, 1912– . (5 per year)
National Academy of Sciences. Proceedings. Washington, D.C., National Academy of Sciences, 1915– . (monthly)
Nature. London, Macmillan Journals, 1869– . (weekly)
Omni. New York, Omni, 1978– . (monthly)
Popular Science. New York, Times Mirror, 1872– . (monthly)
Science. Washington, D.C., American Association for the Advancement of Science, 1880– . (weekly)
Science Digest. New York, Hearst, 1937– . (monthly)
Science 80. Washington, D.C., American Association for the Advancement of Science, 1979– . (bimonthly)
Science News: The Weekly Summary of Current Science. Washington, D.C., Science Service, 1921– . (weekly)
Science Teacher. Washington, D.C., National Science Teachers Association, 1934– . (9 per year)
Scientific American. New York, Scientific American, 1845– . (monthly)
Things of Science. Marion, Ohio, Science Service, Inc., 1940– . (monthly) (science kits, text, and materials for experiments).
Yearbook of Science and the Future. Chicago, Encyclopedia Britannica, 1969– . (annual)

PRIMARY LITERATURE MATERIALS

Bernard Houghton's *Technical Information Sources: A Guide to Patents, Standards and Technical Reports Literature* (Hamden, Conn., Shoe String, 2d edition 1972) contains sections discussing

SCISEARCH   Multidisciplinary index to the literature of science   Coverage: 1965 to present
              and technology, including medicine. Contains all   File size: 7.2 million records
              the records published in Science Citation Index.   Unit record: citation
              Can be searched by author, title, and cited refer-   Vendor, Cost/connect hour:
              ences. DIALOG has three files: file 94 (1978 to   BRS, $46-$60 to subscribers,
              1980), file 34 (1981 to present), and file 186 $106-$120 to nonsubscribers;
              (1974 to 1977). In mid-1982, two additional   DIALOG (34, 94, 186, 187,
              retrospective files will be added to DIALOG: 188), $65 to subscribers,
              187 (1970-1973), 188 (1965-1969). $165 to nonsubscribers
              Prepared by Institute for Scientific Information.

Fig. 3-4. Computer data base; SCISEARCH

patents and where to obtain them, standards and where to obtain them, and technical reports. Coverage is international. There is an index.

Research Reports

Many indexing and abstracting services include research reports.

Since government agencies produce much of the world's report literature, specialized tools that lead to government documents will be described here. *Government Reports Announcements and Index* (Springfield, Va., National Technical Information Service, 1946–) is published every two weeks. The National Technical Information Service is the central source for sale to the public of U.S. government-sponsored research, development, and engineering reports, plus foreign technical reports prepared by government agencies or their contractors. *Government Reports Announcements* is arranged by a subject classification scheme in broad subjects with many subdivisions, and lists reports with an abstract, and price. There are indexes by keyword, personal author, corporate author, contract or grant number, or NTIS order number. There is an indication of where reports listed may be purchased, usually from NTIS, but some different sources are indicated. In addition to these *Government Reports Announcements,* NTIS puts out newsletters and published searches, and makes its data base available for computer searching. Published searches are available at a cost of approximately $30 each, and there are hundreds available on many topics from maternal and child health care to solar power satellites.

Some agencies have their own coverage, for example, *Technical Abstracts Bulletin* from the Department of Defense, *Scientific and Technical Aerospace Reports* from NASA, and *Energy Research Abstracts* from the Department of Energy.

Monthly Catalog of United States Government Publications (Washington, D.C., U.S. Government Printing Office, 1, 1895–) is published monthly. Arrangement is alphabetical by issuing agency within the U.S. government. Publications are listed, together with an indication of where the item may be obtained and whether or not it is deposited in depository libraries. Indexes are in each monthly issue and are cumulated annually, by subject, personal author, and title. *A Selected List of U.S. Government Publications* (Washington, D.C. Government Printing Office, 1, 1928–), issued monthly, may be obtained free from the Superintendent of Documents and lists more popular selected publications with annotation and price.

Most states issue regular listings of state documents, such as *Florida Public Documents* (Tallahassee, Fla., State Library, 1, 1968–), issued monthly with annual cumulations.

Canadian reports are listed in *Canadian Government Publications* (Ottawa, Ontario, Canada, Department of Public Printing and Stationery, 1, 1895–), published monthly with annual cumulations. The same department also puts out *Selected Titles,* giving information on more popular government publications. Official publications from the Canadian provinces are listed in *Canadiana* (Ottawa, Ontario, Canada, National Library of Canada, 1, 1951–), published monthly with annual cumulations.

British government reports are listed in *Government Publications* (London, England, H. M. Stationery Office, 1, 1936–), published monthly with annual cumulations. HMSO also issues a daily list of new publications. *R and D Abstracts* (St. Mary Cray, Orpington, Kent, England, Department of Industry, Technology Report Centre, 1, 1972–) lists and abstracts available British and foreign research and development reports received at the Technology Report Centre.

International documents are listed in *International Bibliography, Information, Documentation* (New York, Bowker, 1, 1973–), published quarterly. Arrangement is in broad subject categories, and documents are listed with an annotation for each telling what the documents is about. Key international scientific organizations included here are United Nations Educational, Scientific and Cultural Organization, UNESCO; Food and Agriculture Organization, FAO; International Atomic Energy Agency, IAEA; and World Meteorological Organization, WMO. These agencies also publish their own complete lists.

Government documents are also included in some abstracting and indexing services.

Conference Proceedings

Many indexing and abstracting services include conference proceedings. Because conference papers are such an important source of original information, there are also specialized indexes for proceedings. *Index to Scientific and Technical Proceedings* (Philadelphia, Pa., Institute for Scientific Information, 1, 1978–   ) is monthly with annual cumulations, giving international coverage for proceedings published in books, reports, or journals. Arrangement is in seven sections, of which the main is "Contents of Proceedings," in which the table of contents of each proceedings is reproduced. Other sections index by category, author and editor, sponsor, meeting location, subject, and corporate author. *Directory of Published Proceedings: Science, Engineering, Medicine, Technology* (Harrison, N.Y., InterDok, 1, 1965–   ) is published ten times per year and cumulated annually, providing bibliographic information on published proceedings of congresses, conferences, symposia, meetings, seminars, and summer schools, worldwide. Arrangement is chronological, with indexing by subject, sponsor of the conference, and title. *Proceedings in Print* (Arlington, Mass., 1, 1964–   ) is issued six times per year plus an annual cumulative index. This index gives international coverage of conference proceedings and symposia that have appeared in print, in all subject areas. Arrangement of the main section is alphabetical by name of the meeting, and there is bibliographic information for the published proceedings. Indexing in each issue and cumulated is by corporate author, sponsor, editor, and subject, all in one alphabetical order.

Patents

In addition to the book by Bernard Houghton described at the beginning of this section on primary resources, Frank Newby's *How To Find Out About Patents* (New York, Pergamon, 1967) is helpful. *Answers to Questions Frequently Asked About Patents* is available free from the United States Patent and Trademark Office, Washington, D.C. 20231. *Patent It Yourself; How to Protect, Patent, and Market Your Inventions* by David Pressman (New York, McGraw-

Hill, 1979) is geared to the inventor or the would-be inventor. Chapters cover record keeping, patent searching, writing the patent application and getting the patent, and selling the invention. There is a bibliography for further reading, and samples of patent forms.

The United States Patent Office *Index of Patents* (Washington, D.C., U.S. Government Printing Office, 1920–) is published annually in two volumes: one alphabetical by patentee and the other by subject of the invention. The main part of the patentee volume is arranged alphabetically by the name of the person holding the patent, and tells the title and number of the patent. This volume also contains lists of reissue patentees, plant patentees, and design patentees. The subject volume first has lists of subject classes and then a listing of patents by these subject class numbers. Information given is patent number only. Another publication put out by the U.S. Patent Office, *Manual of Classification,* should be used in conjunction with these volumes to determine the correct subject class for your topic. The United States Patent and Trademark Office issues an *Official Gazette: Patents* (Washington, D.C., U.S. Government Printing Office, 1872–) weekly. Arrangement is in general topical sections: general and mechanical, chemical, electrical, and design. Patents are listed, with administrative information such as name and when filed and patent number, and a brief description of the item patented, with a drawing of the item. There is an alphabetical index of patentees. The full texts of patents are available in certain collections as mentioned in Chapter 1 of this book and in the appendix.

United Kingdom patents are listed in the Patent Office *Official Journal* (Orpington, Kent, England, Patent Office, 1884–), published weekly. This listing is in numerical order by patent number, with indexes by name and subject. At a later date abstracts of patents are published, arranged in broad subject groups. Indexes are cumulated after every 25,000 patents, or every several months.

Several bulletins from Derwent Publications, London, announce and abstract patents, internationally. These are published in thirteen separate publications by subject matter area.

Standards

The American National Standards Institute *Catalog of American National Standards* (New York, American National Standards Institute, 1923–) is published annually to list American standards for products, materials, or processes that have been registered by American National Standards Institute. Arrangement is in groups by the subject of the standard, for example, machine tool fluids, magnet wire, and so forth. Information given is the title of the standard and its standard number. *Industry Standards* by VSMF Data Control Services (Englewood, Colo., Information Handling Services) indexes standards that are part of the collection available in microform on a subscription basis. The index by society is arranged in sections for each society, for example, American Concrete Institute, and lists standards. The subject index provides access by specific subject or general subject.

The *Index of Federal Specifications and Standards* (Washington, D.C., U.S. General Services Administration, 1952–) and *Index of Specifications and Standards* (Washington, D.C., U.S. Department of Defense, 1951–) index standards of items for government nonmilitary use and military use, respectively.

The United States National Bureau of Standards sponsors the "National Standard Reference Data Series" Published by the United States Government Printing Office and available as a government publication through the Superintendent of Documents. This Series is produced by the National Standard Reference Data System which, as part of the National Bureau of Standards, was set up to compile critically evaluated numerical data and make them available for scientists. In this connection the National Bureau of Standards also co-sponsors the *Journal of Physical and Chemical Reference Data,* mentioned elsewhere in this chapter and described in Chapter 7 of this book.

Again in addition to Houghton's book, a guide to standards is Erasmus J. Struglia's *Standards and Specifications Information Sources* (Detroit, Mich., Gale, 1965). This guide lists general sources and directories, bibliographies and indexes to periodicals, catalogs and indexes of standards and specifications, and then government sources of U.S. standards, and associations and societies that produce standards. There is a subject index by specific subjects of standards. Sections on sources of standards, government and nongovernment, tell addresses of the sources and what is published.

United Kingdom standards are covered by the *British Standards Yearbook* (London, British Standards Institution, 1, 1937–), published anually. Arrangement is by subject of the standard, for example, automobiles, aerospace, and so forth. There is an index.

Theses and Dissertations

The *Comprehensive Dissertation Index, 1861–1972* (Ann Arbor, Mich., University Microfilms International, 1973) is in thirty-seven volumes that according to the introduction, list "virtually all of the dissertations" from U.S. universities during the years covered, and some foreign dissertations. Arrangement is by discipline, each volume or group of volumes being on a discipline, for example, volumes 1–4 chemistry, volume 5 mathematics and statistics, and so forth. These subject volumes are divided by broad subject divisions, for example, in the health and environmental science volume, the subject "Pharmacy and pharmacology" appears, and dissertations within each subject are listed alphabetically by keywords in their titles. Complete bibliographic information is given. Volumes 33–37 are the author index for the entire set and give complete bibliographic information. Supplements have been published annually since 1973 to index dissertations for the preceding year, again arranged by discipline and then by key words in the title, with an index by author. The supplements are cumulated, for example, for 1973–77. Current coverage is provided by *Dissertation Abstracts International* (Ann Arbor, Mich., University Microfilms International, 1969–   ), published monthly in two separate volumes: A on the humanities and social sciences, and B on the sciences and engineering. Earlier titles published in 1935–69 by University Microfilms preceded this one in providing information on dissertations, but did not include European universities. These journals list dissertations from cooperating universities in the United States, Canada and Europe; a list of cooperating institutions is included. Arrangement is by broad subject area with subdivisions; for example, the subject agriculture is subdivided into general, animal culture and nutrition, animal pathology, and so forth. Each entry has biliographic information and an extensive abstract. Indexing is by key word in the title and by author. All dissertations listed are available for order from University Microfilms.

Masters theses have traditionally been more difficult to trace than dissertations. Those in science from U.S. and Canadian colleges and universities are listed in *Masters Theses in the Pure and Applied Sciences* edited by Wade H. Shafer (New York, Plenum, 1, 1956–   ), published annually. There are also specialized lists of theses, from a particular university or in a particular subject field.

CURRENT AWARENESS MATERIALS

World Meetings: United States and Canada (New York, Macmillan, 1963–) is issued quarterly, listing meetings that will take place in the coming two-year period. Arrangement is in eight sections by three-month periods, for example, July to September 1982, and meetings are listed together with location, dates, sponsor, and information such as content, expected attendance, and whethe · the proceedings will be published. There are indexes by subject ke ' word, date, deadline, location, and sponsor. Published separately to complete the international coverage is *World Meetings: Outside United States and Canada* (New York, Macmillan, 1968–). This journal is also issued quarterly, and has the same format. *Scientific Meetings* (San Diego, Calif., Scientific Meetings, 1, 1957–), published quarterly, lists meetings that will take place in the coming one-year period. There are four parts in each issue: (1) an alphabetical list of sponsoring organizations with addresses to write for information; (2) the main section, alphabetical by the organization sponsoring the meeting, and telling dates and place of meeting; (3) chronological list of meetings arranged by month and day; and (4) subject index.

The various subject sections of *Current Contents* (Philadelphia, Pa., Institute for Scientific Information, 1958–) will be described with the subject chapters with which they fit. Because collectively these sections give such a wide coverage of current scientific and technical literature, they are also mentioned here. Published weekly, each section reprints tables of contents of selected journals and multi-author books, worldwide. About one thousand journals are covered by each subject section, with each issue of *Current Contents* reprinting the tables of contents of those items issued most recently. Each issue also includes some regular features such as notes on articles that have been cited many times in other articles. An author index gives addresses for authors so that you may write for reprints of articles you want, or the publisher will provide a copy of the article for a fee. The scientific subject sections and date each began publication are:

Current Contents: Agriculture, Biology and Environmental Sciences
(1970–)
Current Contents: Clinical Practice (1973–)
Current Contents: Engineering, Technology and Applied Sciences
(1970–)

Current Contents: Life Sciences (1958–)
Current Contents: Physical, Chemical and Earth Sciences (1961–)

QUICK REFERENCE TOOLS

Dictionaries

The *McGraw-Hill Dictionary of Scientific and Technical Terms* (New York, McGraw-Hill, 2d edition 1978) is arranged alphabetically by terms and tells the field in which the term is used and a brief definition. Drawings to illustrate meanings are grouped near the margin of the page on which the related terms appear. Appendixes include the metric system, conversion factors, signs and symbols, abbreviations, and brief biographies of historically prominent scientists.

Chambers Dictionary of Science and Technology (Edinburgh, Scotland, Chambers, 1975) includes scientific and technical terms, and abbreviations. The appendix contains information in tabular form. A. Hechtlinger's *Modern Science Dictionary* (Palisades, N.J., Franklin, 2d edition 1975) is arranged in two alphabets, the second being for works with definitions added since the first edition. There is also a list of about 500 hard-to-pronounce words with phonetic aids. The *First Science Dictionary* by David J. Lucas and others defines biological, chemical, and physical terms and phrases likely to be encountered up through undergraduate courses. Definitions are brief.

The *Dictionary of Scientific Units, Including Dimensionless Numbers and Scales* by Harold G. Jerrerd and D. B. McNeill (London, Chapman and Hall, 4th edition 1980) is arranged alphabetically by unit. Information given includes definition, historical facts, and size of the unit. Appendixes include fundamental physical constants, weights and measures, and conversion factors. There are references and an index.

Foreign language dictionaries that specialize in scientific and technical terminology all give word equivalents in the other language. The ones by DeVries also have a special section on grammar and suggestions for translators.

French

DeVries, Louis. *French–English Science and Technology Dictionary.* New York, McGraw-Hill, 4th edition 1976.

Dorian, A. F. *Dictionary of Science and Technology: English–French.* Amsterdam and New York, Elsevier, 1979.
Dorian, A. F. *Dictionary of Science and Technology: French–English.* Amsterdam and New York, Elsevier, 1980.

German:

DeVries, Louis. *German–English Science Dictionary for Students in Chemistry, Physics, Biology, Agriculture, and Related Sciences.* New York, McGraw-Hill, 3d edition 1959.
Dorian, A. F. *Dictionary of Science and Technology: English–German.* Amsterdam and New York, Elsevier, 2d edition 1978.
Dorian, A. F. *Dictionary of Science and Technology: German–English.* Amsterdam and New York, Elsevier, 1978.
Ernst, Richard. *Dictionary of Engineering and Technology, vol. 1 German–English* and vol. 2 *English–German.* New York, Oxford University, 4th edition 1975–1981.

Spanish:

Collazo, Javier L. *Encyclopedic Dictionary of Technical Terms: English–Spanish, Spanish–English.* New York, McGraw-Hill, 1980.

Russian:

Kuznetsov, B. V. *Russian–English Polytechnical Dictionary.* New York, Pergamon, 1981.
Muller, V. K. *English–Russian Dictionary.* New York, Dutton, 14th edition 1973.

Because so many acronyms and abbreviations are used in scientific fields, dictionaries that specialize in these terms are needed in addition to their coverage in more general dictionaries. *Acronyms, Initialisms, and Abbreviations Dictionary* (Detroit, Mich., Gale, 7th edition 1981) includes all fields, not just scientific. Arrangement is alphabetical by acronym or abbreviation, and the full equivalent word or phrase is given. This is kept up to date between editions by supplements called *New Acronyms, Initialisms, and Abbreviations.* There is also a separate volume called *Reverse Acronyms, Initialisms, and Abbrevia-*

tions Dictionary (Detroit, Mich., Gale, 7th edition 1980) that covers the same terms as the dictionary above. Arrangement is alphabetical by what the acronym or abbreviation stands for and tells the acronym or abbreviation. Ralph DeSola's *Abbreviations Dictionary* (New York, Elsevier, 5th edition 1978) is also general, not just scientific, and includes some foreign abbreviations. Arrangement is alphabetical by abbreviation or acronym, and the meaning is given. Also included are some special categories such as geographical equivalents, historical and mythological characters, initials and nicknames, signs and symbols.

Ocran's *Acronyms: A Dictionary of Abbreviations and Acronyms Used in Scientific and Technical Writing* by Emanuel B. Ocran (London and Boston, Mass., Routledge and Kegan Paul, 1978) has as its main part an alphabetical arrangement of abbreviations and acronyms, with meaning and subject fields in which the abbreviation is used. A second part lists subject fields alphabetically, and under each lists abbreviations and acronyms alphabetically, with meaning.

Initialisms of Scientific and Technical Organization edited by Urban J. Sweeney (Roway, Calif., Scientific Meetings, 1978) is arranged alphabetically by initials of organizations and gives the full name of the organization, as well as an alphabetical list of organizations with addresses.

Handbooks

Scientific Tables by J. R. Geigy and A. G. Basel (Ardsley, N.Y., Geigy, 7th edition 1974) contains basic data including mathematical and statistical tables and data on physical chemistry, biochemistry, composition and functions of the body, body fluids, body measurement, hormones, international biological standards, and reference preparations. The *Practicing Scientist's Handbook; a Guide for Physical and Terrestrial Scientists and Engineers* by Alfred J. Moses (New York, Van Nostrand Reinhold, 1978) gives property data for physics, chemistry, and engineering. A chapter on the environment is especially useful to geologists and geophysicists. After introductory materials, information is mostly in tabular form, giving properties of elements, organic and inorganic compounds, alloys, glasses and ceramics, composites, polymers and adhesives, semiconductors, superconductors, the environment, and miscellaneous materials.

Tables of Physical and Chemical Constants by George W. C. Kaye and T. H. Laby, this edition edited by A. E. Bailey and others (New York, Longman, 14th edition 1973), is in three main sections: physics, chemistry, and mathematical functions. References give information sources.

International Critical Tables of Numerical Data, Physics, Chemistry and Technology (New York, McGraw-Hill, 1926–33) is in seven volumes plus index. Contents are mostly tables with accompanying explanatory information. The index volume is a subject index for the set. All data were examined and compiled by experts in the field before being included, and the subject experts were to give the best values possible; this is why the word "critical" is used in the title. Presenting new critically evaluated physical and chemical data is the *Journal of Physical and Chemical Reference Data,* described in Chapter 7 of this book.

Most handbooks are specialized by subject area covered, and are listed in subject chapters of this book. Another guide to help you find the one you need is a bibliography of handbooks, *Handbooks and Tables in Science and Technology* edited by Russell H. Powell (Phoenix, Ariz., Oryx, 1979). Over 2,000 handbooks and tables in science, technology, and medicine are listed. The main part, called the title index, is arranged alphabetically by title and gives bibliographic information and some annotations. There is also an author index, and a subject index. Appendixes list separately medical handbooks and United States National Bureau of Standards data compilations.

Directories

The *World Guide to Scientific Associations and Learned Societies* (Ridgewood, N.J., Saur, 1981) is an international directory for all fields of science and technology. Arrangement is in sections by geographic area: Europe, America, Africa, Asia, Oceania; and then by country. Associations are listed within these sections alphabetically with address and sometimes other information such as number of members or names of officers. There is a subject index.

The *Encyclopedia of Associations* (Detroit, Mich., Gale, 1956–   ), is now published annually in three volumes. Volume 1 *National Organizations of the United States,* lists organizations in subject area groups, the one of interest here being "scientific, engineering and technical organizations," subdivided by field, for example, aerospace, botany, and so forth. Organizations are listed with address and phone, person in charge, and brief information such as founding date and publications. Indexing is alphabetical and by key word. Volume 2, *Geographic and Executive Index,* is arranged alphabetically by state in the geographic part and by name of executive in the executive part. Volume 3, *New Associations and Projects,* is issued between editions to keep the information up to date.

Research Centers Directory and *Industrial Research Laboratories* of the United States were described in Chapter 1 of this book.

Science Guide to Scientific Instruments (Washington, D.C., American Association for the Advancement of Science, 1964–) is published annually as a buyer's guide for laboratory instruments and equipment. Arrangement is alphabetical by name of instrument or equipment, with names of manufacturers listed for each in abbreviated form. A separate section arranged alphabetically by name of manufacturer gives complete name, address, and phone.

Thomas Register of American Manufacturers (New York, Thomas, 1, 1905–) is published annually. The 72d edition, 1982, is in seventeen volumes. The first several volumes of each edition are arranged alphabetically by product or service, and under each product firms are listed in a geographical arrangement by state and city. Name and address and a rating code for approximate minimum total tangible assets are given. Two volumes provide company profiles. Arrangement is alphabetical by company name, and address and phone, asset rating, company executives, and location of sales offices and so forth are given. Other volumes are catalogs of companies, arranged alphabetically by company.

The *Directory of Directories* (Detroit, Mich., Information Enterprises distributed by Gale, 1, 1980–) has a descriptive subtitle: "Annotated guide to business and industrial directories, professional and scientific rosters, and other lists and guides of all kinds." Directories for this purpose are defined basically as lists of names and addresses with little text. The main section is the list of directories, arranged in fifteen subject catagories, for example, science and engineering, and then alphabetically by title within the subject. Information given is bibliographic citation, address and phone of publisher, and an annotation including such information as what is covered, arrangement, indexes, and frequency. There are indexes by subject and by title. *Directory of Scientific Directories: A World Guide to Scientific Directories Including Medicine, Agriculture, Engineering, Manufacturing and Industrial Directories* (Detroit, Gale, 3d edition 1979) lists directories of universities, laboratories, organizations, museums, people, and so forth. Arrangement is by country, with an international section first. Directories are listed with bibliographic information and sometimes an annotation. Indexes are by author, compiler, or editor and by title in the original language and in English.

Biographical

Historical biographical materials and those with lengthy biographies are described above in the section on biographies. A long-standing source for biographical information on scientists who are currently alive and active in their field is *American Men and Women of Science: Physical and Biological Sciences* (New York, Bowker, 15th edition 1982). This multivolume set is arranged alphabetically by names of scientists, and contains brief biographical sketches including birth date and place, areas of interest, education, positions held, and address. Indexing, in the last volume, is by discipline and geographical. The National Academy of Sciences *Biographical Memoirs* (Washington, D.C., National Academy of Sciences, 1, 1877–), published approximately annually, contains biographies of members of the National Academy of Sciences who have died. A biographical sketch, portrait, and list of publications are included for each.

Annual Obituary (New York, St. Martin's, 1, 1980–) is published annually and gives international coverage. Detailed information on the lives and achievements of prominent people who have died during the year is provided. Each entry contains an obituary essay, biographical data, career details, important sources of further information, and usually a photograph. There are indexes by name and profession.

Current Bibliographic Directory of the Arts and Sciences (Philadelphia, Pa., Institute for Scientific Information, 1967–), which had different titles up to 1979, is published annually to list names and addresses of authors who published during the year in any of a large group of journals used for preparing *Current Contents*. Arrangement is alphabetical by name, and information given is the author's address and a list of publications in the year covered. There is also an organization section arranged alphabetically by name of organization that tells location—country, state and city—for each organization, and a geographic section arranged by country, state, and city that lists names of organizations and then names of authors in the organizations.

4
Mathematics, Computer Science

This chapter will be concerned with mathematics, including probability and statistics, and computer science.

GENERAL MATHEMATICS

INTRODUCTORY MATERIALS

Mathematics: An Introduction to its Spirit and Use (San Francisco, Freeman, 1979) is a collection of forty articles from *Scientific American* that provide an excellent overview of the study of mathematics. The articles, written by many different authors, are arranged in sections; history, numbers, algebra, geometry, statistics and probability, symbolic logic and computers, and applications. Many illustrations are used. There is a bibliography, and an index. Another collection is *Mathematics Today! Twelve Informal Essays* edited by Lynn Arthur Steen (New York, Springer-Verlag, 1978), emphasizing the relevance of mathematics for everyone. The book begins with a discussion of mathematics today by editor Steen and then presents papers by various authors. Essays cover the nature, development, and use of mathematical concepts, especially as applied to modern scientific research. One essay contains an interview with three mathematicians. Interesting problems and portraits and biographical information on mathematicians are set off in boxed areas within the essays, and there are many illustrations, suggestions for further reading, and an index. *Mathematics in the Real World* (Boston, Birkhausen, 1979) is the proceedings of an international workshop. Mathematicians from many countries and many different fields of interest met for a two-day workshop, and these approximately twenty-five papers by different authors are the result. The papers stress mathematics today, and implications for its further development and for its usefulness and development in nonmathematical fields. Materials on underdeveloped countries and on educational aspects and teacher training are included. There is a bibliography of books about mathematics.

An Introduction to the History of Mathematics by Howard W. Eves (New York, Holt, Rinehart and Winston, 4th edition 1976) reads easily for general interest reading or for use as a text. It is arranged in chronological sequence, beginning with primitive counting as used in ancient tribes and proceeding into the twentieth century. There are portraits and information including personal anecdotes and stories about mathematicians, as well as many other illustrations of historical documents and of mathematical figures. Suggested problems at the end of each chapter are of varying levels of difficulty so as to be just for fun or for use as class exercises; answers or suggestions for solutions are at the back of the book. A bibliography at the end of each chapter deals with the subject matter of that chapter, and there is a general bibliography at the end of the book. *Historical Roots of Elementary Mathematics* by Lucas N. Bunt and others (Englewood Cliffs, N.J., Prentice-Hall, 1976) is aimed at general readers, high school and college students, and teachers. It covers the historical roots of elementary mathematics, beginning with Egyptian mathematics in about 3000 B.C. and proceeding through Babylonian and Greek mathematics, and into the bases of modern mathematics. Exercises are inserted where they are appropriate, often for each of several sections of a chapter, so the reader can actually carry out long division as the ancient Egyptians did and study geometry as scholars did in Euclid's day. Hints and answers to selected problems are at the back of the book. Quotations from old documents and many illustrations make the book interesting, and its many subsections add to its clarity. There are references with each chapter.

Men and Institutions in American Mathematics (Lubbock, Tex., Texas Tech, 1976) consists of ten papers from a conference on the history of American Mathematics held at Texas Tech University in 1973. The papers, by different authors, are on different historical aspects including the roles of specific people, international relations, mathematics in colonial America, and the rise of modern algebra. Emphasis is twentieth-century American. Another history is by L. C.

Young: *Mathematicians and Their Times: History of Mathematics and Mathematics of History* (New York, Elsevier North-Holland, 1981).

Subject Headings and Classification

Algebra
Calculus
Games of chance (Mathematics)
Geometry
Mathematical literature
Mathematical models
Mathematical recreations
Mathematical statistics
Mathematicians
Mathematics
   (also subdivisions of Mathematics)
   —Bibliography
   —Dictionaries
   —Problems, exercises, etc.
   —Tables
Probabilities
Sampling (Statistics)
Statistics

In the Library of Congress classification mathematics books are classed in the QA class, with computer science being the QA 76 section and probability and statistics the QA 273 to QA 280 section. In the Dewey Decimal Classification mathematics is classed 510, with probability and statistics in 519.

BIBLIOGRAPHIC MATERIALS

Guides to the Literature

Using the Mathematical Literature; a Practical Guide by Barbara K. Schaefer (New York, Dekker, 1979) is for scientists in any field as well as for students, teachers, and practicing mathematicians. Introductory material includes the history of mathematical literature, the nature of mathematics and of mathematical literature, information needs in mathematics, and libraries. The major part of the book is a review of the current literature in pure mathematics, arranged in chapters covering journals and access to them, books and access to them, and reference books. Other chapters cover the literature of applied mathematics, statistics, and operations research. There is an index. A similar, older, guide is John E. Pemberton's *How to Find Out in Mathematics* (Oxford and New York, Pergamon, 2d edition 1969). The book begins with a discussion of careers in mathematics, and then is arranged in chapters by Dewey Decimal Classification classes and covers library guides and bibliographies, reference works, periodicals and indexes, and where to find information on specific areas, for example, probability and statistics. The appendixes provide sources of Russian mathematical information, as well as material on mathematics and the government, and actuarial science. There is an index.

Current Information Sources in Mathematics by Elie M. Dick (Littleton, Colo., Libraries Unlimited, 1973) is a bibliography of materials published from 1960 to 1972. Books are listed in broad subject groups, with complete bibliographic information and annotation. Reference books, periodicals, and professional organizations are also covered. *Guide to the Literature of Mathematics Today* by Joong Fang (Hauppauge, N.Y., Paideia, 1972) is a selected bibliography. In most subject areas materials listed were published before 1967 although in a few areas they go up to 1971. The most important sections are extensive lists of major terms used in mathematics, of key subject headings, and of major series of books with each volume of the series listed.

Use of Mathematical Literature edited by A. R. Dorling (London and Boston, Mass. Butterworths, 1977) is at the more advanced, graduate level. Chapters cover the role of literature in mathematics, discussion of major organizations and journals, reference materials, and subject areas, such as history, logic, and group theory. Each chapter discusses the literature and then has an extensive bibliography.

Bibliographies

Matthew P. Gaffney's *Annotated Bibliography of Expository Writing in the Mathematical Sciences* (Washington, D.C., Mathematical Association of America, 1976) lists mostly periodical articles and some books. Items were chosen for those who want surveys of current mathematical topics. Items are arranged in broad subject groups and then in subdivisions by difficulty of understanding: general, requiring a high school education; elementary and advanced, meaning college undergraduate levels; and research, meaning graduate level. Bibliographic information is given, and usually an annotation. Related references to a given subject are listed with bibliographic information only and a cross-reference to their main listing with annotation. The author index is actually a bibliography arranged by author and giving bibliographic information with reference to full citation in the subject section. The *Bibliography and Research Manual of the History of Mathematics* by Kenneth O. May (Toronto, University of Toronto Press, 1973) is designed for use by mathematicians and historians. There is introductory material on information retrieval, personal information storage, and historical analysis and writing. The bibliography is arranged in sections by topic: biographies, mathematical topics, epimathematical topics, history, and information retrieval, with subdivisions within each topic. Books and periodical articles are listed; coverage is international. The appendixes contain symbols and abbreviations and a list of journals cited in the bibliography.

Indexing and Abstracting Services

Mathematical Reviews (Providence, R.I., American Mathematical Society, 1, 1940–   ) is issued monthly. Periodical articles, books, and reports are listed in the same classed subject arrangement as in *Current Mathematical Publications*, which is described below in the section on current awareness. In addition to bibliographic information, there is an informative review of each item, often 250 or more words in length. Each issue has an author index and a key subject index; the author indexes are cumulated twice a year and the key subject index annually.

Bulletin Signaletique 110: Informatique, Automatique, Recherche Operationnelle, Gestion (Paris, Centre de Documentation, 33, 1972–   ) was preceded by other similar titles. Like others in the series, it has international coverage of journals, books, reports, theses, and proceedings. Arrangement is by subject in a classed grouping by

ISI/COMPUMATH

Multidisciplinary citation index to the world's significant mathematics literature. It is a subset of Science Citation Index (SCISEARCH) with 15% more mathematics literature.

Prepared by Institute for Scientific Information.

Coverage: 1976 to present
File size: 200,000 records
Unit record: citation
Vendor, Cost/connect hour:
ISI, $50 to subscribers,
$150 to nonsubscribers,
(5 hours per year minimum)

Fig. 4-1. Computer data base: ISI/COMPUMATH

broad topics with many subdivisions. Bibliographic information and an abstract are given, with author and subject indexes.

SECONDARY LITERATURE MATERIALS

Encyclopedias

The *VNR Concise Encyclopedia of Mathematics* (New York, Van Nostrand Reinhold, 1977) has as its aim to describe interrelations in mathematics so that nonmathematicians may better understand mathematics for use not only in science but in everyday life. Colors are used to help highlight types of information: yellow background for definitions and formulas, blue for examples, and red for theorems. Illustrations, for example, of geometric figures, are also highlighted in color. Articles are arranged in three main sections: elementary mathematics, for example, higher arithmetical operations, steps toward higher mathematics, for example, set theory, and brief reports on selected topics, for example, number theory. Tables at the back of the volume include meanings of mathematical symbols, squares and cubes, logarithms, and trigonometric and exponential functions. Appendixes include photographs of drawing instruments, historic manuscripts and artifacts, and portraits of famous mathematicians in history. The *Encyclopedic Dictionary of Mathematics* (Cambridge, Mass., MIT Press, 1977) is a two-volume set prepared and translated by the Mathematical Society of Japan with the cooperation of the American Mathematical Society. It is arranged alphabetically by term, and most articles are several pages in length. Brief biographical sketches are given for famous mathematicians. The appendix contains tables of formulas, and there are indexes by name and by subject. The *Universal Encyclopedia of Mathematics* (New York, Simon and Schuster, 1969) is geared to high school and college students. Arranged alphabetically by term, it has brief concise definitions, often followed by a more lengthy discussion with examples. At the back are mathematical formulas and tables.

Learning and Developing Mathematics Skills

Mathematics, the Man-Made Universe: An Introduction to the Spirit of Mathematics by Sherman K. Stein (San Francisco, Freeman, 3d edition 1976) is an introduction to mathematics for general readers or high school and college students. In using the term "man-made universe" the author points out that mathematics is completely the product of the human mind, whereas the natural world is not yet completely understood. Core chapters of this book deal with some fundamentals about numbers, primes, rationals, and irrationals, and other chapters deal with applications including such topics as tiling, memory wheels, probability, and map coloring. Material is often presented as interesting stories and examples. There are exercises with each chapter of three levels of difficulty: those to check understanding of the chapter, those for which one must apply ideas from the chapter, and those that develop ideas tangential to the chapter. Answers for selected problems are at the back of the book. There are references with each chapter. *From Sticks and Stones: Personal Adventures in Mathematics* by Paul B. Johnson (Chicago, Science Research Associates, 1975) is written for those who need to understand and use arithmetic. Arithmetic, statistics and probability, and introductions to algebra and to geometry are included. There are exercises at the end of each chapter, and answers are provided for selected exercises. An appendix deals with problem solving. *Mathematics and the Modern World* by Mario F. Triola (Menlo Park, Calif., Benjamin/Cummings, 2d edition 1978) relates mathematics to the world, through its illustrations, through a historical overview and historical sections in each chapter, and in a chapter on mathematics in the humanities and social sciences. Topics covered are structure of mathematical systems, algebra, probability, statistics, computers, and modern and abstract mathematical systems; appendixes cover geometry and trigonometry. Many examples are used throughout, and exercises are scattered through the chapters, with answers to selected problems at the back of the book. There is a bibliography. *Mathematics: Ideas and Applications* by Daniel D. Benice (New York, Academic, 1978) aims to give a treatment of mathematics for general interest. Arithmetic skills and some algebra background are needed. Topics covered are in areas of logic, number theory, geometry, topology, mathematical analysis, probability and statistics, and computers. There are also interesting introductory problems, applications, and puzzles. Many examples of applications for each concept help to make the information interesting and useful. There are many exercises in each chapter, with answers to selected problems at the back. N. W. Gowar's *Invitation to Mathematics* (New York, Oxford University Press, 1979) also teaches concepts and gives many applications and examples to make them clear.

Algebra

Modern Algebra With Applications by William J. Gilbert (New York, Wiley, 1976) deals with the essential concepts of modern algebra, with a wide variety of applications. Examples are included with each concept. There are exercises at the end of each chapter, with answers to selected problems at the back of the book. A bibliography, glossary of symbols, and index complete the volume. *Introduction to Modern Algebra* by Marvin Marcus (New York, Dekker, 1978) contains concepts of algebra with many examples. There are exercises for each concept, with answers to selected problems at the back of the book. New words are listed with an indication of the page where the word was introduced.

Calculus

A Primer for Calculus by Leonard I. Holder (Belmont, Calif., Wadsworth, 1978) is designed to fill gaps in prior learning and to reinforce and strengthen skills, and could be a text for a college-level precalculus course. It teaches concepts and then has examples and exercises for each concept. There are review exercises at the end of each chapter, and answers to selected problems at the back of the book. Appendixes contain mathematics tables. *Calculus: One and Several Variables* by S. L. Salas and Einar Hille (New York, Wiley, 3d edition 1978) begins with a section answering the question "What is calculus?" and procedes through limits and continuity, differentiation, mean values, integration, logarithms, trigonometric and hyperbolic functions, integration, conic sections, polar coordinates, infinite series, vectors, variables, and integrals. Appendixes deal with sets and induction and proofs of some theorems, and also contain tables. Examples are used throughout, and exercises are scattered through chapters and at the ends of chapters, with the answers to most problems at the back of the book. *Calculus for Business and Life* by

Howard B. Beckwith (Belmont, Calif., Wadsworth, 1978) requires high school algebra for understanding, and a review of algebra is provided in the appendix. In addition to basic calculus, many practical applications are presented in detail, and these applications are stressed rather than the basic mathematics. Exercises at the ends of chapters are of two types: those for review and more difficult ones using principles learned in the chapter. Answers to selected problems are provided. Francis B. Hildebrand's *Advanced Calculus for Applications* (Englewood Cliffs, N.J., Prentice-Hall, 2d edition 1976) deals with topics that have wide application, based on an elementary knowledge of calculus. It is aimed mostly at nonmathematicians, those in other fields wanting to apply calculus. Topics covered include ordinary differential equations, boundary-value problems, vector analysis, partial differential equations, complex variables, and applications of analytic function theory. Problems at the end of each chapter have answers provided at the back of the book.

Geometry

Descriptive Geometry by James H. Earle (Reading, Mass., Addison-Wesley, 2d edition 1978) takes an approach of teaching geometry to be used as a tool for solving problems. As such it is especially useful for engineers and technicians interested in design. Many photographs and many graphs and diagrams are used throughout. There is a summary at the end of each chapter, and a series of exercises. Another basic geometry book is *A First Course in Geometry* by Edward T. Walsh (San Francisco, Rinehart, 1974).

Finite

Finite Mathematics by Daniel P. Maki and Maynard Thompson (New York, McGraw-Hill, 1978) contains basic ideas and techniques, with emphasis on developing methods for problem solving. There is introductory material, and then chapters are grouped in three main sections: probability models, linear models, and applications. Each chapter has examples and applications, and the applications section has more applications which are based on ideas developed in the first two sections, for example, mathematical games, and evaluation of various types of investments of money. Exercises are scattered through the chapters with each topic, and the chapters end with review exercises. Answers to selected problems are at the back of the book. Many books cover the mathematics needed in specific fields of interest. *Mathematical Methods in Science* by George Polya (Washington, D.C., Mathematical Association of America, 1977) aims to make important mathematics ideas interesting and understandable. Topics included are measurement, approximation, statics, dynamics, physical reasoning, and differential equations. Other examples are *Basic Technical Mathematics with Calculus* by Allyn J. Washington (Menlo Park, Calif., Benjamin/Cummings, 1978) for students in technical areas and pre-engineering; *Finite Mathematics and Calculus: Applications in Business and the Social and Life Sciences* by Hugh G. Campbell (New York, Macmillan, 1977); *Mathematics for Students of Business, Economics, and Social Sciences* by James Radlow (North Scituate, Mass., Duxbury, 1979); and *Essential Mathematics for Applied Fields* by Richard M. Meyer (New York, Springer-Verlag, 1979).

Calculators

Science With Pocket Calculators by David R. Green and J. Lewis (London, Wykeham, 1978) is directed to owners or prospective owners of advanced calculators that incorporate some scientific or mathematical functions. There is discussion of types of calculators and their features and how they work; and there are examples of how they may be used, for example, in statistics, probability, solving nonlinear equations, and so forth. The last chapter deals with programmable calculators. The appendix contains a few games to play with calculators, a list of references, and solutions to the problems that are scattered through the chapters. There is an index.

Calculator Users Guide and Dictionary by Charles J. Sippl (Champaign, Ill., Matrix, 1976) begins with a discussion of hand-held and desk-top calculators, including types and capabilities, and presents criteria and evaluation procedures for proper selection of a calculator for one's own use. The main part of this book is the dictionary section. Arrangement of this section is alphabetical by term, with cross-references, and definitions are concise, consisting of seventy-five words or less.

Mathematical Recreations

Mathematics and Humor by John A. Paulos (Chicago, University of Chicago Press, 1980) is a mixture of mathematics and wit. Chapter topics are mathematics and humor; axioms, levels, and iteration; self-reference and paradox; humor, grammar, and philosophy; catastrophe theory model of jokes and humor; odds and the end. A list of references is included. *The Mathematical Gardener* edited by David A. Klarner (Belmont, Calif., Wadsworth, 1981) is a collection of thirty essays written by leading mathematicians, aimed at a nonspecialist or amateur level. Sections are on games, geometry, two-dimensional tiling, three-dimensional tiling, fun and problems, numbers and coding theory.

There are many books of mathematical games. Following is a sample.

Benson, William H. and Jacoby Oswald. *Magic Cubes: New Recreations*. New York, Dover, 1981.

Dunn, Angela. *Mathematical Bafflers*. New York, Dover, revised edition 1980.

Gardner, Martin. *Mathematical Carnival*. New York, Knopf, 1975.

Gardner, Martin. *Scientific American Book of Mathematical Puzzles and Diversions*. New York, Simon and Schuster, 1963.

Gardner, Martin. *Second Scientific American Book of Mathematical Puzzles and Diversions*. New York, Simon and Schuster, 1965.

Schwartz, Benjamin L., editor. *Mathematical Solitaires and Games*. Farmingdale, N.Y., Baywood, 1980.

Taylor, Don. *Mastering Rubik's Cube*. New York, Holt, Rinehart and Winston, 1981.

Prabability and Statistics

Probability, Statistics, and Queueing Theory: With Computer Science Applications by Arnold O. Allen (New York, Academic, 1978) is written so that readers with a college algebra background can follow most of the book, but knowledge of calculus is helpful. Readers also need a basic knowledge of computer hardware and software. Emphasis is on theory used to solve practical computer science problems for those interested in computer science or in using computers to solve problems in other scientific fields. Many examples are used. There are references and exercises at the end of each chapter; answers to selected problems are at the back of the book. *Probability and Statistical Inference* by Robert V. Hogg and E. A. Tanis (New York, Macmillan, 1977) is a text for which some knowledge of calculus is needed. It covers fundamental concepts, including probability and distribution of the discrete type, empirical distributions, distributions of the continuous type, basic sampling distribution, approximation, multivariate distributions, chi-square tests, analysis of variance, and statistical inference. Exercises are scattered through the chapters, with answers to selected ones at the back of the book. There is a list of references, and appendixes contain tables. Other tests also require some knowledge of calculus, and also have exercises with answers to selected ones, and references. *Introduction to Probability and Statistics* by Bernard W. Lindgren (New York, Macmillan, 4th edition 1978) covers basic notions of probability models, statistical inference, and useful statistical methods. *Probability* by Edward J. Dudewicz (New York, Holt, Rinehart and Winston, 1976) is a basic text. *Introduction to Probability and Statistics* by Narayan C. Giri (New York, Dekker, 1974–75) is in two volumes, one for probability and one for statistics. It is written for introductory understanding, at an undergraduate level. *Probability and Statistics: Theory and Applications* by Donald A. S. Fraser (North Scituate, Mass., Duxbury, 1976) introduces basic concepts of probability and statistics, blending theory and application, and also covers basic principles of experimentation. The Schaum's outline series provides *Schaum's Outline of Theory and Problems of Probability and Statistics* by Murray R. Spiegel (New York, McGraw-Hill, 1975).

Principles and Procedures of Statistics: A Biometrical Approach by Robert G. Steel (New York, McGraw-Hill, 1980) takes a nonmathematical approach, stressing the application of statistical methods in all fields. Many examples are used, and there are references with each chapter, and suggested exercises. The appendix contains statistical tables. An *Introduction to the Statistical Analysis of Data* by Theodore W. Anderson and S. L. Sclove (Boston, Mass., Houghton Mifflin, 1978) requires knowledge of only high school algebra. It is an introduction to statistical concepts and methods with many examples of applications from various fields. Main sections are descriptive statistics, probability, statistical inference, and statistical methods for problem solving. Basic information is concise, with extra material often put into the appendixes or separately marked sections. There are exercises at the end of each chapter, with answers at the back of the book. References are also listed for each chapter, and appendixes include statistical tables. *Introductory Statistics* by Thomas H. Wonnacott (New York, Wiley, 3d edition 1977) also requires only high school algebra although calculus is helpful. Topics are basic probability and statistics, basic inference, regression, and some miscellaneous topics such as chi-square and Bayesian methods. There are problems with answers, and statistical tables. *Mathematical Statistics: Basic Ideas and Selected Topics* by Peter J. Bickel (San Francisco, Holden-Day, 1977) requires some knowledge of calculus and of probability theory for understanding. Examples are used throughout, and references are given.

Practical techniques of statistics basic to many fields are discussed in *Statistical Survey Techniques* by Raymond J. Jessen (New York, Wiley, 1978). Many examples are based on real data in actual studies. There are references and exercises with each chapter, and an appendix of tables. *Survey Sampling and Measurement* edited by N. K. Namboodiri (New York, Academic, 1978) contains papers from a symposium held in 1977 at the University of North Carolina, Chapel Hill. There are several papers dealing with each of these topics: design issues in sample surveys, methodological problems, analysis of survey data, nonresponse and undercoverage, time series analysis, applications of survey data and methods, and the gap between theory and practice. References are included with each paper. Another volume on sampling is by Richard L. Schaeffer: *Elementary Survey Sampling* (North Scituate, Mass., Duxbury, 2d edition 1979).

Statistical tables are collected in the *CRC Handbook of Tables for Probability and Statistics* edited by William H. Beyer (Cleveland, Ohio, Chemical Rubber Company, 2d edition 1968). Part one contains tables of probability and statistics, and other, shorter, parts contain tables of normal distributions, student's t-distribution, chi-square, F-distribution, order statistics, range, correlation, non-parametric statistics, quality control, and other miscellaneous tables. *Basic Statistical Tables*, with the same editor and publisher (Cleveland, Ohio, Chemical Rubber Company, 1971), brings together the most commonly used basic tables. *Statistical Tables for Science, Engineering, Management, and Business Studies* by John Murdoch and J. A. Barnes (New York, Halsted, 2d edition 1974) is divided into sections and includes accounting tables in addition to basic mathematical statistical tables.

Take a Chance With Your Calculator by Lennart Rade (Forest Grove, Oreg., Dilithium, 1977) has the descriptive subtitle "Probability problems for programmable calculators." This book is divided into three parts: problems, commentaries, and programs. The user needs access to a programmable calculator, but need not know probability and statistics. The problems part contains sections on topics such as tossing dice or family planning of number and sex of children, with several exercises for each topic. The commentaries part discusses each exercise, and the programs part contains programs for Hewlett-Packard 25 and Texas SR-56 calculators.

Games of chance are analyzed by Richard A. Epstein in *The Theory of Gambling and Statistical Logic* (New York, Academic, 1977). The author does not purport to teach an easy way to win in gambling, but says it's better to "lose intelligently than win ignorantly." Chapters include theory of gambling, coups and games with dice, blackjack, contract bridge, and games of pure skill and competitive computers. *Inequalities for Stochastic Processes: How to Gamble if You Must* by Lester E. Dubins and L. J. Savage (New York, Dover, 1976) is for mathematicians, but the reader does not need a technical knowledge of probability. The pure mathematics behind gambling is explained, with many examples. *The Science of Winning* by Burton P. Fabricand (New York, Van Nostrand Reinhold, 1979), which has the interesting subtitle "A random walk on the road to riches," also deals with games of chance.

Topology

Topology: A First Course by James R. Munkers (Englewood Cliffs, N.J., Prentice-Hall, 1975) is written to be used in an introductory course in topology, laying the foundations for future studies in analysis, geometry, and algebraic topology. Areas covered are set theory and logic, topological spaces, connectedness and compactness, countability and separation axioms, theorems, and the fundamental group and covering spaces. Exercises are scattered through and at the ends of the chapters. There is a bibliography, and an index. *Topics in Topology* by Arlo W. Schurle (New York, North Holland, 1979) is an introduction to topology for courses for students with little mathematical background or at the beginning graduate level but with little background in topology. Basic concepts are considered intuitively and rigorously, and then examples, winding numbers, combinatorial topology, and the fundamental group are covered. Again there are exercises with each chapter, and a bibliography and index.

Modeling

Modeling, the underlying theme of all applications of mathematics to real situations, is introduced by Clive Dym and Elizabeth S. Ivey in *Principles of Mathematical Modeling* (New York, Academic, 1980). The book is divided into two main parts: foundations and applications. In the first part are dimensional analysis, scaling, and elementary ideas of approximation of function curves. In the second part the authors develop a series of models and discuss their origin, validity, and meaning, for example, linear and nonlinear oscillations of a pendulum. Problems are included at the ends of chapters. There is a bibliography, and an index. *Constructive Approaches to Mathematical Models* edited by C. V. Coffman and G. J. Fix (New York, Academic, 1979) is the proceedings of a conference. After introductory materials, papers are included in these sections: graphs and networks, mathematical programming, differential equations, mathematical models, and related areas. There are several papers by different authors in each section, each with reference.

Periodicals

A list of representative mathematical periodicals follows:

Advances in Mathematics. New York, Academic, 1967– . (bimonthly)
American Journal of Mathematics. Baltimore, Md., Johns Hopkins, 1978– . (bimonthly)
American Mathematical Society, Bulletin. Providence, R.I., American Mathematical Society, 1894– , new series 1979– . (bimonthly)
Applied Mathematics and Optimization: An International Journal. New York, Springer, 1974– . (quarterly)

Association of Teachers of Mathematics of New York City. Summation, N.Y., Association of Teachers of Mathematics, n.d. (quarterly)

Communications in Algebra. New York, Dekker, 1974– . (20/year)

Industrial Mathematics. Roseville, Md., Industrial Mathematics Society, 1950– . (semiannual)

International Journal of Mathematical Education in Science and Technology. London, Taylor and Francis, 1970– . (bimonthly)

Journal of Graph Theory. New York, Wiley, 1976– . (quarterly)

Journal of Undergraduate Mathematics. Greensboro, N.C., Guilford College, 1969– . (semiannual)

Mathematics Magazine. Washington, D.C., Mathematics Association of America, 1926– . (bimonthly)

Mathematics Teacher. Reston, Va., National Council of Teachers of Mathematics, 1908– . (monthly)

Operations Research. Baltimore, Md., Operations Research Society of America, 1952– . (bimonthly)

Quarterly Journal of Mechanics and Applied Mathematics. London, Oxford University Press, 1948– . (quarterly)

Rocky Mountain Journal of Mathematics. Tempe, Ariz., Rocky Mountain Mathematics Consortium, 1971– . (quarterly)

SIAM Journal on Applied Mathematics. Philadelphia, Pa., Society for Industrial and Applied Mathematics, 1953– . (bimonthly)

Scripta Mathematica; Devoted to the Philosophy, History and Expository Treatment of Mathematics. New York, 1933– . (quarterly)

CURRENT AWARENESS MATERIALS

Current Mathematical Publications (Providence, R.I., American Mathematical Society, 1, 1969–) is issued biweekly as both a current awareness tool and an index. It is produced in the editorial offices of *Mathematical Reviews*, and lists only materials that will be later reviewed in the publication *Mathematical Reviews*. The main part of each issue is arranged by a subject classification scheme and alphabetically by author within each subject, and lists periodical articles, books, and reports with bibliographic information only. There is an author index, and a very brief key subject index. Tables of contents of a few major journals are reproduced in full. The author and key subject indexes are cumulated twice a year.

QUICK REFERENCE TOOLS

Dictionaries

The *Dictionary of Mathematics* by T. Alaric Millington and W. Millington (New York, Barnes and Noble, 1971) contains brief definitions at a beginner's level. The *Facts on File Dictionary of Mathematics* edited by Carol Gibson (New York, Facts on File, 1981) is also alphabetical by term with cross-references. Illustrative drawings are included.

Glenn James's *Mathematics Dictionary* (New York, Van Nostrand Reinhold, 4th edition 1976) is for amateur and professional mathematicians: students, scientists, engineers, and others. The main section is arranged alphabetically by terms and gives a definition and often an expanded explanation of a page or more in length. Brief biographies of people whose contributions to mathematics have been particularly important are also included in the alphabetical order. Some miscellaneous information such as mathematical symbols and differentiation formulas and integral tables follow. This comprehensive dictionary is completed by multilingual indexes in French, German, Russian, and Spanish, leading to the English equivalent term as used in the main dictionary section. The *English–Greek Dictionary of Pure and Applied Mathematics* by Memas Kolaitis (Athens, Greece, Technical Chamber of Greece, 1976) is alphabetical by English term or phrase and gives the Greek equivalent.

Handbooks, Tables

Mathematics Manual: Methods and Principles of the Various Branches of Mathematics for Reference, Problem Solving, and Review by Frederick Merritt (New York, McGraw-Hill, 1962) contains methods, definitions, and principles for all areas of mathematics from simple arithmetic through higher mathematics. The *Handbook of Mathematical Formulas* by Hans J. Bartsch (New York, Academic, 1974) contains fundamental rules of arithmetic, geometry, calculus, differential equations, infinite and Fourier series, theory of probability, statistics, linear optimization, and Boolean algebra. Treatment includes formulas, explanations, and examples. The *Handbook of Applied Mathematics* by Edward E. Grazda and Martin E. Jansson (New

York, Van Nostrand Reinhold, 4th edition 1966, reprinted 1977) is designed to be used as a reference book or as a text for self-instruction. The first several chapters are a review of arithmetic, algebra, trigonometry, and differential calculus. These chapters are followed by separate sections for various applications, for example, brickwork, or plumbing. Recommended further readings are mentioned in many of the sections; tables and drawings are used. There is an index of tables, and a general index.

For Good Measure by William D. Johnstone (New York, Holt, Rinehart and Winston, 1975) aims to answer any questions involving measurement. The main parts of this book are units of length, surface units, capacity and volume, weight and mass, metric system, and electrical units, and there is a part for miscellaneous measure. Each unit of measure is listed, with information on its size, conversion to metric, other names and spellings and values, and often also brief information on what the unit is used for and its history. There is a general index, and an index of units. The *SI Metric Handbook* by John L. Feirer (New York, Scribner, 1977) is a reference book for those who need metric conversions to the International System of Units in their work. There are two main parts: (A) SI measuring system and ISO standards, which explains the system itself, defines the units, and gives conversions; and (B) applied metrics, which discusses metrics in industrial work, in office practice, and at home. *Conversion Tables for SI Metrication* by William J. Semioli and Paul B. Schubert (New York, Industrial, 1974) contains introductory information about the SI system, metric conversion factors, and conversion tables.

A large volume that brings together many mathematical tables is the *CRC Handbook of Tables for Mathematics* (Boca Raton, Fla., CRC, 1, 1962–   ), the 4th edition published in 1970. This volume is mostly tables and formulas, for example, mensuration formulas, logarithms, formulas and tables for trigonometry, interest tables, and conversion factors. There is some explanation of tables and of basic mathematics, for example, basics of algebra. A list of mathematics symbols and abbreviations gives their meanings. *Mathematical Handbook of Formulas and Tables* by Murray R. Spiegel (New York, McGraw-Hill, 1968) is part of Schaum's outline series. It contains 2,400 formulas and 60 tables useful for students and researchers in mathematics, physics, engineering and other sciences. There are two main parts: (1) mathematical formulas, divided into sections, for example, integrals,

SINE, COSINE, AND EXPONENTIAL INTEGRALS

x	$Si(x)$	δ^2_m	$Ci(x)$	δ^2_m	$Ei(x)$	δ^2_m	$E_1(x) = -Ei(-x)$	δ^2_m
.00	.00000		$-\infty$		$-\infty$		$+\infty$	
.01	.01000	0	-4.02798		-4.01790		4.03790	
.02	.02000	0	-3.33482		-3.31476		3.35476	
.03	.03000	0	-2.92957		-2.89912		2.95912	
.04	.04000	-2	-2.64206		-2.60126		2.68126	
.05	.04999	2	-2.41914		-2.36788		2.46790	
.06	.05999	-2	-2.23709		-2.17528		2.29531	
.07	.06998	0	-2.08327		-2.01080		2.15084	
.08	.07957	0	-1.95011		-1.86688		2.02694	
.09	.08996	-2	-1.83275		-1.73866		1.91874	
.10	.09994	2	-1.72787	-997	-1.62281	-989	1.82292	990
.11	.10993	-3	-1.63308	-829	-1.51696	-816	1.73711	816
.12	.11990	2	-1.54665	-695	-1.41935	-687	1.65954	688
.13	.12988	-1	-1.46723	-594	-1.32866	-582	1.58890	585
.14	.13985	-1	-1.39379	-514	-1.24384	-505	1.52415	503
.15	.14981	0	-1.32552	-449	-1.16409	-436	1.46446	441
.16	.15977	0	-1.26176	-394	-1.08873	-384	1.40919	384
.17	.16973	-1	-1.20196	-349	-1.01723	-341	1.35778	342
.18	.17968	-1	-1.14567	-314	-.94915	-302	1.30980	303
.19	.18962	0	-1.09253	-281	-.88410	-270	1.26486	272
.20	.19956	-1	-1.04221	-254	-.82176	-244	1.22265	245
.21	.20949	-1	-.99444	-231	-.76187	-222	1.18290	223
.22	.21941	1	-.94899	-212	-.70420	-199	1.14538	201
.23	.22933	-3	-.90566	-194	-.64853	-184	1.10988	186
.24	.23923	0	-.86427	-177	-.59470	-166	1.07624	167
.25	.24913	0	-.82466	-166	-.54254	-155	1.04428	158
.26	.25903	-3	-.78671	-153	-.49193	-142	1.01389	142
.27	.26891	-1	-.75029	-142	-.44274	-131	.98493	134
.28	.27878	1	-.71529	-132	-.39486	-122	.95731	122
.29	.28865	-3	-.68161	-124	-.34820	-113	.93092	115
.30	.29850	1	-.64917	-117	-.30267	-105	.90568	107
.31	.30835	-1	-.61790	-107	-.25819	-96	.88151	100
.32	.31819	-2	-.58771	-103	-.21468	-94	.85834	92
.33	.32801	-1	-.55855	-97	-.17210	-83	.83610	90
.34	.33782	1	-.53036	-91	-.13036	-81	.81475	82
.35	.34763	-3	-.50308	-86	-.08943	-76	.79422	77
.36	.35742	-1	-.47666	-84	-.04926	-69	.77446	74
.37	.36720	-3	-.45107	-76	-.00979	-67	.75544	69
.38	.37696	1	-.42625	-76	.02901	-63	.73711	66
.39	.38672	-3	-.40218	-70	.06718	-57	.71944	60
.40	.39646	-1	-.37881	-67	.10477	-58	.70238	59
.41	.40619	-1	-.35611	-65	.14179	-53	.68591	56
.42	.41591	-2	-.33406	-60	.17828	-50	.67000	51
.43	.42561	-2	-.31262	-61	.21427	-47	.65461	51
.44	.43529	1	-.29178	-54	.24979	-45	.63973	48
.45	.44497	-2	-.27149	-56	.28486	-43	.62533	46
.46	.45463	-2	-.25175	-52	.31950	-40	.61139	43
.47	.46427	-1	-.23253	-48	.35374	-39	.59788	41
.48	.47390	-2	-.21380	-50	.38759	-36	.58478	42
.49	.48351	-1	.19556	-46	.42108	-35	.57209	36
.50	.49311	-2	-.17778	-45	.45422	-33	.55977	37

Fig. 4-2. Mathematical tables: *CRC Handbook of Tables for Mathematics*

complex numbers, formulas from *solid analytic* geometry, and Fourier series; and (2) numerical tables, for example, logarithms and Bessel functions. The United States National Bureau of Standards *Handbook of Mathematical Functions With Formulas* (Washington, D.C., U.S. Government Printing Office, 1964) is all tables and equations. There is a subject index, and an index of notations. Many sections include references. *Tables of Higher Functions* by Eugen Jahnke (New York, McGraw-Hill, 6th edition 1960) consists of tables and graphs with explanations. Written material is presented in German and in English, side by side. There is a bibliography, and an index. *Mathematical Functions and Their Approximations* by Yudell Luke (New York, Academic, 1975) consists of tables, equations, and explanations. There is a bibliography, and a notation index and subject index. The *Handbook of Mathematical Tables and Formulas* by Richard S. Burington (New York, McGraw-Hill, 5th edition 1973) also contains tables. *Table of Integrals, Series, and Products* by I. S. Gradshteyn and I. M. Ryzhik, updated and enlarged in this edition by Alan Jeffery (New York, Academic, 1980), has an explanation of the use of the tables and begins with formulas of finite sums, numerical and functional series, and differential calculus. Tables of formulas are in these main sections: elementary functions, indefinite integrals of elementary functions, indefinite integrals of special functions, definite integrals of special functions, special functions, vector field theory, algebraic inequalities, integral inequalities, matrices and related results, determinants, norms, ordinary differential equations, and Fourier and Laplace transforms. For each formula, the bibliographic reference is given by an abbreviation that refers to a list at the back of the book; there is also a supplementary list of references for further study.

COMPUTER SCIENCE

INTRODUCTORY MATERIALS

The *Computer Book* by Fred Lee (Dedham, Mass., Artech, 1978) starts out with an exercise in which the reader "becomes" a computer and goes through a simple program, using pencil and paper. The book aims to provide an introduction for those completely ignorant of computers to come to a basic understanding of them. No technical background is needed. Chapters deal with understanding and programming of a digital computer, number systems and circuits, and FORTRAN and COBOL programming languages. *Computer Consciousness: Surviving the Automated 80's* by H. Dominic Covvey and N. McAlister (Reading, Mass., Addison-Wesley, 1980) deals with fundamentals of computer technology. The main sections are on "hardware," "software," and the "whole system." Lists of new terms appear at the end of each chapter, and there is a glossary. Many drawings for fun and to illustrate facts are used throughout. *How You Can Learn to Live with Computers* by Harry Kleinberg (Philadelphia, Pa., Lippincott, 1977) is an introduction to computers, how they work, and what they can and cannot be expected to do. *Computers for Everybody* by Jerry Willis and Merl Miller (Portland, Oreg., Dilithium, 1981) deals with basics of operation and principles of selection of a computer for a home or small business. Descriptions of popular models are included. There is also information on programs, and a survey of sources of software.

People-Oriented Computer Systems: The Computer in Crisis by Edward A. Tomeski and Harold Lazarus (New York, Van Nostrand Reinhold, 1975) emphasizes the humanistic aspects of computer use rather than the technology. The first part of the book deals with the impact of technology on organizations; the second part summarizes the systems approach, information systems, and computers; and the third part relates computer systems to human systems. Many examples of real-life situations are used. A summary, discussion questions, and bibliography are included with each chapter. *The Social Impact of Computers* by Gerald A. Silber (New York, Harcourt Brace Jovanovich, 1979) is an introduction to computers and their place in society. Treatment is general, without technical language. A summary and exercises are included with each chapter. James Martin's *The Wired Society* (Englewood Cliffs, N.J., Prentice-Hall, 1978) aims to provide nontechnical information for general understanding of computers and their potential in society. Some topics covered are "new uses of television," "instant mail," and "education."

Data Processing; an Introduction by Donald D. Spencer (Columbus, Ohio, Merrill, 1978) is a text for an introductory course in computer data processing. There is no mathematics prerequisite, and no access to a computer is needed. The book provides a general orientation to what computers can and cannot do and how they work, and provides insight into the impact of computers on business organizations and people, with examples being related to business operations. The first chapters deal with components of a data processing system: computers, number systems, some specific computer systems, coding of data, and hardware. Then there are several chapters on programming and language and on management concepts and social issues. Review questions are inserted through the chapters with each major topic. Many cartoons and photographs are used. *Information Processing Systems* by William S. Davis (Reading, Mass., Addison-Wesley, 1978) contains basic information processing and computer concepts presented in a readable fashion. The book is divided into five major parts with chapters in each: "computer impact" or why computers are used, "basic computer concepts," "file processing" covering data management concepts, "information systems," specific technologies and "where do we go from here?" on computer applications with examples. A summary and exercises are included with each chapter.

Learning With Computers by Alfred Bork (Bedford, Mass., Digital, 1981) asks the question "Will computers replace books in American education?" and goes on to discuss the role of computers in education, and the personal computer. Other chapters consider computer graphics, the educational technology at the University of California at Irvine and its teaching functions, computer use in the classroom, producing computer-based learning materials, and concerns of the future. Many chapters have references.

History of Computing in the Twentieth Century: A Collection of Essays (New York, Academic, 1980) is made up of thirty-eight papers that were presented at the International Conference on the History of Computing held in June 1976. There are references with each paper. *Project Whirlwind: The History of a Pioneer Computer* by Kent C. Redmond and Thomas M. Smith (Bedford, Mass., Digital, 1980) tells the interesting story of the development of the Whirlwind computer beginning in 1945 at the Massachusetts Institute of Technology. Whirlwind was the first digital computer to be developed that could be used as a practical device for purposes like directing airplane traffic or controlling a manufacturing process.

The *Making of the Micro* by Christopher Evans (New York, Van

Nostrand Reinhold, 1981) tells the historical story of microcomputers. Both the equipment and the people involved in its development are included.

Subject Headings and Classification

Computer-assisted instruction
Computer crimes
Computer engineering
Computer industry
Computer input–output equipment
Computer programmers
Computer programs
Computer storage devices
Computer terminals
Computers
Computers and civilization
Electronic data processing
Minicomputers
Programming (Electronic computers)
Programming languages (Electronic computers)

Books on computer science will be found shelved in libraries in the QA 76 section of the Library of Congress classification system or in 001.6 section of the Dewey Decimal Classification.

BIBLIOGRAPHIC MATERIALS

Guides to the Literature

Guide to Reference Sources in the Computer Sciences by Ciel M. Carter (New York, Macmillan, 1974) gives international coverage of computer literature, listing about 900 sources. It is divided into chapters, by type of literature, for example, bibliographies, directories and catalogs, handbooks, and manuals, and lists sources with bibliographic information and annotation and a critical evaluation. Separate chapters list professional organizations, and research and information centers with addresses and officers and general information. The appendixes include a selected list of periodicals with notation of what major indexing and abstracting services index each. *Guide to Computer Literature: An Introductory Survey of the Sources of Information* by Alan Pritchard (London, Bingley, 2d edition 1972) is also arranged by type of literature. These guides are still useful even though dated.

Bibliography

A very complete bibliography of early computer literature to 1967 was edited by W. W. Youden, *Computer Literature Bibliography 1946-1967* (New York, Arno, 1970). Books, journal articles, reports, and so forth are included.

Indexing and Abstracting Services

Computing Reviews (New York, Association for Computing Machinery 1, 1960–   ) is published monthly and reviews books, journal articles, and reports on computer science. Arrangement is in subject groups using a classification scheme. For each item listed there is full bibliographic information, including price for books, and then a signed review. There is an author index in each issue, cumulated yearly. The *ACM Guide to Computing Literature* (New York, Association for Computing Machinery, 1977–   ) is published annually by the same association as is *Computing Reviews*. The main part is a bibliographic listing of books, journal articles, proceedings, reports, and master theses, and reviewed materials. Full bibliographic information is given. An author listing and key-word listing lead to this bibliographic section, and there are also indexes by category, *Computing Reviews* reviewer, and source.

Computer and Control Abstracts (London, Institution of Electrical Engineers and New York, Institute of Electrical and Electronics Engineers, 1, 1966–   ) is published monthly to abstract journal articles, books, reports, dissertations, and conference papers. Arrangement is in broad subject groups by a classification scheme, and bibliographic information, author's affiliation, and an abstract are given for each item. Each issue includes a subject guide to broad subject groups, and also an author index. A detailed subject index to individual entries and an author index are cumulated January–June and July–December. In addition to these indexes, there are a bibliography index, book index, corporate author index, and conference index in each issue and cumulated.

Computer Program Abstracts (Washington, D.C., National Aeronautics and Space Administration, 1, 1969–) appears quarterly to list and abstract computer programs that have been developed by NASA and its contractors plus others that are for sale through NASA. Arrangement is in subject categories, with indexes by subject, originating agency, program number, and computer equipment requirements. Programs listed are for sale to the public. The *Directory of Computer Software and Related Technical Reports* (Springfield, Va., NTIS, 1980–), preceded by other similar titles, is published irregularly, listing programs and reports that are available to the public from U.S. government agencies. Arrangement is by broad subjects, for example, aerodynamics, agriculture, atmospheric sciences. Information given is bibliographic information, an abstract, and availability and cost of the item. There are indexes by originating agency name and number, subject, computer hardware required, and computer language used.

SECONDARY LITERATURE MATERIALS

Encyclopedias

The *Encyclopedia of Computer Science and Engineering* edited by Anthony Ralston (New York, Van Nostrand Reinhold Co., 2nd edition, 1982) is a one-volume encyclopedia for nonspecialists made up of signed articles by about 200 different authors. Articles are arranged alphabetically by subject, and there is an index. Articles are often several pages long and include references, and also often refer to other articles on related subjects in the encyclopedia. A "classification of articles" at the beginning lists all articles classified into ten large classes, for example, software, hardware, theory, and so forth. The appendix includes a list of abbreviations and acronyms with meanings, and a few tables. The *Encyclopedia of Computers and Data Processing* (Detroit, Mich., International Electronics Information Services, 1, 1978–) is a multivolume encyclopedia on all aspects of computers and data processing. Articles include bibliographies. The *Encyclopedia of Computer Science and Technology* (New York, Dekker, 1975–80) is a compendium of basic knowledge about com-

164 BASE REGISTER

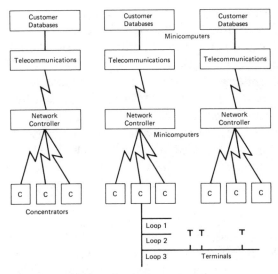

Fig. 3. Distributed banking application.

v.) function is clearly the key to future computerized banking applications.

R. G. MILLS AND E. R. WILLNER

BASE REGISTER

For articles on related subjects *see* ADDRESSING; and IBM 360-370 SERIES.

A base register is used in addressing a computer memory. In a computer that uses base registers, the effective address (i.e., the address field of the instruction, possibly modified by indexing and indirect addressing) is a relative address. The actual memory address used is determined by adding this relative address to the contents of one or more base registers.

The Control Data Cyber series is an example of a computer system that uses a single base register. Every program is written as if it were meant to run in a single memory area, starting at location 0. The program may in fact be loaded starting at any memory location. When the program is run, the operating system places the address of the first word of the program in the base register. The content of the base register is automatically added to every memory reference address, and thus every relative address is converted into an absolute address. This feature is useful in multiprogramming systems, since it permits programs to be loaded wherever space exists, and permits programs to be moved in memory, or to be removed from memory and then resumed in a different area of memory. Such base registers are thus often called *relocation registers.*

Some computers have several base registers. A relative address must then contain a field that indicates which register is selected, and the contents of that register are added to the relative address to form the absolute address. In such a machine a program may be constructed in parts or segments that can be independently loaded into available areas of memory. The Univac 1110 is an example of a machine with two base registers. The Multics machine (Honeywell 68/80) is an example of a machine with multiple base registers.

The term "base register" is sometimes used more or less interchangeably with the term "index register." Thus, the IBM 360 and 370 have 16 general registers, each of which provides a 24-bit base address to which the 12-bit address field (displacement) in an instruction is added to produce the effective address. These registers can be, and usually are, loaded by and stored in the programs that use them. It is conceptually better to think of

Fig. 4–3. Encyclopedia: *Encyclopedia of Computer Science and Engineering* by Anthony Ralston, 2nd Edition, 1982. Van Nostrand Reinhold.

puters. The approximately 2,000 signed articles are arranged alphabetically by topic through the fourteen basic volumes, and there are supplementary volumes. It is aimed at those who use computers extensively to solve problems and at computer professionals. References are included with each article.

Home Computers: A Beginner's Glossary and Guide by Merl K. Miller and Charles J. Sippl (Portland, Oreg., Dilithium, 1978) is a quick reference source for beginners. It has general information on microcomputers, such as their history, uses, and specific models, and information on number systems, and symbols. The largest section is a glossary, alphabetical by term, with brief descriptions.

Fundamentals

Several books provide information of a more technical nature than those mentioned earlier. These are mostly written for use as texts for a first course on computers and data processing. Although use of a computer is not mandatory when reading these books, the information in them would usually be better understood if the reader could also have computer access.

Introduction to the Computer; an Integrative Approach by Jeffrey Frates (Englewood Cliffs, N.J., Prentice-Hall, 1980) brings theory and practice together in each chapter. The first chapters deal with introductory basic concepts, and then there are several groups of chapters on hardware, programming and software, and advanced systems and future trends. Each chapter has a section on applications and implications. Appendixes present programming languages: COBOL, FORTRAN, and PASCAL. Each chapter includes a summary and study questions, and there is a glossary, and a bibliography. *Introduction to Computers and Data Processing* by Harry Katzan (New York, Van Nostrand, 1979) surveys concepts, techniques, and applications of data processing. There are chapters on computer hardware, programming, software, systems and applications, and various specialized topics such as file design concepts, computer networks, and automated offices. Exercises and a list of related reading are included with each chapter, and there is a glossary.

Foundations of Computer Science by M. S. Carberry and others (Potomac, Md., Computer Science, 1979) contains sections on historical perspectives, problem solving, computer and control systems, data structures, and applications. Social issues in the use of computers and artificial intelligence are also discussed. One chapter is devoted to programming a pocket calculator, the Hewlett-Packard HP-65. Problems and references are included where appropriate. *Digital Computer Fundamentals* by Thomas C. Bartee (New York, McGraw-Hill, 5th edition 1981) presents the principles of modern digital computers. Chapters cover uses of computers, basic ideas and principles of all digital computers and digital devices, arithmetic operations, memories, and input–output devices, and control units. Questions are included with each chapter, with answers provided for some at the back of the book. There is a bibliography. *Introduction to Computers and Information Processing with BASIC—COBOL—FORTRAN—PASCAL* by Don Cassel and Martin Jackson (Reston, Va., Reston Publishing, 1981) is an introduction to computers and to major facets of information processing. The major sections are "guide to computers," on computers and what they are, history, number systems, and computing concepts; "computer hardware"; "computer programming" including programming languages; "systems analysis and design"; and "advanced concepts" of operating systems, data communications systems, data-base structures and files and languages, and computers in society. Questions and exercises are included with each chapter. The appendixes include information on careers in computers and a list of periodicals of interest. *Introduction to Computer Data Processing* by Margaret S. Wu (New York, Harcourt Brace Jovanovich, 2d edition 1979) provides fundamental concepts of hardware and software. One series of chapters considers the use of the computer from start to finish of a problem, including design, choosing the language, and testing. Programming languages discussed are FORTRAN, COBOL, PL/I, BASIC, and RPG. There are questions with each chapter, and a glossary and list of references are provided.

Computers in Society by Donald H. Sanders (New York, McGraw-Hill, 3d edition 1981) includes an introduction to computer concepts, technological change, input-output, systems analysis, program preparation, BASIC computer language, hardware, applications in government, health, humanities, business, and engineering, and the social implications for good and for bad uses.

Programming

Programming for Poets: A Gentle Introduction using PL/I by Richard Conway (Cambridge, Mass., Winthrop, 1978) is not really for poets, but is written for readers who do not intend to do programming but who want to know about it. Reading of programs is emphasized, rather than writing them. The first part of the book is an introduction to programming and how to read and write simple programs. Then some longer, more complicated, programs are presented for the reader's understanding, and then the nature and use of computers is discussed. There are exercises with some chapters, and a list of references. *Understanding and Programming Computers* by Samiha Mourad (New York, Exposition, 1978) is an integrated overview of computers and their uses, potentials, and limitations. There is information on the general nature of computers and their evolution, computer hardware, programming, data structure, languages BASIC, FORTRAN, and COBOL, and roles of the computer, for example, as record keeper, controller, and analyzer. Appendixes contain information on electrical and electronic circuits, languages, and lists of computer manufacturers, organizations and periodicals. There is a bibliography, and a glossary. Pal Quittner's *Problems, Programs, Processing, Results: Software Techniques for Sci-Tech Programs* (New York, Crane, Russak, 1977) explains the main features of computer software. It is aimed at those using computers to solve problems, and who have some practical experience. Topics covered are applications, hardware, assembly and compilation of a program, data organization and management, and operating systems. Also two chapters follow the path of a program and its debugging, with analysis of problems occurring in practical programming. References are included with each chapter, and there is a combined glossary and index. *Computers: Programming and Applications* by Herbert Maisel (Chicago, Science Research Associates, 1976) is a text for a first course in computers geared especially to those in mathematics or physical sciences. Topics include how computers work, fundamentals of computers and programming, programming languages FORTRAN, PL/I, and BASIC, and computer applications. Many programming exercises are included to develop skills. There are references and an annotated supplementary bibliography with each chapter. *Program*

Design and Construction by David A. Higgins (Englewood Cliffs, N.J., Prentice-Hall, 1979) tells how to design a program through analyzing a problem and creating a logical process to solve it, and how to construct the program. BASIC language and microcomputers are used. This book is aimed at computer users, from hobbyists to business people to beginning professional programmers. There are exercises with each chapter. *A Bit of BASIC* by Thomas A. Dwyer and M. Critchfield (Reading, Mass., Addison-Wesley, 1980) features the computer language most used by beginners. BASIC originally meant Beginners All-Purpose Symbolic Instruction Code; now it is also used by professionals. Topics included are fundamental features of BASIC, electronic computer hardware, writing programs to produce simple graphics, and an introduction to extended BASIC. Self tests and project ideas are scattered throughout.

Donald D. Spencer's *Problems for Computer Solution* (Ormond Beach, Fla., Camelot, 1977) may be used as a supplement with programming language books to give added practice. The wide selection of problems may be used with any programming language. First there is a group of introductory problems in all areas, and then problems are arranged in chapters by topic, for example, algebra, geometry, number theory, science, fun and games. Within each chapter, problems are arranged in order of difficulty. *Game Playing With Computers* by Donald D. Spencer (Rochelle Park, N.J., Hayden, revised 2d edition 1975) introduces many games that may be programmed for computers. The games vary from those for students and beginning programmers to those for which the programs are extremely complex, and include magic squares, puzzles, casino games, board games, number games, gambling games, and so forth. One chapter is made up of exercises, and there are answers to selected problems.

Hardware

Computer hardware is detailed by Martin Cripps in *An Introduction to Computer Hardware* (Cambridge, Mass., Winthrop, 1977). This book is written for beginners in using computers, or for those just interested in computers; and aims to give information on design, construction, and operation of computers to provide a good understanding of how they work. After introductory discussion of the basic concepts, chapters cover various parts of the computer, such as control circuits, the book ending with bringing these parts together into a discussion of the complete computer and its implementation. Appendixes include glossaries of symbols and terms. Computer software is discussed in the *Tutorial on Software Design Techniques* (Long Beach, Calif., IEEE Computer Society, 2d edition 1977). This volume is made up of twenty-three papers from a conference plus original material. There is also an annotated bibliography on software design.

Management

Several books deal with management aspects of computers. *Computer Fundamentals for Nonspecialists* by Joseph M. Vles (New York, American Management Associations, 1981) is aimed at business managers who supervise people working with computers. Basics about computers are included, as well as hardware and software, computer languages, and information on duties of programmers and other personnel. William M. Taggart's *Information Systems: An Introduction to Computers in Organizations* (Boston, Mass., Allyn and Bacon, 1980) emphasizes that we are all users of information systems in our daily activities, and each chapter has examples of these uses. Main sections are introductory basic concepts, computer technology of hardware and software, information systems organization, application software development, and computer-based applications. Each chapter has questions and exercises, and a situation from real life for thought and discussion. *Computer Data Security* by Harry Katzan (New York, Van Nostrand Reinhold, 1973) is an introduction to data security problems for anyone involved with data processing by computer. There is basic information on computers and data management, and then methods for implementing data security in a computer system. One chapter contains applications of data security measures to real-life situations. *Computer Technology Impact on Management* by George A. Champine (Amsterdam and New York, North-Holland, 1978) aims to bring together what is happening in computer technology and to discuss the impact of this technology and changes in technology on organization management and electronic data processing management.

Home Computers

Home computer users or potential users are the intended audience for Paul M. Chirlain's *Understanding Computers* (Portland Oreg., Dilithium, 1978). This book describes how computers work, the binary number system, and how a computer works with numbers. There are exercises with each chapter. *Buying a Personal Computer* by Carlton Shrum (Sherman Oaks, Calif., Alfred, 1981) is also for those interested in a personal computer and will aid in the selection of one to buy. Uses are discussed by Daniel R. McGlynn in *Personal Computing: Home, Professional, and Small Business Applications* (New York, Wiley, 1979).

Programming of home computers is covered in *Programming in BASIC for Personal Computers* by David L. Heiserman (Englewood Cliffs, N.J., Prentice-Hall, 1981). This book will teach home computer users to go beyond the prerecorded programs to doing their own programs. Information given applies to Radio Shack's TRS–80, the Apple IV, and Commodore PIT, as well as most others on the market. There are many examples throughout. Exercises are included with each chapter, with answers to selected problems at the back of the book. *Programming Techniques* (Peterborough, N.H., BYTE, 1, 1978–) is a series of monographs on aspects of programming for home personal computer users. For example, volume one deals with program design, volume two simulation, and volume three numbers in theory and practice. Each volume contains articles from *BYTE* magazine as well as original material. Bruce Presley's *Guide to Programming Applesoft* (New York, Van Nostrand Reinhold, 1982) is a manual for use with Apple home computers. The user does not need a mathematics background. Games and graphics are included.

Conspicuous Computing—Or—Informal Choices for the Computer Age by H. Dominic Covvey and Neil H. McAlister (Reading, Mass., Addison-Wesley, 1981) deals with data security, evaluating and selecting computer systems, and the personal computer revolution. *The Best of Creative Computing* (Morristown, N.J., Creative

Computing Press, 1976–) is issued irregularly as a book containing articles reprinted from the magazine *Creative Computing*. This is a lively collection, with serious information and humor, poems, cartoons, computer puzzles, and games. It is geared to home computer users and professionals.

Periodicals

A sampling of computer journals follows:

ACM Computing Surveys. New York, Association for Computing Machinery, 1969– . (quarterly)
Association for Computing Machinery. Communications. New York, ACM, 1958– . (monthly)
Byte; the small systems journal. Peterborough, N.H., McGraw-Hill, 1957– . (monthly)
Computer. Long Beach, Calif., Institute of Electrical and Electronics Engineers, 1966– . (monthly)
Computers and People. Newtonville, Mass., Berkeley Enterprises, 1951– . (monthly)
Computers and the Humanities. Amsterdam, North-Holland, 1966– . (quarterly)
Computerworld; Newsweekly for the Computer Community. Newton, Mass, Computerworld, 1967– . (weekly)
Mini-Micro Systems. Denver, Colo., Cahners, 1968– . (monthly)
Computer Decisions; Information Systems, Automated Processing, Problem Solving. Rochelle Park, N.J., Hayden, 1969– . (monthly)
Datamation. New York, Technical, 1957– . (monthly)
SIGBIO Newsletter. New York, Association for Computing Machinery, 1970– . (quarterly)
Also many other SIG (Special Interest Group of Association for Computing Machinery) publications of different special interest groups.

CURRENT AWARENESS MATERIALS

Current Papers on Computers and Control/CPC (Piscataway, N.J., Institute of Electrical and Electronics Engineers, 1969–) is published monthly. This is the current awareness publication from the same associations that put out *Computer and Control Abstracts,* described above in the section on indexing and abstracting services.

QUICK REFERENCE TOOLS

Dictionaries

The *Standard Dictionary of Computers and Information Processing* by Martin H. Weik (Rochelle Park, N.J., Hayden, revised 2d edition 1977) is alphabetical by term, with cross-references. Acronyms are included in the regular alphabetical order like words. Terms with modifiers are also listed separately as words, so that there are separate definitions—for example, for card: card, aperture, and card, aspect. A brief phrase defines each term, and then supplementary information is given in essay form ranging from a few to about fifty words. The *Dictionary of Data Processing* by Jeff Maynard (New York, Crane, Russak, 1976) is alphabetical by term, with "see" references as needed. Defintions are brief. The appendixes include common acronyms, abbreviations, and symbols with meanings, tables of information, and a list of British and U.S. standards relating to data processing. *The Dictionary of Microcomputing* by Philip E. Burton (New York, Garland, 1976) is alphabetical by term with brief definitions. This book features an interesting introductory essay by the author on microprocessors and their development. Some other dictionaries are Anthony Chander's *Facts on File Dictionary of Microcomputers* (New York, Facts on File, 1981), Jack Hern's *Systems/Data Processing A-Z Factomatic* (Englewood Cliffs, N.J., Prentice-Hall, 1978), Charles J. Sippl's *Computer Dictionary and Handbook* (Indianapolis, Ind., Sams, 3d edition 1980), Charles J. Sippl's *Microcomputer Dictionary* (Indianapolis, Ind., Sams, 2d edition 1981), and Donald D. Spencer's *Computing Dictionary* (Ormond Beach, Fla., Camelot, 2d edition 1979).

Computer Acronyms, Abbreviations, Etc. by Claude P. Wrathall (New York, Petrocelli, 1981) is arranged alphabetically by acronym or abbreviation and gives the equivalent word meaning. Greek letters are listed at the end of the alphabetical arrangement. At the back of the book is a brief bibliography of reference works on computers.

A dictionary for foreign terms is the *Dictionary of Data Processing* by Alfred Wittmann (Amsterdam and New York, Elsevier, 3d edition

1977). The first section is alphabetical by term in English and gives equivalent terms in each of the other languages: German and French. There are indexes in German and French. The *Multilingual Computer Dictionary* edited by Alan Isaacs (New York, Facts on File, 1981) contains 1,600 common computer terms. Terms are listed in English, with word equivalents in French, German, Spanish, Italian, and Portugese.

Directories

The *Computer Directory and Buyers' Guide* (Newtonville, Mass. Berkely, 1974–   ) is issued annually as a publication of the staff of the journal *Computers and People*. It provides up-to-date information on computer firms and products. The journal *Byte* also lists many computer-related products in each issue.

5
Astronomy

INTRODUCTORY MATERIALS

An interesting introductory book of astronomy is *Space Shots: An Album of the Universe* by Fred Hapgood (New York, Times Books, 1979). This lovely volume is made up of photographs, mostly in color, with a description of each. Included are the earth, moon, asteroids, comets, planets, stars, nebulae, supernovae, galaxies, black holes, and quasars. Beautiful color photographs also illustrate Herbert Friedman's *The Amazing Universe* (Washington, D.C., National Geographic Society, 1975). Text includes the history of astronomy and discussions of the sun, stars, galaxies, cosmic order, and the search for life. There is also a brief glossary. Also a picture book of astronomy, filled with lovely photographs and some explanation, is *Pictorial Astronomy* by Dinsmore Alter and others (New York, Harper, 5th edition 1982). *Children of the Universe* by Hoimar von Ditfurth (New York, Atheneum, 1976) is an astronomical history of the universe, our solar system, and the earth. Several excellent black and white photographs are included.

Colin A. Ronan's *Practical Astronomer* (New York, Macmillan, 1981) is geared to amateur astronomer's, especially young people. An encyclopedia format is used to arrange the approximately sixty articles alphabetically by topic, and there are many illustrations, some in color. Topics include stars, comets, planets, galaxies, and so forth, and simple experiments are also included. The *Cambridge Encyclopedia of Astronomy* by Simon Mitton (New York, Prentice-Hall, 1977) is aimed at beginners in astronomy but also has much information for more advanced amateurs. An introduction to the study of the universe is followed by chapters on stars and the nature of cosmic matter, the sun, the solar system and its members, intergalactic space and the galaxies, and cosmology and life in the universe.

Exploration of the Universe by George O. Abell (Philadelphia, Pa., Saunders College, 4th edition 1982) is an introductory astronomy text. Many beautiful photographs are included, some in color. Most areas of astronomy are covered, including information obtained from space exploration. Exercises are included at the ends of some chapters, with answers to some of the problems. There is bibliography, and a glossary. Another thorough and reliable text is *The Physical Universe: An Introduction to Astronomy* by Frank H. Shu (Mill Valley, Calif., University Science Books, 1982). *Introduction to Astronomy* by Laurence W. Frederick and Robert H. Baker (New York, Van Nostrand Reinhold, 9th edition 1981) deals with such topics as the moon and Apollo program results, planets, moons of Jupiter, origin and evolution of stars, theories of the nature of the universe, black holes, and attempts to communicate with life elsewhere. Another book of general coverage is *Astronomy* by Dinah Moché (New York, Wiley, 2d edition 1981). *The Universe: From Flat Earth to Black Holes—and Beyond,* by Isaac Asimov (New York, Walker, 3d edition 1980) considers the earth, the solar system, stars, galaxies, the sun, the universe, and radio astronomy. A brief list of suggested further readings is included.

Interesting reading on individuals working in astronomy may be found in Colin A. Ronan's *The Astronomers* (New York, Hill and Wang, 1964). This book begins with a discussion of the early history of the study of the heavens, from before the Greeks, and then has a chapter on each of several individual astronomers including Kepler, Galileo, Halley, and Einstein. A brief bibliography and index complete the book.

Two books by Harlow Shapley provide a synposis of writings in astronomy from 1500 to 1950: *Source Book in Astronomy* (New York, McGraw-Hill, 1929) and *Source Book in Astronomy, 1900–1950* (Cambridge, Mass., Harvard University Press, 1960). The first volume covers the 400 years from 1500 to 1900 with excerpts from classic works, and the second covers 1900 to 1950 with extracts of sixty-nine classic works with citation of original works. Arrangement is in chapters by subject, for example, instrumentation which contains extracts by Hale, Schmidt, and others. A third volume of similar type brings us more up to date: *Source Book in Astronomy and Astrophysics, 1900–1975* edited by Kenneth R. Lang and Owen Gingerich (Cambridge, Mass., Harvard University Press, 1979). This is a collection of 132 classical papers, with reference to where they were originally published. Arrangement is by subject area, for example, solar system.

History of Astronomy by A. A. Pannekoek (Totowa, N.J., Rowman and Littlefield, 1961), though old, is a famous text on the history of astronomy, translated from the Dutch. This book stresses the part astronomy has played in the history of civilization, for example, in religious beliefs and observances. Otto Neugebauer's *History of Ancient Mathematical Astronomy* (Berlin and New York, Springer-Verlag, 1975) is a three-volume set divided and subsivided into many sections so as to be valuable as a reference work even though written in continuing form. There is a subject index, and references.

This Wild Abyss: The Story of the Men Who Made Modern Astronomy by Gale E. Christianson (New York, Free Press, 1978) is arranged broadly in chronological order, from the dawn of human consciousness through the time of Copernicus, about 1470, to the time of Newton, about 1700, and ending with a discussion of the nature of scientific discovery. It is a historical account of people and their work, in very readable form. *Astronomy, a Popular History* by J. Dorschner and others (New York, Van Nostrand Reinhold, 1975) is a translation of a work also written in 1975. In addition to the historical information, there are many photographs, and the appendixes contain astronomical data and a glossary.

Subject Headings and Classification

Astrographic catalog and chart
Astronomers
Astronomical instruments
Astronomical observatories
Astronomy
    (also subdivisions of Astronomy)
    —Charts, diagrams, etc.
    —Observations
    —Observatories
    —Observers' manuals
    —Pictorial works
    —Research
Astronomy, Ancient

Astronomy, Medieval
Astronomy, Spherical and practical
Astrophysics
Comets
Constellations
Earth
Ephemerides
Life on other planets
Meteorites
Meteors
Milky Way
Moon
Nautical almanacs
Orbits
Planets
Quasars
Radio astronomy
Satellites
Solar system
Stars
   (also subdivision of Stars)
   —Atlases
Sun
(names of planets)

Materials on astronomy will usually be found shelved in libraries in the QB class of the Library of Congress classification, or in the 520 to 528 class of the Dewey Decimal Classification.

BIBLIOGRAPHIC MATERIALS

Guides to the Literature

Guide to the Literature of Astronomy by Robert A. Seal (Littleton, Colo. Libraries Unlimited, 1977) is an introduction to the literature of astronomy, aimed mainly at beginning or amateur astronomers and librarians but also serving as a reference for astronomers. Arrangement is in chapters: reference sources in astronomy, general materials, descriptive astronomy, and special topics. Each chapter has many subdivisions, either by type of material, for example, handbooks, or by subject. Materials are listed, with detailed annotations. The appendix contains a list of basic reference materials in astronomy with a key indicating whether the work would be found primarily in an astronomy library, a public library, or a university library. Indexes are by author and title, and by subject. Material in this guide is updated somewhat by another book by the same author: *Bibliography of Astronomy 1970-79* by Robert A. Seal and Sarah S. Martin (Littleton, Colo., Libraries Unlimited, 1982).

Astronomy and Astrophysics: A Bibliographical Guide by D. A. Kemp (Hamden, Conn., Archon, 1970) is geared more to the professional astronomer than the amateur. Both books and periodical articles are covered, in sections by subject area. The first section lists and briefly annotates reference sources including bibliographies, lists of periodicals, and abstracting services. Other sections do the same for works in astronomy and astrophysics, arranged in broad subject areas, for example, catalogs and atlases, infrared astronomy, and the moon. There is a glossary of abbreviations, and author and subject indexes.

Bibliographies

The historical literature of astronomy is listed in *Bibliographie Astronomique* by J. J. F. de Lalande (Paris, Imprimerie de la Republique, 1803). This bibliography lists writings from ancient times, beginning in 480 B.C., through 1802, in a chronological arrangement. Indexes are by author and subject. *Bibliographie Générale de l'astronomie Jusqu'en 1880* was first published in 1882-89 by J. C. Houzeau and A. Lancaster; a recent edition by D. W. Dewhirst (London, Holland Press, new edition 1964) is a bibliography of astronomy to the year 1880. Books, manuscripts, society publications, and journal articles are listed. *Bibliography of Astronomy, 1881-1898* (Buckinghamshire, England, University Microfilms Ltd., 1970) is on microfilm. Beginning with the literature of 1899 and published annually through 1968, *Astronomischer Jahresbericht* (Berlin, Reimer, 1900-10 and W. de Gruyter, 1920-68) provides a complete international listing of books, book reviews, journal articles, and astronomical observations. Arrangement is in broad subject groups, and bibliographic information is given, in some cases accompanied by an abstract. Thus the astronomical literature through the years is listed, up to *Astronomy and Astrophysics Abstracts,* which began in 1969 and will be described in the section on indexing and abstracting services.

Basil J. W. Brown in *Astronomical Atlases, Maps and Charts: An Historical and General Guide* (London, Search, 1932, reprinted Dawson, 1968) lists star atlases, charts, and catalogs, plus other categories of materials such as celestial globes. Much historical information is included, with details on individual items. Biographical information on the astronomers and cartographers who made the maps and charts is included, as well as pictures of some of the old maps and charts. Catalogs published more recently are listed in *Astronomical Catalogues 1951–75,* compiled by Mike Collins (London, Institution of Electrical Engineers, 1977). This is a bibliography of all astronomical catalogs published in the years 1952 to 1975, about 2,500 items. Included are those published separately as catalogs and those done as part of a journal article or book. Arrangement is in broad subject categories, for example, "stars," with subdivisions, for example, "positional catalogues." There is an index by author. Catalogs and atlases are also listed in the guides to the literature listed earlier in this chapter.

Reviews of the Literature

The *Annual Review of Astronomy and Astrophysics* (Palo Alto, Calif., Annual Reviews, 1, 1963–) contains review articles on various subjects, each about thirty to forty pages long, each with references. Indexes are by author and subject. *Vistas in Astronomy,* edited until 1980 by Arthur Beer and now by his son Peter Beer (New York, Pergamon, 1955–), is also published annually, and contains review articles, with references.

Indexing and Abstracting Services

Astronomy and Astrophysics Abstracts (Berlin and New York, Springer-Verlag, 1, 1969–) is published twice a year under the auspices of the International Astronomical Union. Coverage is international and includes books, periodical articles, reports, and conference proceedings. Entries are arranged in subject groups using a classification scheme, with cross-references leading from entries under secondary subjects to that under the main subject. Bibliographic information and an abstract of the work are given; titles are usually given in English even if the work was not originally in English; abstracts are in English, French, or German. There are author and subject indexes in each volume, with cumulations periodically.

Bulletin Signaletique 120: Astronomie, Physique Spatiale, Geophysique (Paris, Centre de Documentation, 30, 1969–) continues earlier titles of the *Bulletin Signaletique* on astronomy, and is similar to other sections of the *Bulletin*. It is published monthly and gives international coverage. Arrangement is in broad subject sections, and it has a subject index, an author index, and a geographic index to the location an article is about. The bibliographic citation is given for each article, plus an abstract, written in French.

SECONDARY LITERATURE MATERIALS

Encyclopedias

1001 Questions Answered About Astronomy by James S. Pickering, revised by Patrick Moore (New York, Dodd, Mead, 1976), is arranged in question-and-answer form within chapters. The chapters deal with different subjects, for example, "the sun," "earth and moon," and "mechanics and physics." Diagrams and a few photographs are used to illustrate answers. There is a subject index. *Astronomy: A Handbook* by Günter D. Roth (Berlin and New York, Springer-Verlag, 2d edition 1975) is also made up of brief information on many subjects, arranged in chapters. Examples of chapter subjects are "astronomical literature and nomenclature," "observing instruments," and "radio astronomy." There is a bibliography, and index. The *Illustrated Encyclopedia of Astronomy and Space* edited by Ian Ridpath (New York, Crowell, 1976) contains expanded definitions illustrated by drawings, diagrams, and photographs, and tables and an index. The *New Space Encyclopedia: A guide to Astronomy and Space Exploration* (New York, Dutton, 2d edition 1975) is written at a popular level, with definitions and brief articles. Miscellaneous information in the appendixes includes brief summaries of the Apollo space flights.

Kenneth Gatland's *Illustrated Encyclopedia of Space Technology* (Worcester, Mass., Harmony, 1981) is a comprehensive history of space exploration. Photographs are used extensively, 400 in color and black and white, and there is a space diary of about 200 pages.

ASTRONOMICAL CATALOGS AND ATLASES

The *Sky Explored: Celestial Cartography 1500–1800* by Deborah J. Warner (New York, Liss, 1979) contains lovely reproductions of star maps of history, with descriptions. Arrangement is alphabetical by names of astronomers, and for each astronomer there is brief biographical information and then a list of his star maps with descriptions, and a sample reproduced.

A guide to the information in star catalogs may be found in *Astronomy of Star Positions; a Critical Investigation of Star Catalogues, the Methods of Their Construction, and Their Purpose* by Heinrich Eichhorn (New York, Ungar, 1974). Information is given on positional astronomy, including astronomical coordinate systems, acquisition of astronomical data, general discussion of star catalogs, compilation catalogs, and systematic zone catalogs.

Patrick Moore's *New Concise Atlas of the Universe* (New York, Rand McNally, 1978) is an oversize volume made up mostly of photographs, many in color, with explanations of the photographs. Main sections are an atlas of the earth from space, an atlas of the moon, an atlas of the solar system, and an atlas of the stars. The appendixes contain a brief catalog of stellar objects. There is a glossary, and an index. *Catalog of the Universe* by Paul Murdin and David Allen (New York, Crown, 1979) contains hundreds of photographs of objects in the sky: galaxies, stars, planets, the sun, moon, and so forth. Detailed explanations of the photographs are given. There is a glossary. *Burnham's Celestial Handbook: An Observer's Guide to the Universe Beyond the Solar System* by Robert Burnham (New York, Dover, revised edition 1978) is a three-volume set directed at both amateurs and advanced astronomers. The first volume contains introductory information, and then begins an alphabetical sequence of constellations, which extends through the other two volumes. Information given for each constellation is a list of stars and descriptive notes, with illustrations, tables, and diagrams as needed. There is a subject index at the end of volume three.

Arthur P. Norton's *Star Atlas and Reference Handbook* (Cambridge, Mass., Sky, 1973) is written primarily for amateurs who have telescopes. It covers the whole star sphere, showing over 9,000 stars, nebulae, and clusters. Star charts, astronomical tables, symbols, and lists of objects for viewing are included. Patrick Moore's *Color Star Atlas* (New York, Crown, 1973) is for beginners. Star maps in color and annotated charts of constellations are included in addition to discussion of astronomy and handsome photographic illustrations.

The Smithsonian Institution Astrophysical Observatory, Cambridge, Massachusetts, puts out companion titles: *Star Catalog* (Washington, D.C., Smithsonian Institution, 1966) and *Star Atlas of Reference Stars and Nonstellar Objects* (Cambridge, Mass., MIT Press, 1969). The *Star Catalog* is a four-volume set, all tables giving, among other information, positions and proper motions for about 259,000 stars. The *Star Atlas* contains plates and charts for use with the *Catalog,* and a bibliography. The 152 star charts cover the whole sky.

The National Geographic Society sponsored a sky survey by the Palomar Observatory, resulting in a photographic atlas, *Palomar Observatory Sky Atlas* (Pasadena, Calif., California Institute of Technology, 1954). Made up of paper copies of photographic plates, this atlas covers the sky from $-33°$ to $+90°$ declination. It has been reprinted several times. For nonstellar objects, the *Revised New General Catalogue of Nonstellar Astronomical Objects* by Jack W. Sulentic and William G. Tifft (Tuscon, Ariz., University of Arizona, 1973) gives basic data such as type, positions, brightness, and description. This catalog is tied to the *Palomar Observatory Sky Atlas* by giving rectangular coordinates for the *Sky Atlas* for each object.

Antonín Bečaár has done several important atlases and a catalog that, although published in Czechoslovakia, are written in English. All are published by Akademie Ved, Czechoslovakia, and distributed by Sky Publishing Corporation in Cambridge, Massachusetts. His *Atlas Australis* (1964) shows stars south of declination $-30°$, and his *Atlas Borealis* (1962) shows stars north of $+30°$. *Atlas Eclipticalis* (1964) covers stars between declinations $-30°$ and $+30°$. *Atlas Coeli* (1962) is a basic sky atlas including stars, galaxies, nebulae, clouds of interstellar gas and dust, and constellations. The catalog companion for this atlas is Bečvár's *Atlas Coeli-II Katalog* (1964).

Observers' Manuals

George Reed's *Naked I Astronomy* (Dubuque, Iowa, Kendall/Hunt, 1976) contains sixteen "activities" for amateur learning, with no telescope needed.

J. Headley Robinson and James Muirden's *Astronomy Data Book* (New York, Wiley, 2d edition 1979) is a reference tool for amateur astronomers and for students. Designed to be used in conjunction with a star atlas, it contains a glossary, tables of data, and chapters on telescopes and on the earth, sun, moon, each planet, comets, meteors, stars, and galaxies. Each chapter includes general information and then information on specific features; for example, in the chapter on the moon there are sections on the moon's surface, lunar phenomena, formations, and information on observing the moon. The *Amateur Astronomer's Handbook* by James Muirden (New York, Crowell, 1974) is in these parts by topic: equipment, solar system, stars and nebulae, and optical work for amateurs. There is a brief bibliography, and a list of amateur astronomical societies in the United States, and the book is completed with an index. The *Larousse Guide to Astronomy* by David Baker (New York, Larousse, 1980) is also an amateur guide, containing photographs, data, and information on individual stars. *Beginner's Guide to the Skies* by Clarence H. Cleminshaw (New York, Crowell, 1977) is described by its subtitle as "a month-by-month handbook for stargazers and planet watchers." Twenty-four star maps are included, one for evening and one for the predawn sky for each month, showing principal stars and constellations. A table below each star map gives locations for Mars, Jupiter, and Saturn. There are also stories of the constellations, and information on each planet and on the sun and moon. Many illustrative drawings are used. The Royal Astronomical Society of Canada puts out yearly an *Observer's Handbook* (Toronto, Royal Astronomical Society of Canada, 74th edition 1982). This useful handbook includes information on the sun and planets, with positions on particular dates, information on the brightest stars, star maps, and a month-by-month listing of astronomical phenomena for the year covered.

The *Manual of Astronomy* by Robert W. Shaw and Samuel L. Boothroyd (Dubuque, Iowa, Brown, 5th edition 1967) has the subtitle "a guide to the observation and laboratory interpretation in elementary astronomy." It contains exercises for use with any text in elementary astronomy. *Mathematical Astronomy With a Pocket Calculator* by Aubrey Jones (New York, Wiley, 1978) provides methods to enable one to calculate such things as Local Sidereal time for any location, visual binary star orbits, and ephemerides of comets. Actual problems are given, with step-by-step solutions.

Telescopes

Astronomy Through The Telescope by Richard Lerner (New York, Van Nostrand Reinhold, 1981) tells the history of telescopes as scientific instruments. Many attractive illustrations are included.

The *Complete Manual of Amateur Astronomy: Tools and Techniques for Astronomical Observation* by P. Clay Sherrod and T. L. Koed (Englewood Cliffs, N.J., Prentice-Hall, 1981) is designed for serious amateurs. Telescopes and photography are discussed, as well as methods of observation. Techniques for observing meteors, comets, asteroids, the moon, Mars, Jupiter, Saturn, the sun, and stars are included.

Using the Telescope: A Handbook for Astronomers by Robinson J. Hedley (New York, Wiley, 1978) contains information for the amateur astronomer on different types of telescopes and on instruments for use with the telescopes, for example, cameras and clocks. There is also information on observing specific planets, observing comets, and observing the stars. A glossary, bibliography, and index complete this useful volume. A similar book is the *Telescope Handbook and Star Atlas* by Neale E. Howard (New York, Crowell, 1975), which begins with a discussion of telescopes and their capabilities and limitations. Most of the book is composed of chapters devoted to what can be seen with most amateur telescopes, and how to photograph those objects. Star maps and a gazeteer are included.

Telescopes for the 1980's edited by G. Burbridge and A. Hewitt (Palo Alto, Calif., Annual Reviews, 1981) discusses history, planning, and completion of new kinds of telescopes in the United States. There are separate chapters on the multiple-mirror telescope, the space telescope, the Einstein observatory, and future X-ray telescopes.

Solar System

The New Solar System edited by J. Kelly Beatty and others (Cambridge, Mass., Sky, 1981) provides enjoyable reading in a collection of articles by different experts. This is a review of current knowledge about the solar system. Arrangement is in chapters, some dealing with one planet and some with a broader topic, such as exploration, the sun, terrestrial planets, the moon, Mars, asteroids, Voyager, encounters, Jupiter and Saturn, planetary rings, and the outer solar system. Outstanding color photographs as well as drawings, illustrate the book. A list of suggested readings is at the back, as are tables of data on planets and satellites. *Solar System* by Peter Ryan (New York, Viking, 1978) is illustrated by many lovely paintings by Ludek Pesek. There is a chapter on the solar system and then separate chapters for each planet and on the sun, asteroids, and comets.

Daytime Star: The Story of Our Sun by Simon Mitton (New York, Scribner, 1981) is on the sun, the solar system, and the universe, from history, including ancient myths about the sun, to the latest solar energy developments.

Planets

If the title of Richard M. Baum's *The Planets: Some Myths and Realities* (New York, Wiley, 1981) doesn't pique your interest, the headings of some of the chapters will: "The Himalayas of Venus," "An Unexplained Observation," and "A Strange Celestial Visitor." There is also a bibliography, and an index. *The Solar Planets* by Valdemar A. Firsoff (New York, Crane, Russak, 1977) was given this title to emphasize that there are other planetary systems besides our solar system, which is the topic of this book. The book contains chapters on individual planets and on the moon in addition to more general information, illustrated by black and white photographs. There is also a bibliography, and an index.

Joseph H. Jackson's *Pictorial Guide to the Planets* (New York, Crowell, 3d edition 1981) is written at a popular level giving much information on the planet earth and the other planets, with many illustrations. There is brief discussion of interplanetary spaces, asteroids, meteors, comets, the sun, and the universe beyond the solar system. Tables of data, a bibliography, and an index are included.

Earthlike Planets: Surfaces of Mercury, Venus, Earth, Moon, and Mars by Bruce G. Murray and others (San Francisco, Freeman, 1981) is written for nonspecialists and for reference use for specialists. Emphasis is on surface features. The NASA planetary geology program is summarized.

Moon

Dinsmore Alter's *Pictorial Guide to the Moon* (New York, Crowell, 3d revised edition 1973) is illustrated with many black and white photographs. Chapters are concerned with historical information on early observations of the moon, lunar features, craters and domes, lunar rays, and more, topped off by two special chapters of photographs taken from space vehicles and from the moon's surface.

The *New Guide to the Moon* by Patrick Moore (New York, Norton, 1976) is also illustrated by several black and white photographs. Chapters deal with general information, movements of the moon, craters, atmosphere and life, and explaining the moon. The appendixes include techniques for observing the moon, miscellaneous data, and, highlighting the book, a detailed description of the moon's surface, with maps, occupying about seventy pages. *Photographic Atlas of the Moon* by Zdenek Kopal (New York, Taplinger, 1971) contains about 200 photographs, including photographs from space exploration. There is also historical discussion.

Galaxies

Galaxies by Timothy Ferris (San Francisco, Sierra Club, 1980) is a lovely oversize volume containing ninety-nine photographs, many in color, with text written in an interesting fashion. Arrangement is in chapters with discussion and photographs for each, including the milky way, local group of galaxies, form and variety of galaxies, interacting galaxies, clusters of galaxies, galaxies and the universe. There is a bibliography, and a glossary.

Periodicals

Astronomical Journal, sponsored by American Astronomical Society. New York, American Institute of Physics, 1849– . (monthly)

Astronomy. Milwaukee, Wis., AstroMedia, 1973– . (monthly)

Astrophysical Journal; an international review of astronomy and astronomical physics, sponsored by American Astronomical Society. Chicago, University of Chicago Press, 1895– . (semimonthly)

Junior Astronomy News. New York, Junior Astronomy Club, 1929– . (bimonthly)

Mercury. San Francisco, Astronomical Society of the Pacific, 1972– . (bimonthly)

Monthly Notices of the Royal Astronomical Society. Oxford, Blackwell, 1827– . (monthly)
Moon and the Planets; an international journal of comparative planetology. Dordrecht, Netherlands, 1969– . (8/year)
Planetary and Space Science. Oxford, Pergamon, 1959– . (monthly)
Publications of the Astronomical Society of the Pacific. San Francisco, Astronomical Society of the Pacific, 1880– . (bimonthly)
Sky and Telescope. Cambridge, Mass., Sky, 1941– . (monthly)

QUICK REFERENCE TOOLS

Dictionaries

Patrick Moore's *The A–Z of Astronomy* (New York, Scribner, 1977), alphabetical by term, contains definitions meant to be amateur or popular in content. Illustrations, tables, and diagrams are used as needed.

The *Dictionary of Astronomy, Space, and Atmospheric Phenomena* by David F. Tver (New York, Van Nostrand Reinhold, 1979) is alphabetical by term and gives concise definitions with diagrams as needed. The appendixes include miscellaneous information, for example, the metric system, and tables of information on the planets, constellations, and stars.

Facts on File Dictionary of Astronomy by Valerie Illingworth (New York, Facts on File, 1979) contains brief definitions, with diagrams, graphs, and so forth as needed. Miscellaneous information at the back includes tables of constants, a list of famous astronomers, and a list of major observatories.

Alfred Weigert's *Concise Encyclopedia of Astronomy* (London, Hilger, 2d edition 1976) gives concise definitions and usually some explanation, often with diagrams. Tables of stars and star maps are included. The *Glossary of Astronomy and Astrophysics* by Jeanne Hopkins (Chicago, University of Chicago Press, 2d edition 1980) is scholarly in content, with definitions coming mostly from articles in the *Astrophysical Journal*, which the author edits.

The foreign language dictionaries do not give definitions. *Astronomical Dictionary* by Josip Kleczek (New York, Academic, 1961) is polyglot, containing astronomical terms in English, Russian, German, French, Italian, and Czech. The terms are divided into subject sections, for example, general, astronomical objects, astrophysics, and so forth, and then listed in English and translated into each of the other languages. A separate index for each language lists terms in that language, and refers to the original listing.

For English-Russian translations, the *Anglo-Russkii Astronomicheskii Slovar'* by O. A. Mel'nikov (Moscow, Soc. Entsiklopediia, 1971) lists English words and phrases with the Russian equivalent, and has an index by Russian terms. Hong-yee Chiu's *Chinese-English, English-Chinese Astronomical Dictionary* (New York, Consultants Bureau, 1966) is in two sections. The Chinese-English section gives the English equivalent word meaning, and the English-Chinese section is alphabetical by the English term and gives the Chinese characters.

Ephemeris and Handbooks

The *Astronomical Almanac* (Washington, D.C., U.S. Government Printing Office and London, H. M. Stationery Office, 1981–) is published annually. This new title replaces two titles that previously provided much of the same type of information: *American Ephemeris and Nautical Almanac* and the *Astronomical Ephemeris*. The purpose of this *Almanac* is to provide current, accurate astronomical data including positions of bodies, eclipses, and so forth, for use in making observations, for reductions, and for general purposes, and it is made up mostly of tables. A list of observatories, worldwide, is included. Related publications that are prepared for particular applications, such as navigation, are listed. There is a glossary, and an index. *Yearbook of Astronomy* (New York, Norton, 1962–) now edited by Patrick Moore, is published annually. It contains articles reporting astronomical events for the year, such as an eclipse or meteor showers. Also there are data for observing, including, for example, new and full moon, positions of the planets, and information on stars and celestial occurrences month by month, and star charts and tables.

Astrophysical Quantities by Clabon W. Allen (London, Athlone, 3d edition 1973) consists entirely of tabular information, with information as to how to use the data as needed. Included is essential quantitative information of astrophysics in a form designed to be readily usable. There is an index.

Field Guide to the Stars and Planets by Donald H. Menzel (Boston,

Mass. Houghton Mifflin, 1975) is a simple observers' manual designed for quick reference.

Directories

Thornton Page's *Observatories of the World* (Cambridge, Mass., Smithsonian Institution Astrophysical Observatory, 1967) is a directory of major observatories throughout the world, arranged by country, with information on location, founding date, apertures, and type of telescope or antennas, observing programs, and wavelengths of radio telescopes. There is also some introductory information on the history of observatories and on observatory equipment.

U.S. Observatories by Henry T. Kirby-Smith (New York, Van Nostrand Reinhold, 1976) is, as its subtitle states, "a directory and travel guide," designed to be useful for astronomers in setting up cooperative studies or as a historical survey, and to assist amateur astronomers in finding observatories in their area and in their travels. There are detailed descriptions of fifteen major U.S. observatories, including the United States Naval Observatory in Washington, D.C., Yerkes Observatory in Wisconsin, and Lick Observatory in California. Other observatories, museums, and planetariums are listed alphabetically by state, with brief information about each. A bibliography is included.

A much more up-to-date directory is *Observatories of the World* by Marx Siegfried and Wener Pfaer (New York, Van Nostrand Reinhold, 1982).

6
Physics

INTRODUCTORY MATERIALS

Most of the introductory physics books to be described here are designed as textbooks for introductory physics courses, but all are also suitable for self study.

Physics in Everyday Life by Richard Dittman and Glenn Schmieg (New York, McGraw-Hill, 1979) stresses the practical aspects of physics in such topics as motion and forces, energy, fluids, heat, sound, electricity and magnetism, and so forth. Many illustrations are used. Each chapter includes an annotated bibliography, as well as problems and discussion questions at the end of the chapter. Answers to selected problems and to the discussion questions are at the back of the book. *Physics* by Arthur Beiser (Menlo Park, Calif., Benjamin/Cummings, 2d edition 1978) also has many illustrations. In addition to basic physics material each chapter has a section for a special topic that examines something of special interest from the subject of the chapter. Each chapter lists important terms with meanings, and important formulas. Questions and exercises are included, with answers to selected problems at the back. An appendix contains mathematics information and useful tables. Two other similar texts are *Introductory College Physics* by Atam P. Arya (New York, Macmillan, 1979) and *Introduction to Physics for Scientists and Engineers* by Frederick J. Bueche (New York, McGraw-Hill, 3d edition 1980). *Physics, Including Human Applications* by Harold Q. Fuller and others (New York, Harper and Row, 1978) covers general principles of physics, plus their interrelationships with other fields, mainly life sciences. A summary, questions, and exercises are included with each chapter. There is a glossary, and a bibliography. The appendix contains a self-study supplement of background mathematics. *Physics for Science and Engineering* by John P. McKelvey and Howard Grotch

(New York, Harper and Row, 1978) is an introductory text for students in science or engineering, with a more detailed presentation than most introductory level books. Appendixes include background information on mathematics.

The Physicists by C. P. Snow (Boston, Mass., Little, Brown, 1981) is a very readable book intended mostly for lay readers. Developments in physics in the 1900s are interspersed with interesting remarks on personalities by the author. *Directions in Physics* by Paul A. M. Dirac (New York, Wiley, 1978) is a description of triumphs and problems of modern physics presented in the form of several papers that were lectures to a conference.

An interesting history of physics covering 2,500 years is *Physical Thought From the Presocratics to the Quantum Physicists* (New York, Pica, 1975). From the mid–sixth century B.C. into the twentieth century, excerpts from writings of the time are arranged chronologically, with discussion. Brief biographical information on the authors is included. *Early Physics and Astronomy* by Olaf Pedersen and Mogens Pihl (New York, Elsevier, 1974) is written at a lay or undergraduate level to provide a first introduction to the history of physics and astronomy. However, it can also serve as a guide for more detailed study through use of its extensive bibliography and biographical appendix which tells brief information about early scientists and gives references to more information. Most of the book is in chapters on historical topics, for example, "conception of light and sound." *History of Twentieth Century Physics* by Charles Weiner (New York, Academic, 1977) contains articles by several authors, both historians and physicists. Articles cover such topics as the beginnings of quantum theory, history of atomic physics, and historical roots of modern physics. References are included with some articles.

Great Experiments in Physics edited by Morris H. Shamos (New York, Holt, 1959) contains detailed studies of twenty historical experiments. Each section has a short description of the subject, and then the original account of the experiment, with illustrations.

Subject Headings and Classification

Astrophysics
Biological physics
Cosmic physics

Elasticity
Electricity
Electrons
Fluids
Gases
Gravitation
Heat
Light
Magnetism
Matter
Mechanics
Motion
Optics
Physicists
Physics
   (also subdivisions of Physics)
   —Bibliography
   —Experiments
   —Formulae
   —History
   —Research
Physics literature
Quantum theory
Radiation
Solid state physics
Sound
Thermodynamics

Materials on physics in libraries will usually be found shelved in the QC section of the Library of Congress classification or in the 530 to 539 section of the Dewey Decimal Classification.

BIBLIOGRAPHIC MATERIALS

Guides to the Literature

Introductory Guide to Information Sources in Physics by L. R. A. Melton (Philadelphia, Pa., Heyden, 1978) is designed for quick reference for students or scientists. Arrangement is in three main parts: (1)

introduction and use of libraries, (2) search techniques and sources, and (3) guide to report writing. *Use of Physics Literature* edited by Herbert Coblans (London, Butterworths, 1975) is aimed at scientists and engineers, as well as students and librarians. Chapters by seventeen contributors, both scientists and librarians, cover the literature of physics, science libraries, reference materials, bibliographies, patents and translation, and specific literature sources in the history of physics, theoretical physics, astrophysics, mechanics and sound, heat and thermodynamics, light, electricity and magnetism, nuclear and atomic physics, crystallography, instrumentation, and computer applications. Appendixes include acronyms with meanings.

Nathan G. Parke's *Guide to the Literature of Mathematics and Physics* (New York, Dover, 2d edition 1958) has chapters on the principles of reading and study and on literature searching. The bibliography covers literature to 1956, arranged in about 120 subject groups, alphabetized by subject, with indexes by author and subject. Other guides are Robert H. Whitford's *Physics Literature* (Metuchen, N.J., Scarecrow, 2d edition 1968) and Bryan Yates's *How to Find Out About Physics* (Oxford, Pergamon, 1965), both of which bring coverage of literature up into the mid-1960s. Although these sources are old, they are still useful in some areas.

Bibliography

Resources for the History of Physics edited by Stephen G. Brush (Hanover, N.H., University Press of New England, 1972) has two main parts: (1) a guide to books and audiovisual materials, and (2) a guide to original works of historical importance and their translations into other languages. The first part is in sections by topic, for example, general books on the history of physics, physical sciences in the sixteenth, seventeenth, and eighteenth centuries, and so forth, and gives bibliographic information, annotation, and age level of expected users. The second part is a bibliography of original works, arranged alphabetically by author.

Reviews of the Literature

Reports of Progress in Physics (London, Institute of Physics, 1, 1934–) is published in association with the American Institute of Physics, and appears monthly. Each issue consists of long review articles with extensive bibliographies. All areas of physics are covered. *Reviews of Modern Physics* (New York, American Institute of Physics, 1, 1929–), published in association with the American Physical Society, appears quarterly. This review journal also contains long articles with extensive lists of references. An especially helpful added feature is a listing at the back of each issue of review articles in other current physics review journals, of which there are several.

Indexing and Abstracting Services

Physics Abstracts (London, Institution of Electrical Engineers, 1898–) gives the most comprehensive coverage of physics literature. This was formerly published as part one of *Science Abstracts*. Published twice per month, the service provides international coverage of journals, reports, books, dissertations, patents, and conference papers in the whole field of physics. It is arranged in broad subject areas by use of a classified scheme, and each item has complete bibliographic information and a brief descriptive abstract, as well as the author's affiliation. Indexing is by subject and author, and, where appropriate, by bibliography, book, corporate author, and conference. Indexes are in each issue and cumulated twice a year.

Physics Briefs (New York, American Institute of Physics, 1920–) is published semimonthly with semiannual indexes. This was called *Physikalische Berichte* up to 1978. It gives international coverage of all areas of physics and related topics, including journals, books, patents, reports, theses, and conference papers. Bibliographic information and an abstract are given.

Two sections of *Bulletin Signaltique* are applicable: part 130, *Physique, Mathematique, Optique, Acoustique, Mechanique, Chaleur,* and part 160, *Physique de l'etat Condense* (Paris, Centre National de la Recherche Scientifique, 1961–). These titles have varied slightly over the years. Arrangement is in broad subject areas, and coverage is international. Citations include bibliographic information, the author's affiliation, and in most cases a brief abstract. As in other sections, abstracts are in French, but titles of English language papers are cited in English. Indexes are by subject and author.

Some indexing and abstracting services are specific to narrower topics within physics. For example, *Science Research Abstracts Journal* (Riverdale, Md., Cambridge Scientific Abstracts, 1972–) is published ten times per year in two separate parts covering the literature of

Physics Abstracts Vol. 85 No. 1184 (17 May 1982)

62.65 ACOUSTIC PROPERTIES OF SOLIDS

(see also 62.80 Ultrasonic relaxation; for sound propagation, see 43.; for lattice dynamics and phonons, see 63.; for magnetoacoustic effects, see 72.55; for acoustoelectric effects, see 72.50; for acousto-optical effects, see 78.20H)

40490 Ultrasonic attenuation in molecular crystals. B.Perrin (Dept. de Recherches Phys., Univ. Pièrre et Marie Curie, Paris, France).
Phys. Rev. B (USA). vol.24, no.10, p.6104-13 (15 Nov. 1981).
It is now well established from an experimental point of view that, concerning the ultrasonic attenuation, molecular crystals exhibit a specific behavior among dielectric crystals. This fact suggests the presence of a relaxation process. Liebermann (1959), who has introduced this field, has proposed a way to analyze this problem and in particular has given an expression for the ultrasonic absorption coefficient in terms of a relaxation time and some thermodynamic quantities. In contrast to Liebermann's approach, a solid-state viewpoint is presented here, and it is shown that this ultrasonic relaxation can be taken into account in the framework of Akhieser's theory (1939). A general expression of the ultrasonic absorption coefficient is calculated in terms of the phonon collision operator using the Boltzmann-equation approach of Woodruff and Ehrenreich (1961). The collision-time approximation widely used in dielectric crystals fails in molecular crystals for which the presence of slow relaxation times in the collision operator prevents the thermalization of the whole set of phonons and gives rise to an ultrasonic relaxation. Thus a more suitable approximation is suggested here, which leads to a new expression of the ultrasonic attenuation valid in molecular crystals. Different forms of this expression are discussed, and comparison with Liebermann's expression used in most of the previous papers shows that the present treatment takes better account of the anisotropy of the solid state. The fit of experimental results obtained for some ionic-molecular crystals also shows that the expression derived here gives better agreement than does Liebermann's. Finally, it is shown that in the framework of the present treatment and under rather general conditions, the anisotropy affects primarily the magnitude of the ultrasonic absorption due to the molecular relaxation, but it does not affect its frequency dependence. (29 refs.)

40491 Piezoelectric attenuation in InP subjected to hydrostatic pressure.
D.N.Nichols, R.J.Sladek (Dept. of Phys., Purdue Univ., West Lafayette, IN, USA).
Phys. Rev. B (USA). vol.24, no.10, p.6161-2 (15 Nov. 1981).
The authors have measured the attenuation of 30-MHz longitudinal ultrasonic waves traveling in the [111] direction in Cr-doped, n-type InP subjected to 2 kbar of hydrostatic pressure between 273 and 350K. A piezoelectric attenuation peak is found which is very nearly equal in height to that observed at 1 bar indicating that the pressure did not change the piezoelectric constant significantly. The peak is located at higher temperatures at 2 kbar than at 1 bar in order for a given amount of screening of the piezoelectric field to be

40496 Vibrational relaxation in liquid carbon disulfide. K.Takagi (Inst. of Industrial Sci., Univ. of Tokyo, Tokyo, Japan).
J. Acoust. Soc. Am. (USA), vol.71, no.1, p.74-7 (Jan. 1982).
Ultrasonic velocity and absorption were measured in liquid carbon disulfide at 10°, 20°, and 30°C over a frequency range from 3 MHz to 5 GHz. Three experimental techniques were used: pulse-echo overlap at 3 MHz, HRB (high-resolution Bragg reflection) from 50 MHz to 1.5 GHz, and Brillouin scattering in the hypersonic region. The obtained spectra of the velocity dispersion and absorption suggested two relaxation processes, one at 100 MHz and the other at ~6 MHz. A hypothesis of vibrational double relaxation was proposed, in which the lower two fundamental modes, ν_1, and ν_2 have a common V-T relaxation time at 2.2 ns while the highest ν_3 relaxes independently at 30 ns. (18 refs.)

40497 Ultrasonic studies of the complexation kinetics of cadmium nitrate in nonaqueous solvents. S.Yamada, R.E.Verrall (Dept. of Chem. & Engng., Univ. of Saskatchewan, Saskatoon, Canada).
J. Phys. Chem. (USA), vol.85, no.21, p.3145-50 (15 Oct. 1981).
Ultrasonic absorption data obtained over the frequency range 5-95 MHz by the pulse method are reported for cadmium nitrate in methanol, dimethylformamide, and dimethyl sulfoxide in the temperature range 15-45°C and the concentration range 0.02-0.25 mol. dm^{-3}. Ultrasonic relaxation spectra show a single relaxation. The kinetic data have been interpreted in terms of the Eigen mechanism. The rate constants for solvent exchange in the first coordination sphere of Cd^{2+} were estimated at 25°C to be $1.1×10^8$ s^{-1} in methanol, $6.5×10^7$ s^{-1} in dimethylformamide, and $5.3×10^7$ s^{-1} in dimethyl sulfoxide. Large negative values of the activation entropy suggest that an associative interchange mechanism I_a is operative in this process. (52 refs.)

Seventh International Conference on Internal Friction and Ultrasonic Attenuation in Solids ....See Entry 38360

Ultrasonic attenuation in molecular crystals ....See Entry 40490

63.00 LATTICE DYNAMICS AND CRYSTAL STATISTICS

(see also 05.50 Lattice theory, 65. Thermal properties, 66.70 Thermal conduction, 68.30 Dynamics of surface and interface vibrations, 78.30 Infrared and Raman spectra)

63.20 PHONONS AND VIBRATIONS IN CRYSTAL LATTICES

Indexing and abstracting service: Physics Abstracts

Fig. 6-1. Indexing and abstracting service: Physics Abstracts

(A) superconductivity, magnetohydrodynamics, plasmas, and theoretical physics, and (B) laser and electrooptic reviews, quantum electronics, and unconventional energy sources. Subject and author indexes appear in each issue and are cumulated annually. *Solid State Abstracts* (Riverdale, Md., Cambridge Scientific Abstracts, 1957–), also published ten times per year, indexes and abstracts the literature of the physics, metallurgy, crystallography, chemistry, and device technology of solids.

SECONDARY LITERATURE MATERIALS

Encyclopedias

The *Encyclopedia of Physics* edited by Rita G. Lerner and George L. Trigg (Reading, Mass., Addison-Wesley, 1981) is a one-volume encyclopedia that aims to make a broad range of concepts of modern physics readily accessible to scientists, students, and interested nonscientists. It is made up of signed articles by experts in the various fields covered. Arrangement is alphabetical by topic, and articles range from one paragraph to several pages in length, each including a brief bibliography. Drawings, graphs, and so forth are used as needed. There is a subject index. The one-volume *Encyclopedia of Physics* edited by Robert M. Besancon (New York, Van Nostrand Reinhold, 2d edition 1974) was written by many contributors for physicists who need information outside their area of specialization and for teachers, librarians, students, engineers, and scientists. Articles are arranged alphabetically by subject, and are written at varied levels, with general articles on general topics and then more advanced articles on subdivisions of those topics, with references for further study. Most are two to four pages in length. Terms are defined and explained. There is an index by author and subject.

Articles of about 100 words make up the *New Dictionary of Physics* by Harold J. Gray and Alan Isaacs (London, Longman, 2d edition, 1975), directed toward physicists and physical chemists in addition to more general users. Arrangement is again alphabetical by term, and diagrams and illustrations are included in the definitions as needed. Also included are a few tables, for example, fundamental constants and a table of nuclides.

The *Encyclopaedic Dictionary of Physics* edited by James Thewlis (New York, Pergamon, 1961–64 and supplements 1966–) has a sub-

| INSPEC | Worldwide coverage of physics, electrical engineering, computer science, control engineering, meteorology, astrophysics, hydrology, glaciology, and oceans. Corresponds to Physics Abstracts, Electrical and Electronic Abstracts, and Computer and Control Abstracts. BRS has 1972 to 1976 offline, and 1977 to present online. DIALOG has two files: 1969 to 1976, and 1977 to present. SDC has two files: 1969 to 1976, and 1977 to present.

Prepared by Institution of Electrical Engineers. | Coverage: BRS, 1972 to present; DIALOG and SDC, 1969 to present; CAN/OLE, 1970 to present
File size: 1,715,279 records
Unit record: citation, abstract
Vendor, Cost/connect hour:
BRS, $51-$65;
CAN/OLE, $40 plus royalty;
DIALOG (12, 13), $75;
SDC, $80 |

Fig. 6-2. Computer data base: INSPEC

title that shows its broad coverage: general, nuclear, solid state, molecular, chemical, metal, and vacuum physics, astronomy, geophysics, biophysics, and related subjects. The basic set consists of nine volumes, of which volume 9 is a multilingual glossary. Arrangement is alphabetical by term, and articles range from a paragraph to several pages in length. Articles are by many contributors, and include references. Indexes, in volume 8, are by subject and author. Supplements are published irregularly.

The *Handbuch der Physik* edited by S. Flugge (Berlin, Springer-Verlag, 2d edition 1955-73) is in fifty-four volumes, each covering a different area of physics. Each volume has chapters by different authors written in English, German, or French, containing anywhere from 60 to 200 pages on the subject as well as references for further study. The subject index in each volume is in German and in English, and also in French in some volumes. Volumes are on specific topics, for example, acoustics, fundamentals of optics, geophysics, or astrophysics.

Not really an encyclopedia, but a series of volumes on various topics in physics is William Bolton's *Study Topics in Physics* (Boston, Mass., Butterworth, 1980). Each volume is approximately 100 pages long, and covers basic theories in the topics mentioned, with bibliography and index. Book 1 is on motion and force; book 2 on solids, structures, fluids, fluid flow, structure of materials; book 3 on concept of energy, heat, engines, energy resources; and book 4 on electric circuits, current and charge, electromagnetism.

Some encyclopedias present physical properties. *Thermophysical Properties of Matter* edited by Y. S. Touloukian and C. Y. Ho (New York, Plenum, 1970-76) is in thirteen volumes, each volume or group of volumes covering properties of a different type. Volumes 1-3 cover thermal conductivity, volumes 4-6 specific heat, volumes 7-9 thermal radiative properties, volume 10 thermal diffusivity, volume 11 viscosity, and volumes 12–13 thermal expansion. The data are presented mostly in table form or graphs, with explanation. A reference is given to the source of the information. An index to volumes 1–13 was published separately: *Index to Materials and Properties* (New York, Plenum, 1979). According to information in the set, new volumes will be published as needed to update or add to the store of information.

A very complex collection of data, sometimes known as Landolt-Börnstein, is *Zahlenwerte and Funktionen* by Hans H. Landolt and R. Börnstein (Berlin, Springer-Verlag, 6th edition 1950– and new series 1961–). The new series supplements the 6th edition and takes the place of new editions. Volumes are issued irregularly. The subtitle describes this encyclopedia: "numerical data and functional relationships in science and technology." Material is in English and German, and consists mostly of tables.

Other Data

Table of Isotopes edited by Charles M. Lederer and others (New York, Wiley, 7th edition 1978) contains two main sections: an isotope index arranged in order by atomic number and subarranged by mass number, and a table of isotopes arranged in order by mass number and subarranged by atomic number. Appendixes provide information on constants and conversion factors, nuclear spectroscopic standards, atomic levels, absorption of radiation in matter, nuclear decay rates, theoretical nuclear level diagrams, and nuclear moments. There is a bibliography.

Atomic Data and Nuclear Data Tables (New York, Academic, 1969–) is published monthly. These tables are compilations and evaluations of experimental and theoretical data in atomic physics. Arrangement is in articles by various authors. There is a cumulated subject index. *Nuclear Data Sheets* (New York, Academic, 1, 1966–) is also published monthly. It is made up of compilations and evaluations of experimental and theoretical results in nuclear physics, assembled from a computer file of nuclear structure data maintained by the Nuclear Data Project, Oak Ridge National Laboratory.

Steam Tables: Thermodynamic Properties of Water Including Vapor, Liquid and Solid Phases (New York, Wiley, 2d edition 1978) is made up of tables, with references.

Biographical

Nobel Prize Winners in Physics 1901–1950 by N. H. deV. Heathcote (New York, Schuman, 1953 reprinted by Arno, 1976) has information on fifty-four Nobel prize winners. Arrangement is chronological, and for each person there is a biographical sketch, as well as a description of the work that led to the Nobel prize. This same type of information is brought more up to date by Robert L. Weber in *Pioneers of Science* (London, Institute of Physics, 1980), which provides biographical sketches of Nobel Prize winners in physics from 1901 to 1979. There is a bibliography, and an index.

Experiments

Experimentation has always been an integral part of the study of physics, and early experiments are described in the books listed earlier on the history of physics. *Landmark Experiments in Twentieth Century Physics* by George L. Trigg (New York, Crane, Russak, 1975) describes "investigations which have signaled a marked change in ideas about some aspect of nature or in our capability of learning more," according to the preface. A bibliography is included with the description of each experiment. The American Association of Physics Teachers has sponsored a project that brings together the best demonstration equipment and techniques of the past 30 years. The result is *Physics Demonstration Experiments* edited by Harry F. Meiners (New York, Ronald, 1970), published in two volumes: (1) mechanics and wave motion; (2) heat, electricity and magnetism, optics, atomic and nuclear physics. There are chapters on the principles of demonstrating and on lecture techniques, and detailed descriptions of materials and experiments. *Novel Experiments in Physics* (Stony Brook, N.Y., State University of New York, 1, 1964–) consists of volumes prepared by the Committee on Apparatus of the American Association of Physics Teachers and published at irregular intervals. These are not laboratory manuals, but aim to describe laboratory experiments in many areas as a selection from which to choose. Experiments are at different levels from simple through challenging, with some quite sophisticated, and are prepared by different people.

Discoveries in Physics for Scientists and Engineers by Leonard H. Greenberg (Philadelphia, Pa., Saunders, 2d edition 1975) is a laboratory manual for college level or for advanced high school students. Directions are given for performing laboratory experiments, record keeping, and writing up the results. References are included with each experiment.

Periodicals

Annals of Physics. New York, Academic, 1957– . (monthly)
Applied Physics Letters. New York, American Institute of Physics, 1962– . (monthly)
Australian Journal of Physics. Melbourne, Commonwealth Scientific and Industrial Research Organization, 1948– . (quarterly)
Fortschritte der Physik. Berlin, Akademie-Verlag, 1953– . (monthly)
Japanese Journal of Applied Physics. Tokyo, University of Tokyo, 1962– . (monthly)
Journal of Physics. London, Institute of Physics. (monthly)
    section *A Mathematical and General* 1968– .
    section *B Atomic and Molecular.* 1968– .
    section *C Solid State.* 1968– .
    section *D Applied Physics.* 1968– .
    section *E Scientific Instruments.* 1968– .
    section *F Metal Physics.* 1971– .
    section *G Nuclear Physics.* 1975– .
Perspective of Physics. London and New York, Gordon and Breach, 1976– . (annual)
Physics of Fluids. New York, American Institute of Physics, 1958– . (bimonthly)
Physics Today. New York, American Institute of Physics, 1948– . (monthly)
Soviet Physics JEPT. New York, American Institute of Physics, 1955– . (monthly) (translation of *Journal of Experimental and Theoretical Physics of the Academy of Sciences of the USSR)*

CURRENT AWARENESS MATERIALS

Current Contents: Physical, Chemical and Earth Sciences (Philadelphia, Pa., Institute for Scientific Information, 1961–) is published weekly and reproduces the tables of contents of the most recent issues of selected journals in the subject areas covered. Journals are grouped by broad subject. Indexes are by subject and author, and the author index also gives the author's address. Additional regular features of each issue include contents lists for a few new books, and informative abstracts of a few current articles of general interest.

CPP: Current Papers in Physics (London, Institution of Electrical Engineers and New York, Institute of Electrical and Electronics Engineers, 1966–   ) is published twice monthly with the aim of helping scientists and engineers keep abreast of newly published information. Each issue is arranged in a classified subject arrangement, the same as is used in *Physics Abstracts,* and simply lists articles without abstracting them. This periodical is intended for browsing; there are no indexes. The whole field of physics is covered, and papers listed are selected from physics journals, worldwide, considered to be most important and productive. *Current Physics Index* (New York, American Institute of Physics, 1975–   ) is published quarterly, giving international coverage of about forty primary research journals. Arrangement is in subject classes, and bibliographic information and an abstract are given. There is an author index in each issue, and subject and author indexes appear annually.

QUICK REFERENCE TOOLS

Dictionaries

The *Concise Dictionary of Physics and Related Subjects* by James Thewlis (Oxford, Pergamon, 2d edition 1979) is arranged alphabetically by term with cross-references to connect interrelated terms. Definitions are brief with few equations and no illustrations, and subject coverage is broad: physics, astronomy, astrophysics, physical chemistry, and so forth. The appendix includes metric equivalents to some fundamental physical constants. The *Facts on File Dictionary of Physics* edited by Eric Deeson (New York, Facts on File, 1981) also contains brief definitions, arranged alphabetically by term with cross-references. Drawings are used as needed to illustrate.

More detailed definitions are given in the *McGraw-Hill Dictionary of Physics and Mathematics* (New York, McGraw-Hill, 1978), directed toward students, teachers, librarians, engineers, researchers, and the general public. More than 20,000 terms are listed alphabetically, with an indication of what field the term is used in, such as acoustics or aerospace, and a brief definition with diagrams and illustrations where needed. The appendix includes SI units, properties of the chemical elements and of planets and stars, and other information.

The *Penguin Dictionary of Physics* edited by Valerie H. Pitt (New York, Penguin, 1977) is an abridgement of Harold Gray's *New Dictionary of Physics* described earlier in the section on encyclopedias.

Elsevier's Dictionary of General Physics (Amsterdam, Elsevier, 1962) covers six languages: English, French, Spanish, Italian, Dutch, and German. The main part is alphabetical by term in English, with definition, and then lists synonyms in the other languages. Each term is numbered, and alphabetical indexes from each language other than English refer to the English entry in the main part. A multilingual glossary was mentioned earlier as part of James Thewlis's *Encyclopedic Dictionary of Physics*. This glossary is in English, French, German, Spanish, Russian, and Japanese. Other foreign-language dictionaries for physics are:

Emin, Irving. *Russian–English Physics Dictionary*. New York, Wiley, 1963.
Hyman, Charles J. and Ralph Idlin. *Dictionary of Physics and Allied Sciences: German–English and English–German*. New York, Ungar, 1978.
Tolstoi, D. M. *English–Russian Physics Dictionary*. New York, Pergamon, 1978.

Handbooks

The American Institute of Physics puts out a *Handbook* (New York, McGraw-Hill, 3d edition, 1972). Mostly tables, it is arranged in chapters by subject: mechanics, acoustics, heat, electricity and magnetism, optics, atomic and molecular physics, nuclear physics, and solid state physics, each contributed by an authority in the subject area. There is also a bibliography, and information on SI units.

The *Handbook of Chemistry and Physics* (Boca Raton, Fla., Chemical Rubber Co., 62d edition 1981), published yearly, is a large volume crammed with chemical and physical data. It also consists mostly of tables, with some explanations and references. It is arranged in general sections, for example, mathematical tables, general physical constants. There is a detailed index. The *Handbook of Physics* by Edward Condon and Hugh Odishaw (New York, McGraw-Hill, 2d edition 1967) is arranged in chapters by subject and consists mostly of discussion and formulas. Bibliographies are included.

Jan J. Tuma's *Handbook of Physical Calculations* (New York, McGraw-Hill, 1976) is a summary of definitions, formulas, tables, and examples. Arrangement is in four parts: applications of technical physics, physical tables, systems of units and their relationship, and an index. There is a bibliography. *Fundamental Formulas of Physics* edited by Donald H. Menzel (New York, Dover, 2d revised edition 1963) is in two volumes. This is a comprehensive reference book of fundamental formulas in physics and some other related disciplines. Arrangement is in chapters, for example, basic mathematical formulas, by subject specialists, with a bibliography for each chapter.

Directory

The *Directory of Physics and Astronomy Staff Members* (New York, American Institute of Physics, 1959/60–   ) is published annually. It gives the address and phone number of departments of physics or astronomy, and lists faculty and staff. Arrangement is in three sections: a geographic listing of institutions in the United States, Canada, Mexico, and Central America, and alphabetical lists of staff membes and of colleges and universities.

7
Chemistry

INTRODUCTORY MATERIALS

There are many general chemistry books, most written for possible textbook use. Only a few examples will be mentioned here. A very basic general book intended for advanced high school or beginning college use is Jesse S. Binford's *Foundations of Chemistry* (New York, Macmillan, 1977). In addition to discussion, each chapter has problems to be solved, with answers to selected problems appearing in the appendix. There is an index. *General Chemistry* by Ralph S. Becker and Wayne E. Wentworth (Boston, Mass., Houghton Mifflin, 2d edition 1980) is written as a text for an introductory course in chemistry for students of chemistry, science, or engineering, and also has exercises with each chapter, and an index. *Chemical Principles* by Richard E. Dickerson and others (Menlo Park, Calif., Benjamin/Cummings, 3d edition 1979) is written for nonspecialists or for future chemistry majors. It has several survey chapters and more detailed information, with suggested readings, self-study questions, and problems with each chapter. In *Chemistry: The Central Science* by Theodore Brown and H. Eugene LeMay, Jr. (Englewood Cliffs, N.J., Prentice-Hall, 1977) the authors stress the study of chemistry as essential to agriculture, engineering, geology, microbiology, and so forth. Introductory material begins with history, and the book progresses through discussions of general chemistry. Each chapter ends with a summary, a section called ''learning goals'' for the chapter, key terms with definitions, and exercises. Appendixes contain answers to selected exercises and tables of information. Other general chemistrys are *Fundamentals of Chemistry* by Frank Brescia (New York, Academic, 3d edition 1976), *Chemistry: A Conceptual Approach* by Charles E. Mortimer (New York, Van Nostrand Reinhold, 4th edition

1979), *Chemistry: A Systematic Approach* by Harry H. Sisler (New York, Oxford, 1980), and, with more popular appeal, *Chemistry for the Consumer* by William R. Stine (Boston, Allyn and Bacon, 1978). *What's Happening in Chemistry?* (Washington, D.C., American Chemical Society, 1981–) consists of articles on recent research. Its aim is to promote a better understanding of science and technology. For example, articles on computers in chemistry and on splitting water by mock photosynthesis were included in the 1981 volume.

It is interesting to read of the history of a science through its people. *Great Chemists* edited by Eduard Farber (New York, Interscience, 1961) contains long biographies of about 100 chemists of history, with portraits. Henry M. Smith's *Torchbearers of Chemistry* (New York, Academic, 1949) has the descriptive subtitle "portraits and brief biographies of scientists who have contributed to the making of modern chemistry." The portraits, of about 200 people, are from a collection at the Massachusetts Institute of Technology.

Subject Headings and Classification

Chemical apparatus
Chemical elements
Chemical engineering
Chemical industries
Chemical libraries
Chemical literature
Chemical plants
Chemical processes
Chemical research
Chemicals
Chemistry
   (also subdivisions of Chemistry)
   —Bibliography
   —Experiments
   —History
   —Laboratory manuals
Chemistry, Inorganic
Chemistry, Organic
Chemistry, Physical and theoretical
Chemists

Materials on chemistry will usually be found shelved in libraries in the QD section of the Library of Congress classification or in the 540 to 549 section of the Dewey Decimal Classification.

BIBLIOGRAPHIC MATERIALS

Guides to the Literature

Guide to Basic Informaton Sources in Chemistry by Arthur Antony (New York, Wiley, 1979), directed mainly to chemistry students, is also for librarians, teachers, researchers, technicians, and anyone else wanting information in chemistry. It is arranged in chapters by type of literature, for example, guides, abstracts and indexes, periodicals, dictionaries and encyclopedias, and so forth, with separate chapters on the use of *Chemical Abstracts,* computer searching, and search strategy. Each chapter includes a brief discussion and then lists of sources with bibliographic information and annotation. The search strategy chapter includes eleven "cases" where a specific problem and search technique are described as if being explored, for example, "Lola is a student and needs . . ." The book is completed by indexes by author and title and by subject. *How to Find Chemical Information* by Robert E. Maizell (New York, Wiley, 1979) is subtitled "a guide for practicing chemists, teachers, and students." This guide is different from most in that it is written more in the form of an informal help for chemists, primarily those in the United States. There is discussion of chemical information and of strategies for searching out and obtaining information, and much practical information, in addition to chapters on the use of *Chemical Abstracts,* computer searching, patents, and safety. Another practical guide is *Using the Chemical Literature* by Henry M. Woodburn (New York, Dekker, 1974). Again this guide is not for use as a bibliography but contains discussions of library classification systems, and of types of materials, for example, government documents, reviews, reference books. Specific information is given on how to use basic sources where use may present problems. R. T. Bottle's *Use of Chemical Literature* (Woburn, Mass., Butterworth, 3d edition 1979) stresses British chemical literature. Chapters by various authors include the use of libraries, translations, abstracting and indexing services, patent literature, government publications, and the practical use of chemical literature, in addition to chapters on specific subject areas and their reference works. A whole chapter is devoted to the use of Beilstein's *Handbuch der Organischen Chemie*. Exercises are included, with notes on their solution.

The patent literature is treated separately by John T. Maynard in *Understanding Chemical Patents: A Guide for the Inventor* (Washington, D.C., American Chemical Society, 1978), written as practical information for practicing chemists and chemical engineers. The book discusses how to use patents as sources of information, how to work with attorneys in seeking a patent for an invention, record keeping, and so forth. There is a glossary, and an index.

Bibliographies

Two standard bibliographies in chemistry are useful for finding older sources of information. *Gmelin's Handbuch der Anorganischen Chemie* by Leopold Gmelin (Leipzig, Germany, Verlag Chemie, 8th edition 1924–), published in many volumes, covers the research literature in inorganic chemistry. The *Handbuch der Organischen Chemie* by Freidrich K. Beilstein (Berlin, Springer-Verlag, 4th edition 1918–) contains research literature of organic chemistry. The main work of twenty-seven volumes covered the literature through 1909, and supplements published since cover the literature of designated periods: 1910–19, 1920–29, 1930–49, 1950–59, and 1960–79.

Indexing and Abstracting Services

Chemical Abstracts (Easton, Pa., American Chemical Society, 1, 1907–) is a massive, very detailed index of international literature in chemistry and chemical engineering: journals, patents, reviews, technical reports, books, conference proceedings, symposia, and dissertations. Issues are published weekly, containing abstracts and three indexes: key word, author, and patent. The citations are arranged in broad subject groups, and full bibliographic information and an abstract are given for each item. Two volumes are issued a year, each having the following indexes: author, subject, chemical substance, patent number, and formula or ring system. These indexes are then cumulated into collective indexes covering five or ten years. A separate source index issued every few years tells where one may find the journals that were indexed, in libraries throughout the world. This index lists each journal and some other sources such as conference proceedings, gives bibliographic information, and lists initials of libraries that have the item together with what volumes they own. A list of the libraries gives addresses.

Bulletin Signlaetique 170: Chimie (Paris, Centre de Documentation Scientifique et Technique, 30, 1969–) continues other *Bulletin Signaletique* sections covering chemistry over the years. It is issued monthly and indexes mostly periodicals, internationally. Arrangement is by subject areas, and bibliographic information and a brief abstract are given. There are subject and author indexes in each issue and cumulated annually.

SECONDARY LITERATURE MATERIALS

Encyclopedias

The *Encyclopedia of Chemistry* edited by Clifford A. Hampel and G. G. Hawley (New York, Van Nostrand Reinhold, 3d edition 1973) has as its purpose to present a concise cross-sectional view of chemistry for students, laymen, and experts outside their field, in one volume. Arrangement is alphabetical by topic, with a subject index, and articles are written by specialists in the various areas.

The *Kirk-Othmer Encyclopedia of Chemical Technology* (New York, Wiley, 3d edition 1978–) contains articles several pages in length, each by a specialist in the field, and each with a bibliography. Arrangement is alphabetical by topic through the many volumes, with cross-references as needed and a subject index. Emphasis in this set is on important present-day topics of health, safety, toxicology, and new materials. About half of the articles deal with chemical substances, and information includes properties, manufacture, and uses.

Chemical Technology: An Encyclopedic Treatment (New York, Barnes and Noble, 1968–75) is an eight-volume set designed with the nonspecialist in mind. It provides a guide to raw materials and the manufacturing and agricultural processes involved. Articles are arranged systematically, in chapters, so that related subjects are together, and there is an index in each volume, and a general index for the set in the last volume. Articles are written by subject specialists and include references.

The *Encyclopedia of Industrial Chemical Analysis* edited by Foster

Dee Snell and C. L. Hilton (New York, Interscience, 1966–74) is a twenty-volume work giving general techniques of analysis, and articles on chemicals important in industry. Arrangement is alphabetical by subject, with subject indexes. Bibliographies are included. *Encyclopedia of Chemical Processing and Design* (New York, Dekker, 1, 1976–) is aimed at readers planning to develop or design a product or process, and covers in its volumes the entire field of chemical processing and design for professional chemical engineers, designers, managers, and technical workers. The long articles by specialists are arranged alphabetically by topic, with cross-references, and include bibliographies.

Compilations and Handbooks

Handbooks of data in table form for quick reference will be described in the quick reference section of this chapter. Some handbooks are in the nature of compilations of information, some in table form and some not. For example, the *Chemist's Companion: A Handbook of Practical Data, Techniques and References* (New York, Wiley, 1972) has information presented in these sections: properties of molecular systems, properties of atoms and bonds, kinetics and energetics, spectroscopy, photochemistry, chromatography, experimental techniques, mathematical and numerical information, and miscellaneous. Information is mostly in table form. An index of suppliers lists manufacturers by page numbers leading to discussion of the materials they supply. References and a subject index are included. The *New Handbook of Chemistry* by Philip S. Chen (Camarillo, Calif., Chemical Elements, 1975) is on a more popular level than the above title, or for beginning students. It includes a glossary.

Some handbooks are designed especially with the technician in mind. The *Chemical Technology Handbook* by the Writing Team for the Chemical Technician Curriculum Project (Washington, D.C., American Chemical Society, 1975) is to be used as a text or for reference. It begins with a refresher and quick reference to first aid techniques, then has chapters on safety, toxic chemicals, radiation and electrical hazards, using laboratory tools and equipment, and so forth. A brief review of the chemical literature, a glossary, and an index complete the book. *Handbook for Chemical Technicians* by Howard J. Strauss (New York, McGraw-Hill, 1976) is for students, laboratory workers, chemical plant operators, and so forth. There are tables and graphs, with an explanation of the theory behind them and how to use them. Arrangement is in chapters, for example, "units and measurements," "thermal, electrical and mechanical units," "metals and alloys," and there is an index. The *Chemical Technicians' Ready Reference Handbook* by Gershon J. Shugar (New York, McGraw-Hill, 2d edition 1981) is designed to aid chemical technicians, high school and college chemistry students, and professional chemists in laboratory work. It provides instructions for all commonly used laboratory procedures, including equipment needed and how to use it, steps to take, cautions, and tables of data needed to utilize data from the experiment. There is also a section of practical reference information on common hazardous chemicals.

A third type of handbook provides information on properties of chemicals, for either identification or use of the chemicals. The *Merck Index: An Encyclopedia of Chemicals and Drugs* (Rahway, N.J., Merck, 1, 1889–   ) is an encyclopedia of chemicals, drugs, and biological substances. It is published at irregular intervals, the 9th edition appearing in 1977. It is arranged alphabetically by name, whether the generic, trivial, or simple chemical name, and then gives for each entry the alternate names, data on the substance, and a list of references. There is an index by formula, and a cross-index to names. *Physical Properties of Inorganic Compounds: SI Units* by Arisztid L. Horvath (New York, Crane, Russak, 1975) contains selected physical properties most frequently used by research workers, engineers, and designers in the chemical and gas industries, with references. *Thermochemical Properties of Inorganic Substances* by Ihsan Barin (Berlin and New York, Springer-Verlag, 1973), and its supplement for 1977 by the same author and publisher, is a collection of tables based on existing compilations of thermochemical properties and on original research. The supplement contains data and functions for 800 additional inorganic substances and updates data as needed for the first volume. The *Handbook of Tables for Organic Compound Identification* by Zvi Rappoport (Cleveland, Ohio, Chemical Rubber Company, 3d edition, 1967) contains tables of information to assist chemists in identification of organic compounds, and some miscellaneous tables such as logarithms and atomic weights. There is an index by names of inorganic compounds. The *Atlas of Spectral Data and Physical Constants for Organic Compounds* by Jeanette G. Grasselli (Cleveland, Ohio, Chemical Rubber Company, 2d edition 1975) is a six-volume set giving data for 21,000 organic compounds. *Sadtler*

Standard Spectra (Philadelphia, Pa., Sadtler Research Laboratories, 196?–) is a collection of reference spectra. The set consists of many volumes, with new volumes published as needed to add spectra of more materials. Loose-leaf replacement pages are also issued to correct or update existing spectra. Spectra are grouped in sections with several volumes for each: infrared prism, infrared grating, nuclear magnetic resonance, Raman, ultraviolet, fluorescence, and 13C-nuclear magnetic spectra. For each spectrum there is information about the compound being analyzed, including its molecular formula, molecular weight, structural formula, physical and optical constants, the source of the sample, and literature references. All spectra are indexed by chemical name and by molecular formula, and there are other indexes as applicable to certain sections of the collection. The indexes are cumulated periodically, and also refer the user to some other standard spectra collections.

An additional source of chemical data, which is not in handbook form, is the *Journal of Physical and Chemical Reference Data* (Washington, D.C., American Chemical Society and American Institute of Physics for National Bureau of Standards, 1, 1972–). This journal is issued quarterly to provide critically evaluated physical and chemical property data. Each issue consists of articles with references, and an index leads to properties for which data are given.

The home chemist may be interested in Henry Goldschmiedt's handbook *Practical Formulas for Hobby or Profit* (New York, Chemical Publishing, 1973). This volume tells how to make some commonly needed items: adhesives and cements; chemical specialities such as automobile products and laundry products; cosmetics and drugs; farm, garden, and home specialities; food products; paints and coatings; and laboratory equipment. *Chemical Formulary* edited by H. Bennett (New York, Chemical Publishing, 1, 1933–) is issued irregularly, with volume 20 issued in 1977. These volumes provide commercial formulas for making thousands of products. All volumes are useful, as the formulas in each volume are different from those in all other volumes. An extensive introduction, repeated in each volume, gives information to enable anyone to start making simple products, according to the author. Formulas are then given in groups by type of product, for example, adhesives, coatings, drugs, and so forth. The appendix contains miscellaneous information including a list of suppliers of chemicals. There is an index.

Safety

Dangerous Properties of Industrial Materials by N. Irving Sax (New York, Van Nostrand Reinhold, 5th edition 1979) has as its purpose to provide "quick, up-to-date, concise, hazard analysis information for nearly 15,000 common industrial laboratory materials," according to its preface. Substances are listed alphabetically, and for each general information, hazard analysis, and countermeasures are given. Other brief chapters discuss such topics as industrial hygiene, industrial noise, industrial waste handling, and labeling of hazardous materials. The *Handbook of Reaction Chemical Hazards* by L. Bretherick (London, Butterworths, 2d edition 1979) is designed to allow the chemist to assess "likely reaction hazard-potential associated with existing or proposed chemical compounds or reaction systems," according to the book. There is some general discussion of hazards, then an alphabetical listing of classes or groups of chemicals and their behavior, and then a listing by formula of elements and compounds giving detailed information on hazardous properties. References and an index complete this book.

The *Manufacturing Chemists' Association Guide for Safety in the Chemical Laboratory* (New York, Van Nostrand Reinhold, 2d edition 1972) would be helpful in school and industrial safety programs. Included are methods and equipment for laboratory safety, and chapters discussing various topics, such as evaluating the hazards of unstable substances. Appendixes include a bibliography, and a chart by name of substance giving waste disposal procedures, flammability limits, and other data. The *CRC Handbook of Laboratory Safety* compiled by Norman V. Steere (Cleveland, Ohio, Chemical Rubber Company, 2d edition 1971) contains practical information for hazard recognition and control in laboratories in schools, hospitals, industry, or elsewhere. There is a section of tables of chemical hazard information listing the chemical names and formulas of about 2,000 chemicals, with data such as relative hazard to health from exposure, hazard identification signals, flammable limits, and so forth.

Laboratory Methods; Mathematics and Statistics

Integrated Experimental Chemistry by David A. Aikens and others (Boston, Mass., Allyn and Bacon, 1977) is a two-volume set. The first volume contains general information on laboratory safety, information sources in chemistry, and experimental methods and techniques. In the second volume are thirty-five experiments, with detailed information on how to do each, and a list of references. *Chemical Experimentation: An Integrated Course in Inorganic, Analytical, and Physical Chemistry* by Ursula A. Hofacker (San Francisco, Freeman, 1972) contains sixteen exercises giving practice in a variety of areas, for example, preparative methods and structure determination methods. Also included is a list of nineteen "projects" to be constructed from experiments in the manual, each of which draws together several experiments. *Techniques of Chemistry* edited by Arnold Weissberger (New York, Wiley, 1, 1971–) is a series of volumes by many authors who are specialists in the fields, giving a comprehensive presentation of techniques. Theoretical background is included in addition to a description of techniques and tools. An example of one volume in this series is *Laboratory Engineering and Manipulations* edited by Edmond S. Perry and Arnold Weissberger (New York, Wiley, 3d edition 1979).

Dorothy M. Goldish's *Basic Mathematics for Beginning Chemistry* (New York, Macmillan, 2d edition 1979) is elementary mathematics, written for students who consider themselves "no good at math" but are taking a chemistry course. *Mathematics for Chemists* by Charles L. Perrin (New York, Wiley-Interscience, 1970) is suitable for self study or for a course text. It has exercises, with answers provided for some. Another is *Mathematical Techniques in Chemistry* by Joseph B. Dence (New York, Wiley, 1975). Edward L. Bauer's *Statistical Manual for Chemists* (New York, Academic, 2d edition 1971) is a practical elementary manual on statistical techniques for the working chemist. Many examples are detailed, and there is a subject index. References list sources of further study.

Periodicals

Acta Crystallographica, parts A and B. Copenhagen, Denmark, 1948– . (part A bimonthly, part B monthly)
American Chemical Society. Journal. Washington, D.C., American Chemical Society, 1879– . (fortnightly)

Association of Official Analytical Chemists. Journal. Arlington, Va., Association, 1915– . (bimonthly)

Catalyst, Philadelphia Section of American Chemical Society. Philadelphia, Pa., University of Pennsylvania, 1916– . (monthly)

Chemical Marketing Reporter. New York, Schnell, 1871– . (weekly)

Chemical Reviews. Washington, D.C., American Chemical Society, 1924– . (bimonthly)

Chemical Society, London. Reviews. London, Chemical Society, 1972– . (4/year)

Chemical Times and Trends. Washington, D.C., Chemical Specialities Manufacturers Association, 1977– . (quarterly)

Chemist. Washington, D.C., American Institute of Chemists, 1923– . (monthly)

Chemistry International. New York, Pergamon, 1977– (bimonthly)

Current Awareness Profile on Quantum Chemistry. Bloomington, Ind., Indiana University, 1973– . (fortnightly)

Food Chemistry; an International Journal. Essex, England, Applied Science, 1976– . (2/year)

Inorganic Chemistry. Washington, D.C., American Chemical Society, 1962– . (monthly)

International Journal of Quantum Chemistry. New York, Wiley, 1966– . (monthly)

Journal of Chemical Education. New York, American Chemical Society, 1924– . (monthly)

Journal of Chemical Information and Computer Sciences. Washington, D.C., American Chemical Society, 1961– . (quarterly)

Journal of Molecular Structure. Amsterdam, Elsevier, 1967– (monthly)

Journal of the Chemical Society, Chemical Communications; a Journal for Urgent Preliminary Accounts of Important Chemical Research. London, Chemical Society, 1965– . (semiannual)

Polymer. Surrey, England, IPC, 1960– . (monthly)

Polymer Bulletin. New York, Springer-Verlag, 1978– . (24/year)

Progress in Solid State Chemistry. New York, Pergamon, 1964– (4/year).

Pure and Applied Chemistry. New York, International Union of Pure and Applied Chemistry, Pergamon, 1960– . (monthly)

CURRENT AWARENESS MATERIALS

Current Contents: Physical, Chemical and Earth Sciences (Philadelphia, Pa., Institute for Scientific Information, 1961–) is published weekly and reproduces the contents lists of current journals in the subject fields listed in its title. Each list contains indexes by subject and author and addresses of authors. *Chemical Titles* (Easton, Pa., American Chemical Society, 1, 1960–) is issued biweekly and aims to be so current as to index journals the same month they are published. Coverage is international. Each issue has two sections: indexes by key subject words in the title of each article and by author's name, and a bibliography section. The bibliography section lists full bibliographic information for articles indexed. It is arranged alphabetically by the name of the journal and then lists articles in that journal. A code number is used to get from the index to the article listing in the bibliography.

QUICK REFERENCE TOOLS

Dictionaries

The *Condensed Chemical Dictionary* revised by Gessner Hawley (New York, Van Nostrand Reinhold, 10th edition 1981) is mainly alphabetical by term including names of chemicals, chemistry terms, and abbreviations, and giving brief definitons. Other miscellaneous information is included in the volume, such as a periodic chart of the elements, information on safety and on trademarks, a temperature conversion table, and derivations of chemical terms. A special feature is that for each chemical a number refers to a list of manufacturers to show the manufacturer of that chemical. The *Facts on File Dictionary of Chemistry* edited by John Daintith (New York, Facts on File, 1981) is arranged alphabetically by term, with cross-references as needed. Drawings are used to illustrate. *Glossary of Chemical Terms* by Clifford A. Hampel (New York, Van Nostrand Reinhold, 1976) is also arranged alphabetically by term and gives a definition. Included in addition to general chemical terms are major chemical classifications, functional terms, basic processes, chemical elements, many compounds, and biographies of outstanding chemists. *Hackh's Chemical Dictionary, American and British Usage* revised and edited by Julius

NM476

RADIOCHEMICAL
AND RADIOANALYTICAL
LETTERS

Elsevier Sequoia S.A.
Akademiai Kiado

Multilingual Journal (Largely English)–Each Abstract in English and
the Language of the Article

VOL. 51 NO. 4   APRIL 8 1982

C

H

E

NN104

JOURNAL OF
LIQUID CHROMATOGRAPHY

Marcel Dekker

Abstracts in English

M

I

S

VOL. 5 SUPPL. 1 1982

T

R

Y

NN311

Chemické listy

Academia

Articles in Czech or Slovak–Abstracts in English

VOL. 76 NO. 4 1982

Fig. 7-1. Current awareness source: *Current Contents: Physical, Chemical and Earth Sciences*

PHYSICAL CONSTANTS OF INORGANIC COMPOUNDS (Continued)

No.	Name	Synonyms and Formulae	Mol. wt.	Crystalline form, properties and index of refraction	Density or spec. gravity	Melting point, °C	Boiling point, °C	Solubility, in grams per 100 cc — Cold water	Hot water	Other solvents
	Lead									
1139	dithionate	$PbS_2O_6.4H_2O$	439.38	trig, 1.635, 1.653	3.22	d		115.0^{00}		
1140	thiosulfate	PbS_2O_3	319.32	wh cr	5.18	d		0.03		s, $Na_2S_2O_3$
1141	metatitanate	$PbTiO_3$	303.09	yel. rhomb-pyr.	7.52	917		i	i	
1142	telluride	Nat. altaite. $PbTe$	334.79	wh, cub.	8.164^{20}_4	917				i a
1143	thiocyanate	$Pb(SCN)_2$	323.35	wh, monocl.	3.82	d 190		0.05^{30}	0.2^{100}	s KCNS, HNO_3
1144	tungstate	Nat. stolzite. $PbWO_4$	455.04	tetr, 2.269, 2.182	8.23			i	i	i HNO_3, s KOH
1145	tungstate	Nat. raspite. $PbWO_4$	455.04	col, monocl, 2.27, 2.27, 2.30	1123			0.03		d a; i al
1146	metavanadate	$Pb(VO_3)_2$	405.07	yel powd		d		sl s		d HCl; s dil HNO_3
1147	**Lithium**	Li	6.939	silver white, soft.	0.534^{20}	180.54	1317	d		
1148	acetate	$LiC_2H_3O_2.2H_2O$	102.01	wh, rhomb, α 1.40, β 1.50		70	d	300^{15}	v s	21.5 al
1149	acetylsalicylate	$LiC_9H_7O_3$	186.09	wh powd hygr, d in moist air				100		25 al
1150	metaaluminate	$LiAlO_2$ (or $Li_2Al_2O_4$)	65.92	wh, rhomb, 1.604, 1.614	2.55^{25}_4	1900–2000		i		
1151	aluminum hydride	$LiAlH_4$	37.95	wh cr powd.	0.917	d 125		d	d	ca 30 eth
1152	amide	$LiNH_2$	22.96	col need, cub.	$1.178^{17.5}$	380–400	d 750–200 subl	s		sl s liq NH_3, al; i eth, bz
1153	antimonide	$LiSb$	142.57	wh powd, rhomb.	3.2^{17}	>950		d	d	d a
1154	orthoarsenate	Li_3AsO_4	159.74	wh powd, rhomb.	3.07^{16}			v al s		s dil ac a; i pyr
1155	azide	LiN_3	48.96	col cr, hygr.		d 115–298		66.41^{14}		20.26^{14} abs al; i eth
1156	benzoate	$LiC_7H_5O_2$	128.06	wh cr or powd.	$1.397^{4.7}$	845		33^4	40^{100}	7.7^{75} al, 10^{75} al
1157	metaborate	$LiBO_2$	49.75	wh, tricl.		47		2.57^{20}	11.83^{30}	
1158	metaborate	$LiBO_2.8H_2O$	193.87	col, trig.	$1.38^{4.3}$	300–350		36.3^4	194^{100}	3.9^{30} al; 22^{18} glycerine; i bz
1159	pentaborate	$LiB_5O_8.8H_2O$	522.10	wh.	1.72	300–350 −$8H_2O$		2.89^{20}	5.45^{100}	i org solv
1160	tetraborate	LiB_4O_7	169.11	wh cr.	0.66	930		s d		s eth
1161	borohydrate	$LiBH_4$	21.78	rhomb cr.	0.66	d 279		s d		d al; 2.5 eth
1162	borohydrate	$LiBH_4$	21.78	wh, orthorhomb.	0.666	275 d		v s l		d al; 2.5 eth
1163	bromide	$LiBr$	86.85	wh, cub, deliq, 1.784	3.464^{25}	550	1265	145^4	254^{90}	73^{40} al; 8 MeOH; s al,eth; sl s pyrid

Fig. 7-2. Quick reference handbook: *CRC Handbook of Chemistry and Physics*

CA SEARCH | Provides worldwide coverage of the chemical science literature from journals, patents, conference proceedings, and government research reports. Coverage corresponds to the printed Chemical Abstracts. BRS has 1970 to 1976 offline, 1977 to present online. DIALOG has five files, and SDC has three files. See CAS-ED, CAST, and ONTAP CA SEARCH for training files.

Prepared by Chemical Abstracts Service.

Coverage: BRS, 1970 to present; CAN/OLE, 1973 to present; DIALOG and SDC, 1967 to present
File size: CAN/OLE 3,200,000; DIALOG and SDC 5,092,753
Unit record: citation, CAS registry number
Vendor, Cost/connect hour: BRS, $40-$54; CAN/OLE, $40 plus royalty; DIALOG (2, 3, 4, 104, 311), $64; SDC, $68

Fig. 7-3. Computer data base: CA SEARCH

Grant (New York, McGraw-Hill, 4th edition 1969) gives brief definitions for terms and the chemical formula for chemical substances. A more specialized dictionary is *Chemical Engineering Drawing Symbols* by D. G. Austin (London, Godwin, 1979) intended for chemical engineers, students, and industry. It contains graphic symbols, divided into three types: general equipment, piping systems, and instrumentation and control. Symbols are arranged alphabetically. Equivalent symbols are given from British standards, American National Standards Institute, and selected industrial design offices. There is an index. *Chemical Synonyms and Trade Names* by William Gardner (London, Technical Press, 7th edition 1971) is subtitled "a dictionary and commercial handbook" and gives brief definitions.

The *International Encyclopedia of Chemical Science* (Princeton, N.J., Van Nostrand Reinhold, 1964) is alphabetical by term and gives definitions, but is made multilingual by its indexes: French–English, German–English, Russian–English, and Spanish–English. The *Dictionary of Chemistry and Chemical Technology in Six Languages* edited by Z. Sobecka and others (Oxford, Pergamon, 1966) is alphabetical by English word or phrase, and gives the equivalent terms in German, Spanish, French, Polish, and Russian. There is an index for each language. Austin M. Patterson's *German–English Dictionary for Chemists* (New York, Wiley, 3d edition 1950) contains terms from chemistry, chemical engineering, and related fields. Arrangement is alphabetical by term in German, and the English equivalent is given, often several different equivalents as the term might be used in different ways. The *Russian–English Chemical and Polytechnical Dictionary* by Ludmilla I. Callaham (New York, Wiley, 3d edition 1975) is alphabetical by Russian terms with definitions in English.

Handbooks

Probably the best known handbook of tables in this field is the *Handbook of Chemistry and Physics* (Boca Raton, Fla., CRC, 1913–), which appeared in its 62d edition in 1981. In this large volume tables giving a wealth of information are arranged in these sections: mathematics tables, elements and inorganic compounds, organic compounds, general chemical information, general physical constants, and miscellaneous. A special added feature is a list of sources of critical data, listing indexes, journal articles, and books that lead to or contain additional data that might be needed. *Lange's Handbook of Chemistry* by Norbert A. Lange (New York, McGraw-Hill, 12th edition 1979) also contains tables arranged in general sections, for example, mathematics, general information, inorganic chemistry, and so forth. There is a subject index. *Chemical Tables* by Bela A. Nemeth (New York, Wiley, 1975) has as its object to provide a handbook for plant workers and technicians. Information is all tables with brief explanations as needed. *Tables of Physical and Chemical Constants and Some Mathematical Functions* by George W. C. Kaye and T. H. Laby (London, Longman, 14th edition 1973) is mostly in table form, with some explanations. There is an index.

Directories

Chemical Business Handbook by John H. Perry (New York, McGraw-Hill, 1954) gives practical information for industrial users on finance, market research, sales, and so forth.

The following four buyer's guides are all published annually. *Chemical Guide to the United States* (Park Ridge, N.J., Noyes Data Corp., 1963–) lists the largest U.S. chemical firms. The same publisher also has guides to other countries. *Chem-Sources—U.S.A.* (Flemington, N.J., Directories Publishing Company, 1958–) lists chemical products alphabetically by chemical name. A code number leads from the product to the manufacturer, with index to manufacturers by code and alphabetically. *Chemical Week Buyers Guide* (New York, McGraw-Hill, 1914–) is issued with the journal *Chemical Week* and is a guide to chemicals, raw materials, specialities, packaging, shipping, and bulk containers. *OPD Chemical Buyers Directory* (New York, Schnell, 1973/74–) lists commercial chemicals and other products and tells suppliers.

8
Earth Sciences

Earth sciences as used here will cover the fields of geology, including mineralogy; oceanography; and meteorology and climatology.

INTRODUCTORY MATERIALS

Planet Earth in Color by Peter L. Brown (New York, Macmillan, 1976) is a small pocket-size book that provides an introduction to the earth sciences. There are eighty pages of color photographs and illustrations, in addition to chapters on the "earth in space," "earth as a planet," "changing face of the earth," and "earth as a habitat." These chapter subjects illustrate how closely the study of earth sciences is linked to astronomy, chemistry, and biology. A chart occupying several pages and called the "spectrum of time" graphically illustrates time periods throughout the history of the earth, with related events in the development of life on earth. *Earth* by Frank Press and R. Siever (San Francisco, Freeman, 2d edition 1978), written as a text for beginning students with no previous science courses, covers the earth sciences. There is a bibliography with each chapter, and a glossary of terms.

The *Cambridge Encyclopedia of Earth Sciences* edited by David G. Smith (New York, Cambridge University Press, 1981) provides an overview of the entire earth sciences area, with illustrations. *Planet We Live On; Illustrated Encyclopedia of the Earth Sciences,* edited by Cornelius Hurlbut, Jr. (New York, Abrams, 1976) is arranged alphabetically by topic with brief articles of one to several paragraphs. Many photographs and drawings are used throughout, with a section at the front of about thirty pages of color photography and drawings called a "color portfolio of the earth sciences." The appendixes include tables; a list of principal features of the earth with location, size, and so forth; and a guide to entries by broad subject area.

The *Encyclopedia of Prehistoric Life* edited by Rodney Steel and Anthony P. Harvey (New York, McGraw-Hill, 1979) has articles arranged alphabetically by topic, for example, an animal or plant name, a scientist's name, or a more general topic. Articles are usually about 150 words in length, and most include illustrative drawings. Several charts show graphically the evolution of various specific groups, for example, fish. There is a bibliography, and a glossary. Donald F. Glut's *Dinosaur Dictionary* (Secaucus, N.J., Citadel, 1972) attempts to list every genus known to paleontologists. Arrangement is alphabetical by genus, and for each the author gives the suborder and family the genus belongs to, and the Mesozoic period in which it lived. There are many drawings and photographs of bones, parts, and models. There is a bibliography.

Applications of earth sciences in urban planning and development are the subject of *Nature to be Commanded; Earth-Science Maps Applied to Land and Water Management* edited by G. D. Robinson and Andrew Spieker (Washington, D.C., U.S. Government Printing Office, 1978). This is U.S. Geological Survey Professional Paper number 950. Earth science information is given for urban environments, with many maps and photographs, and discussion. Such topics as erosion, resource protection, and water are included. It is mostly done as discussion of applications in different environments, for example, coastal, arid, and mountain.

Subject Headings and Classification

Atmosphere
Climatology
Crystallography
Earth
Earth sciences
Geology
   (also subdivisions of Geology)
   —Bibliography
   —History
   —Research
   —Terminology

Geophysics
Hydrology
Meteorological instruments
Meteorological research
Meteorology
 (also subdivisions of Meteorology)
 —Bibliography
 —Observations
Mineralogy
Mountains
Ocean
Oceanographic research
Oceanography
Physical geography
Rocks
Sea-water
Water
Weather
Weather forecasting

Materials on earth sciences in libraries will usually be found in the QE, GC, and QC sections of the Library of Congress classification and the 550 section of Dewey Decimal Classification. Specifically, geology materials are classified in QE or 550 to 559, oceanography in GC or 551.46 to 551.49, meteorology in QC 851 to QC 999 or 551.5 to 551.59, and climatology in QC 851 to QC 999 or 551.6 to 551.69.

BIBLIOGRAPHIC MATERIALS

Guides to the Literature

Geologic References Sources by Dederick C. Ward, Marjorie Wheeler, and Robert Bier (Metuchen, N.J., Scarecrow, 3d edition 1981) is a subject and regional bibliography of publications and maps in the geological sciences. This bibliography has a section for general reference works such as dictionaries and encyclopedias, a section arranged by subjects such as earth science and oceanography, a regional section, and a section listing geologic maps. Bibliographic information is given, with some brief annotations. Stuart R. Kaplan's *Guide*

80-3. Maps showing ground-water conditions in the Hopi area, Coconino and Navajo Counties, ARIZONA—1977, by C. D. Farrar. 4 over-size sheets, scale 1:63,360 (1 inch = 1 mile). (NC, M; USGS, Federal Bldg., 301 West Congress St., Tucson, AZ 85701.)

80-4. Machine-independent Fortran coding of the Lehmer random number generators, by W. Kirby. 13 p. (NC; USGS, Surface Water Hydrology, 430 National Ctr., Room 5B112, 12201 Sunrise Valley Dr., Reston, VA 22092.)

80-5. Water-level records for the northern High Plains of COLORADO, 1975-79, by R. G. Borman. 31 p. (NC, Da, Db; USGS, WRD, Room H-2106, Bldg. 53, Denver Federal Ctr. (Box 25046, Mail Stop 415), Denver, CO 80225.)

80-6. Summaries of technical reports, Volume IX—National Earthquake Hazards Reduction Program, by J. F. Evernden. 598 p. (NC, Da, M.)

80-7. Hydrologic response of aquifers to droughts in the Great Plains, U.S.A., by M. S. Bedinger. 21 p. (NC, Da; USGS, WRD (Mail Stop 406, Box 25046), Denver Federal Ctr., Denver, CO 80225.)

80-8. Water-level contour and salt front map, Hialeah-Miami Springs well-field area, Dade County, FLORIDA, October 13, 1978, by L. J. Swayze. 1 over-size sheet. (NC; USGS, WRD, Suite F-240, 325 John Knox Rd., Tallahassee, FL 32303; USGS, WRD, Suite 110, 7815 Coral Way, Miami, FL 33155.)

80-9. Surficial geology of part of Ellisburg quadrangle, Oswego County, NEW YORK, by T. S. Miller. 1 over-size sheet, scale 1:24,000 (1 inch = 2,000 feet). (NC; USGS, WRD (P.O. Box 1350), 343 U.S. Post Office and Courthouse, Albany, NY 12201.) (Water-Resources Investigations.)

80-10. Retreat of Columbia Glacier—A preliminary prediction, by M. F. Meier, A. Post, L. A. Rasmussen, W. G. Sikonia, and L. R. Mayo. 12 p. (NC, M; USGS, Office of the Regional Hydrologist, WRD, 1201 Pacific Ave., Suite 850, Tacoma, WA 98402.)

80-11. Program objectives for the National Water Data Exchange (NAWDEX) for fiscal year 1980, by M. D. Edwards. 9 p. (NC; USGS, WRD, National Water Data Exchange Program, Room 5A130, 421 National Ctr., 12201 Sunrise Valley Dr., Reston, VA 22092.)

80-12. Reconnaissance of ground-water resources in the vicinity of Gunnison and Crested Butte, west-central COLORADO, by T. F. Giles. 2 over-size sheets. (NC; USGS, WRD, Bldg. 53, Denver Federal Ctr., Denver, CO 80225; USGS (Box 25046, Mail Stop 914), Denver Federal Ctr., Denver, CO 80225; USGS, WRD (Box 25046, Mail Stop 415), Denver Federal Ctr., Denver, CO 80225; USGS, WRD, 321 Seventh Ave., Meeker, CO 81641; USGS, WRD, Room 223, Wayne Aspinall Federal Bldg., Fourth St. and Rood Ave., Grand Junction, CO 81501; Colorado State Engineer's Office, 818 Centennial Bldg., 1313 Sherman St., Denver, CO 80203.) (Water-Resources Investigations.)

80-13. Map showing potential geothermal-resource areas, as indicated by the chemical character of ground water, in Verde Valley, Yavapai County, ARIZONA, by P. P. Ross and C. D. Farrar. 1 over-size sheet, scale 1:125,000 (1 inch = about 2 miles). (NC; USGS, WRD, Federal Bldg., 301 West Congress St., Tucson, AZ 85701.) (Water-Resources Investigations.)

80-14. Submarine features and bottom configuration in the Port Townsend quadrangle, Puget Sound region, WASHINGTON, by M. J. Chrzastowski. 1 over-size sheet, scale 1:100,000 (1 inch = about 1.6 miles). (NC; USGS, WRD, University District Bldg., 1107 NE. Forty-Fifth St., Suite 125, Seattle, WA 98105.) (Water-Resources Investigations.)

Fig. 8-1. Bibliography of government publications: *Publications of the Geological Survey* by U.S. Department of the Interior

to Information Sources in Mining, Minerals, and Geosciences (New York, Interscience, 1965) is in two sections, one for organizations with addresses and how each is useful for information, and one for literature. The literature section is arranged in subject areas, for example, lapidary, and gives bibliographic information and sometimes a brief annotation. *Information Sources in the Earth Sciences* by Jessie B. Watkins (Syracuse, N.Y., Syracuse University, 1976) is a guide to materials in the Natural Science Library at Syracuse. There are abstracts for some items.

Use of Earth Science Literature edited by David N. Wood (Hamden, Conn., Archon, 1973) covers materials published through 1970, plus selected items through 1972. There is introductory material on using libraries and literature and on translations and maps, and then discussion of the geological literature by subject area, for example, structural, soil science, and so forth.

Bibliographies

Geological Survey publications are very important in the earth sciences. *Publications of the Geological Survey* (Washington, D.C., U.S. Department of the Interior, 1971-   ) lists these books, reports, and maps yearly with a monthly supplementary list called *New Publications of the Geological Survey.* Older publications are listed in *Publications of the Geological Survey, 1879-1961* and *Publications of the Geological Survey, 1962-70. Maps and Geological Publications of the United States: A layman's guide* compiled by William R. Pampe (Falls Church, Va., American Geological Institute, 1978) is a bibliography arranged by state with subdivisions such as "bibliographies," "caves," and "general geology." Each category contains a list of publications from the state or from commercial publishers about that state. There is a list of publishers with addresses at the back, and brief information on where to get additional information, especially maps.

Catalogs

Two catalogs of libraries that have outstanding collections in the earth sciences are useful as bibliographies. The *Catalog of the United States Geological Survey Library* (Boston, Mass., G. K. Hall, 1964) reproduces in twenty-five volumes the cards from the catalog of the United

States Geological Survey, the largest collection of its kind on geology and related subjects. This bibliography is kept up to date by supplements published since 1972. The *Dictionary Catalog of the Department Library* (Boston, Mass., G. K. Hall, 1968–   ) is made from the catalog of the United States Department of the Interior library, and includes geology and related disciplines, as well as special collections on mines and minerals, petroleum, and coal.

Review of the Literature

Annual Review of Earth and Planetary Sciences (Palo Alto, Calif., Annual Reviews, 1, 1973–   ) is published annually. Each volume is made up of bibliographic essays surveying work currently being done by researchers in the earth sciences. References are given.

Indexing and Abstracting Services

The *Bibliography and Index of Geology* (Falls Church, Va., American Geological Institute, 1, 1933–   ) is a monthly publication with annual cumulations. It covers the earth sciences literature, internationally, including books, journals, reports, maps, and theses. Arrangement is in broad subject groups, and for each item listed it tells full bibliographic information and selected descriptive subject terms to supplement the title. There are indexes by subject and by author. From 1922 to 1968 this publication was called the *Bibliography and Index of Geology Exclusive of North America*. These volumes also are arranged in broad subject groups and give bibliographic information and selected descriptive subject terms to supplement the title. Indexing is by subject and author. For this older literature on North America, consult the U.S. Geological Survey's *Bibliography of North American Geology* (Washington, D.C., Geological Survey, 1785–1973), which covers the literature for 1785–1970. The title varies; early volumes were called *Geologic Literature of North America*. Arrangement is alphabetical by author with an index by subject, and bibliographic information is given. Geology of the North American continent, Greenland, the West Indies and adjacent islands, Hawaii, and Guam is covered, as it appears in American or foreign publications. *Geophysical Abstracts* (Norwich, England, GeoAbstracts Ltd., 1, 1977–   ) is

GEOREF | International geological reference file, covering geology, geochemistry, geophysics, mineralogy, paleontology, petrology, and seismology. Includes citations from Bibliography and Index of Geology. Prepared by American Geological Institute. | Coverage: 1961 to present File size: 678,000 records Unit record: citation Vendor, Cost/connect hour: CAN/OLE, $40 plus royalty;. DIALOG (89), $70; SDC, $95

Fig. 8–2. Computer data base: GEOREF

issued six times per year plus an annual index by subject and author and region. Coverage is international, of journals, reports, and proceedings. Arrangement is by subject categories, and in addition to bibliographic information there is an informative abstract usually written by the author of the articles being cited. *Geo Abstracts* (Norwich, England, Geo Abstracts, Ltd., 1972–), formerly called *Geographical Abstracts,* also gives international coverage. It is published in several sections, three of which are useful in geology: A on "landforms and the quarternary," B on "climatology and hydrology," and E on "sedimentology." Six issues of each section are published per year, plus yearly indexes by author and region and periodic cumulated indexes. Arrangement is in broad subject areas, for example, soil mechanics, and bibliographic information and an abstract are given for each item.

Bulletin Signaletique; Bibliographie des Sciences de la Terre (Paris, Centre de Documentation, 1, 1948–) is published in several sections of interest:

220—"Mineralogie, Geochimie, Geologie extraterrestre"
221—Mineral economics
222—Crystalline rocks
223—Sedimentary rocks, marine geology
224—"Stratigraphie, Geologie regional, Geologie generale"
225—"Tectonique"
226—"Hydrologie, Geologie de l'ingenieur, formations superficielles"
227—Paleontology

The bulletin is bilingual, in French and English. Each section is published monthly and gives international coverage of more than 9,000 periodicals of the whole field of earth sciences plus proceedings, books, reports, and dissertations. Arrangement is in broad subject groups, giving bibliographic information and a brief abstract for each item. There are indexes by author and subject and a geographical index, and some sections have other appropriate indexes.

Mineralogical Abstracts (London, published jointly by Mineralogical Society of Great Britain and Mineralogical Society of America, 1, 1920–) is issued four times per year plus an annual index. Coverage is international, of journal articles and reports, with new books listed in a separate "book notices" section. Arrangement is in broad subject categories, such as "clay minerals," "gemstones," and "new minerals," and there is an author index in each issue. The annual index issue is a cumulative index by author and subject.

Oceanic Abstracts (Bethesda, Md., Cambridge Scientific Abstracts, 1972–) is published bimonthly to give international coverage of oceanic research and related engineering studies for serious researchers. Arrangement is in broad subject groups, for example, "marine biology" and "biological oceanography," with subheadings, and items are cited from journals, proceedings, government reports, and trade publications. Bibliographic information and an informative abstract up to 200 words in length are given. A separate section lists books and conferences.

Oceanographic Literature Review (New York, Pergamon, 1953–) is issued as part B of the journal *Deep-Sea Research,* and was formerly called *Oceanographic Abstracts and Bibliography.* It is issued monthly and gives international coverage of articles in journals. Items are arranged in six main subject categories: physical oceanography, marine meteorology, chemical oceanography, submarine geology and geophysics, biological oceanography, and general, with subsections in each category. For each article cited, bibliographic information is given, and most have a short annotation or abstract. There are indexes by author and subject issued quarterly and cumulated yearly.

Meteorological and Geoastrophysical Abstracts (Boston, Mass., American Meteorological Society, 1950–) is published monthly, providing international coverage of meteorological and geoastrophysical materials. Journals, annuals, and numbered monographic series are included. Citations are in the original language, with foreign language titles translated into English in brackets just after the original title; all abstracts are in English. There is usually an indication of at least one library where the item may be found. Arrangement is in broad subject groups: environmental sciences, meteorology, astrophysics, hydrosphere/hydrology, glaciology, and physical oceanography. Indexes by author, subject, and geographic area are included in each issue, and cumulated annually.

SECONDARY LITERATURE MATERIALS

Geology

Two general encyclopedias are the *McGraw-Hill Encyclopedia of the Geological Sciences* (New York, McGraw-Hill, 1978) and the *Encyclopedia of World Regional Geology* by Rhodes W. Fairbridge (Stroudsburg, Pa., Dowden, Hutchinson and Ross, 1975). The McGraw-Hill encyclopedia is alphabetical by topic with cross-references in the articles and an index, and contains articles that are usually several pages in length. Articles are illustrated with photographs and drawings, and there is a bibliography with each. The Fairbridge encyclopedia is in two volumes, one for the Western Hemisphere and one for the Eastern Hemisphere. Articles are arranged alphabetically by topic, with cross-references and indexes by author and subject. There are references with each article.

The *Standard Encyclopedia of the World's Mountains* by Anthony J. Huxley (New York, Putnam, 1969) contains approximately 300 articles of several pages each, arranged alphabetically by the name of the mountain range or mountain, peak, or pass. Also included are some introductory materials, brief biographies of "mountaineering pioneers," a glossary, maps, gazetteer, and index. The *Standard Encyclopedia of the World's Oceans and Islands* by Anthony J. Huxley (New York, Putnam, 1969) has about 350 articles, also of several pages each, arranged alphabetically by the name of the ocean, sea, island, bay, coast, cape, or related topic. It containes brief introductory material, and maps, gazetteer, and index. The *Standard Encyclopedia of the World's Rivers and Lakes* by R. Kay Gresswell and Anthony J. Huxley (New York, Putnam, 1965) is arranged alphabetically by names of rivers and lakes. Information is given as to location, length or size, a brief description, and history, in one to several paragraphs, on each river or lake. There is also some introductory discussion, and a set of ten pages of maps showing positions of principal rivers and lakes of the world. A gazetteer and index complete this volume. *Volcanoes of the World; a Regional Directory, Gazetteer, and Chronology of Volcanism during the Last 10,000 Years* (Stroudsburg, Pa., Hutchinson and Ross, 1981) contains data table summaries, volcano data, eruption data, and historic records. There are also a directory of volcanoes and a chronology of eruptions. A gazetteer and bibliography complete this book.

Geological names are recorded in a dictionary series, *Lexicon of Geologic Names of the United States* (Washington, U.S. Government Printing Office). The first publication is by Mary G. Wilmarth and was issued in 1938 as *U.S. Geological Survey Bulletin 896.* The second, by Grace C. Keroher and others, covering names for 1936–60, was published in 1966 as *U.S. Geological Survey Bulletin 1200;* and the third, by the same principal author and covering names for 1961–67, was published in 1970 as *U.S. Geological Survey Bulletin 1350.* Each gives names with definitions and bibliographic references.

Geological Maps by Brian Simpson (Oxford, Pergamon, 1968) is intended for students studying geology for the first time, as an introduction to geological maps and their interpretation. The author tells how to read maps, with many maps and diagrams used to illustrate. There is an index. *Landforms Illustrated* by C. R. Twidale and M. R. Foale (Sydney, Australia, Thomas Nelson, 1969) starts out with simple geological features and goes on to specific features such as boulders, volcanoes, weathering, and coastal landforms. The book is made up mostly of black and white photographs with notes. The *World Atlas of Geomorphic Features* by Rodman E. Snead (New York, Van Nostrand Reinhold/Krieger, 1980) is a comprehensive atlas illustrating and explaining all geological and geographical landforms. Maps and satellite photographs are used. The atlas covers plate tectonics, continental drift, earthquake-sensitive regions, distribution of soils, drainage patterns, tidal patterns, highest and lowest elevations, worldwide distribution of deserts, waterfalls, meteorite craters, large artificial lakes, and glaciers.

Physical Geology by Arthur N. Strahler (New York, Harper and Row, 1981) is a text for students in earth sciences. The user does not need to know mathematics, but elementary chemistry is needed. The book begins with an overview of geology and a review of matter and energy. Then there are sections on minerals, igneous and sedimentary and metamorphic rocks, earthquakes, oceans, water and its geologic effects, astrogeology, and geologic resources. Illustrations are used throughout, and there is a bibliography, and a glossary.

Earth, Time, and Life by Charles W. Barnes (New York, Wiley, 1980) contains fundamental concepts of geology, clearly written, with a historical approach throughout. There are references with each chapter, and a glossary, and the book is illustrated with photographs and drawings. Another general geology text is William L. Stokes's *Introduction to Geology, Physical and Historical* (Englewood Cliffs, N.J., Prentice-Hall, 2d edition 1978). This book begins with an interesting chapter on the "astronomical background" of the earth. Also included is a table of minerals and their properties. There are illustrations, a glossary, and suggested readings. *Powers of Nature* (Washington, D.C., National Geographic Society, 1978) is about earthquakes, volcanoes, rain and snow, wind and storm, drought, and water, illustrated with lovely color photographs throughout.

A history of the study of geology is called *Two Hundred Years of Geology in America* (Hanover, N.H., University of New Hampshire, 1979). This book is based on the New Hampshire Bicentennial Conference on the History of Geology, and contains several papers by different authors. The papers are arranged in groups in chapters, and most include a bibliography. There is an index.

Mineralogy

The *Encyclopedia of Minerals* by Willard L. Roberts (New York, Van Nostrand Reinhold, 1974) is illustrated with beautiful color photographs of minerals. The minerals are listed in alphabetical order, and information given for each includes the chemical formula, hardness, density, and occurrence, along with one or two references to the literature. There is also a glossary of terms. James D. Dana's *Manual of Mineralogy* (New York, Wiley, 19th edition 1977), this section by Cornelius S. Hurlbut and Cornelis Klein, is a classic in the field in all of its editions through the years. Written as a text for a beginning course in mineralogy and for reference, there are chapters on crystallography, physical and optical properties of minerals, and mineral associations. Several chapters systematically cover all of the common minerals, about 200, telling for each its crystallography, physical properties, composition and structure, diagnostic features, occurrence, and use. There are also determinative tables included to identify common minerals, and a mineral index. There are references with each chapter, and a subject index.

The *Illustrated Encyclopedia of the Mineral Kingdom* (New York, Larousse, 1978) contains lovely color photographs. It is arranged in chapters by subject, each by a subject specialist, with many clearly marked subdivisions to facilitate its use as an encyclopedia. Chapters include properties and study of minerals, gemstones, and building a collection. One chapter, called "The Mineral Kingdom," gives descriptions of about 300 of the most widely distributed minerals, many with a photograph, and with information on chemical composition, color and transparency, distinguishing features, and uses. The *Encyclopedia of Minerals and Gemstones* edited by Michael O'Donoghue (New York, Putnam, 1976) begins with information in chapters on the chemistry of minerals, the crystalline state, minerals valuable to man, how minerals are identified, fashioning of gemstones into jewelry and so forth, and conserving and displaying minerals, with a large section on collecting. The second half of the book lists about 1,000 minerals arranged in groups such as elements and their alloys, oxides, silicates, and so forth. There is an index by mineral name. Information given for each mineral varies but generally includes a description, occurrence, and treatment, and in many cases a color photograph. There are identification tables for more common materials most likely to be found in the field by collectors.

The *Larousse Guide to Minerals, Rocks, and Fossils* by William R. Hamilton (New York, Larousse, 1978) begins with brief general information on collecting, and then has sections on minerals, rocks, meteorites and tektites, and fossils. Each section begins with brief general information; for example, the section on minerals has information on structure, crystal systems and forms, aggregates, and so forth. Each species is listed with a photograph and description that includes distinguishing features, occurrence, and physical characteristics. The lovely color photographs are of specimens in the British Museum. This guide ends with a bibliography for further reading, and an index.

Gemstone and Mineral Data Book by John Sinkankas (New York, Collier, 1972) is a compilation of data, recipes, formulas, and instructions for mineralogists, gemologists, and collectors.

Simon and Schuster's Guide to Rocks and Minerals (New York, Simon and Schuster, 1978) is in two parts: minerals and rocks. Similar to the above guide, each part has several pages of introductory information and then a list of species with description and a color photograph. The description includes properties, appearance, occurrence, and uses. There is a glossary, and an index. Two other guides are the *Field Guide to Rocks and Minerals* by Frederick H. Pough (Boston, Mass., Houghton, Mifflin, 4th edition 1976), from the Peterson Field Guide Series, and *Field Guide to North American Rocks and Minerals* by Charles W. Chesterman (New York, Knopf, 1979), in the Audubon series.

Richard V. Dietrich's *Mineral Tables; Hand-Specimen Properties of 1500 Minerals* (New York, McGraw, Hill, 1969) has as its purpose to enable one to identify many minerals without a microscope or other equipment. Identification is based on appearance and physical properties that can be determined by performing simple tests. The beginning division for identification is between minerals with metallic luster and those without, and then identification is made by color within each of those two divisions. There is a glossary, and an index by name of mineral.

Mineral Names: What Do They Mean? by Richard S. Mitchell (New York, Van Nostrand Reinhold, 1979), contains derivations of all mineral names currently used. The main part of this book is an alphabetical list of mineral names, with the derivation of the name, for example, "Feldspar . . . from Swedish names for field . . . and spar . . . , in reference to the spar in tilled fields overlying granite . . . ." There is also a discussion of mineral names, including how names are derived from people, places, chemical composition, physical properties, and Greek and Latin terms. Also included are a glossary, bibliography, and index. The *Manual of New Mineral Names 1892–1978* edited by Peter G. Embrey and John P. Fuller (Oxford, Oxford University Press, 1980) is a compilation of thirty lists published in *Mineralogical Magazine* from 1897 to 1978. Arrangement is by mineral name, and the first reference in the literature to that name is cited, along with a description of the mineral. There is an index by author. The *Glossary of Mineral Species* by Michael Fleischer (Tuscon, Ariz., Mineralogical Record, revised edition 1980) is arranged alphabetically by the names of minerals. Information given for each is chemical formula, crystal system, color, relations to other minerals, and reference to its first description. Supplements are issued irregularly, to make corrections and add new species. The *Color Encyclopedia of Gemstones* by Joel

E. Arem (New York, Van Nostrand Reinhold, 1977) is arranged alphabetically by species name. Information given is chemical formula, crystal structure, color, luster, hardness, density, cleavage, optics, spectral data, occurrence, luminescence, size, comments, and meaning of name. Sometimes other data are included such as dispersion or streak. There are lovely color photographs of many species.

Oceanography

When we stop to realize that oceans cover about 72% of our planet earth, we can appreciate how important their study is. There are many introductory text-type books that give a broad overview of oceanography, but also provide answers to many specific questions, especially through the use of their indexes. J. J. Bhatt's *Oceanography: Exploring the Planet Ocean* (New York, Van Nostrand, 1978) is written for students with a limited background in science, to introduce fundamental concepts and to relate them to contemporary problems. It has a glossary and an index, and suggested readings with each chapter. *Principles of Oceanography* by Richard A. Davis, Jr. (Reading, Mass., Addison-Wesley, 2d edition 1977) is written with the intention of stimulating broad interest in the subject. There are references with each chapter, and a glossary and an index. John G. Weilhaupt's *Exploration of the Oceans: An Introduction to Oceanography* (New York, Macmillan, 1979) also assumes no previous knowledge of the subject. Each chapter ends with a summary and suggestions for further reading, and at the end of the book there is an extensive list of references, as well as a glossary and an index. *Oceanography: An Introduction* by Dale Ingmanson and W. J. Wallace (Belmont, Calif., Wadsworth, 2d edition 1979) has extensive illustrations, photographs and drawings, and like the others has references, glossary, and index.

Oceanography: A View of the Earth by Meredith G. Gross (Englewood Cliffs, N.J., 2d edition 1977) includes a history of oceanography and then chapters on sediments, seawater, waves, tides, shoreline, marine biology, and more. *The Oceans* by Robert Barton (New York, Facts on File, 1981) contains chapters on composition of the sea, maritime life, economic aspects of oceans such as commercial fishing and mineral wealth, and undersea diving. Many color photographs illustrate the book. *Opportunities and Uses of the Ocean* by David A. Ross (New York, Springer-Verlag, 1978) includes basic information on pollution, military uses, and the coastal zone, and finishes with a chapter on innovative uses of the ocean. There are references, and an index.

Ocean Science: Readings from Scientific American (San Francisco, Freeman, 1977) is made up of articles by different authors, taken from *Scientific American* magazine. Articles are grouped in chapters by general subject. At the end of the book is a bibliography for each chapter, and an index.

Two histories of oceanography are Tjeerd Andel's *Tales of an Old Ocean* (New York, Norton, 1978) and Susan Schlee's *Edge of an Unfamiliar World: A History of Oceanography* (New York, Dutton, 1973).

Ocean World Encyclopedia by Donald Groves and Lee Hunt (New York, McGraw-Hill, 1980) is geared toward nonspecialists, and includes all major divisions of oceanograpy and related subjects. Arrangement of articles is alphabetical by topic, with cross-references as needed. Articles, all written by the two authors of the encyclopedia, are mostly a few paragraphs in length, but some are quite long, with subdivisions. Black and white photographs, maps, and diagrams illustrate the articles, and there is an index. The *McGraw-Hill Encyclopedia of Ocean and Atmospheric Sciences* (New York, McGraw-Hill, 1980) contains 236 articles by different specialists. Arrangement is alphabetical by topic, with cross-references as needed. Most articles are lengthy, with topic subdivisions, and they are illustrated by photographs, maps, diagrams, and tables. There is a bibliography with each article.

The *Rand McNally Atlas of the Oceans* edited by Martyn Bramwell (New York, Rand McNally, 1977) is a large-size volume. Arrangement is in sections: "the ocean realm," "man's oceanic quest," "life in the oceans," "the great resource," and "face of the deep"; and an encyclopedia of marine life. Each section has many subsections done as two-page spreads consisting of written material, photographs, drawings, and maps. Examples of these topics are "the surging tides," "the ocean pathfinders," and "life between the tides." The encyclopedia of marine life section consists of a list of plant species and a list of animal species found in the oceans, with descriptions. The *Gazetteer of Undersea Features* (Washington, D.C., Defense Mapping Agency, 3d edition 1981) contains approximately 6,000 names for undersea features of the world, meaning parts of the ocean floor or seabed that have measurable relief. Arrangement is alphabetical by names of features, and information given is the kind of feature, for example, "canyon" or "gap"; latitude; and longitude. A separate section lists the same names in groups by geographic location and gives the same information about each.

Meteorology and Climatology

The United States National Oceanic and Atmospheric Administration puts out a wealth of publications through the United States Government Printing Office, Washington, D.C. These are listed each month in the *Monthly Catalog of United States Government Publications*, described earlier. Examples of these publications are monthly climatic data, storm data, and the monthly weather outlook.

Climates of the States (Detroit, Mich., Gale, 1980) is in two volumes, containing a narrative account and statistical information. National Oceanic and Atmospheric Administration narrative summaries are included, together with tables and maps. *Weather of U.S. Cities* (Detroit, Mich., Gale, 1981) is a reference work of weather data in two volumes. Arrangement is alphabetical by state and then by city.

Periodicals

Earth Science:

American Journal of Science, devoted to the geological sciences and to related fields. New Haven, Conn., Kline Geology Laboratory, Yale University, 1818– . (monthly)

Earth Science. Colorado Springs, Colo., Earth Science Publishing Company, 1946– . (quarterly) (on fossils)

Earth Science Bulletin. Casper, Wyo., Wyoming Geological Association, 1968– . (quarterly)

Earth Science Reviews; the international geological journal bridging the gap between research articles and text books. Amsterdam, Elsevier, 1966– . (quarterly)

Geotimes; news of the earth sciences. Falls Church, Va., American Geological Institute, 1956– . (12/year)

Physics and Chemistry of the Earth. New York, Pergamon, 1956– . (quarterly)

Geology:

Cascade Caver; international journal of vulcanospeleology. Seattle, Wash., University of Washington, National Speleological Society, 1961– . (10/year)
Environmental Geology. New York, Springer-Verlag, 1975– . (quarterly)
Geological Society of America. Bulletin. Boulder, Colo., Geological Society of America, 1888– . (monthly)
Journal of Geological Education. Lawrence, Kans., National Association of Geology Teachers, 1951– . (5/year)
Journal of Geology. Chicago, University of Chicago Press, 1893– . (bimonthly)
Journal of Petrology. London, Oxford University Press, 1960– . (quarterly)
Pennsylvania Geology. Harrisburg, Pa., Department of Environmental Resources, 1970– . (bimonthly)

Mineralogy:

Rocks and Minerals; mineralogy, geology, lapidary. Washington, D.C., Heldref, 1926– . (bimonthly)

Oceanography:

Bulletin of Marine Science. Miami, Fla., Rosenstiel School of Marine and Atmospheric Science, 1951– . (4/year)
Coastal Research. Tallahassee, Fla., Florida State University, 1962– . (3/year)
Journal of Marine Research. New Haven, Conn., Sears Foundation for Marine Research, 1937– . (4/year)
Ocean Engineering; an International Journal. New York, Pergamon, 1968– . (bimonthly)
Ocean Science News. Washington, D.C., Nautilus Press, 1958– . (weekly)
Underwater Naturalist. Highlands, N.J., American Littoral Society, 1962– . (quarterly)

Meteorology:

American Meteorological Society. Bulletin. Boston, Mass., American
Meteorological Society, 1920– . (monthly)
Journal of the Atmospheric Sciences. Boston, Mass., American Me-
teorological Society, 1944– . (monthly)
Monthly Weather Review. Boston, Mass., American Meteorological
Society, 1872– . (monthly)
Weatherwise; Popular Weather Magazine. Washington, D.C.
Heldref, 1948– . (bimonthly)

CURRENT AWARENESS MATERIALS

Current Contents: Physical, Chemical, and Earth Sciences has been
described elsewhere. *Geotitles Weekly* (London, GeoServices, 1,
1969–) is published weekly, to give international coverage of current
materials. There are three sections in each issue: news, subject
classification, and source and author indexes.

QUICK REFERENCE TOOLS

Dictionaries

The *Glossary of Geology* edited by Robert L. Bates and Julia A.
Jackson (Falls Church, Va., American Geological Institute, 2d edition 1980) defines 36,000 terms, including mineral names and abbreviations. Arrangement is alphabetical by term, and definitions are
one phrase or sentence to approximately 100 words. Fields covered include archaeology, climatology, engineering, geology, oceanography,
and so forth.

The *Dictionary of Geology* by John Challinor (Cardiff, England,
University of Wales, 5th edition 1978) is arranged alphabetically by
term and gives an explanation in more detail than do most dictionaries. There is a classified index by type of term, that is, classes of
terms are listed, such as the branches of geology and parts of the earth,
and there is a list of terms used in each. Another special feature is a list
of abbreviations of periodical titles in geology, giving the full title of
the periodical. The *Dictionary of Geological Terms* (Garden City,
N.Y., Anchor, revised edition 1976) contains over 8,000 of the more

commonly used terms in geology and related earth sciences, with definitions. The *Dictionary of Earth Sciences* edited by Stella E. Stiegler (New York, Pica, 1976) is also alphabetical by term with definitions of one to several sentences.

For foreign terms S. A. Cooper's *Concise International Dictionary of Mechanics and Geology* (New York, Philosophical Library, 1958) is alphabetical by term in English and gives the equivalent terms in French, German, and Spanish. Indexes from each other language lead to the English sections. There are no definitions. The *Russian–English Dictionary of Earth Sciences* by Mark E. Burgunker (New York, Telberg, 1961) and the *Russian–English Dictionary of Paleontological Terms* by Vladir Telberg (New York, Telberg, 1966) are alphabetical by Russian term and give the English equivalents.

The *International Dictionary of Metallurgy, Mineralogy, Geology, and the Mining and Oil Industries* by Angel Cagnacci-Schwicker (New York, McGraw-Hill, 1970) is a polyglot dictionary. Languages covered are English, French, German, and Italian. Arrangement is alphabetical by term in English, with equivalents in the other languages.

The *Ocean and Marine Dictionary* by David F. Tver (Centreville, Md., Cornell Maritime Press, 1979) is arranged alphabetically by term and has a brief concise definition for each. The scope, according to the author is "all aspects of marine and ocean environment, and activities relating to the oceans and seas . . . from sailing ships and nautical terms to seashells and seaweeds."

Handbooks

The *Concise World Atlas of Geology and Mineral Deposits* by Duncan R. Derry (New York, Wiley, 1980) includes information on landscape and geology, structures and history of earth, distribution of earthquakes and volcanoes, mineral resources, and life, and then map sheets divided by geographical area: Americas, Northern Europe, and so forth. There is a bibliography, and a glossary.

Smithsonian Meteorological Tables (Washington, D.C., U.S. Government Printing Office, 6th edition revised 1951) contains tables for use in interpreting and compiling meteorological information.

9
Natural History

BIOLOGY, NATURE CONSERVATION

INTRODUCTORY MATERIALS

The *Living World: Exploring Modern Biology* by Jean Macqueen (Englewood Cliffs, N.J., Prentice-Hall, 1978) is written for all readers with an interest in the world of living things, including students. Basic information is given on both plants and animals, and much information on man. The many illustrations add to the interest of the book. There is a bibliography, and an index. *Life on Earth* by Edward O. Wilson (Sunderland, Mass., Sinauer, 2d edition 1978) covers general biology, including the cell, multicellular life, diversity of life, and alternative futures. A few readings are listed with each chapter, and a glossary and index complete this text. Robert D. Allen's *Science of Life* (New York, Harper and Row, 1977) is a general text, also featuring suggested readings with each chapter, a glossary, and an index. *Biology: A Human Approach* by Irwin W. Sherman (New York, Oxford University Press, 2d edition 1977) is another basic text. A helpful feature is a detailed summary at the end of each chapter, together with questions and topics for review. An appendix includes a discussion of simple chemistry as applied to biology. Some other general texts are *Biology* by James F. Case (New York, Macmillan, 2d edition 1979) and *Biological Science* by William T. Keeton (New York, Norton, 3d edition 1980).

Some of the social aspects of biology are discussed by David G. Lygre in *Life Manipulation: From Test-tube Babies to Aging* (New York, Walker, 1979). Topics included are artificial insemination, overcoming infertility, cloning and virgin birth, genetics, aging, controlling intelligence and behavior, and freedoms and restrictions of scientific inquiry. References for each chapter are listed together at the end of the book, along with additional suggested readings. There is an index. *Contemporary Issues in Bioethics* edited by Tom L. Beauchamp and LeRoy Walters (Belmont, Calif., Wadsworth, 1978) is made up of eighty-seven essays by different authors to provide a selection of readings on important issues in bioethics. The essays are arranged in chapters, with an introduction for each chapter by one of the editors. In many cases, essays with conflicting viewpoints are placed next to each other to show all sides of an issue. Each chapter includes a bibliography of suggested readings, and a list of bibliographies. A comprehensive view of population is presented in Edward O. Wilson's *Sociobiology* (Cambridge, Mass., Harvard University, 1975).

Specialized areas of the study of biology are examined in *Biology in Profile: An Introduction to the Many Branches of Biology* edited by P. N. Campbell (New York, Pergamon, 1981). Twenty essays by subject experts provide an overview of the various specializations.

The many illustrations of *The Science of Life: A Picture History of Biology* by Gordon R. Taylor (New York, McGraw-Hill, 1963) provide an interesting history of biological science. The illustrations include reproductions of old pictures, drawings, and photographs. It is written in historical sequence, from Aristotle's time to about 1960, with an emphasis on people. A special feature is a chronological table of the history of biology. There is an index. Lois N. Magner's *History of the Life Sciences* (New York, Dekker, 1979) begins with ancient civilizations, proceeding through the Greek and Roman worlds, the Middle Ages, and the Renaissance, and on to the foundations of modern scientific tradition. Then such modern topics as problems in reproduction and development, cell theory, evolution, and genetics are discussed. There are references with each chapter, and an index. *Changing Scenes in Natural Sciences, 1776-1976* (Philadelphia, Pa., Academy of Natural Sciences, 1977) is the result of a symposium held in 1976. It is made up of articles by different authors, most including a bibliography.

Great Experiments in Biology by Mordecai L. Gabriel (Englewood Cliffs, N.J., Prentice-Hall, 1955) contains historical articles by many scientists. It is arranged in chapters by general subject: cell theory, general physiology, microbiology, plant physiology, embryology, genetics, and evolution. Within each chapter is a chronology of the history of that subject area to the 1900s, and then articles by different scientists in that field, reprinted from journals of their time.

Discovery Process in Modern Biology: People and Processes in Biological Discovery edited by W. R. Klemm (Huntington, N.Y., Krieger, 1977) contains contributions by contemporary prominent biologists, stressing the personal side of their careers in biology. Essays are written in the first person, and most begin with childhood and educational experiences. Each essay is accompanied by personal biographical data such as birth date, education, positions held, and research interests, and a photograph and introduction by the editor. References are included with each essay.

Subject Headings and Classification

Agriculture
Animal industry
Biological chemistry
Biological libraries
Biological research
Biological warfare
Biology
   (also subdivisions of Biology)
   —Bibliography
   —Field work
   —Nomenclature
   —Terminology
Biology, Economic
Biology, Experimental
Biologists
Cells
Crops and soils
Evolution
Fertilizers and manures
Field crops
Food crops
Genetics
Heredity
Natural history
Population biology

Reproduction
Soils

Library materials on biology will generally be found shelved in the
QH 301 to QH 705 section of the Library of Congress section, or 574
to 579 section of the Dewey Decimal Classification. Materials on
agriculture will be found in the S to SK section of the Library of Congress classification and the 630 to 639 section of the Dewey Decimal
Classification.

BIBLIOGRAPHIC MATERIALS

Guides to the Literature

Guide to the Literature of the Life Sciences by Roger C. Smith, W.
Malcolm Reid, and A. E. Luchsinger (Minneapolis, Minn. Burgess,
9th edition 1980) is not a bibliography or list of references but deals
with literature problems of life scientists, with limited examples of
specific books. Information is included on libraries and classification,
books, bibliographies, abstract journals, ready reference works, journals, and literature searching and preparation of scientific papers.
There is an index. *The Library Research Guide to Biology: Illustrated
Search Strategy and Sources* by Thomas G. Kirk (Ann Arbor, Mich.,
Pierian Press, 1978) is a guide and a bibliography. There is detailed information on using some major indexes of biological science: *Science
Citation Index, Biological Abstracts, Biological and Agricultural Index, Chemical Abstracts,* and *Zoological Record,* and on how to
search the card catalog. Also included is a bibliography of reference
works by subject.

Author Elizabeth B. Davis in *Using the Biological Literature: A
Practical Guide* (New York, Dekker, 1981) aims to acquaint biology
students and others with important resources of biology, both primary and secondary sources. Emphasis is on current English language
materials. Arrangement is in chapters by broad subjects, subdivided
by form, for example, handbooks, and books are listed together with
an informative annotation and bibliographic information. A helpful
feature is a list with each chapter of subject headings applicable to that
subject, which is useful in searching a card catalog. *Use of Biological
Literature* edited by R. T. Bottle and H. V. Wyatt (London, Butter-

worths, 2d edition 1971) contains chapters by various authors on the different subjects of biological science. Emphasis is on British sources. At the end of the book is a section of exercises, with notes on their solution. Helpful additions are a glossary of terms, abbreviations, and acronyms.

An audiovisual aid to the use of biological literature is *A Guide to Searching the Biological Literature* by Michael M. King and Linda S. King (J. Huley Associates, Inc., 1978) which consists of two cassette tapes and seventy-eight slides. Discussion is mainly on the use of *Excerpta Medica, Biological Abstracts, Index Medicus, Chemical Abstracts,* and *Science Citation Index.*

Fundamental to the applied life sciences is *Guide to Sources for Agricultural and Biological Research* by J. Richard Blanchard (Berkeley, Calif., University of California, 1981). This guide covers the fields of agriculture, plant science, crop production, animal science, physical sciences where applicable to agriculture, food science and nutrition, environmental sciences, social sciences, and computerized data base searching. It gives international coverage. Arrangement is in chapters containing a brief introduction and list of sources, with annotations. Indexes are by author, title, and subject. An appendix gives meanings of acronyms and abbreviations.

Bibliographies

Theodore Besterman's *Biological Sciences: A Bibliography of Bibliographies* (Totowa, N.J., Rowman and Littlefield, 1971) contains bibliographic entries taken from Besterman's *World Bibliography of Bibliographies.* Arrangement is by subject, and for each citation there is full bibliographic information plus an indication of the number of entries in the bibliography being cited. Sources for historical studies are listed by Pieter Smit in *History of the Life Sciences: An Annotated Bibliography* (New York, Hafner, 1974). International coverage is given for general reference works and historical works of the life and medical sciences, divided into ancient and medieval, renaissance, and later works. Citations give bibliographic information and a brief annotation.

Indexing and Abstracting Services

Biological and Agricultural Index (New York, Wilson, 1916–) is very much like the *Readers Guide to Periodical Literature.* It is published monthly and indexes articles about biology, agriculture, and related sciences from about 150 English-language periodicals. Arrangement is alphabetical by subject, and only bibliographic information is given for each article cited. The monthly issues are cumulated quarterly and again at the end of the year, which runs from August through July. This is the most straightforward and easily used index to the biological literature.

Biological Abstracts (Philadelphia, Pa., BioSciences Information Service, 1, 1926–) is a much more comprehensive index than the preceding one. It is published twice a month and indexes periodical articles from countries all over the world. Arrangement is in broad subject sections with more specific subdivisions, and bibliographic information is given, plus the author's address, and a concise summary of the article. Each issue also contains indexes by author and specific subject, by broad subject areas called concept, by genus and species called generic, and by taxonomic categories called biosystematic indexes. Indexes are cumulated twice a year. This abstracting service covers the journal literature, while its companion title *Biological Abstracts RRM* (Philadelphia, Pa., BioSciences Information, 1, 1965–) covers the report, conference, and book literature. This service has had title changes; it has been called *Bioresearch Index* and *Bioresearch Titles,* with the present title beginning in 1980. It is now published twice a month.

International Abstracts of Biological Sciences (London, Pergamon, 1, 1965–), published monthly, is also arranged by subject categories. Coverage is international. The author and subject indexes are cumulated quarterly.

The *Bibliography of Agriculture With Subject Index* (Phoenix, Ariz., Oryx, 1, 1942–) is published monthly from data provided by the National Agricultural Library. Up to 1975 the subject section was published separately. This service provides international coverage of

BIOSIS [PREVIEWS] Includes the contents of Biological Abstracts and Biological Abstracts/RRM (Reports, Reviews, Meetings), formerly BioResearch Index, covering the entire life sciences. DIALOG has two files: 1969 to 1976 (file 55), and 1977 to present (file 5). SDC has three files: 1969 to 1973, 1974 to 1979, and 1980 to present.

Prepared by Biosciences Information Service.

Coverage: BRS, Jan 1970 to present; CAN/OLE, 1972 to present; DIALOG and SDC, 1969 to present
File size: over 3 million records; CAN/OLE 2.2 million records
Unit record: citation; abstract since 1978
Vendor, Cost/connect hour: BRS, $41-$55; CAN/OLE, $40 plus royalty; DIALOG (5, 55), $58; SDC, $65

Fig. 9-1. Computer data base: BIOSIS

journal articles, pamphlets, government documents, special reports, proceedings, and so forth. The first section of each issue, called the "main entry section," is arranged by broad subjects, for example, plant science, and for each subject there is a list of references arranged in groups alphabetically by the journal from which they came. Five subsections of this main entry section list USDA publications, state agricultural experiment station publications, state agricultural extension service publications, FAO publications, and translated publications. There are indexes by geographic area covered by articles, corporate author, personal author, and subject. Indexes are cumulated annually. In the references, the names of journals are abbreviated; a separate list by the same publisher called *Agricultural Journal Titles and Abbreviations* may be consulted if needed to find the full title.

SECONDARY LITERATURE MATERIALS

Encyclopedias

The *Encyclopedia of the Biological Sciences* edited by Peter Gray (New York, Van Nostrand Reinhold, 2d edition 1970) is also arranged alphabetically, by subject, and defines and explains in articles of 500 words or more. Each article is by a specialist, whose name is included, and there are references with each article. Drawings are used as needed to make meanings clear. A subject index leads not only to the main article on a given subject but also to significant mentions in other articles. The *Illustrated Encyclopedia of Plants and Animals* (New York, Exeter, 1979) is a large one-volume encyclopedia with articles arranged in groups by general topic: "origin and evolution of species," "world of plants," "world of animals," and "plant and animal habitats." Plants and animals are discussed as groups, for example, algae, bacteria, Protozoa, birds. The article on birds in the "world of animals" section covers anatomy, flight, migration, mating and breeding, and ecology and conservation of birds. In addition to the discussion there are lovely color photographs, drawings and maps. There is an index.

Origins of Life

Grzimek's Encyclopedia of Evolution (New York, Van Nostrand Reinhold, 1976) is a one-volume encyclopedia covering the theory of evolution, including geological and evolutionary factors that have influenced the development of all animal species including man. Arrangement is in chapters, with introductory material on the history of the theory of evolution and on paleontology, then phylogenetic relationships of the animal kingdom, origin of life, and then different geological periods and epochs, up to the evolution of domestic animals in modern times. Each chapter is by a subject specialist. There are bibliographies, and illustrations, many in color, are used throughout. Indexing is by personal name, plant and animal names, and subjects.

Roots of Life: A Layman's Guide to Genes, Evolution, and the Ways of Cells by Mahlon B. Hoagland (Boston, Mass., Houghton Mifflin, 1978) is primarily for nonscientists. There is a brief glossary, and an index. The *New Evolutionary Timetable: Fossils, Genes, and the Origin of Species* by Steven M. Stanley (New York, Basic, 1981) discusses recent ideas about evolution in a historical context.

Life History of a Fossil: An Introduction to Taphonomy and Paleoecology by Pat Shipman (Cambridge, Mass., Harvard University Press, 1981) considers the events that occur between the time of death of an organism and its subsequent fossilization, which is taphonomy. The author emphasizes the procedure for bones and teeth. A guide for fossil identification is that written by Gerard R. Case: *Pictorial Guide to Fossils* (New York, Van Nostrand Reinhold, 1982).

In *The Selfish Gene* by Richard Dawkins (New York, Oxford University Press, 1976), the author takes the view that the animal or plant is simply the gene's way of reproducing itself, and stresses the ultimate selfishness of the gene in reproducing itself. There is a bibliography, and an index to both the text and the bibliography.

The *Primer of Population Genetics* by Daniel L. Hartl (Sunderland, Mass., Sinauer, 1981) is an introduction to population genetics. It covers the orgin, maintenance, and significance of genetic variation; measurement of variation as a function of mating patterns, evolutionary effects of mutation, selection, size of population, and other factors; and artifical insemination for genetic improvement. Many illustrations are used, and there is a bibliography.

Laboratory Work; Research

Methods in Experimental Biology by Robert Ralph (New York, Wiley, 1975) tells how instruments work, for example, the pH meter for measuring acidity/alkalinity. The approach is practical, stressing the general principles but not background equations. There is a bibliography of further suggested reading. *Research Problems in Biology: Investigations for Students* was prepared by the Biological Science Curriculum Study Committe of the American Institute of Biological Sciences (New York, Oxford University Press, 2d edition 1976). This book was written by experts as a guide for biology students in scientific investigation. Each experiment is presented by a different author, and includes references. There is also a general bibliography at the back of the book.

Agricultural Experimentation: Design and Analysis by Thomas M. Little and F. J. Hills (New York, Wiley, 1978) is a text covering the basics of experimentation and inductive reasoning, along with the major types of experimental methods such as block design, Latin squares design, and split-plat design. It discusses linear correlation and regression, curvilinear relations and so forth, and has tips on improving precision. Tables are included, and there is an index. Statistical methods are discussed more fully by the same authors in *Statistical Methods in Agricultural Research* (Davis, Calif., University of California, 1972.)

Mathematical data for research are gathered in *Statistical Tables for Biological, Agricultural and Medical Research* by Ronald A. Fisher and Frank Yates (New York, Hafner, 6th edition 1974). This volume contains basic statistical tables, with explanation of how to use them. There is also a bibliography of information on statistical methods. Another useful compliation for the laboratory is Colin Pennycuick's *Handy Matrices of Unit Conversion Factors for Biology and Mechanics* (New York, Wiley, 1974).

Biology Data Book complied and edited by Philip L. Altman and Dorothy Dittmer (Bethesda, Md., Federation of American Societies for Experimental Biology, 2d edition 1972–74) is in three volumes. Volume one deals with genetics, cytology, reproduction, development and growth, properties of biological substances, and materials and methods of culture. The appendixes include a list of scientific names of animals and plants with the equivalent common name, and a reverse list of common names with scientific equivalents. Volume two deals with biological regulators, biological effects of the environment, parasitism, and sensory and neurobiology. The third volume of this set covers nutrition, digestion, and excretion; metabolism; respiration and circulation; and blood and other body fluids. Each volume is indexed and so is complete in itself.

Taxonomy

Biological Nomenclature by Charles Jeffrey (New York, Crane Russak, 2d edition 1977) is a practical guide to the use of nomenclature in taxonomic literature, designed to promote understanding of biological nomenclature and to introduce the official Codes of Nomenclature. It has a bibliography, glossary, and index.

Synopsis and Classification of Living Organisms edited by Sybil P. Parker (New York, McGraw-Hill, 1982) is in two volumes, consisting of articles covering the classification characteristics, life cycle, ecology, and geographic distribution of taxonomic groups. Many drawings and diagrams are used to illustrate, and there are more than 100 full-page photograpns. There is an index.

Periodicals

American Biology Teacher. Reston, Va., National Association of Biology Teachers, 1938– . (monthly)

American Midland Naturalist. Notre Dame, Ind., University of Notre Dame, 1909– . (quarterly)

American Naturalist. Chicago, University of Chicago, 1867– . (monthly)

Annals of Applied Biology. Warwick, England, Association of Applied Biologists, 1914– . (9/year)

Audubon Magazine. New York, National Audubon Society, 1899– . (bimonthly)

Behavioral Ecology and Sociobiology. New York, Springer-Verlag, 1976– . (8/year)

Biologist. London, Institute of Biology, 1953– . (5/year)

Biology and Human Affairs. London, British Social Biology Council, 1935– . (semiannual)

Bioscience. Arlington, Va., American Institute of Biological Sciences, 1951– . (monthly)

Biotechnology and Bioengineering. New York, Wiley, 1958– . (monthly)

Biotropica. Pullman, Wash., Association for Tropical Biology, 1969–   . (quarterly)

Developmental Biology. New York, Academic, 1959–   . (monthly)

Freshwater Biology. Oxford, Blackwell, 1971–   . (bimonthly)

Human Biology. Detroit, Mich., Wayne State University, Human Biology Council, 1929–   . (quarterly)

Journal of Biological Standardization. New York, Academic, 1973–   . (quarterly)

Journal of Experimental Biology. Cambridge, Cambridge University Press, 1923–   . (6/year)

Journal of the History of Biology. Dordrecht, Netherlands, Reidel, 1968–   . (semiannual)

Journal of Theoretical Biology. London, Academic, 1961–   . (fortnightly)

National Wildlife; Dedicated to the Wise Use of our Natural Resources. Washington, D.C., National Wildlife Federation, 1962–   . (bimonthly)

Natural History. New York, American Museum of Natural History, 1900–   . (monthly)

Nature. London, Macmillan, 1869–   . (weekly)

Parks and Recreation. London, Institute of Parks and Recreation, 1936–   . (monthly)

Sierra. San Francisco, Sierra Club, 1893–   . (bimonthly)

Society for Experimental Biology and Medicine. Proceedings. New York, Society for Experimental Biology and Medicine, 1903–   . (11/year)

CURRENT AWARENESS MATERIALS

Current Contents: Agriculture, Biology, and Environmental Sciences (Philadelphia, Pa., Institute for Scientific Information 1970–   ) is published weekly, and contains reprints of the tables of contents of many journals in its area published that week. Each issue has a subject index and an author index, with the address of each author.

QUICK REFERENCE TOOLS

Dictionaries

The *Facts on File Dictionary of Biology* edited by Elizabeth Tootill (New York, Facts on File, 1981) defines approximately 3,000 terms of life sciences. Arrangement is alphabetical by term, with cross-references as needed. Drawings are used to illustrate.

The *McGraw-Hill Dictionary of the Life Sciences* (New York, McGraw-Hill, 1976) contains about 20,000 terms of biology and related disciplines. Definitions are brief, usually one sentence. In addition to the definitions there is an indication of the field in which the term is used, for example, zoology, and sometimes an illustration. Arrangement is alphabetical, and cross-references lead from synonyms to the definition. An appendix includes the metric system and conversion, and animal, plant, and bacterial taxonomy, for example, phyla, classes, and orders. The *Dictionary of Life Sciences* edited by E. H. Martin (New York, Pica, 1976) is arranged alphabetically by term, with cross-references. Definitions range in length from a sentence to a paragraph, and a few are illustrated by drawings. Michael Abercrombie's *Penquin Dictionary of Biology* (New York, Viking, 7th edition 1977) defines about 3,000 terms with a few to 200 words each. Peter Gray's *Dictionary of the Biological Sciences* (New York, Reinhold, 1967) and the abridged *Student Dictionary of Biology* (New York, Van Nostrand, 1972) briefly define about 40,000 terms and about 8,000 terms, respectively.

A Source-book of Biological Names and Terms by Edmund C. Jaeger (Springfield, Ill., Thomas, 3d edition 1955, reprinted 1978) is a dictionary of elements that have been used to make up three kinds of words: genus and species names and technical terms. Arrangement is alphabetical by the word element, and information given is the origin, usually Greek or Latin, and examples of how the element is used in generic or specific or technical terms. At the back of the book is a section of very brief biographies of about 280 people in whose honor commemorative names have been given.

For foreign terms, the *Dictionary of Biology* by Günter Haensch (Amsterdam and New York, Elsevier, 1976) is polyglot in English, German, French, and Spanish. Arrangement is alphabetical by term in English, with the word equivalents for each other language given in columns. The indexes list the same terms in German, French, and Spanish and for each refer to the number of the term in the main section so that one can find the English meaning and equivalents in the other two languages. The *Russian–English Biological and Medical Dictionary* by Eugene A. Carpovich (New York, Technical Dictionaries, 2d edition 1960) is arranged alphabetically by Russian terms and gives the English equivalent, all in the Russian Cyrillic characters.

For the reverse, the *English–Russian Biological Dictionary* edited by O. I. Chibisova and L. A. Kozyar (London, Pergamon, 1981) contains about 60,000 terms on all areas of biology.

Directories

John W. Thompson's *Index to Illustrations of the Natural World: Where to Find Pictures of the Living Things of North America* (Syracuse, N.Y., Gaylord, 1977) is arranged alphabetically by the common names of the plants, animals, and birds and tells where illustrations of each may be found. The illustrations listed were chosen from 178 books selected in part because they are available in most medium- and large-size libraries. There is an index by scientific names, and a list of the books in which the illustrations are to be found. *Index to Illustrations of Living Things Oustide North America: Where to Find Pictures of Flora and Fauna* by Lucille Thompson Munz and N. G. Slauson (New York, Archon, 1981) gives locations for illustrations of more than 9,000 species of plants and animals. The illustrations are found in 206 books, most published in the 1970s and widely available in medium-size and larger libraries. Arrangement is alphabetical by common name, with an index by scientific names. *Topic-aids: Biology* edited by R. S. Egan (College Station, Tex., Texas A & M University Press, 1977) lists instructional aids: films, filmstrips, audiocassettes, charts, and models. For each item, information given is title, format, a short description, and distribution.

The National Park Foundation has put out a *Complete Guide to America's National Parks* (Washington, D.C., National Park Foundation, 1979), which lists 353 national parks areas and affiliated sites in the United States. Arrangement is alphabetical by state, with a state map with the parks marked on it and then a listing of the parks with information including address, directions, visitor activities, and general information. A special feature is a listing of peak visitation times for each park so visitors may avoid those times if they wish.

The *Conservation Directory* (Washington, D.C., National Wildlife Federation, 1956–) has a descriptive subtitle: "a listing of organizations, agencies, and officials concerned with natural resource use and management." Published annually, this directory lists U.S. government agencies concerned with conservation, conservation organizations in the United States and other countries, for example, the Sierra

Club, state agencies and citizens groups for the United States and Canada arranged alphabetically by state, and for each listing the address and contact person and usually some information about the organization. A smaller section lists U.S. national parks, forests, wildlife refuges, and national seashores; colleges; and foreign conservation offices. There is an index by personal name.

The *Naturalists' Directory International* (Marlton, N.J., World Natural History, 1878–) gives international coverage. The main part is a listing of individual naturalists, arranged by country, and alphabetically by state for the United States. Each person's address and area of special interest or expertise is given. Other sections list natural history museums, associations, and so forth, and natural science periodicals.

Directory of Biologicals (London and New York, Macmillan, Journals, 1, 1982–) is published annually as a supplement to the journal *Nature*. This directory contains information on obtaining biological materials, excluding instruments. The first section is arranged alphabetically by name of company and tells what products are manufactured. The second part is alphabetical by product, for example, culture media, enzymes, or living organisms, and lists companies that manufacture or sell the product.

ECOLOGY

Because of the enormous interest in ecology, it will be treated separately from biology. Although the basic principles of biology are needed in the study of ecology, one can read and understand much of the literature of ecology without knowing those basic principles and perhaps even without being interested in them.

INTRODUCTORY MATERIALS

Nature's Economy: The Roots of Ecology by Donald E. Worster (San Francisco, Sierra Club, 1977) is a history of the study of ecology, beginning with the eighteenth century. According to the preface, the book is divided by the five "major formative moments in the life history of modern ecology," with several chapters in each part. It also has a glossary, a brief bibliography, and an index.

Edward O. Wilson has collected readings from the magazine *Scientific American* in *Ecology, Evolution and Population* (San Francisco, Freeman, 1974). Articles are grouped into four sections: evolutionary process, multiplication and dispersal of species, growth and interaction of populations, and ecosystems. Each section has several articles by different authors. Bibliographies for all articles are grouped together at the end of the volume, and there is an index. *Handbook of Contemporary Developments in World Ecology* (Westport, Conn., Greenwood, 1981) is made up of thirty-three essays by different authors, and is international in scope. The theme is the state of the science, including the historical development of ecology in the various countries. Also included are lists of professional societies and journals, and government organizations sponsoring research.

Ecology Out of Joint: New Environments and Why They Happen by Lorus J. Milne and Margery Milne (New York, Scribner, 1977) discusses the effects of the spread of civilization on nature worldwide. A few interesting chapter titles will indicate the nature of the book: "Cast-off Pets," about the walking cat-fish discovered in Florida in 1967, and others; "Something New to Eat"; and "Giving Time." References for each chapter are collected at the end of the book. Of similar interest is Paul A. Colinvaux's *Why Big Fierce Animals are Rare: An Ecologist's Perspective* (Princeton, N.J., Princeton University Press, 1978). *Ecology of Invasions by Animals and Plants* by Charles S. Elton (London, Chapman and Hall, distributed by Halsted Press, N.Y., 1977) is about ecological explosions. By this the author means an enormous increase in numbers of a living organism, for example, a disease like potato disease or an insect such as the African mosquito. Written in an interesting way and illustrated, chapters deal with invasions of continents, islands, and the sea, food chains, and more. References are included.

Subject Headings and Classification

Ecological surveys
Ecologists
Ecology
   (subdivision—Environmental aspects under types of industries, chemicals, and so forth, e.g., Atomic power-plants—Environmental aspects)

Library materials on ecology will generally be found shelved in the QH 540 to QH 541 section of the Library of Congress classification, or in the 574.5 section of the Dewey Decimal Classification.

BIBLIOGRAPHIC MATERIALS

Guides to the Literature

Guide to Ecology Information and Organizations by John G. Burke (New York, Wilson, 1976) is arranged in chapters by the type of material covered. Included are a wide range of materials: citizen action guides, reference materials, books and periodicals, government publications, non-print media, organizations, and U.S. government officials. Items are listed in each chapter with bibliographic information and/or address as appropriate, and an annotation. There is an index. *Sourcebook on the Environment; a Guide to the Literature* edited by Kenneth A. Hammond and others (Chicago, University of Chicago Press, 1978) is a broad guide to selected environmental literature, using twenty-six subject specialists to write a review of the literature in their fields with a list of references at the end with full bibliographic information. The literature is grouped into four main sections: environmental perspectives and prospects; environmental modification case studies; major elements of the environment, that is, landforms, vegetation, and so forth; and research aids. Appendixes contain a selected list of environmental periodicals, a review of U.S. government legislation on the environment, and a list of selected U.S. environmental organizations with addresses.

Bibliographies

The Chicorel Index to Environment and Ecology by Marietta Chicorel (New York, Chicorel Library Publishing, 1975) is a two-volume set listing books on the environment and ecology. It is arranged in sixteen major subject categories subdivided by topic. Only bibliographic information is given. A very brief subject index leads to the topic under which an item will be found. *Conservation/Ecology, Resources for Environmental Education* by David F. Harrah and Barbara Harrah (Metuchen, N.J. Scarecrow, 1975) has several sections, beginning with an annotated list of books arranged alphabetically by author. It also lists other books, giving bibliographic information only; periodical articles of interest to educators, with a list of periodicals; U.S. government agencies with addresses and U.S. government publications; and other public agencies with addresses.

Indexing and Abstracting Services

Environment Abstracts (New York, Environment Information Center, 1971–), called *Environment Information Access* for the first three volumes, is published monthly to give international coverage of journal articles, conference papers, and reports. The main section, which is the review section, is arranged in about twenty broad subject areas and gives bibliographic citation and an informative abstract for each item listed. There are indexes by subject and by personal and corporate author. The subject and corporate author indexes give bibliographic information but refer to the item number in the review section for an abstract. Items listed may be ordered from the publisher in most cases. Annual indexing is provided by a companion title, the *Environment Index* (New York, Environment Information Center, 1971–), published each year. This publication has two main sections: the review section and the index section. The review section contains articles, a review of the literature for the year, legislation, a list of conferences, and lists of books and films. The index section includes indexes by subject, SIC code, geographic term, and author. Indexes give bibliographic information and refer to the number of the abstract in *Environment Abstracts*. *Environmental Periodicals Bibliography* (Santa Barbara, Calif., Environmental Studies Institute, 1973–) has six issues per year and an annual index. Only journal articles are included; coverage is international. Arrangement is in six main subject categories, and the tables of contents of journals within each subject area are reproduced in alphabetical order by the name of the journal. There are subject and author indexes.

Pollution Abstracts (Riverdale, Md., Cambridge Scientific Abstracts, 1970–) is published six times per year plus an annual index, providing international coverage of journals, conference proceedings, books, and government reports. Arrangement is in broad subject groups, for example, "air pollution" and "marine pollution," and bibliographic information is given along with the author's address and an abstract of up to 200 words in length. There are indexes by subject and author in each issue and cumulated yearly.

Ecology Abstracts (London, Information Retrieval, 1975–), called *Applied Ecology Abstracts* for its first five volumes is published monthly. This service covers journal articles and reports. Items are listed in broad subject groups, and give bibliographic information and an abstract. There are indexes by author and subject. *Ecological Abstracts* (Norwich, England, Geo Abstracts, 1974–) is published bimonthly and also has a broad subject arrangement.

SECONDARY LITERATURE MATERIALS

The *Environmental Impact Book* (Ann Arbor, Mich., Ann Arbor Science, 1979) is a compilation of data for preparing environmental impact statements. Following introductory information on techniques and data bases, information is mostly in tabular form. There are references with each section, and there is an index.

There are several ecology books that were written primarily as textbooks but are also useful for general study or reference. *Plants, People, and Environment* edited by Peter B. Kaufman and J. Donald LeCroix (New York, Macmillan, 1979) is arranged in three sections, each of which contains several articles by different subject specialists. The three sections are titled "plants: their way of life," "probing the nature of our environment," and "constructive action and solutions to our environmental problems." This action-oriented text has questions for consideration at the beginning of each article, and ends each with a summary. There is a glossary, and an index. *Environmental Science* (Philadelphia, Saunders, 2d edition 1978) is divided into six units: introduction, biological background, human population, resources and energy, rural land use, and pollution. An interesting feature at the end of each chapter is a section of "take-home experiments," for example, making a solar collector of ice cube trays to determine which direction of placement is best and the effects of insulation. There are a glossary, a bibliography, and an index. *Principles of Ecology* by Richard Brewer (Philadelphia, Pa., Saunders, 1979) is a text for sophomore–junior level of college, with a bibliography with each chapter for added reading, and a glossary. Chapter titles include "Ecology as a Science," "Ecology of Individual Organisms," "Population Ecology," "Community and Ecosystem Ecology," and "Practical Ecologist." *Environmental Science: Managing the Environment* by P. Walter Purdom (Columbus, Ohio, Merrill, 1980) also has references with each chapter, and study questions and a glossary. Appendixes include a selected list of environmental periodicals, a list of U.S. environmental organizations with addresses, and a selected bibliography for further reading.

The *McGraw-Hill Encyclopedia of Environmental Science* (New York, McGraw-Hill, 2d edition 1980) is written by experts but designed for the nonspecialist. Much of the material is taken from the publisher's general scientific encyclopedia. The volume begins with five articles of several pages each on topics of general interest: environmental protection, precedents for weather extremes, environmental satellites, urban planning, and environmental analysis. Then there are about 250 mostly shorter articles, arranged alphabetically. Articles are illustrated by photographs and drawings, and many include a bibliography. There is an index. *Grzimek's Encyclopedia of Ecology* (New York, Van Nostrand Reinhold, 1976) is arranged in chapters grouped into two main parts: environment of animals and environment of man. Articles by different authors cover animal adaptation to the abiotic environment, the biotic environment, habitats and their fauna, and man as a factor, in the first part. The second part includes chapters on changes in the natural landscape, the sea in danger, waste explosion, and air pollution. Several lovely color photographs are used to illustrate; supplementary readings are listed. There is an index.

Periodicals

Most of the periodicals listed under biology would contain articles on ecology. A few periodicals will be listed here that are more strictly concerned with ecology.

Ambio; a Journal of the Human Environment Research and Management, Royal Swedish Academy of Sciences. New York, Pergamon, 1972– . (bimonthly)

Australian Journal of Ecology, Ecological Society of Australia. Oxford, Blackwell, 1976– . (quarterly)

Bio Cycle. Emmaus, Pa., J G Press, 1960– . (bimonthly)
Biological Conservation. Essex, England, Applied Science, 1968– .
(8/year)
Ecological Society of America. Bulletin. Durham, N.C., Duke University Press, 1917– . (quarterly)
Ecology: All Forms of Life in Relation to Environment, Ecological Society of America. Durham, N.C., Duke University Press, 1920– . (6/year)
Environment. Washington, D.C., Heldref, 1958– . (10/year)
Human Ecology: An Interdisciplinary Journal. New York, Plenum, 1972– . (quarterly)
International Wildlife. Washington, D.C., National Wildlife Federation, 1971– . (bimonthly)
Journal of Applied Ecology, British Ecological Society. Oxford, Blackwell, 1964– . (3/year)
Journal of Ecology, British Ecological Society. Oxford, Blackwell, 1913– . (3/year)
Journal of Environmental Quality. Madison, Wis., American Society of Agronomy, 1972– . (quarterly)
Journal of Wildlife Management. Washington, D.C., Wildlife Society, 1937– . (quarterly)
Living Wilderness. Washington, D.C., Wilderness Society, 1935– .
(quarterly)
Nature Study. Jersey City, N.J., American Nature Study Society, 1946– . (quarterly)
Theoretical Population Biology. New York, Academic, 1970– .
(6/year)
Tropical Ecology. Varanasi, India, International Society for Tropical Ecology, 1960– . (semiannual)

CURRENT AWARENESS MATERIALS

The specialized current awareness tool is *Current Advances in Ecological Sciences* (New York, Pergamon, 1975–). This journal is published monthly, with international coverage. Books and journal articles are listed in subject categories with an author index, and each entry gives bibliographic information and author's address. There are also short articles in some issues.

QUICK REFERENCE TOOLS

Dictionaries

The *Ecology Field Glossary: A Naturalist's Vocabulary* (Westport, Conn., Greenwood, 1977) is a dictionary for nonspecialists or beginners in the field. Arrangement is alphabetical by term with cross-references as needed, and brief definitions. A special feature is a glossary outline at the beginning of the book that gives the subject beginner an introduction to terms by listing them in broad subject headings of "terrestrial ecosystems," "aquatic ecosystems," "soil ecosystems," and "man's impact on ecosystems," each with subdivision headings. There is a bibliography, and an index. Michael Allaby's *Dictionary of the Environment* (London, Macmillan, 1977) is alphabetical by term, with definitions of one sentence to a paragraph. This dictionary is directed toward both lay users and scientists. Alan Gilpin's *Dictionary of Environmental Terms* (St. Lucia, Queensland, University of Queensland, 1976) is arranged alphabetically by term, with definitions of one sentence to several paragraphs. A few photographs and drawings are used to illustrate, and there is a bibliography. The appendix contains the proclamation and principles resulting from the United Nations Conference on the Human Environment, Stockholm, June 1972.

Handbooks

The *Handbook of Contemporary Developments in World Ecology* by Edward Kormondy and Frank McCormick (Westport, Conn., Greenwood, 1981) contains state-of-the-art articles on ecological science in thirty-four nations. Appendixes list bibliographic and organizational resources.

Directories

The *World Environmental Directory* (Silver Spring, Md., Business Publishers, 1974–) is published annually and is international in scope. It lists companies, organizations, agencies, institutions, and people. The *World Directory of Environmental Organizations* (Claremont, Calif., Institute of Public Affairs, 2d edition 1975) is published with the Sierra Club. It lists international organizations and national, regional, and local organizations for each country of the world.

The *Directory of Nature Centers and Related Environmental Education Facilities* (New York, National Audubon Society, 1979) lists nature centers and outdoor laboratories in the United States and Canada.

10
Botany

INTRODUCTORY MATERIALS

The *Short History of Botany in the United States* edited by Joseph A. Evan (New York, Hafner, 1969) is, of course, tied in with the whole world, but it stresses U.S. centers of activity such as Harvard University. The book is written by twelve authors, each covering a different subject such as plant physiology, phycology, taxonomy, and so forth. An interesting feature is a "calendar of events" from 300 B.C. to recent years. The entry for 300 B.C. shows surprisingly advanced "storage baskets made of yucca leaves, juniper berry skewers, and wooden dice in use by natives who lived near Tularosa Cave, New Mexico." For further information there is a list of suggested readings, and there is an index to personal names mentioned. Another interesting history is the *Illustrated History of the Herbals* by Frank J. Anderson (New York, Columbia University Press, 1977).

The histories reflect the large amount of legend connected with plants. Three sources of pleasurable reading along these lines are William A. Emboden's *Bizarre Plants: Magical, Monstrous, Mythical* (New York, Macmillan, 1974), Lesley Gordon's *Green Magic: Flowers, Plants, and Herbs in Lore and Legend* (New York, Viking, 1977), and Brendan Lehane's *Power of Plants* (New York, McGraw-Hill, 1977).

The *New York Botanical Garden Illustrated Encyclopedia of Horticulture* by Thomas H. Everett (New York, Garland, 1980) is an encyclopedic dictionary for both popular and professional use. The ten volumes are arranged in alphabetical order by plant name, usually genus, with cross-references from other names. Information given for each plant is characteristics, identification, uses in garden and landscape, cultivation, and pests and diseases. Other articles treat other subjects. There are thousands of photographs, many in color, to aid in identification of the plants.

Wild Flowers of the United States by Harold W. Rickett (New York, McGraw-Hill, 1966–) was prepared in conjunction with the New York Botanical Garden. This lovely multivolume set gives comprehensive coverage of wildflowers of the United States with nontechnical language. The volumes cover different geographical areas, for example, northeastern states, southeastern states. Arrangement is by plant family, with descriptions of each species and photographs or diagrams of most.

An introduction to all areas of botany may be found in *Botany: An Introduction to Plant Biology* by T. Elliot Weier and others (New York, Wiley, 6th edition 1981). Plants whose continuing existence is endangered are listed in *Endangered and Threatened Plants of the United States* by Edward S. Ayensu and Robert A. DeFillipps (Washington, D.C., Smithsonian Institution and World Wildlife Fund, 1978). This volume is an outgrowth of a review and report by the Smithsonian Institution as required by the Endangered Species Act of 1973, reviewing species of plants that are or may become endangered or threatened. There is introductory discussion of how these lists were made, and of such topics as plant habitats, conservation, and preservation in botanical gardens. Then, endangered, threatened, and extinct plant species are listed. The lists are divided into sections, such as commercially exploited species, extinct species, and state lists of endangered and threatened species. There is a bibliography, as well as several lists of addenda at the back of the book.

Subject Headings and Classification

Botanical gardens
Botanical laboratories
Botanical literature
Botanical museums
Botanical research
Botanical societies
Botanists
Botany
    (also subdivisions of Botany)
    —Bibliography

—Classification
—Dictionaries
—Ecology
—Nomenclature
Botany, Economic
Botany, Medical
Dangerous plants
Ferns
Floriculture
Flowers
Fruit
Gardening
Herbaria
Horticulture
House plants
Mycology
(headings beginning with "plant," e.g., Plant diseases)
Poisonous plants
Seeds
Shrubs
Trees
Weeds
(names of individual plants)
(divisions of the plant kingdom, e.g., Algae)

Most materials of the type described here will be found in libraries shelved in the Library of Congress classification QK section or in the Dewey Decimal Classification 580 to 589 section. Plant culture and gardening are also classified in class SB 110 to SB 999 in the Library of Congress classification.

BIBLIOGRAPHIC MATERIALS

Bibliographies

A listing of bibliographies of general botany and specific subject areas is *Botanical Bibliographies* by Lloyd H. Swift (Minneapolis, Minn., Burgess, 1970). This is a guide to bibliographic materials, listing both complete publications and specific sections within publications in sixty-five subject divisions. The index lists each work cited by author and title, and also subjects.

Taxonomic Literature by Frans A. Stafleu and Richard S. Cowan (Utrecht, Netherlands, Bohn, Scheltema and Holkema, 2d edition 1976–) is a selective guide to botanical publications and collections. Arrangement is alphabetical by author through the four volumes. Each entry gives brief biographical information on the author, herbaria and types of the author, publications, and references to other information. There are two indexes in each volume, one to names and one to titles of books.

Catalog

The *Plant Science Catalog: Botany Subject Index* (Boston, Mass., G. K. Hall, 1958) was compiled by the United States Department of Agriculture Library. In fifteen volumes, it photo-reproduces the catalog cards in the subject section of the catalog alphabetically by subject. International in coverage, the bibliography spans early times to 1952.

Review

Advances in Botanical Research (London and New York, Academic, 1963–) is published somewhat irregularly but has appeared annually in recent years. It contains long articles on very specific topics by different authors, with extensive bibliographies.

Indexing and Abstracting Services

Excerpta Botanica (Stuttgart and New York, Fischer, 1, 1959–) is issued in two sections. Section A, taxonomica et chrologica, issued ten times per year, is arranged by broad subject and lists articles with an abstract. Abstracts are in German, English, or French. Section B, sociologica, published quarterly, lists monographs on plant geography and ecology, with no abstracts for this section. Coverage is international. *Bulletin Signaletique, part 370: Biologie et Physiologie Vegetales Sylviculture* (Paris, Centre National de le Recherche Scientifique, 1961–) is published monthly, and also provides international coverage. Arrangement is in broad subject groups, and bibliographic information and an abstract are given.

There are several indexing and abstracting services that cover very specialized materials, for example, *Horticultural Abstracts* (Farnham Royal, England, Commonwealth Agricultural Bureaux, 1931-).

Historically, botanical literature was indexed and abstracted in *Botanical Abstracts* (Baltimore, Md., Williams and Wilkins, 1918–26). This index was published monthly to 1926, when its coverage was taken over by *Biological Abstracts,* discussed in the chapter of this book on natural history. Arrangement is by broad subject categories. The botanical literature for 1900 to 1913 is covered by the *International Catalogue of Scientific Literature* (London, Royal Society, 1902–16).

SECONDARY LITERATURE MATERIALS

Research Methods

Research Methods in Plant Science by Richard M. and Deana T. Klein (Garden City, N.Y., Natural History Press, 1970) was published in connection with the American Museum of Natural History. It discusses methods of doing research with plants; it is not a book of experiments. Illustrations are used as needed, and references are included in the discussion.

Plant Geography and Population Biology

The Geographical Guide to Floras of the World by Sidney F. Blake (Washington, D.C., U.S. Government Printing Office, 1942–61) is an annotated listing with specific reference to plant common names and to useful plants, prepared by the Bureau of Plant Industry and the United States Department of Agriculture Library. Rexford Daubenmire's *Plant Geography* (New York, Academic, 1978) studies North American plants from two approaches: floristic, which is the study of their evolutionary divergence, migration, and decline as influenced by past events in the history of the earth, and ecologic, which takes plant communities as units and uses sociological and physiological considerations to interpret their ranges. Maps and photographs aid discussion of the various areas such as tundra region, subarctic-subalpine forest region, and temperate mesophytic forest region. It has an extensive bibliography, a glossary, and an index.

Population Biology of Plants by John L. Harper (New York, Academic, 1977) is concerned with the numbers of organisms and the consequences of these numbers. There are sections on dispersal, effects of neighbors and predators, natural dynamics, and plant evolution, followed by an extensive list of references, and author and subject indexes. *Demography and Evolution in Plant Populations* edited by Otto T. Solbrig (Berkeley, Calif., University of California Press, 1980) has chapters by seven botanists dealing with flowering plants. It contains an extensive annotated bibliography, and taxonomic and subject indexes.

Ecological Succession edited by Frank B. Golley (Stroudsburg; Pa., Dowden, Hutchinson and Ross, 1977) is made up of papers by twenty-seven different authors. Comments by the editor tie together the five main sections, which deal with precursors, pattern, mechanisms, interpretation, and community stability. There are references, and indexes by author and subject. The *Dictionary of Cultivated Plants and Their Centres of Diversity* by A. C. Zeven (Wageningen, Centre for Agricultural Publishing and Documentation, 1975) excludes ornamentals, forest trees, and lower plants. The book is divided into twelve sections corresponding to geographical areas of the world, such as Chinese–Japanese, African, and North American, and for each area lists plant species that originated there. For each species brief information is given such as where the plant was first found in that area, how it spread, and why it is cultivated. There is an extensive bibliography, and an index of botanical names. In *Plant Diversification* by Theodore Delevoryas (New York, Holt, Rinehart and Winston, 2d edition 1977) the author has chosen certain topics in evolution of special interest and developed them more fully than surveys that include all plants can. Emphasis is on evolution of flowering plants. Fossil records are included where applicable.

Biographical

Pioneers of Plant Study by Ellison Hawks and George S. Boulger (New York, Arno, 1928) is an interesting historical study. Arrangement is in chapters beginning with "plants of Ancient Egypt" and going on through in historical sequence to the middle of the nineteenth century. Some chapters are on individual botanists, but most are intertwining accounts of history and its makers. Some portraits are included. There is an index.

Dictionary of British and Irish Botanists and Horticulturists Including Plant Collectors and Botanical Artists by Ray Desmond (London, Taylor and Francis, 1977) was first published in 1893 under a slightly different title. Arrangement is alphabetical by name, and biographical information is presented in concise form, usually about fifty words, including place and dates of birth and death, education and career, selected publications, biographical references in books and periodicals, locations of plant collections or manuscripts, and plants commemorating the person. The subject index includes geographic areas and plant groups as well as such terms as "artists" and "paleobotany." *Biographical Notes Upon Botanists* compiled by John H. Barnhart (Boston, Mass., G. K. Hall, 1965) consists of three volumes that reproduce a file of biographical information maintained in the New York Botanical Library. Brief information on more than 44,000 botanists is included: dates of birth and death, education, honors, professional positions held, memberships, outstanding contributions and publications, and biographical works.

Plant Identification

Taxonomy of Vascular Plants by George H. M. Lawrence (New York, Macmillan, 1951) begins with a discussion of taxonomy, its history, principles and systems in use, nomenclature, and identification. Part two covers selected families of vascular plants. There is an illustrated glossary, and indexing is by both common and scientific plant names. *Vascular Plant Systematics* by Albert E. Radford and others (New York, Harper and Row, 1974) is a reference text for a basic course in taxonomy, and a source book of information, procedures, and references. It begins with a discussion of taxonomy, including its history, and of names and naming; then there is an extensive section on evidence, principles, and concepts fundamental to vascular plant taxonomic studies and research; then laboratory and field exercises and problems, techniques, terminology, and bibliographies. The appendix contains drawings of angiosperm families. There is an index.

The *International Code of Botanical Nomenclature of the International Botanical Congress* (Utrecht, Netherlands, Bohn, Scheltema and Hokema, 1, 1867–   ) is published as revised at each meeting of the congress, about every five years. For example, the code as revised at the 12th Botanical Congress in 1975 was published in 1978. Each edition supersedes all previous editions. This code is the foundation upon which the classification of plants is now built, providing a stable method of naming taxonomic groups, avoiding and rejecting names that may cause error or ambiguity. It is made up of principles of naming, rules and recommendations, and provisions for modification of the code. The text is presented first in English, and then repeated in French and German. Following the text is a list of approved names. There is an index.

Manuals

Manual of Cultivated Plants Most Commonly Grown in the Continental United States and Canada by Liberty Hyde Bailey (New York, Macmillan, revised edition 1949) is a classic manual, the first edition having appeared in 1924. Another classic manual, first published in 1848, is *Gray's Manual of Botany: A Handbook of the Flowering Plants and Ferns of the Central and Northeastern United States and Adjacent Canada* by Asa Gray (New York, Van Nostrand Reinhold, 8th edition 1970), the 8th edition largely rewritten and expanded by Merritt L. Fernald. Its purpose is to provide a means for identification of plants in the geographic area covered. Arrangement is by families, with keys to identification of genera and species.

Arthur Cronquist's *Integrated System of Classification of Flowering Plants* (New York, Columbia University, 1981) is a synoptic description and discussion of the classes, subclasses, orders, and families of plants. There are drawings of representative species of each family, and keys for identification. References are included. The book *100 Families of Flowering Plants* by M. Hickey and C. J. King (New York, Cambridge University Press, 1981) provides a comprehensive overview of flowering plants, intended to be at an undergraduate level. There is detailed information on principal economic and ornamental species in each family, and floral, distribution, and vegetative characteristics of each family. Drawings and charts are used, and a glossary and bibliography are included.

Richard Headstrom's *Families of Flowering Plants* (New York, A. S. Barnes, 1978) is a more popular treatment geared to general readers, to provide a readable narrative account of the families of flowering plants with a minimum of technical terminology. Arrangement is alphabetical by family names, and individual species of plants are described as to their "virtues and vices and legends and folk tales," according to the preface. Often a drawing is included. The appendix is a check list of species giving common and scientific names. The book has a glossary, a bibliography, and an index. Another lovely volume of interest to general readers is the *Audubon Society Book of Wildflowers* by Les Line (New York, Abrams, 1978), composed primarily of full-page color photographs of wildflowers, grouped by habitat, for example, climbers, or floating gardens. Indexing is by both scientific and common names of plants.

The United States Department of Agriculture, Soil Conservation Service *National List of Scientific Plant Names* (Washington, D.C., USDA, 1982) is in two volumes: (1) list of plant names and (2) synonymy. The first volume lists accepted plant names for genera, species, subspecies, and varieties, and also lists accepted family names. There are symbols for plant habitats and for regions of distribution. The second volume, the synonym section, directs the user from various forms of names to the accepted names. This is important, for example, for botanists using various plant lists that may employ different names for the same plant.

Dictionaries

Botanical dictionaries are of two types, those giving word definitions and those listing plants. The word definition dictionaries will be described in the section of this chapter on quick reference tools. The ones listing plants will be described here.

Hortus Third by Liberty Hyde Bailey (New York, Macmillan, 1976) is a concise dictionary of plants cultivated in the United States and Canada, with various editions published since 1930. Arrangement is alphabetical by family and generic names and by key word for general topics, and the amount of information supplied ranges from a paragraph to several pages. Information includes species with descriptions, authors for that name, synonyms, and common names. There are plant drawings as needed, a glossary of botanical terms, and an index from common names of plants.

Also by Liberty Hyde Bailey is the *Standard Cyclopedia of Hor-*

ticulture (New York, Macmillan, 1935), published in three volumes. This work covers the plants that are normally considered to be part of the nursery or horticulture trade. Included is a key to the families and genera, and a name list. There is also a glossary of botanical and horticultural terms, and a synopsis of the plant kingdom. Articles are arranged by topic or name of plant, usually the common name. There are long articles under major crops, such as apples, with descriptions of varieties. Some articles under general topics, such as bedding or bulbs, are included. The Royal Horticultural Society *Dictionary of Gardening: A Practical and Scientific Encyclopedia of Horticulture* (Oxford, Clarendon, 2d edition 1956 reprinted with corrections 1974) is in four volumes and supplements. Arrangement is alphabetical by topic, which may be a plant name, family, insect pest, or more general subject such as arbour. Articles, written by subject specialists, include a definition or description, sometimes a drawing, sometimes a key to identification of species, and references to the literature.

Die Naturlichen Pflanzenfamilien (Leipzig, Engelmann, 1887–1909 and 2d edition 1924–) is commonly known among botanists as Engler and Prantl. This is one of the major works of plant taxonomy, and is used by many herbaria to organize their collections. It includes keys and descriptions of all plants. Many volumes of the second edition have been issued, and new volues are still being issued at irregular intervals.

The Harvard University *Gray Herbarium Index* (Boston, Mass., G. K. Hall, 1968–) is in ten oversize volumes and supplements. The supplements are now coming out in card form. This index lists taxonomic names of plants of the Western Hemisphere, beginning with the literature of 1886. Arrangement in the volumes is alphabetical by plant scientific name, and the source of the first taxonomic listing of the plant is given. The cards, now issued quarterly, list new names.

Some dictionaries specialize in certain types of plants, such as plants used by man. The *Dictionary of Useful Plants* by Nelson Coon (Emmaus, Pa., Rodale, 1974) intends to include the "most valuable useful plants of all parts of the United States, calling attention to the special merits of the plants," according to the preface. The dictionary is arranged by plant families and then alphabetically by the scientific names of the plants. Information is given on the family and on each plant, including the common name, where found, and uses. Drawings often illustrate characteristics of the plant for identification. The book is written in an informal and interesting style and includes, in addition to the dictionary, introductory sections on American Indians and their use of plant life, medicinal plants, poison plants, and so forth, each with a bibliography. There is an index by common and botanical plant names and by uses, for example, hair tonic. The *Dictionary of Useful and Everyday Plants and Their Common Names* by Frank N. Howes (Cambridge, Cambridge University Press, 1975) is arranged alphabetically by plant name, usually the common name, for example, carrot, with cross-references as needed. Trade names and names of economic or commercial plant products are included. Information given is the scientific name of the plant, where it is found, and its uses. Coverage is international, and there is a bibliography. The *Dictionary of Plants Used by Man* by George Usher (New York, Hafner, 1974) is arranged alphabetically by generic name and gives a brief description of the distribution of the genus and the number of species, and then a list of species with name authority, origin, and uses.

The *Gardener's Guide to Plant Names* by B. J. Healey (New York, Scribner, 1972) includes only plants that can be grown in open gardens and are generally available through plant nurseries. The main part is alphabetical by scientific name and gives such information as plant description, where found, and common names. A list of common names tells equivalent scientific names, and there is a brief glossary. The *Gardener's Dictionary of Plant Names* by Archibald W. Smith (New York, St. Martin's, 1972) treats the origin and meaning of some plant names. The main part is alphabetical by Latin name, genus, or species, and tells the meaning of the word, for example, "dioc'cus: Furnished with two berries or nuts."

Floras

North American Flora (New York, New York Botanical Garden, 1905–49 and series II 1954–   ) covers the flora of North America, including Mexico, Central America, and the West Indies. Volumes are issued irregularly, each one devoted to an order, family, or smaller group. The aim is to present descriptions of all plants growing in North America. In general each volume is made up of keys for identification, descriptions, a bibliography, and an index.

Two other major floras of the United States are the *New Britton and Brown Illustrated Flora of the Northeastern United States and Adjacent Canada* by Henry A. Gleason (New York, New York

D. anthelmintica Kuntze. The leaves are used by the natives of S.Africa to treat intestinal worms.

D. barbigera (Moore) Kuntze. Himalayan area. The rhizomes are used locally to treat intestinal worms.

D. blandfordii (Hope) C. Chr. Himalayas. The rhizome is used locally to treat intestinal worms.

D. filix-mas (L.) Schott.=Aspidium felixmas. (Male Fern, Male Shield Fern). The dried rhizome is used medicinally to combat tapeworms.

D. heterocarpa (Blume) Kuntze. Tropical Asia. In Malaya the fronds are rubbed on the skin to treat leucodermia. They are eaten as a vegetable in Penang.

D. odontoloma (Moore) C. Chr. Himalayas. The rhizomes are used locally to treat intestinal worms.

D. paleacea (Sw.) C. Chr. Tropical America. In Colombia the rhizome is used to treat intestinal worms.

D. pteroides Kuntze. Philippines. The stems are used locally to decorate baskets.

D. schimperiana (Hochst.) C. Chr. Himalayas. The rhizomes are used locally to treat intestinal worms.

D. spinulosum (O. F. Muell.) Sw. Temperate Europe, Asia and N.America. The rhizome (Rhizoma Filicis Maris) is used medicinally to treat intestinal worms. They are also eaten cooked on hot stones by the Eskimos.

DRYPETES Vahl. Euphorbiaceae. 200 spp. Tropics, S.Africa, E.Asia. Trees.

D. bisacata Gagnep.=Putranjiva roxburghii. India, Indochina. A decoction of the leaves and fruits is used locally in India to treat liver complaints and fevers and in Thailand to treat rheumatism. The leaves are also used to feed livestock.

D. longifolia Pax. and Hoffm.=Cyclostemon longifolius. Indonesia. The wood is fairly hard and durable. It is used locally for general construction work.

D. ovalis Pax. and Hoffm.=Hemicycla ovalis. (Melamon, Mentaos). Malaysia. The wood is yellow, very hard and heavy, but easy to work. It is used locally for house construction. The older wood darkens and is much used for making walking sticks.

D. simaluresis J. J. Sm. (Lebool fatooh). Indonesia. The heavy wood is immune to attack by insects. It is used for house-building and general construction work.

D. subsymmetrica J. J. Sm. See D. simaluresis.

DUABANGA Buch.-Ham. Sonneratiaceae. 3 spp. Indomalaya. Trees.

D. moluccana Blume. Malaysia. The wood is strong, though light. It is used locally for boards. The bark is ground with that of Mallotus moluccana to make a black dye used locally to stain baskets.

D. sonneratioides Buch.-Ham. India. The soft yellowish wood is used to make boats and canoes and tea boxes.

Duahi – Wrightia tinctoria.

Duahi – Wrightia tomentosa.

DUBOISIA R. Br. Solanaceae. 2 spp. Australia, New Caledonia. Woody shrubs.

D. hopwoodii F. v. Muell. Australia. The leaves and small twigs are chewed by the natives as a stimulant.

D. myoporoides R. Br. (Corkwood, Mgmeo). Australia. The plant contains hyoscine and hyoscyamine of which it is a potential commercial source. It is used locally to stupify fish.

DUCHESNEA Smith. Rosaceae. 6 spp. India, E.Asia. Herbs.

D. filipendula (Hemsl.) Focke.=Fragaria filipendula. China. The fruits (She-p'aotzu) are like strawberries and are eaten in China. The plant is cultivated locally.

Duck Acorn – Nelumbo pentapetala.

Duck Potato – Sagittaria latifolia.

Duckweed – Lemna minor.

Duckweed, Tropical – Pistia stratiotes.

Dudhali – Eryngium coeruleum.

Dudoa – Hydnocarpus alcalae.

Duffin Bean – Phaseolus lunatus.

Duggal Fibre – Sarcochlamys pulcherrima.

DUGUETIA A. St.-Hil. Annonaceae. 70 spp. Tropical America, W.Indies. Trees.

D. quitarensis Benth. W.Indies. (Cuban Lancewood, Jamaican Lancewood). The elastic wood is used for whip handles, fishing rods, cart shafts etc.

D. vallicola MacBride. (Yaya). Colombia. The wood is used locally for making tool handles.

Dugulu – Radlkofera calodendron.

Duhnual Balsam – Commiphora opobalsamum.

Dulgonia laticuspis Turcz.=Phyllonoma laticuspis.

Dulce, Pepper – Laurencia pinnatifida.

Dulse – Rhodymenia palmata.

Dumb Plant – Dieffenbachia seguina.

Fig. 10-1. Plant dictionary: *Dictionary of Plants Used by Man* by George Usher

Botanical Garden, 1952) and *Manual of the Vascular Plants of the Northeastern United States and Adjacent Canada* by Henry A. Gleason and Arthur Cronquist (New York, Van Nostrand Reinhold, 1963). Many floras cover plants of a smaller geographic area such as a state.

Field Guides

Guides for identification of plants are many and varied. Usually a guide will deal with only one kind of plant, for example, flowering plants, and/or one geographical area, for example, *Trees, Shrubs, and Flowers of the Midwest* by G. Eric Hultman (Chicago, Contemporary Books, 1978). Guides are often in a form called a "key," in which the user starts by observing a basic fact about a plant, for example, whether a tree has needles or is broad-leaved, for which he uses a certain section of the guide; then he narrows down the identification gradually, for example, if broad are the leaves simple or compound? opposite or alternate? and so forth—always leading to a more specific section of the guide until the plant is identified.

An example of a guide is from the Peterson Field Guide series: *Field Guide to the Trees and Shrubs* by George A. Petrides (Boston, Mass., Houghton Mifflin, 2d edition 1972). This guide is the same convenient small size as others in the series and uses the same schematic approach to point out visual or field differences between species. All illustrations are drawings with important features marked. It has five main sections: plants with needlelike or scalelike leaves, broad-leaved plants with opposite compound leaves, broad-leaved plants with opposite simple leaves, broad-leaved plants with alternate compound leaves, and broad-leaved plants with alternate simple leaves. Appendixes include winter keys to plants and keys to trees in leafy and leafless condition, and a glossary. A special feature is tree silhouette drawings of some trees that can be identified in that way.

Following is a listing of identification guides including those from the Peterson Field Guide series, published by Houghton Mifflin, and the Audubon Society series, published by Knopf.

Identification of algae and fungi:

Bigelow, Howard E. *Mushroom Pocket Field Guide.* New York, Macmillan, 1979.

Hale, Mason E. *How to Know the Lichens.* Dubuque, Iowa, Brown, 1969.
Lincoff, Gary H. *Audubon Field Guide to North American Mushrooms.* New York, Knopf, 1981.
Miller, Orson K. and Hope Miller. *Mushrooms in Color.* New York, Dutton, 1981.
Neuner, Andreas. *Mushrooms and Fungi.* Lawrence, Mass., Merrimack, 1979.
Prescott, G. W. *How to Know the Freshwater Algae.* Dubuque, Iowa, Brown, 3rd edition 1978.
Smith, Alexander and Nancy Weber. *The Mushroom Hunter's Field Guide.* Ann Arbor, Mich., University of Michigan, 1980.
Smith, Gilbert M. *The Fresh-Water Algae of the United States.* New York, McGraw-Hill, 2d edition 1950.

Identification of mosses and liverworts:

Conrad, Henry Shoemaker. *How to Know the Mosses and Liverworts: Pictured-Keys for Determining Many of the North American Mosses and Liverworts, with Suggestions and Aids for Their Study.* Dubuque, Iowa, Brown, revised edition 1956.
Crum, Howard A. and Lewis E. Anderson. *Mosses of Eastern North America.* New York, Columbia University Press, 1981.
Grout, A. J. *Mosses with Hand Lens and Microscope.* New York, Johnson, reprint 1972.

Identification of vascular plants:

Brown, Lauren. *Grasses; an Identification Guide.* Boston, Mass., Houghton Mifflin, 1979.
Cobb, Boughton. *Field Guide to the Ferns and Their Related Families.* Boston, Mass., Houghton Mifflin, 1977.
Edlin, Herbert L. *The Tree Key; a Guide to Identification in Garden, Field and Forest.* New York, Scribner, 1978.
Little, Elbert L. *Field Guide to North American Trees, Eastern Edition.* New York, Knopf, 1980.
Little, Elbert L. *Field Guide to North American Trees, Western Edition.* New York, Knopf, 1980.
Loewer, H. Peter. *Evergreens: A Guide to Landscape, Lawn and Garden.* Louisville, Ky., Walker, 1982.

Key: Hardwood Group B

Leaves alternate and simple (consisting of 1 blade).

A. Leaves deciduous.

   1. Flowers lacking petals.

      a. Flowers male or female.

         (1) Flowers produced in catkins; floral parts attached above the ovary (inferior), except for the corkwood family.

            (a) Leaves with leaf-like growths (stipules) at leafstalk base sometimes falling away; fruits dry capsule, winged, or acorns partly to totally enclosed by a cup or bur.

               (a1) Fruits many seeded, each seed with a tuft of hairs at the end; flowers lacking a calyx; family includes willows and poplars **Willow Family (Salicaceae), p. 456**

               (a2) Fruits 1-seeded, without a tuft of hairs at the end; flowers with a calyx.

                  (a2a) Leaves with many, usually fine, teeth; winged seeds or nuts in a catkin, the seeds usually covered by bracts; family includes birches, alders, hornbeams **Birch Family (Betulaceae), p. 385**
                  (a2b) Leaves entire, lobed, or coarsely toothed; fruit a nut enclosed in a bur or cup; family includes beeches, oaks, chestnut, chinkapins, tanoak **Beech Family (Fagaceae), p. 298**

            (b) Leaves without stipules; fruits fleshy to leathery, enclosing a hard stone fruit **Corkwood Family (Leitneriaceae), p. 264**

         (2) Flowers produced in dense heads or elongated clusters; flower parts attached at or near the base of the ovary.

Quaking Aspen

Black Willow

Eastern Hop Hornbeam

American Beech

Oregon White Oak

Pin Oak

Fig. 10–2. Field guide: *Complete Trees of North America* by Thomas S. Elias

Mickel, John T. *How to Know the Ferns and Fern Allies*. Dubuque, Iowa, Brown, 1979.

Niehaus, Theodore F. *Field Guide to Pacific States Wildflowers*. Boston, Mass., Houghton Mifflin, 1981.

Niering, William and Nancy Olmstead. *Field Guide to North American Wildflowers, Eastern Region*. New York, Knopf, 1979.

Peterson, Roger Tory and Margaret McKenny. *Field Guide to Wildflowers of Northeastern and North-Central North America*. Boston, Mass., Houghton Mifflin, 1968.

Spellenberg, Richard. *Field Guide to North American Wildflowers: Western Region*. New York, Knopf, 1979.

Usher, George. *Complete Trees of North America*. New York, Van Nostrand Reinhold, 1980.

Identification of wild plants:

Crockett, Lawrence J. *Wildly Successful Plants: A Handbook of North American Weeds*. New York, Macmillan, 1977.

Kirk, Donald R. *Wild Edible Plants of the Western United States*. Healdsburg, Calif., Naturegraph, 1970.

Muenscher, Walter C. *Weeds*. Ithaca, N.Y., Comstock, 1980.

Peterson, Lee. *Field Guide to Edible Wild Plants of Eastern and Central North America*. Boston, Mass., Houghton Mifflin, 1978.

Poisonous Plants

Dangerous Plants by John Tampion (New York, Universe, 1977) is intended for use by parents, gardeners, and teachers, and also possibly by physicians. It describes 100 plants in three groupings: those commonly cultivated, those frequently growing wild, and fungi. For each plant discussed it gives a sketch, a description, information on distribution and habitat and dangers, and a list of related plants. There are also chapters on plant poisons, allergies, and harmful substances in food. The appendix lists other plants with reference to where more information can be found. The book has a bibliography, and indexes of common names, scientific names, and subjects. *Know Your Poisonous Plants* by Wilma R. James (Healdsburg, Calif., Naturegraph, 1973) is arranged alphabetically by common names of plants. For each, it gives a drawing of the plant, a description, and signs of poisoning. General information on poisoning prevention and on first aid are also included. References, a glossary, and an index complete this useful volume. *Poisonous Plants* by Robert E. Arnold (Jeffersontown, Ky., Terra, 1978) is a pocket-size guide arranged alphabetically by common names of plants. A color photograph and description of each of the ninety-six poisonous plants are given, together with information as to what poisoning each can cause and brief information on treatment. There is an index.

Frequently books are available on poisonous plants in specific geographical areas, for example, Julio F. Morton's *Plants Poisonous to People in Florida and Other Warm Areas* (Miami, Fla., Fairchild Tropical Gardens, 1977).

Poisonous Plants of the United States and Canada by John M. Kingsbury (Englewood Cliffs, N.J., Prentice-Hall, 1964) is a reference book for physicians, veterinarians, and others interested in this subject. It includes all plants of the United States and Canada that at the time of publication were known to have poisoned people or livestock. There is some general discussion of the literature and history of poisons. Most of the book is arranged in chapters by plant group: algae, fungi, ferns, horsetails, gymnosperms, and angiosperms, with individual plants listed alphabetically in these chapters, with information on each, including specific antidotes to poisoning if known. Drawings are used as needed to help in identification.

Gardening

Principles of Gardening: A Guide to the Art, History, Science and Practice by Hugh Johnson (New York, Simon and Schuster, 1979) is a large volume packed with lovely color photographs of gardens and plants. There is a discussion of gardening, including hardiness, climate, soil, pests, and so forth, and then plants in general. Then there are sections by type of plant, for example, trees, hedges, climbing plants, and so forth. There is also a section on providing settings for the plants by use of paving, ponds and streams, decks, and so forth. The book ends with photographs and descriptions of gardens from history and of other countries. It has a brief bibliography, a glossary, and an index. The *Time-Life Encyclopedia of Gardening* (Alexandria, Va., Time-Life, 1, 1971-   ) is a series of slim volumes, issued at irregular intervals, on various gardening topics. Volumes are prepared by different authors, and each is complete in itself. For example, volume 27, *Shade Gardens* by Oliver E. Allen, has chapters on gardening in shade; working with shape, texture, and color; green plants; and flowers for shady areas. Then a plant dictionary section, arranged alphabetically by plant name, contains a color picture and information on each plant, including characteristics and how to grow the plant. Many lovely color photographs are used throughout the volume, some full-page or double-page spreads. The appendix includes characteristics of shade-garden plants in table form, and there is a bibliography, and an index. Other volumes in this series cover such topics as annuals, lawns and ground covers, flowering shrubs, vegetables and fruits, and greenhouse gardening. A comprehensive book on ornamentals is *Ornamental Plants, Their Care, Use, Propagation and Identification* by D. Dwight Wait (Dubuque, Iowa, Kendall/Hunt, 1977).

Andrew R. Addkinson's *100 Garden Plans* (New York, Random House, 1977) is a fascinating book able to spark anyone's imagination. The main part of the book consists of 100 plans for different home gardens, from formal to low-maintenance, ornamentals to wildflowers, each on a two-page spread with a perspective drawing to show how the garden would look and a plan drawing to visualize the space, and then an illustration of each suggested plant with information on its growth conditions, size, and so forth. Those interested in or working in landscape development will prefer *Plants in the Landscape* by Philip Lee Carpenter (San Francisco, Freeman, 1975). This book includes principles of landscape design and construction, and has many photographs and diagrams.

Most common gardening questions will be found answered in *10,000 Garden Questions Answered by 20 Experts* edited by Marjorie J. Dietz (Garden City, N.Y., Doubleday, 3d edition 1974). Arrangement is in sixteen sections by topic, for example, "soils and fertilizers" and "planning and landscaping." Each section is written by a sepecialist in that area, and contains questions with brief answers. A bibliography of sources for more information includes societies and botanical gardens. There is an index. *Getting the Most From Your Garden; Using Advanced Intensive Gardening Techniques* (Emmaus, Pa., Rodale, 1980) was prepared by the editors of *Organic Gardening* magazine. There are sections on intensive gardening using growing beds, interplanted gardens, and extending the growing season. First-hand accounts of people who do intensive gardening in several geographic areas of the United States complete the book. There is a bibliography, and an index.

New Plants From Old: Pruning and Propagating for the Indoor Garden by Charles M. Evans (New York, Random House, 1976) includes propagating plants from plant parts and from seeds, and pruning to keep the plants healthy and attractive. *Plant Propagation: Principles and Practices* by Hudson T. Hartmann (Englewood Cliffs, N.J., Prentice-Hall, 3d edition 1975) discusses propagation in general and also has information on specific selected annuals and herbaceous perennials used as ornamentals. There are references with each chapter. *Propagation* by Alan Toogood (New York, Stein and Day, 1981) contains techniques for getting new plants from old. It includes an extensive list of plants with proper methods of propagating them.

Westcott's Plant Disease Handbook by R. K. Horst (New York, Van Nostrand Reinhold, 4th edition 1979) contains a list of garden chemicals and describes methods of applying the chemicals. One chapter of the book lists plant diseases alphabetically by type, for example, bacterial diseases, blackspot, powdery mildews, and then for each type lists the pathogens alphabetically and then the common name of the disease with description and method of control. The next chapter lists the host plants: trees, shrubs, vines, flowers and vegetables, alphabetically by common name, and for each lists the heading as used in the previous disease section, and then the specific pathogens causing the disease, so that one can refer back to the disease chapter for discussion and control measures. The book has a glossary, a bibliography, and an index. The author suggests that because chemicals for treatment of plants change so rapidly, one should go to an agricultural agent for the latest information on chemicals, and also stresses the importance of not jumping to conclusions in home diagnosis of plant diseases.

J. Van der Plank has written *Disease Resistance in Plants* (New York, Academic, 1968) for plant pathologists, plant breeders, and those interested in ecology. This book discusses the nature of resistance to plant disease and how this can be used to protect crops. For up-to-date information, the Commonwealth Agricultural Bureaux in Kew, England publishes various indexes and reviews. For example, the *Index of Fungi,* published once a year, lists fungi and lichens alphabetically by generic name and gives bibliographic citations to information. The *Review of Plant Pathology,* published monthly, is arranged alphabetically by subject, for example, antibiotics, and gives bibliographic information and abstract. Most articles cited are available as photocopies from the Commonwealth Agricultural Bureaux. The *Multilingual Compendium of Plant Diseases* by Paul R. Miller (St. Paul, Minn., American Phytopathological Society, 1976–) includes only diseases with economic importance on a worldwide basis, and only those caused by fungi and bacteria. The name and description of each disease are given in English, with equivalent names in twenty-one languages and descriptions in French, Spanish, and Interlingua, which is a common language derived from most languages of the world. There are host indexes in various languages, and a brief annotated bibliography. Breeding plants for resistance to disease is discussed by Zoltan Kiraly in *Methods in Plant Pathology* (Amsterdam and New York, Elsevier, 1974). There is an extensive bibliography.

The *Ball Red Book* (West Chicago, Ill., George J. Ball, 13th edition 1975) is concerned with marketing of ornamentals. The first section of the book contains practical information on growing bedding plants to sell, including when to sow, containers, medium, pest and disease control, greenhouses, and more. The second part is arranged alphabetically by plant name, and gives information on plant culture, which is useful for home or commercial growers. *Introduction to Floriculture* edited by Roy A. Larson (New York, Academic, 1980) is aimed at both students and commercial growers. The first part of the book deals with cut flowers, including chrysanthemums, carnations, roses, snapdragons, orchids, gladioli, and other minor plants. Other sections cover potted plants, including bulbous plants, azaleas, chrysanthemums, gloxinias and violets, poinsettias, Easter lilies, hydrangeas, cyclamen, begonias, and kalanchoe; bedding plants; hanging baskets; and foliage plants. Illustrations and references are included in each chapter, and there is a glossary, and an index.

The *Complete Guide to Flower and Foliage Arrangement* edited by Iris Webb (New York, Doubleday, 1979) contains many color illustrations covering various areas discussed, such as basic principles of arrangement, drying and preserving, church flowers, and ikebana.

Periodicals

Listed here are a fiew of the many journals devoted to botany.

American Journal of Botany; Official Publication of the Botanical Society of America. Lancaster, Pa., Botanical Society of America, 1914– . (10/year)

Annals of Botany. London, Academic, 1887– . (monthly)

Annual Review of Plant Physiology. Palo Alto, Calif., Annual Reviews, 1950– . (annual)

Arnold Arboretum. Journal. Cambridge, Mass., Harvard University, 1919– . (quarterly)

Arnoldia. Cambridge, Mass., Harvard University, 1941– . (6/year)

Bonsai Bulletin. New York, Bonsai Society of Greater New York, 1963– . (quarterly)

Botanical Gazette. Chicago, University of Chicago Press, 1875– . (quarterly)

Botanical Magazine. Tokyo, Botanical Society of Japan, 1887– . (quarterly) (in English)

Brittonia. New York, New York Botanical Garden, 1931– . (quarterly)

Canadian Journal of Botany. Ottawa, Canada, National Research Council of Canada, 1929– . (monthly)

Economic Botany, Society for Economic Botany. New York, New York Botanical Garden, 1947– . (quarterly)

Harvard University Botanical Museum. Botanical Museum Leaflets. Cambridge, Mass., Botanical Museum, 1932– . (irregular, approx. 5/year)

Journal of Experimental Botany, Society for Experimental Biology. London, Oxford University, 1950– . (bimonthly)

New York Botanical Garden Memoirs. New York, Botanical Garden, 1900– . (irregular)

Plant Physiology. Lancaster, Pa., American Society of Plant Physiologists, 1926– . (monthly)

Watsonia: Journal and Proceedings of the Botanical Society of the British Isles. London, Botanical Society of the British Isles, 1949– . (semiannual)

Here are some of the journals devoted to gardening and horticulture.

American Horticulturist. Mount Vernon, Va., American Horticultural Society, 1922– . (bimonthly)

American Orchid Society Bulletin. Cambridge, Mass., Harvard University Botanical Museum, 1932– . (monthly)

American Rose Magazine. Shreveport, La., American Rose Society, 1933– . (monthly)

American Society for Horticultural Science. Journal. Alexandria, Va., Society, 1903– . (bimonthly)

Cactus Comments. Brooklyn, N.Y., New York Cactus and Succulent Society, 1962– . (monthly)

Camellia Journal. Fort Valley, Ga., American Camellia Society, 1946– . (4/year)

Flower and Garden, in three editions, Northern, Southern, and Western. Kansas City, Mo., Mid-America, 1957– . (monthly)

Garden. New York, New York Botanical Garden, 1977– . (bimonthly)

Gardener. Des Moines, Iowa, Men's Garden Clubs of America, 1958– . (bimonthly)

Horticulture. Boston, Mass., Massachusetts Horticultural Society, 1904– . (monthly)

Hortscience. Alexandria, Va., American Society for Horticultural Science, 1966– . (quarterly)

Missouri Botanical Garden Bulletin. St. Louis, Mo., Missouri Botanical Garden, 1913– . (6/year)

Organic Gardening. Emmaus, Pa., Rodale, 1942– . (monthly)

Plants Alive. Seattle, Wash., Plants, Inc., 1972– . (monthly)

Plants and Gardens. Brooklyn, N.Y., Brooklyn Botanic Garden, 1945– . (quarterly)

CURRENT AWARENESS MATERIALS

Current Advances in Plant Science (Oxford, Pergamon, 1972–), published monthly, is arranged in broad subject categories, with an author index. It gives bibliographic information on new works in all areas of plant sciences including forestry, ecology, conservation, and pollution, in addition to general botany. Coverage is international.

QUICK REFERENCE TOOLS

Dictionaries

The *Dictionary of Botany* by R. John Little and C. E. Jones (New York, Van Nostrand Reinhold, 1980) contains approximately 5,500 definitions from all fields of botany. Arrangement is alphabetical by term, and definitions range from a phrase to a few sentences, with drawings to illustrate as needed. Most taxonomic and common plant names are omitted. A brief bibliography is included. *Collegiate Dictionary of Botany* by Delbert Swartz (New York, Ronald, 1971) according to the preface contains "nearly 24,000 entries compiled from more than 170 sources." Because it excludes botanical terms in general use that would be found in the average dictionary, its size is especially impressive. Arrangement is alphabetical, with brief definitions. Plant names are not included.

Elsevier's Dictionary of Horticulture (Amsterdam, Elsevier, 1970) is a foreign language dictionary for French, Dutch, German, Danish, Swedish, Spanish, Italian, and Latin terms. The basic part is alphabetical by term in the English language and gives synonyms in each other language. Indexes in each other language lead to numbered entries in the basic part so that one can translate from any of the languages represented into any other languages. No definitions are given. *Elsevier's Dictionary of Botany* (New York, Elsevier, 1979–) is also a foreign language dictionary, in two volumes. Volume one covers names of plants, trees, shrubs, mushrooms, and lichens, and volume two covers general botanical terms other than plant names. Arrangement of the first section is alphabetical by term in English, with equivalents in French, German, and Latin. Indexes from French, German, and Latin terms refer to the first section. Russian equivalents in the Cyrillic alphabet are in a separate section.

B-P-H: Botanico-Periodicum-Huntianum edited by G. H. M. Lawrence and others (Pittsburgh, Pa., Hunt Botanical Library, 1968) is a listing of abbreviations of periodical titles for botanical literature.

Information is given as to the full title of the periodical, volumes and dates published, title changes if any, and place of publication.

Directories

The Green Thumbook by Marion Schroeder (Cary, Ill., Valley Crafts, 2d edition 1975) is a directory of garden sources. The main part is arranged by product: seeds, herbs, vegetable plants, and so forth, and also many specialities such as wildflowers, rock and alpine plants, and orchids, and is an annotated directory of dealers in the United States. Information and sources are given for some special products such as plant lights, and there is a selected list of garden books and periodicals. An address is included to which one may write for supplements issued to keep this volume up to date. Most areas or states have nurserymen and growers associations with lists of nurserymen in those areas.

The *Flowering Plant Index of Illustration and Information* compiled by R. T. Isaacson (Boston, Mass., G. K. Hall, 1979) is a three-volume set listing sources of pictures of flowering plants. Approach is by common or botanical scientific name.

Directories of Botanical Gardens

Explorers were surprised by the botanical gardens in early Aztec Mexico, but by the mid-sixteenth century Italy, Holland, and Germany had such gardens. Today there are display gardens in most countries of the world, varying in size from part of an acre to over 1,000 acres, and the few hundred species represented in the early gardens have grown to tens of thousands of species in some gardens.

The *Gardener's Directory* by Joseph W. Stephenson (Garden City, N.Y., Hanover House, 1960) has a traveler's guide to places of horticultural interest in the United States. Botanical gardens and arboretums, garden centers, and other places of horticultural interest are listed alphabetically by state, with brief information on each. An international horticulture section, alphabetical by country, lists more than 1,200 gardens, arboretums, and other places outside the United States with location and, for some, a brief description. This book also lists horticultural organizations in the United States with addresses and information on activities, and government agencies and other sources of information.

Edward S. Hyam's *Great Botanical Gardens of the World* (New York, Macmillan, 1969) is a larger volume with beautiful photographs, both in color and in black and white, and also drawings. It is arranged geographically: Europe, North America, the Soviet Union, the Tropics, the Southern Hemisphere, and Japan; and it gives general history and information about gardens in each country and then information on specific gardens, often with lovely photographs and a map of the garden. At the back of the book is a list of the world's botanical gardens with addresses, and a world map marking their locations. The *International Directory of Botanical Gardens* compiled by D. M. Henderson and H. T. Prentice (Utrecht, Netherlands, Bohn, Scheltema and Holkema, 3d edition 1977) is arranged alphabetically by country and then by city, and gives such information about botanical gardens as address, administration, area, rainfall, facilities such as herbarium or greenhouse, and when and to whom the garden is open as well as the name of the director. There is an index to personal names and to names of cities and gardens.

11
Zoology

INTRODUCTORY MATERIALS

A good introduction to the field of zoology may be found in many pictorial works. The *Audubon Society Book of Wild Animals* by Les Line and Edward Ricciuti (New York, Abrams, 1977) is a large-size volume containing 181 beautiful color photographs of mammals, most on double-page spreads. Arrangement is in chapters such as "Life in the Trees," "Marsupial Marvels," and "Mammals with Wings," with an informative essay and the photographs making up each chapter. *Wild America* by James Lockhart (Nashville, Tenn., Thomas Nelson, 1979), also an oversize volume, contains some of the paintings and drawings of the author done over the preceding twenty-five years, with the aim of showing the beauty of American wildlife in its natural habitats. Narrative discussion of conservation and ecology is woven through the pages of photographs. *Wild Mammals of Northwest America* by Arthur Savage and Candace Savage (Baltimore, Md., Johns Hopkins University Press, 1981) explores the behavior, ecology, and natural history of seventy different North American mammals, with many color photographs included.

Wildlife by Robert B. Smith (Portland, Oreg., Belding, 1976) contains lovely color photographs from Western North America by the author, with a brief description of the photographs and text by Robert M. Storm. *Wild Creatures* by Russell Franklin (New York, Simon and Schuster, 1975), described by its subtitle as "a pagent of the untamed," is a handsome volume with glossy color photographs, many of them two-page spreads. It is arranged in sections by type of habitat, for example, sea, shore, wetlands, and desert, and gives introductory information and then the photographs with a description of each. The *Audubon Wildlife Treasury* (Philadelphia, Pa., Lippincott, 1976) was published in cooperation with the National Audubon Society. It consists of a series of essays on natural history by leading naturalists, most focusing on a particular animal, and includes beautiful full-page color photographs. *The Amazing World of Animals* (New York, Praeger, 1975) is arranged in sections by type of animal: large mammals, smaller mammals, birds, amphibians and reptiles, fish, insects, and evolution, and it also includes lovely color photographs.

There are many textbook-type sources of information on general zoology. Two examples of these are *Integrated Principles of Zoology* by Cleveland P. Hickman (St. Louis, Mo., Mosby, 6th edition 1979) and *Zoology: An Introduction to the Study of Animals* by Richard A. Boolootian (New York, Macmillan, 1979), which is divided into five main parts: approach to zoology; animal diversity, invertebrates; animal diversity, vertebrates; design and function of organ systems; and continuity of life. There is usually a glossary, as well as references for further study. The index will lead the user to answers to specific questions.

Interesting reading on history may be found in George Jennison's *Noah's Cargo: Some Curious Chapters of Natural History* (New York, B. Blom, 1971) and Hoffman R. Hays's *Birds, Beasts, and Men: A Humanist History of Zoology* (New York, Putnam, 1972). *Turning Points in Zoological Science* (London, Royal Society, 1977) contains eight articles, each by a different author, all of which were part of a discussion meeting. The papers were chosen to illustrate advances in zoology in the past 150 years, and there are references with each paper. *The History of Life* by Arcie Lee McAlester (Englewood Cliffs, N.J., Prentice-Hall, 2d edition 1977) begins with the first primitive organisms of several billion years ago and carries through to about 5,000 years ago. The evolutionary sequence of fossils is stressed.

Subject Headings and Classification

Animal ecology
Animals
Entomology
Herpetology
Ichthyology

Laboratory animals
Ornithology
Poisonous animals
Variation (Biology)
Zoo animals
Zoogeography
Zoological gardens
Zoological research
Zoological specimens—Collection and Preservation
Zoologists
Zoology
  (also subdivisions of Zoology)
  —Classification
  —Pictorial works
  —Terminology
Zoology, Experimental
Zoonoses

Materials on zoology will usually be found shelved in libraries in the QL section of the Library of Congress classification or in the 590 to 599 section of the Dewey Decimal Classification.

BIBLIOGRAPHIC MATERIALS

Catalog

The *Catalogue of the Library of the Museum of Comparative Zoology, Harvard University* (Boston, Mass., G. K. Hall, 1968) consists of eight volumes and covers works published to 1966 with supplements for later works. This bibliography is composed of reproductions of catalog cards from this outstanding library collection of more than 250,000 volumes. Arrangement is alphabetical by author and title; there is no subject approach. Books and periodicals are included.

Indexing and Abstracting Services

Zoological Record (London, Zoological Society, 1, 1864–) is published annually, covering books and periodical literature. The *Record* is divided into sections. The first section covers new literature on comprehensive, general zoology, and following are sections for many phyla or classes; the final section lists the new genera and subgenera contained in the volume for that year. *Bulletin Signaletique part 364: Protozoaires et Invertebres Zoologie Generale et Appliquee* and *part 365: Zoologie des Vertebres, Ecologie Animale, Physiologie Appliquee Humaine* (Paris, Centre de Documentation, 1961–) are arranged in subject groups and give bibliographic information and a brief abstract. There are indexes by subject and author in each issue and cumulated yearly. This service provides up-to-date international coverage of articles in periodicals and of reports and meetings, in twelve issues per year. *Wildlife Review* (Washington, D.C., U.S. Fish and Wildlife Service, 1, 1935–), published quarterly, gives bibliographic information only, no abstract, and in most cases the address of the author. Arrangement is in subject groups and then alphabetical by author; indexes are by author and subject, and there is a geographic index.

Several indexing and abstracting services cover materials of specialized areas of zoology. Five of these are listed here as examples:

Abstracts of Entomology. Philadelphia, Pa., BioSciences Information Service, 1970– . (monthly)

Animal Behavior Abstracts. Association for the Study of Animal Behavior. London, Information Retrieval, 1973– . (quarterly)

Animal Breeding Abstracts: A Monthly Abstract of World Literature. Slough, England, Commonwealth Agricultural Bureaux, 1933– . (monthly)

Entomology Abstracts. London, Informational Retrieval, 1969– . (monthly)

Sport Fishery Abstracts: An Abstracting Service for Fishery Research and Management. Washington, D.C., U.S. Fish and Wildlife Service, 1955– . (quarterly)

SECONDARY LITERATURE MATERIALS

Encyclopedias

Grzimek's Animal Life Encyclopedia by Bernhard Grzimek (New York, Van Nostrand Reinhold, 1972–75) is in thirteen volumes arranged by these animal groups: lower animals, insects, mollusks and echinoderms, fish and amphibians, reptiles, birds, and mammals. Each volume contains chapters arranged by appropriate groupings, which include articles by subject specialists; a systematic classification index for animals covered by that volume; a polyglot dictionary of animal names in English, German, French, and Russian; a bibliography; and an index. The *World Encyclopedia of Animals* edited by Maurice Burton (New York, World, 1972), in one volume, begins with a review of classification and nomenclature and information on each animal phylum and its classes. Then there are articles of about 200 words on specific animals arranged alphabetically by the common name of the animal, and including diagrams as needed and photographs, some in lovely color. The *New Larousse Encyclopedia of Animal Life* (New York, Larousse, 1980) is one large volume. Arrangement is in chapters by animal phyla. Each chapter begins with discussion of the phylum as a whole; for example, the chapter on birds includes sections on feathers and pigmentation, beak and alimentary canal, wings and flight, legs, and so forth. Depending on the size and diversity of the phylum, information may also be given on classes, orders, and families. There are many lovely color photographs used throughout, and drawings and diagrams. The book is completed by a glossary, a bibliography, and an index.

International Wildlife Encyclopedia by Maurice Burton and Robert Burton (New York, Cavendish, 1969) is made up of twenty slim volumes consisting of articles of from one to several pages, often with several color photographs. Arrangement is alphabetical by the common name of the animal, or by topic in the case of the few articles on other topics such as adaptation. There are three indexes: by animal name, by subject, and systematic.

Classification

Two textbooks that discuss classification and naming of animals are *Principles of Animal Taxonomy* by George G. Simpson (New York, Columbia University Press, 1961) and *Taxonomy* by Richard E. Blackwelder (New York, Wiley, 1967). Each of these books contains a bibliography for further study, and another bibliography is the *Guide to the Taxonomic Literature of Vertebrates* by Richard E. Blackwelder (Ames, Iowa, Iowa State University Press, 1972).

A listing of scientific names officially accepted up to 1955 may be found in Sheffield Neave's *Nomenclator Zoologicus* (London, Zoological Society of London, 1939–66), published in six volumes over the years indicated. These are generic names, arranged alphabetically. This list is kept up to date by the *Zoological Record,* mentioned earlier.

Classification of Living Animals by Nathaniel Rothschild (New York, Wiley, 1961) is a sort of table to be used to find out how the animal kingdom or parts of it are classified. The main part is a classification of living animals. For each phylum, it lists classes and subclasses, and for each of these lists orders and suborders, with examples of animals in each order by scientific and common names. There is a list of references including those on which the classification is based and sources for futher reading, as well as an index to phyla, classes, and so forth, and to genera. The index also lists genera not mentioned in the classification and tells where they would be classified.

Invertebrates

How Invertebrates Live by Kaye Mash (London, Elsevier-Phaidon, 1975) is arranged in chapters by topic, for example, food chains, parasites, reproduction, colors, and venoms. This is an interesting book with many color photographs, and diagrams as needed. *Invertebrates* by W. D. Russell-Hunter (New York, Macmillan, 1979) is a text for beginning students of invertebrates. Its arrangement is in chapters by groups of invertebrates, such as Protozoa, and some chapters of general information, including fossils. A review gives references for further reading. *Animals Without Backbones* by Ralph M. Buchsbaum (Chicago, University of Chicago Press, 2d edition 1975) contains introductory-level material on invertebrates.

Techniques for collecting and preserving invertebrates are discussed in *Invertebrate Animals, Collection and Preservation* (London, British Museum and Cambridge University Press, 1979). The first part treats each of thirty-nine main groupings of invertebrates by phyla and classes, and gives for each a brief description, habitat, and methods of collection and preservation. Each group is illustrated by drawings. Other parts of the book deal with collecting methods and apparatus, methods of killing, fixing, and preserving, and general treatment of collections. Insects are not included in this book.

Seashell Parade by A. Gordon Melvin (Rutland, Vt., Tuttle, 1973) is subtitled "fascinating facts, pictures and stories," which describes the book well. There are stories about shells and information on their curious and interesting aspects, as well as information on collecting them. *The Seas and Their Shells: A Collector's Guide to the Seashells of the World* by Sergio Angeletti (Garden City, N.Y., Doubleday, 1978) is, according to the preface, a "tourist guide to the most important shells." The first part of the book discusses shells in general; the second part briefly discusses each sea in the world, and presents color photographs of many of the shells found in each sea, giving the name of the shell, where found, and its size; whereas the third part discusses shell collecting: where and how to collect shells and how to arrange them.

Insects

The Insects (San Francisco, Freeman, 1977) contains readings by different authors taken from the magazine *Scientific American*. There are several articles on each of the following areas: anatomy and physiology, neurobiology and behavior, processes of evolution and ecology, life styles, and insects and mankind. There are photographs and drawings, and a bibliography. *Insects in Perspective* by Michael D. Atkins (New York, Macmillan, 1978) is written as a text for background reading for students taking course in entomology. There is a glossary, and the appendix lists and describes the orders of insects with drawings to illustrate each. C. P. Friedlander's *Biology of Insects* (New York, Pica, 1976) assumes an advanced knowledge of biology, with the aim, according to the preface, of giving students information on the "nature of insects as animals that are perfectly and widely adapted to life on land, and the influence on man's economy that stems from the perfection of their adaptation."

Textbook of Entomology by A. D. Imms and others (New York, Halsted, 10th revised edition 1978) is in two volumes: (1) *Structure, Physiology, and Development* and (2) *Classification and Biology*. The first volume has chapters on individual parts of anatomy and physiology, such as the thorax, muscular system, and so forth; and on embryology and postembryonic development. References are included with each chapter, and there is an index for volume one. The second volume is arranged by orders of insects, and contains several pages on each, including a description, and lists and descriptions of families in the order. References are included for each order. Another basic text is Donald J. Borror's *Introduction to the Study of Insects* (New York, Holt, Rinehart and Winston, 4th edition 1976).

The hobbyist interested in collecting insects will enjoy Richard L. Ford's *Practical Entomology; Guide to Collecting Butterflies, Moths, and Other Insects* (London and New York, Warne, 1963). Catching, killing, and displaying insects are covered, as well as breeding, attracting butterflies and moths, and making a sub-terrarium to observe life as it is underground. There is a list of recommended reading. Alvah Peterson's *Entomological Techniques: How to Work with Insects* (Los Angeles, Entomological Reprint Specialists, 10th edition 1964, 1976 printing) is aimed at amateurs or professionals, but is especially good for amateurs, teachers, and professional biologists with little training in entomology. Included are techniques of collecting, preserving, and rearing, and illustrations and instructions for making cages and other equipment.

Fundamentals of beekeeping are presented in *Practical Beekeeping* by Enoch H. Thompkins (Charlotte, Vt., Garden Way, 1977). Also for the beginner is *Guide to Bees and Honey* by Ted Hooper (Emmaus, Pa., Rodale, 1977). The author begins with information on bees such as behavior, and then goes on to provide practical information on beekeeping and harvesting the honey. There is a bibliography, and an index. *Bees, Beekeeping, Honey and Pollination* by Walter L. Gojmerac (Westport, Conn., Avi, 1980) is designed to be a text for bee-keeping courses, including those in adult education or extension. The purpose of the book is to organize information on bees, beekeeping, honey production, and polination, concentrating on the rationale behind specific operations rather than "how to" aspects. The book has a bibliography with each chapter, a glossary, and an index.

Fish

How Fishes Live by Peter Whitehead (London, Elsevier-Phaidon, 1975) has chapters on such topics as feeding, breeding, senses, and distribution of fish. Color photographs make the book especially interesting. Carl E. Bond's *Biology of Fishes* (Philadelphia, Pa., Saunders, 1979) is intended to be an introduction to the study of fish for students and general readers. There are three sections: (1) introduction and structure of fish, (2) relationships and diversification of fish, and (3) biology and special topics. The book has a glossary and references. *Fun with Fish; A Hobby Guide for Fishermen* by Bob Frankowick (Milwaukee, Wis., Milwaukee Public Museum, 1972) covers taxidermy, photography, and fish prints.

Reptiles and Amphibians

Reptiles and Amphibians of North America by Alan E. Leviton (New York, Doubleday, 1970) is in sections grouping these animals by the orders to which they belong: amphibians—salamanders, frogs, and toads; and reptiles—lizards, snakes, turtles, crocodiles, and alligators. In each case there is information on the order, and then a section for each family, including information on the genera and species in that family, illustrated by lovely color photographs.

Birds

When we think of books about birds, both the names Audubon and Peterson are likely to come to mind. These names are combined in a volume edited by Roger Tory Peterson, *Audubon Birds of America* (New York, Crown, 1978), which contains prints of 102 paintings by John James Audubon with commentaries by Peterson, and also a brief biographical sketch of Audubon by Peterson.

Audubon Society Encyclopedia of North American Birds by John K. Terres (New York, Knopf, 1980) contains detailed descriptions of 847 birds of North America. Arrangement is alphabetical by name of bird. Many drawings and color plates are included. There is a bibliography.

The *Great Book of Birds* by John Gooders (New York, Dial, 1975) contains introductory material including historical information on birds, and general information on birds including an interesting chart showing different forms of bill and foot structure. The main part of the book is arranged by families of birds and gives information and usually a color photograph. There is a selected bibliography.

Introduced Birds of the World: The Worldwide History, Distribution, and Influence of Birds Introduced to New Environments by John L. Long (New York, Universe, 1981) includes all known introductions of birds around the world. The impact of the birds is discussed from the standpoint of crop damage, competition with native species, hybridization, disease transfer, and habitat range fluctuations.

Behaviors of birds such as running and swimming, individual and social actions, birdsongs, and egg laying and nesting are discussed by Robert Burton in *How Birds Live* (London, Elsevier-Phaidon, 1975). There are also beautiful color photographs. Another book on this topic is *Guide to the Behavior of Common Birds* by Donald W. Stokes (Boston, Mass., Little, Brown, 1979), which also includes a bibliography for further reading. The serious bird watcher may be interested in books that give information in more depth on specific topics about birds. Two examples, each of which includes bibliographies for further reading, are *Bird Sounds and Their Meaning* by Rosemary Jellis (London, British Broadcasting Corporation, 1977) and Georg Rüpperll's *Bird Flight* (New York, Van Nostrand Reinhold, 1975).

Backyard Bird Watcher by George H. Harrison (New York, Simon and Schuster, 1979) includes some excellent ideas for planting your yard to attact birds, feeding stations, bird photography, and suggested readings. *Beyond The Bird Feeder* by John W. Dennis (New York, Knopf, 1981) has the descriptive subtitle "the habits and behavior of feeding-station birds when they are not at your feeder." Information is included on feeders, types of food, bathing, anting, and so forth, with references.

Audubon Society Handbook for Birders by Stephen W. Kress (New York, Scribner, 1981) is a handbook for amateur birders, but not a field guide. Included are field trip techniques, record keeping, photography, lists of educational programs, bird tours, research programs, and ornithological societies. Michael Scofield's *Complete Outfitting and Source Book for Bird Watching* (Marshall, Calif., Great Outdoors Trading Company, 1978) is a fascinating book for the bird watcher, including a history of bird watching and information on equipment. Equipment includes binoculars, scopes, telephoto lenses, portable tape recorders, and microphones, and there is information on how to choose them and on specific items on the market. The book also contains an annotated bibliography of books and magazines, a list of bird watching clubs, general information on good places to see birds and a list alphabetically by state of wildlife refuges and other excellent sites, information about tours specializing in bird watching and list of some of them worldwide, a glossary, and much useful miscellaneous information such as plants to attact birds to your home. *Guide to North American Bird Clubs* (Elizabethtown, Ky., Avian, 1978) has sections for national organizations, and then for state and local clubs in the United States, Canada, and other North American areas. In addition to information about each organization such as contact person and meeting times, a "field trip" note for each club lists specific places where birding is especially good in that area. Outline maps of states have club locations marked.

Birds of the World: A Checklist by James Clements (New York, Facts on File, 1981) lists the classification and status, that is, rare or endangered, for more than 10,000 birds. Important sightings, nesting habits, and so forth are given. There is a bibliography, and indexing is by scientific and common name.

Mammals

Between one and 1.5 million animal species have been described, and of these about 12,000 are species of mammals living today. *Mammalogy* by Harvey L. Gunderson (New York, McGraw-Hill, 1976) has as its theme how mammals have adapted to change and have survived through time. There are chapters on internal environment, hibernation, reproduction, homes, and behavior, in addition to general information on characteristics of mammals, and their classification. Also titled *Mammalogy* is a book by Terry A. Vaughan (Philadelphia, Pa., Saunders, 2d edition 1978). Preliminary material deals with characteristics of mammals, evolution, and an introduction to classification of mammals. Each order of mammals is discussed in subsequent chapters, including the families of each, and the book ends with topics such as ecology, zoogeography, behavior, and reproduction. Both mammalogy books include bibliographies.

Mammals of North America by E. Raymond Hall (New York, Wiley, 2d edition 1981) is in two volumes. The first edition of this book has established it as the standard taxonomic work on North American mammals. All native North American mammals are listed in evolutionary sequence. Detailed physical descriptions and measurements are given for most. There is a bibliography. Indexing is by scientific and common names.

Some books deal with a particular aspect or a particular mammal. Examples of these are:

Anderson, Rudolph Martin. *Methods of Collecting and Preserving Vertebrate Animals.* Ottawa, Canada, Cloutier, King's Printer, 2d edition 1948.
Barkalow, Frederick S. J. and Monica Shorten. *The World of the Grey Squirrel.* Philadelphia, Pa., Lippincott, 1973.
Big Game of North America, prepared under the auspices of the Wildlife Management Institute. Harrisburgh, Pa., Stackpole Books, 1978.
Leyhausen, Paul C. *Cat Behavior.* New York, Garland, 1979.
Young, J. Z. *Life of Mammals: Their Anatomy and Physiology.* Oxford, Clarendon, 2d edition 1975.

Animal Habits and Behavior

Author Bernard Stonehouse in *Young Animals* (New York, Viking, 1973) explores the struggle for survival in mammals and in some animals that receive little or no parental care, including insects, amphibians, birds, and reptiles. Color photographs, diagrams, and charts add to the interest of this book. *Complete Care of Orphaned or Abandoned Baby Animals* by C. E. Spaulding and Jackie Spaulding (Emmaus, Pa., Rodale, 1979) begins with fascinating tales of animal babies raised by the authors, and then has chapters on various animals, for example, foals, calves, fawns, raccoons, birds, and poultry. Each chapter contains specific instructions for care and includes, where appropriate, how to prepare the animal for release into the wild. The book has a glossary, a bibliography, and information on first aid equipment needed.

A lovely introduction to ethology, the study of animal behavior, is *The Living Forest: A World of Animals* by Rien Poortvliet (New York, Abrams, 1979). This volume contains paintings by the author with several pages of introductory discussion on each animal and then notes with drawings to show features such as foot and tracks, habitat, and how an animal pounces on its food. Another pictorial introduction is *Private Lives of Animals* by Milton A. Rugoff (New York, Grosset and Dunlap, 1974).

Grzimek's Encyclopedia of Ethology (New York, Van Nostrand

Reinhold, 1977) is a one-volume encyclopedia of animal behavior, for nonspecialists although chapters are written by subject experts and do use some technical language. Some topics included are history of ethology, visual sense, chemical sense, mechanical senses, electrical senses, hormones and behavior, learning and play, courtship, and language of the bees. There is a list of supplementary readings, as well as a glossary and an index.

In *Cult of the Wild* (Garden City, N.Y., Anchor, 1977) Boyce Rensberger deals with ten major species about which zoological research has now invalidated many long-held popular beliefs: lions, wolves, gorillas, elephants, sharks, baboons, hyenas, bears, crocodiles, whales, and dolphins. *Just Like an Animal* by Maurice Burton (New York, Scribner, 1978) contains some fascinating stories of humanlike behavior in animals that seems to indicate intelligence. Chapters have such interesting titles as "Compassionate Elephants," "Graves and Graveyards," "Heroism Investigated," and "Midwives and Nursemaids."

Also of interest by Maurice Burton is *How Mammals Live* (London, Elsevier, 1975), which illustrates with lovely color photographs chapters on exploratory behavior and curiosity, food and feeding, breeding, territory, hibernation, and grooming. *Secret Life of Animals: Pioneering Discoveries in Animal Behavior* by Lorus Milne and Margery Milne (New York, Dutton, 1975) has chapters on the senses, migration, mating, parenting, hunting, and other such topics, illustrated with color photography. Donald A. Dewsbury's *Comparative Animal Behavior* (New York, McGraw-Hill, 1978) is written on the level of a text in a first undergraduate course in animal behavior and comparative psychology. After some introductory material, aspects of behavior are explored, including locomotion, exploration, reproductive patterns, social patterns, development of behavior through genetics and experience, mechanisms correlated with behavior, evolution of behavior, functions of behavior, and learning. References are included, and indexing is by name, animal species, and subject.

Animal Communication

Look Who's Talking! by Emily Hahn (New York, Crowell, 1978) provides interesting reading on communication, illustrated by black and white photographs. Flora Davis's *Eloquent Animals* (New York, Coward, McCann, and Geoghegan, 1978), subtitled "a study in animal communication: how chimps lie, whales sing, and slime molds pass the message along," consists mostly of chapters on particular animals including chimps, ants, bears, whales, and birds, with a bibliography for further study.

Secret Languages of the Sea by Robert F. Burgess (New York, Dodd, 1981) is a survey of marine animal communication. Sharks, whales, Florida manatees, and dolphins are discussed. The work of researcher John Lilly is included. *Communication Between Man and Dolphin: The Possibilities of Talking with Other Species* by John C. Lilly (New York, Crown, 1978) is the story of John Lilly's research and findings, and that of his co-workers, which have led to the new belief about dolphins being very intelligent. An extensive annotated bibliography is included. *Animal Communication* by Hubert Frings (Norman, Okla., University of Oklahoma Press, 2d edition 1977) also includes an extensive bibliography.

Zoonoses

Diseases of animals that affect man, called zoonoses, are the subject of *Diseases Transmitted from Animals to Man* by William T. Hubbert (Springfield, Ill., Thomas, 6th edition, 1975). The book is in sections by type of disease: bacterial, mycotic, parasitic, and viral, with additional sections on noninfectious diseases and vectors of disease, and a summary in table form of diseases, hosts, and transmission. Chapters in each section are by different authors, specialists in the field, and discuss the disease and methods of its control. References are also included in each chapter.

The *CRC Handbook Series in Zoonoses* (Boca Raton, Fla., CRC, 1979–   ) is designed to be used in isolating and describing the agent, diagnosis and treatment of the disease in people, and control by health officials. Each section, written by an authority in that field, brings together information known to date, and includes references.

Zoogeography

Zoogeography edited by Carl L. Hubbs (New York, Arno, 1974) contains fifteen papers from two symposia held in 1957 by the American

Institute of Biological Sciences and American Association for the Advancement of Science. These papers serve as a review of the subject, with a bibliography included in each, and with general conclusions by the editor. *Wandering Lands and Animals* by Edwin H. Colbert (New York, Dutton, 1973) is a discussion of the land masses and the animals inhabiting them through geologic time, ending with a discussion of man and other animals in the modern world. There is a glossary, and a bibliography.

Geographic distribution of animals is approached from a climatic standpoint by Mary Parker Buckles in *Animals of the World* (New York, Grosset and Dunlap, 1978). The book is in sections by major climatic zones of the earth, called biomes: tropical rain forest, temperate deciduous forest, coniferous forest, tropical grasslands, temperate grasslands, desert tundra, and ocean. Each habitat is discussed, and then mammals inhabiting the area are listed with a description of about 150 words and often a photograph. There is a brief bibliography. *Terrestrial Environments* by J. L. Cloudsley-Thompson (New York, Wiley, 1975) also describes the more important terrestrial environments of the earth with respect to their influence on the animals that live there. For each area, climate and vegetation are described, together with the fauna found there with specific examples. A bibliography is included.

An atlas of animal life is the *Rand McNally Atlas of World Wildlife* (New York, Rand McNally, 1973), produced in consultation with the Zoological Society of London. This oversize volume has two-page spreads on many subjects, including such topics as survival, mimicry, hunters of the plains, and primates, with brief discussion and maps, photographs, and diagrams. These topical presentations are arranged in sections by geographical area, for example, North America, Central and South America, Africa, and so forth. There is an index. Another atlas is the *Animal Atlas of the World* by Emil L. Jordon (Maplewood, N.J., Hammond, 1969).

Wildlife Conservation, Ecology

In *Lost Wild Worlds: The Story of Extinct and Vanishing Wildlife of the Eastern Hemisphere* (New York, Morrow, 1976) author Robert M. McClung surveys the past and present wildlife of Europe, Asia, Africa, Madagascar, and islands of the Indian Ocean, the Malay archipelago, Australia, and New Zealand. The *Doomsday Book of Animals: A Natural History of Vanished Species* by David Day (New York, Viking, 1981) is about animals that have become extinct since 1680. Information is based on the author's research in the British Museum in naturalists' journals, ship logs, and observers' descriptions. The book tells when, where, and why each animal became extinct.

American wildlife conservation is surveyed by Hal Glen Borland in *The History of Wildlife in America* (Washington, D.C., National Wildlife Federation, 1975). Illustrated with beautiful color photographs and drawings, sections of the book are "migrants to a new world," "taming the forest wilderness," "wagon wheels follow buffalo trails," "frontier closes," "tide turns," and "an enduring place for wildlife." A list of endangered or threatened species concludes this interesting book. *An American Crusade for Wildlife* by James B. Trefethen (New York, Winchester Press, 1975) is a history of wildlife conservation with implications for the future. References are included. *These Are the Endangered* by Charles Cadieux (Washington, D.C., Stone Wall, 1981) lists endangered American species and federally managed lands where they are found. There is a detailed examination of thirty-one species.

Behavioral Aspects of Ecology by Peter H. Klopfer (Englewood Cliffs, N.J., Prentice-Hall, 2d edition 1973) discusses these questions: "Why don't predators overeat their prey?" "How are food and space shared between species?" "Why does species diversity vary?" "How are species kept distinct?" "How are communities organized?" There is a final chapter on human behavior as it is related to that of animals.

Experiments, Laboratory Animals

John L. Gill's *Design and Analysis of Experiments in the Animal and Medical Sciences* (Ames, Iowa, Iowa State University Press, 1978) is concerned with the application of statistics to experiments, using real examples from animal science. It is in two volumes with appendixes in the third volume consisting of tables and charts, a glossary, and solutions to exercises.

Examples of other books on experimentation are:

Gay, William I. *Methods of American Experimentation*. New York, Academic, 1965.

Holman, H. H. *Biological Research Method: A Practical Guide.* New York, Hafner, 1969.
Mahoney, Roy. *Laboratory Techniques in Zoology.* New York, Wiley, 2d edition 1973.
Storer, Tracy I. *Laboratory Manual for General Zoology.* New York, McGraw-Hill, 2d edition 1951.

Animal Behavior in Laboratory and Field (San Francisco, Freeman, 2d edition 1975) provides ideas for study but not a "cookbook" approach. Exercises, most of which are to be done in a laboratory setting but some in the field, are by different authors, and methods have been tested carefully. At the end of each experiment, additional studies are suggested, with references.

Reproduction and Breeding Techniques for Laboratory Animals edited by E. S. E. Hafez (Philadelphia, Pa., Lea and Febiger, 1970) is in two parts: (1) information about comparative aspects of endocrinology, anatomy, behavior, physiology, and biochemistry of mammals and (2) modern methods of breeding common laboratory animals. There is a bibliography with each section, and a general bibliography for further reading. The Universities Federation for Animal Welfare puts out a *Handbook on the Care and Management of Laboratory Animals* (London, Livingstone, 5th edition, 1976). The *CRC Handbook of Laboratory Animal Science* (Cleveland, Ohio, Chemical Rubber Company, 1974–) is published irregularly to bring together and update information.

Zoos

A tourist-type book with color photographs and brief interesting information describes the national zoo, which was created in 1889 by an act of Congress: *Zoobook* by the National Zoological Park, Washington, D.C. (Washington, D.C., Smithsonian, 1976). Photographs and narrative illustrate the zoo today: variety of species, creating natural settings, breeding, feeding, research and health. *What's For Lunch: Animal Feeding at the Zoo* by Sally Tongren (New York, GMG, 1981) includes specific diets for sixty animals at the National Zoo, Washington, D.C. *Man and Animal in the Zoo: Zoo Biology* by Heini Hediger (New York, Delacorte, 1969) discusses the basic principles of keeping animals in captivity, and includes references. *My Wild World*

(New York, Delacorte, 1980) contains interesting tales by Joan Embery, the "animal lady" who has appeared on NBC's "Tonight Show." As a representative of the San Diego Zoo, Ms. Embery has trained and shown a large variety of animals both at the zoo and in presentations elsewhere, and she describes these things in interesting detail.

Some books about zoos also contain directories of zoos and aquaria. *Zoos of the World: The Story of Animals in Captivity* by James Fisher (New York, Natural History Press, 1967) provides interesting reading about zoos, with many photographs scattered throughout. The appendix is a list of zoos and aquariums of the world, alphabetical by country and city, with very brief information as to size and number of species. *The World of Zoos: A Survey and Gazetteer* edited by Rosl Kirchscofer (New York, Viking, 1968) has introductory material on zoo animals and threatened species, some chapters by subject specialists on zoos, and 112 pages of photographs of zoo animals, many in color. The gazeteer of zoological gardens of the world is arranged alphabetically by country and city and gives a description and location of each zoo, mentioning special features.

Breeding Endangered Species in Captivity (New York, Academic, 1975) contains papers from a conference on breeding as part of a conservation program to be carried out in a laboratory or zoo setting. Chapters by various authorities are on specific animals or types of animals, for example, reptiles, giant tortoises, waterfowl, and tigers.

Veterinary work in zoos is discussed by Bruce Buchenholz in *Doctor in the Zoo* (New York, Viking, 1974) and by David Taylor in *Zoo Vet: Adventures of a Wild Animal Doctor* (Philadelphia, Pa., Lippincott, 1977).

Field Guides

Guides to identification usually consist mainly of drawings of the animals with distinguishing features clearly marked and briefly described in accompanying text. In some cases the guides are general as to geographical area covered, but more often they cover a specific area. They are also specific as to what animal group they cover, for example, birds.

There are many guides available. If you plan to do much watching, you will probably want to own one or more that apply to your interests and geographical area. The Peterson guide series, started by Roger Tory Peterson after the enormous success of his field guides to the birds, and the Audubon Society field guides are examples of the excellent guides available. One of the Peterson guides, *Field Guide to Animal Tracks* by Olaus J. Murie (Boston, Mass., Houghton Mifflin, 2d edition 1974) is mostly for identification of North American mammals but also covers a few representative birds, reptiles and amphibians, and some insects, by their tracks and sometimes droppings. The main part of the book is in sections by families of mammals, and has drawings of tracks and/or droppings and information on the animal. Introductory discussion covers reading tracks and how to preserve tracks with plaster of Paris. There is a bibliography, and an index. Other volumes in this series are on specific animal groups.

Following is a list of some guides, including the Peterson guides published by Houghton Mifflin and the Audubon guides published by Knopf.

Shells and seashore creatures:

Abbott, R. T. *American Seashells.* New York, Van Nostrand Reinhold, 2d edition 1974.
Meinkoth, Norman A. *Audubon Society Field Guide to North American Seashore Creatures.* New York, Knopf, 1981.
Morris, Percy A. *Field Guide to the Shells of Our Atlantic and Gulf Coasts and the West Indies.* Boston, Mass., Houghton Mifflin, 3d edition 1973.
Morris, Percy A. *Field Guide to Pacific Coast Shells.* Boston, Mass., Houghton Mifflin, n.d.
Rehder, Harold A. *Audubon Society Field Guide to North American Seashells.* New York, Knopf, 1981.

Fish:

Lindberg, Georgii U. *Fishes of the World: A Key to Families and a Checklist.* New York, Wiley, 1974.
Paysan, Klaus. *Larousse Guide to Aquarium Fishes.* New York, Larousse, 1981.

Insects:

Borror, Donald J. and Richard E. White. *Field Guide to the Insects of America North of Mexico.* Boston, Mass., Houghton Mifflin, 1970.

Klots, Alexander. *Field Guide to the Butterflies of North America, East of the Great Plains.* Boston, Mass., Houghton Mifflin, 1951.

Milne, Lorus and Margery Milne. *Field Guide to North American Insects.* New York, Knopf, 1980.

Pyle, Robert M. *Field Guide to North American Butterflies.* New York, Knopf, 1981.

Reptiles and amphibians:

Carr, A. F. *Handbook of Turtles.* Ithaca, N.Y., Comstock, 1952.

Conant, Roger. *Field Guide to Reptiles and Amphibians of Eastern and Central North America.* Boston, Mass., Houghton Mifflin, 2d edition 1975.

King, F. Wayne and John Behler. *Field Guide to North American Reptiles and Amphibians.* New York, Knopf, 1979.

Birds:

Bull, John and John Farrand. *Field Guide to North American Birds.* New York, Knopf, 1977. (eastern region)

Harrison, Hal H. *Field Guide to Bird's Nests Found East of the Mississippi River.* Boston, Mass., Houghton Mifflin, 1975.

Harrison, Hal H. *Field Guide to Western Bird's Nests in the United States West of the Mississippi River.* Boston, Mass., Houghton Mifflin, 1979.

Peterson, Roger Tory and others. *Field Guide to Bird Songs.* Boston, Mass., Houghton Mifflin, 1959. (2 records)

Peterson, Roger Tory. *Field Guide to the Birds.* Boston, Mass., Houghton Mifflin, 1980.

Peterson, Roger Tory. *Field Guide to Western Birds.* Boston, Mass., Houghton Mifflin, 1981.

Peterson, Roger Tory and others. *Western Bird Songs.* Boston, Mass., Houghton Mifflin, 1962. (3 records)

Udvardy, M. D. F. *Field Guide to North American Birds.* New York, Knopf, 1977. (western region)

Mammals:

Burt, William H. *Field Guide to the Mammals.* Boston, Mass., Houghton Mifflin, 3d edition 1976.
Van Gelder, Richard G. *Mammals of the National Parks.* Baltimore, Md., Johns Hopkins University Press, 1982.
Whitaker, John. *Field Guide to North American Mammals.* New York, Knopf, 1980.

Taxidermy

Taxidermy and its practical step-by-step methods are covered in the following titles. Even the oldest of these is still in print.

McFall, Waddy F. *Taxidermy Step by Step.* Tulsa, Okla., Winchester, 1975.
Pray, Leon L. *Taxidermy.* New York, Macmillan, 1943.
Taxidermy. New York, State Mutual, 1981.
Tinsley, Russel. *Taxidermy Guide.* South Hackensack, N.J., Stoeger, 1977.

Periodicals

American Birds; Devoted to Reporting the Distribution, Migration and Abundance of North American Birds. New York, National Audubon Society, 1947– . (bimonthly)
American Zoologist. Thousand Oaks, Calif., American Society of Zoologists, 1961– . (quarterly)
Animal Behaviour. London, Association for the Study of Animal Behaviour, 1953– . (quarterly)
Animal Kingdom. New York, Zoological Society, 1897– . (bimonthly)
Auk. Chicago, American Ornithologists' Union, 1884– . (quarterly)
Bat Research News. Potsdam, N.Y., State University of New York, 1960– . (quarterly)

Birding. Austin, Tex., American Birding Association, 1969– . (bimonthly)

Brookfield Bison. Brookfield, Ill., Chicago Zoological Society, 1966– . (10/year)

Bulletin of Entomological Research; Containing Original and Review Articles on Economic Entomology. Slough, England, Commonwealth Agricultural Bureaux, 1910– . (quarterly)

Canadian Entomologist. Ottawa, Canada, Entomological Society of Canada, 1868– . (monthly)

Canadian Journal of Zoology. Ottawa, Canada, National Research Council of Canada, 1929– . (monthly)

Condor. Lebanon, N.H., Cooper Ornithological Society, 1899– . (quarterly)

Copeia, American Society of Ichthyologists and Herpetologists. Washington, D.C., U.S. National Museum, 1913– . (quarterly)

Ecological Entomology, Royal Entomological Society. Oxford, Blackwell, 1976– . (quarterly)

Entomological Society of America Annals; Devoted to the Interest of Classical Entomology. College Park, Md., Entomological Society of America, 1908– . (bimonthly); *General Interest, 1955– .* (quarterly)

Environmental Entomology. College Park, Md., Entomological Society of America, 1972– . (bimonthly)

Gleanings in Bee Culture. Medina, Ohio, Root, 1872– . (monthly)

Journal of Experimental Zoology. New York, Liss, 1904– . (monthly)

Journal of Field Ornithology. Manomet, Mass., Northeastern Bird Banding Association, 1930– . (quarterly)

Journal of Fish Biology. New York, Academic, 1929– . (monthly)

Journal of Mammalogy. Pittsburgh, Pa., American Society of Mammalogists, 1919– . (quarterly)

Journal of Zoology. New York, Academic Press for Zoological Society of London, 1830– . (monthly)

North American Bird Bander. Carefree, Ariz., Eldon, 1923– . (quarterly)

Physiological Zoology; a Quarterly Journal of Zoological Research. Chicago, University of Chicago Press, 1928– . (quarterly)

Systematic Zoology, Society of Systematic Zoology. Lawrence, Kans., Allen, 1952– . (4/year)

Wildlife; the International Wildlife Magazine. London, Wildlife Publications, 1963– . (monthly)

Wilson Bulletin; a Quarterly Magazine of Ornithology. Toronto, Wilson, Ornithological Society, 1889– . (quarterly)

QUICK REFERENCE TOOLS

Dictionaries

The *Dictionary of Zoology* by A. W. Leftwich (London, Constable, 3d edition 1973) consists mainly of definitions of technical terms of zoology and related branches of biology. Arrangement is alphabetical by term with cross-references as needed, and definitions often include examples. There is also a bibliography, and brief information of principles of classification and nomenclature. A list of common names of about 800 common or well-known animals gives a brief description of the animal or a cross-reference to the main part of the dictionary.

Directories

International Zoo Yearbook (London, Zoological Society of London, 1, 1959–) is published annually and has sections with articles about zoos and zoo animals, but of main interest here is the reference section which lists worldwide zoos, aquaria, and a number of other institutions with important animal collections such as universities and bird parks. This section is alphabetical by country and then by state or city, and tells zoo location and also number of specimens of each type, for example, mammals, birds, and so forth.

Two directories of zoos and acquariums in the United States are *Zoos and Aquariums in the Americas* edited by William Hoff (Wheeling, W.Va., American Association of Zoological Parks and Aquariums, 6th edition 1966) and *The Animals Next Door* by Harry Gersh (New York, Fleet, 1971), done in cooperation with the National Recreation and Park Association of Washington, D.C.

12
Medicine

INTRODUCTORY MATERIALS

A pleasant introduction to medical topics is the *Dictionary of Medical Folklore* by Carol Ann Rinzler (New York, Crowell, 1979). This volume is arranged alphabetically by topic, for example, acne, aging, air conditioning, and alcoholism. Statements from old wives' tales, some familiar and some not, are listed for each topic. In each case the author explains what is behind the particular statement and why it is not true, or in many cases why it is partly true and partly not. There is an index, but this book is especially fun just to browse through.

The Healers: The Rise of the Medical Establishment by John Duffy (New York, McGraw-Hill, 1976) is concerned with the medical field in America. It begins with historical chapters on myths of Indian medicine and health conditions in early America, and follows developments in medicine on through to modern times. In addition to chapters on historical development, there are chapters on medical education, military medicine, women and minorities in medicine, and medical licensure. There is a bibliography, and an index. *Patients, Physicians, and Illness: A Sourcebook in Behavioral Science and Health* edited by E. Gartly Jace (New York, Free Press, 3d edition 1979) is a collection of articles by many contributors, with emphasis on the United States. It begins with an overview of American health care and then has sections on society, illness, and use of health services; health and illness behavior; and society and organization of health service systems. Each section has an introduction and then several chapters by different authors. Statistics are included on many subjects. There is an index by name and by subject.

An annual report of health status of the United States is *Health,*

United States (Washington, D.C., U.S. Department of Health and Human Services, 1, 1975–). Each volume contains discussion of current health issues, and statistics on recent trends in health care. Articles on current issues are by different authors. The 1981 volume, for example, includes articles on birth weight, mortality among the elderly, long-term care for the elderly, and more, each with references. There are many statistical tables of data on the nation's health, detailing for example, death rates for various causes of death, interval between physical check-ups, and length of stay in hospitals.

Human Life Science by Kenneth L. Fitch and Perry B. Johnson (New York, Holt, Rinehart and Winston, 1977) gives an overview of medical topics. It is designed as a text for a general education course or a more specific course in human biology. Chapters include heredity, the female, the male, sexual development, pregnancy and birth, nutrition, some specific diseases such as heart disease, some specific body functions such as respiration, and some specific body parts such as skin. Each chapter includes a list of references and suggested additional readings. There is a glossary, and an index.

There are several medical encyclopedias for general or home use. Each of these described is in one volume. The *Good Housekeeping Dictionary of Symptoms* (New York, Good Housekeeping, 1976) is arranged alphabetically by symptom, for example, abdominal distension, or backache, and describes the symptom and what it may mean in articles of about 100 to 200 words. "See" references are used as needed. There are shorter sections on personal health and medical treatment, nursing at home, and first aid. The *Family Health Guide and Medical Encyclopedia* (Pleasantville, N.Y., Reader's Digest, revised edition 1976) is in three sections: first, a family health guide including general information on maintaining good health; second, first aid, arranged alphabetically by emergency, such as convulsions, and telling what to do; and third, a medical encyclopedia, arranged alphabetically by term and giving definitions and explanations. Diagrams are used throughout this volume, and there is an index. *Dr. Fishbein's Popular Illustrated Medical Encyclopedia* by Morris Fishbein (New York, Doubleday, 1979) is alphabetical by term and has articles of one paragraph to several pages. Illustrations are used as needed for clarity. The *Family Medical Guide* (New York, Better Homes and Gardens, 1973) contains twenty-eight chapters on health care topics, each by a specialist. Topics include home care to a patient, infectious diseases, heart and circulatory system, and so forth, and there is a section on first aid. There is a glossary, and an index. Better Homes and Gardens has also a *Women's Health and Medical Guide* (Des Moines, Iowa, Meredith, 1981). This volume gathers together information about women's normal health and development and provides the knowledge to make decisions about health care. There are thirty-one sections on different subjects, each by a subject expert, for example, woman's body, woman's psychology, mental health, sexuality, abortion, pregnancy, and so forth. References are included for each section. There is an index.

The introduction to the history of medicine by Albert S. Lyone and R. Joseph Petrucelli, *Medicine: An Illustrated History* (New York, Abrams, 1978), is a lovely oversize volume crammed with photographs and drawings, many full-page size and in color. The book begins with prehistoric medicine and goes through the periods of history, for example, ancient civilizations, Greece and Rome, fifteenth and sixteenth centuries, and so forth, ending with the twentieth century. Discussion is interspersed with illustrations. There is a bibliography, and an index. *Images of Healing: A Portfolio of American Medical and Pharmaceutical Practice in the 18th, 19th and Early 20th Centuries* (New York, Macmillan, 1980) is a collection of pictures showing people, artifacts, documents, institutions, and techniques. There is a brief bibliography, and an index. John Camp's *The Healer's Art: The Doctor Through History* (New York, Taplinger, 1977) begins with discussion of primitive medicine, for example, witch doctors and medical men who existed as long ago as 30,000 years, and then discusses medical healers of Egypt and Babylon, ancient Greece, Rome, and the Middle Ages. Then there are chapters on some specific subjects, for example, anatomists and surgeons, quack doctors and importers, and microbe men, and the book ends with discussion of doctors in the twentieth century. There is a bibliography. Irving I. Edgar's *Origins of the Healing Art* (New York, Philosophical, 1978) is about the practice of medicine from its primitive origins to the present. It is organized in sections by topic, for example, infections, preventive medicine, psychiatry, and so forth.

Adventures in Medical Research: A Century of Discovery at Johns Hopkins by A. McGehee Harvey (Baltimore, Md., Johns Hopkins University Press, 1976) is the history of the Johns Hopkins medical school, and includes portraits of physicians. There is a bibliography.

Subject Headings and Classification

Aged—Medical care
Anatomy
Bioethics
Child health services
Death
Dental care
Dentistry
Diseases
Drugs
First aid in illness and injury
Health
Health facilities
Medical care
Medical education
Medical emergencies
Medical ethics
Medical instruments and apparatus
Medical laws and legislation
Medical libraries
Medical literature
Medical research
Medicine
  (also subdivisions of Medicine)
  —History
  —Terminology
Medicine, Ancient
Medicine, Experimental
Medicine, Medieval
Medicine, Preventive
Medicines
Nursing
Obstetrics
Pediatrics
Pharmacy
Public health
Right to die
Self medication

Materials on medical subjects will usually be found in libraries shelved in the R section of the Library of Congress classification or in the 610 to 619 section of the Dewey Decimal Classification.

BIBLIOGRAPHIC MATERIALS

Guides to the Literature

The most comprehensive current guide to the literature is Ching-Chih Chen's *Health Sciences Information Sources* (Cambridge, Mass., MIT Press, 1981). This volume is arranged in chapters by types of literature, for example, guides to the literature, bibliographies, encyclopedias, and so forth, with subdivision for each subject area covered, for example, anatomy. Books are listed with full bibliographic information, a brief annotation, and a list of other places where information on the book may be found, usually in standard reference lists of books. Also included are lists of sources of non-print materials, professional societies, and computer data bases with vendor and coverage. Indexes are by author and title. *Use of Medical Literature* by L. T. Morton (London, Butterworths, 2d edition 1977) is a guide to the general and specialist literature of medical science. There is discussion of libraries, primary sources, indexes, abstracts, bibliographies, standard reference sources, and mechanized information retrieval. Then chapters are by topic, for example, anatomy and physiology, public health, and so forth. There is an index. *Health Sciences and Services: A Guide to Information Sources* by Lois F. Lunin (Detroit, Mich., Gale, 1979) first treats the field as a whole, and then each area of specialization such as microbiology and immunology, oncology, nursing, and so forth. For each area items are listed with bibliographic information and an annotation. Included are publications, mostly reference works, data bases, and organizations. Indexing is by author and title.

Since medical science is such a wide-ranging and diverse field, many literature guides cover only a specific subject area and are generally directed to health professionals. *Guide to Drug Information* by Winifred Sewell (Hamilton, Ill., Drug Intelligence Publications, 1976) discusses drug handbooks, periodicals, books, reference sources, how to search and how to obtain literature wanted, and ideas for personal systems for keeping up with the literature. Many reference tools are

described, and there are bibliographies of other materials. There is an index.
Examples of literature guides in other medical subject areas are:

Ennis, Bernice. *Guide to the Literature in Psychiatry.* Los Angeles, Partridge, 1971.
Greenberg, Bette, ed. *How to Find Out in Psychiatry: A Guide to Sources of Medical Health Information.* New York, Pergamon, 1978.
Kerker, Ann E. and Henry T. Murphy, eds. *Comparative and Veterinary Medicine, A Guide to the Resource Literature.* Madison, Wis., University of Wisconsin Press, 1973.
Kowitz, Aletha, comp. *Basic Dental Reference Works.* Chicago, American Dental Association, 1975.

Bibliographies

Current Works in the History of Medicine: An International Bibliography (London, Wellcome Historical Medical Library, 1965–) is issued quarterly as a bibliography of new historical works. Coverage is international. Items are arranged in subject groups, with an author index. There is also a list of new books on the history of medicine. The *Bibliography of the History of Medicine* (Bethesda, Md., National Library of Medicine, 1965–) is issued annually, with a cumulation every five years. Coverage is international, and materials included are journal articles, books, chapters in books, symposia, and congresses. The first part lists biographies in two sections: collective and individual, with indexes chronological and geographical. Part two, the subject section of the bibliography, is arranged by subject, for example, aerospace medicine, anatomy, and so forth, subdivided by chronological and geographical subheadings. There is an author index for the biographical and subject sections.

Some guides have been prepared especially for nonmedical readers. *Medical Books for the Layperson* by Marilyn M. Philbrook (Boston, Mass., Boston Public Library, 1976) is a basic annotated bibliography directed to nonspecialists. A supplement to this bibliography was issued by the author in 1978. The *Consumer Health Information Source Book* by Alan M. Rees and Blanche A. Young (New York, Bowker, 1981) was prepared based on the premise that the individual is the one to decide about his medical care: when to seek help, where, and from whom, what information to give, what advice to accept, and what self care to practice. This book is designed to tell lay individuals where to get the information needed to make these decisions. The book is arranged in three parts: (1) description and bibliographies of health information needs of the public, (2) bibliographies and information on consumer health and on major topics such as alcoholism, and (3) descriptions of sources on health information for consumers. The third part, the most important for consumers, is arranged by specific health aspect or problem, for example, wellness, children, cancer, and so forth, and lists books, pamphlets, audiovisual producers and distibutors, and resource organizations. There is an informative abstract of each book listed. Indexes are by author, title, and subject. A guide to information on care of children is by Andrew Garoogian and Rhoda Garoogian, entitled *Child Care Issues for Parents and Society: A Guide to Information Sources* (Detroit, Mich., Gale, 1977).

Medical Books and Serials in Print (New York, Bowker, 1971–), published annually, lists books that are in print and published or distributed in the United States, and serials that are published anywhere in the world. Materials on health sciences and allied fields are included. The first section lists books alphabetically by topic and then by author, then by titles, and gives bibliographic information and price. The serials section is arranged alphabetically by subject with an index by title, and tells bibliographic information, price, and in what indexing and abstracting service the serial is indexed, if any. This large volume is completed by a list of publishers with addresses.

Indexing and Abstracting Services

The most used indexing service for medical sciences, put out by the National Library of Medicine, is called *Index Medicus* (Bethesda, Md., National Library of Medicine, 1, 1879–), continuing its earlier title to 1959: *Current List of Medical Literature*. Published monthly with annual cumulations, this service indexes current journal articles from about 2,600 journals in biomedical fields. Annual cumulations consist of many volumes, for example, fourteen volumes for 1980. The main part is alphabetical by subject and lists articles with bibliographic information only, no abstract, and an indication of language if other than English. A separate author section is arranged alphabetically by author and also tells bibliographic information and language. There is also a "medical reviews" section that lists surveys of recent biomedical literature. These reviews are included in the main part by subject, but are also grouped together in both the monthly and annual editions. Supplementing these sections is *Medical Subject Headings,* published as part two of the January issue of *Index Medicus* and also available separately. This list is very important in finding the correct subject term to consult, as there are no "see" references or "see also" references in the monthly issues and few in the cumulations. *Abridged Index Medicus* (Bethesda, Md., National Library of Medicine, 1, 1970–) is a separate publication designed especially for practicing physicians. This abridged version is also published monthly with annual cumulations, and indexes about 100 journals, English-language only. The main section is the subject section, arranged alphabetically by subject. Both specific and broad subject terms are used, for example, abdomen and acetaminophen. Bibliographic information is given. The author section is arranged alphabetically by author and also gives bibliographic information.

Excerpta Medica (Amsterdam, Excerpta Medica, 1947–) is published in many separate subject sections as separate journals, the sections numbering forty-three in 1982. Sections are specialized, for example, anesthesiology, cancer, human genetics, pharmacology and toxicology, and so forth. Different sections started at different times and are published with varying frequencies. This indexing and abstracting service gives international coverage of journal articles. Arrangement in each issue is by subject with subdivisions for more specific subjects, and information given is bibliographic citation, an abstract, and the author's address. There are indexes by subject and author, and these are cumulated annually.

There are other indexing and abstracting services for specialized subject areas. An example is *International Pharmaceutical Abstracts* (Bethesda, Md., American Society of Hospital Pharmacists, 1, 1904–). This service is published twice a month, giving international coverage of journal articles. Arrangement is by broad subjects with subdivisions, and informatin given for each article is bibliographic citation and abstract. There are indexes by author and subject in each issue and cumulated semiannually.

SECONDARY LITERATURE MATERIALS

Books and encyclopedias on a number of specific topics will be discussed here, beginning with those applicable in most areas of medicine: anatomy, bioethics, diagnosis, and drugs; and going on to some narrower topics. Most of these items are aimed at health care professionals, but interested nonprofessionals will be able to gain some information from them. A few are designed specifically for lay use as indicated in their titles or in the discussion.

Anatomy

The classic source for information on human anatomy is *Gray's Anatomy* (London, Longman, 35th edition 1973), edited by Roger Warwick and Peter L. Williams. This large volume is divided into sections by area of study, for example, cytology, embryology, osteology, and so forth, with introductory discussion for each of these areas and then many subsections covering various topics. Many illustrations are used, both photographs and drawings. There is an extensive bibliography, and an index. David A. Langebartel's *Anatomical Primer: An Embryological Explanation of Human Gross Morphology* (Baltimore, Md., University Park, 1977) stresses patterns of organization of body structures that begin in the embryo and carry over into the adult. The book begins with an explanation of anatomical terms and then goes through the stages of development of the embryo to the fetus. Subsequent sections deal with tissues of the body wall, the nervous system and related structures, the cardiovascular system, and viscera. These sections are made up of drawings and explanatory discussion. There is a bibliography, and an index.

The *Atlas of Medical Anatomy* by Jan Langman and M. W. Woerdman (Philadelphia, Pa., Saunders, 1978) contains photographs, radiographs, and schematic drawings, with explanatory text. Embryos are included as well as adult anatomy.

The *Photographic Anatomy of the Human Body* by Chihire Yokochi and J. W. Rohen (Baltimore, Md., University Park, 2d edition 1978) contains photographs, in color, to illustrate structures. It is divided into sections: skeletal system, muscular system, digestive system, respiratory system, urinary system, reproductive system, endocrine organs, circulatory system, nervous system, sensory organs, and cross sections of the body. Each section has several pages of photographs, well labeled and with explanatory material as needed. The book is aimed at general readers, students, nurses, and physicians. Another book designed to be of use to general readers as well as others is *Human Body* by the Diagram Group (New York, Facts on File, 1980). This volume covers the body's functioning, care, and development. Brief concise information is arranged in two sections: (1) man's body, woman's body, and (2) child's body. The book includes discussion, as well as illustrations, tables, graphs, and diagrams. At the back are reference diagrams of man and woman, showing body parts. There is an index.

Bioethics

The *Encyclopedia of Bioethics* edited by Warren T. Reich (New York, Free Press, 1978) is in four volumes. Its aim is to synthesize, analyze, and compare positions taken on problems of bioethics. The approach is both historical and modern, in articles done by many contributors. Arrangement is alphabetical by topic, for example, abortion, and articles generally cover ethical and legal problems and underlying concepts. For some topics there is more than one article, by different authors, on different aspects. Each article includes a bibliography. The appendix contains the texts of codes and statements related to medical ethics, for example, the oath of Hippocrates. There is an index. The *Dictionary of Medical Ethics* edited by A. S. Duncan and others (London, Darton, Longman and Todd, 1977) is a one-volume survey of ethical issues in medicine. Religious views are included, as are texts of current codes of medical ethics.

Making Medical Choices: Who is Responsible? by Jane J. Stein (Boston, Mass., Houghton Mifflin, 1978) has as its premise that technological advances in medicine have created many new choices for individuals. The main sections covered are birth, life, and death, with several chapters in each. The book begins with a chapter on medical mores and ends with a discussion of a new medical morality. An important feature is the section called "guide to information about medical choices," which discusses literature sources related to each chapter. There is an index. *Life Span: Values and Life-Extending Technologies* edited by Robert M. Veatch (New York, Harper and Row, 1979) is a collection of articles. The book begins and ends with discussion of life-extending technologies, and has sections on values and guidelines, natural death and aging, and ethical issues. Each section contains several chapters by different authors, and most chapters include a bibliography. At the end of the book is a bibliography of related books and articles. There is an index.

The *Bibliography of Bioethics* (New York, Free Press, 1, 1975–) is an annual bibliography of current English-language materials, print and non-print, including journal and newspaper articles, books, parts of books, court decisions, bibliographies, audiovisual materials, and unpublished documents. The main part is arranged by subject in about eighty major headings, subdivided as needed and with cross-references as needed. Each entry includes bibliographic information and descriptive terms to indicate subjects dealt with. There is a thesarus of terms, as well as author and title indexing.

Diagnosis and Treatment

The Common Symptom Guide: A Guide to the Evaluation of 100 Common and Pediatric Symptoms by John Wasson (New York, McGraw-Hill, 1975) is arranged by symptom and gives information to evaluate the meaning of each symptom. It is written at the level of medical students, residents, and physician's assistants. The *Merck Manual of Diagnosis and Therapy* (Rahway, N.H., Merck 1, 1899–) is issued irregularly, the 13th edition having appeared in 1977, and is designed for use by practicing physicians. Arrangement is in sections by type of disease, for example, infectious and parasitic, and for each there is general information followed by subdivisions by more specific types of disease, for example, viral, and then specific diseases, for example, chickenpox. For each specific disease, information given includes description, etiology, symptoms, diagnosis, and treatment. Although specific drugs for treatment are not given, there is a drug section that discusses groups of drugs. A special section is included on poisoning from bites and stings. There is an index. *Current Medical Diagnosis and Treatment* (Los Altos, Calif., Lange, 1962–) is issued annually as a desk reference for practicing physicians. It contains chapters by different authors, beginning with general symptoms and then many specific areas of medicine, for example, fluid and electrolyte disorders, eye, blood, and so forth. The appendix adds miscellaneous information. There is an index. The *Handbook of Medical*

Treatment by Milton A. Chatton (Greenbrai, Calif., Jones, 1, 1949–) is issued irregularly, the 16th edition appearing in 1979. It is small in size for easy reference, and covers essentials of current treatment. The first section treats general symptoms, for example, pain or fever, and subsequent sections are on specific disorders, for example, diseases of the skin. Such information as symptoms, treatment, prevention, complications, and prognosis is included. The appendix has some emergency treatments. There is an index.

Information designed especially for use by patients is contained in *Instructions for Patients* by H. Winter Griffith (Philadelphia, Pa., Saunders, 2d edition 1975). Arrangement is alphabetical by ailment, for example, allergy, angina pectoris, back pain, and so forth, and for each ailment general information, treatment, and precautions are given. Diagrams are included at the back of the book. There is an index.

Solomon Garb's *Laboratory Tests in Common Use* (New York, Springer, 6th edition 1976) summarizes knowledge about tests. Directions for performing tests are not included. The first part is arranged by type of specimen, for example, microbiological tests, tests on blood, and so forth, and describes the test procedure. The second part includes tables and reference data. There is a bibliography, and an index. *Medical Tests and You* by Aaron E. Klein (New York, Grosset and Dunlap, 1977) is arranged alphabetically by name of diagnostic test, for example, amniocentesis, bronchography, or dacryocystography. The purpose of the test, what is done, preparation, procedure, pain involved, aftereffects, and risk are included. There is an index.

Drugs

The *Physicians' Drug Manual* (Garden City, N.Y., Biomedical, 1981) is intended for use by physicians and for home use. Some of its information is written especially to help lay readers. It covers more than 95% of all drugs prescribed, plus frequently used nonprescription drugs. Arrangement is according to disease or problem area, for example, cardiovascular, with subdivisions for specific diseases, for example, asthma. Each section begins with general discussion, and then information on various drugs including dosage, side effects, and precautions. There is also a discussion on "achieving good health," and a glossary of medical and drug-related terms. A separate drug identification section shows color pictures of tablets and capsules for identification, giving brand name and manufacturer. This information-packed volume ends with a brief bibliography, a directory of major pharmaceutical manufacturers with address and phone number, and an index. The information is kept up to date by a monthly publication, *PDM Update*. The *United States Pharmacopeia Dispensing Information* (Rockville, Md., Pharmacopeial Convention, 1, 1980–) is published annually with a supplementary update every two months. It is divided into two sections, the first being monographs arranged alphabetically by generic name of drug. The term monograph in this case and in other publications about drugs means a summary of information about the drug including such information as action, precautions, side effects, and dosage. The second section is advice for the patient, again alphabetical by generic name and giving basically the same information as in the first section but in easily understood language. There is an index.

Physician's Desk Reference (Oradell, N.J., Medical Economics, 1, 1947–) is published annually, and kept up to date by supplements. Most of the book is product information on drugs, prepared by manufacturers. Arrangement is alphabetical by manufacturer, then by brand name, and each drug is described as to composition, action and uses, dosage, precautions, side effects, and so forth. There are indexes by manufacturer, product name, product category, and generic and chemical names. A separate product identification section has color pictures of capsules and tablets for identification. There is also a section giving information on products used in diagnosis, and a list of poison control centers. Inside the back cover is a guide to management of drug overdoses by prescription drugs. A companion publication is *Physician's Desk Reference for Nonprescription Drugs* (Oradell, N.J., Medical Economics, 1, 1980–), also annual. Arrangement and contents of the main section are about the same as the above, but for nonprescription drugs. Information given includes a guide to self treatment of minor health problems, a directory of poison control centers, first aid for poisoning, and a glossary.

Facts and Comparisons (St. Louis, Mo., Facts and Comparisons, 1, 1947–) is issued in annual bound volumes, or loose-leaf and updated monthly, or in microfiche with monthly updates. Arrangement is in sections by category, for example, nutritional products, blood modi-

The management of chronic constipation should also include attention to fluid intake, diet and bowel habits.

Contraindications: Sensitivity to phenolphthalein.

(Taken at bedtime, laxation may be expected the next morning.)

	Adults	Children over 6 years	2 to 4
Agoral Plain without phenolphthalein	1 to 2 tablespoonful	1 to 1 tablespoonful	1 to 2 teaspoonfuls
Agoral Raspberry	½ to 1 tablespoonful		1 to 2 teaspoonfuls
Agoral Marshmallow	½ to 1 tablespoonful		1 to 2 teaspoonfuls

Take at bedtime only, unless other time is advised by physician.

Agoral may be taken alone or in milk, water, fruit juice, or any miscible food.

Expectant or nursing mothers, bedridden or aged patients, young children or infants should use only on advice of physician.

Supplied: Agoral Plain (without phenolphthalein), plastic bottles of 16 fl oz (N 0071-2071-23). Agoral (raspberry flavor), plastic bottles of 16 fl oz (N 0071-2072-23). Agoral (marshmallow flavor), plastic bottles of 8 fl oz (N 0071-2070-20) and 16 fl oz (N 0071-2070-23).

AMCILL®
(ampicillin, USP) as the trihydrate
Ampicillin Capsules, USP—250 mg and 500 mg
Ampicillin for Oral Suspension, USP 125 mg/5 ml and 250 mg/5 ml

Description: Ampicillin is a semisynthetic penicillin derived from the basic penicillin nucleus, 6-aminopenicillanic acid.

Actions: **Microbiology:** In vitro studies have coli, *H influenzae*, *P mirabilis*, and *N gonorrhoeae*. Ampicillin may also be indicated in certain infections caused by susceptible gram positive organisms: penicillin G-sensitive staphylococci, streptococci, pneumococci, and enterococci.

Bacteriology studies to determine the causative organisms and their sensitivity to ampicillin should be performed. Therapy may be instituted prior to the results of sensitivity testing.

Contraindication: Ampicillin is contraindicated in patients with a history of a hypersensitivity reaction to the penicillins.

Warning: Serious and occasionally fatal hypersensitivity (anaphylactic) reactions have been reported in patients on penicillin therapy. Although anaphylaxis is more frequent following parenteral therapy, it has occurred in patients on oral penicillins. These reactions are more apt to occur in individuals with a history of sensitivity to multiple allergens.

There have been reports of individuals with a history of penicillin hypersensitivity who experienced severe reactions when treated with cephalosporins. Before therapy with any penicillin, careful inquiry should be made concerning previous hypersensitivity reactions to penicillins, cephalosporins, or other allergens. Serious anaphylactoid reactions require immediate emergency treatment with epinephrine. Oxygen, intravenous steroids, and airway management, including intubation, should also be administered as indicated.

Usage in Pregnancy: Safety for use in pregnancy has not been established.

Precautions: As with any potent drug, periodic assessment of renal, hepatic, and hematopoietic functions should be made during prolonged therapy.

The possibility of superinfections with mycotic or bacterial pathogens should be kept in mind during therapy. If superinfections occur, appropriate therapy should be instituted.

Adverse Reactions: As with other penicillins, Other—Since infectious mononucleosis is viral in origin, ampicillin should not be used in the treatment. A high percentage of patients with mononucleosis who received ampicillin developed a skin rash.

Dosage and Administration:
Infections of the respiratory tract and soft tissues

Patients weighing 20 kg (44 lb) or more: 250 mg every six hours

Patients weighing less than 20 kg (44 lb): 50 mg/kg/day in equally divided doses at 6- or 8-hour intervals

Infections of the gastrointestinal and genito-urinary tracts

Patients weighing 20 kg (44 lb) or more: 500 mg every six hours

Patients weighing less than 20 kg (44 lb): 100 mg/kg/day in equally divided doses at 6- or 8-hour intervals

In the treatment of chronic urinary tract and intestinal infections, frequent bacteriologic and clinical appraisal is necessary. Smaller doses than those recommended above should not be used. Higher doses should be used for stubborn or severe infections. In stubborn infections, therapy may be required for several weeks. It may be necessary to continue clinical and/or bacteriologic follow-up for several months after cessation of therapy.

Urethritis in males or females due to *N gonorrhoeae:*

3.5 grams with 1 gram probenecid, administered simultaneously.

In the treatment of complications of gonorrheal urethritis, such as prostatitis and epididymitis, prolonged and intensive therapy is recommended. Cases of gonorrhea with a suspected primary lesion of syphilis should have darkfield examinations before receiving treatment. In all other cases where concomitant syphilis is suspected, monthly serologic tests should be made for a minimum of four months.

B

Fig. 12–1. Drug information: *Physicians' Desk Reference*

fiers, and so forth. Specific drugs are listed, with such information as indications, administration, and dosage, in addition to general information about the group of drugs covered in each section. The *Modern Drug Encyclopedia and Therapeutic Index* (New York, Yorke, 16th edition 1981) is arranged alphabetically by drug name. Information given for each drug is description, indications, contraindications, warnings, precautions, adverse reactions, dosage and administration, and availability including names of manufacturers. There are three indexes: therapeutic, manufacturers, and general. Also included are a glossary and data on drug and chemical blood levels. The *United States Dispensatory* (Philadelphia, Pa., Lippincott, 1, 1951–) is issued irregularly, the 27th edition being 1973. Arrangement is alphabetical by name of drug, with about one page of information on each, including chemical, generic, and brand names, chemical structure, preparation, actions and uses, contraindications, drug interactions, and so forth. There is an index, and also a list by categories of use, for example, acidifier, with names of drugs in each category. Articles of several pages on some classes of drugs, for example, adrenergic inhibiting drugs, appear right in the same alphabetical order.

The following sources of information on drugs are for use of health care professionals; those not in the field would be unlikely to find useful information in them. Most present information in a brief or coded form.

American Drug Index. Philadelphia, Pa., Lippincott, 26th edition 1982.
Current Drug Handbook. Philadelphia, Saunders, 1958– . (annual)
Handbook of Non-prescription Drugs. Washington, D.C., American Pharmaceutical Association, 6th edition 1979.
Merck Index: An Encyclopedia of Chemicals and Drugs. Rahway, N.J., Merck, 9th edition 1976.
Tallarida, Ronald J. *Top 200: A Compendium of Pharmacologic and Therapeutic Information on the Most Widely Prescribed Drugs in America*. New York, Springer-Verlag, 1981.
USAN and the USP Dictionary of Drug Names. Rockville, Md., U.S. Pharmacopeial Convention, 1981.

Some publications are geared toward use by non-health-care professionals. *Your Prescription and You; A Pharmacy Handbook for*

Consumers by Steven Strauss (Ambler, Pa., Medical Business Services, 4th edition 1979) is a very practical guide. Its purpose is to call attention to the common side effects, proper storage, and correct use of U.S. drugs, both prescription and over-the-counter. Arrangement is alphabetical by brand name with a notation of whether the drug is prescription or over-the-counter, generic name or formula, manufacturer, and information about what the drug is for, how it should be used, and side effects. There are also sections on how to administer certain forms, for example, eye drops and ear drops; and information for diabetics, and persons taking anticoagulant drugs. Indexing is by generic name. The American Society of Hospital Pharmacists' *Consumer Drug Digest* (New York, Facts on File, 1982) is also a guide to prescription and over-the-counter drugs.

James Long's *Essential Guide to Prescription Drugs: What You Need to Know for Safe Drug Use* (New York, Harper and Row, 1977) contains information on drug actions and reactions, and patients' guidelines for safe drug use. The main part consists of "drug profiles" arranged by drug name and giving brand names, dosage, therapeutic effects, possible side effects, precautions, and so forth. Other information includes lists of drug families, a glossary, and tables of drug information. *Drug Information for Patients* by H. Winter Griffith (Philadelphia, Pa., Saunders, 1978) is in loose-leaf form. Arrangement is alphabetical by drug name, and information given includes instructions, precautions, possible side effects, refills, what to do in case of overdose, and sometimes other information.

Some sources of drug information are specialized by use. Two of these, which may be of special interest, will be used as examples. The *Handbook for Prescribing Medications During Pregnancy* (Boston, Mass., Little, Brown, 1981) was prepared by many contributors. The first section is arranged alphabetically by drug name and gives indications and recommendations, special considerations in pregnancy, dosage, adverse effects, mechanism of action, absorption, and five or six recommended readings. There are indexes by drug classification and by generic and trade names. *Pediatric Dosage Handbook* by Harry C. Shirkey (Washington, D.C., American Pharmaceutical Association, 1, 1964–   ) is published irregularly. Arrangement is alphabetical by drug name, and information is included on dosage, warnings, contraindications, trade names, and dosage forms. A list of pharmacological categories at the front of the book gives categories of use, for example, anticonvulsants, and lists of drug names. There is an index.

Sources of information on some more narrow or specific topics will now be described. These topics are aging, alcoholism and drug abuse, birth and OB-GYN, death and dying, emergencies, mental health, nutrition, poisoning, and sports medicine.

Aging

The *Sourcebook on Aging* (Chicago, Marquis, 1, 1977–) is a collection of information on the current status of the elderly in America. Areas covered are aging, health, economic status, housing, employment, education, transportation, leisure and retirement, special concerns and problems, and government programs. There are several articles by different authors in each of these areas, giving facts, statistics, discussion, lists of agencies, and references. There is a subject index, and a geographic index. The *Older American's Handbook* by Craig Norback and Peter Norback (New York, Van Nostrand Reinhold, 1977) contains information on associations such as the Administration on Aging and American Association of Retired Persons. The book is mostly listings of agencies and associations, for example, area and state agencies on aging, home health agencies, housing, and mental health centers, with name and address. There is a list of publications of interest to older people. The *Student's Guide to Geriatrics* by Howell Trevor (Springfield, Ill., Thomas, 2d edition 1970) discusses common diseases of elderly people. Also covered are anatomical and physiological changes, psychology and mental disorders, surgery, rehabilitation, and social medicine. The *Handbook of Geriatric Nutrition: Principles and Applications for Nutrition and Diet in Aging* (Park Ridge, N.J., Noyes, 1982) is written by many expert contributors. Articles cover present knowledge, and the relationship between nutrients and aging and disease; modification of nutrition to take into account medical, surgical, economic, and psychological problems; improving nutrition in the elderly; and some fads and folklore in nutrition.

Geriatric Medicine: An Education Resource Guide (Cambridge, Mass., Ballinger, 1981) first describes geriatric medical education activities at medical schools. The part of principal interest here is a list and critical reviews of books in geriatric medicine, medical gerontology, and related fields. Arrangement is by broad topic, for example, general, geropsychiatry, neurology, and so forth, and then alphabetically. The book also contains a bibliography of periodical articles, audiovisual materials, and other miscellaneous information in the appendixes. *Current Literature on Aging* (New York, National Council on the Aging, 1, 1957–) is published quarterly. Arrangement is by subject, for example, aging process, and bibliographic information is given together with an annotation. Indexes by author and subject are issued yearly.

Alcoholism and Drug Abuse

Alcohol and Drug Abuse Yearbook/Directory (New York, Van Nostrand Reinhold, 1, 1979/80–) is published every other year. It presents information about alcoholism, including causes and understanding the effects. A list of alcohol treatment centers follows, arranged alphabetically by state and then name of center, with address and phone number, contact person, type of program, services, and admission requirements. A separate section gives information on drug abuse and lists treatment programs, arranged by state. *Alcoholism and Drug Abuse Treatment Centers* (Santa Monica, Calif., Ready Reference, 1981–) lists treatment centers. Arrangement is alphabetical by state and then city, and information given is address and phone number.

Birth, Obstetrics and Gynecology

The *Birth Defects Compendium* edited by Daniel Bergsma (New York, Liss, 1979) is published in cooperation with the March of Dimes, and is a collective work by many authors. The first section, called an "atlas," has color photographs of conditions. Section two, the "compendium," is arranged alphabetically by name of condition and describes the condition and its treatment, with references. The third section contains information presented in tables and diagrams. There is an author index, and a general index. Ralph C. Benson's *Handbook of Obstetrics and Gynecology* (Los Altos, Calif., Lange, 6th edition 1977) contains much practical information. It is intended primarily for physicians, but is also useful for nurses, midwives, and paramedics.

Death and Dying

Ethical Issues in Death and Dying edited by Tom L. Beauchamp and Seymour Perlin (Englewood Cliffs, N.J., Prentice-Hall, 1978) takes an interdisciplinary approach in a collection of articles by different authors. There are sections on definition and determination of death, suicide, rights of the dying patient, euthanasia and natural death, and the significance of life and death. Each section contains several articles by different authors, and a list of suggested readings. There is a comprehensive bibliography at the end of the book.

There are several bibliographies on death and dying. The *Comprehensive Bibliography of Thanatology Literature* (New York, MSS, 1975) is arranged alphabetically by author and gives bibliographic information only, for books and journal articles in the English language. There is a detailed subject index. *Death, Grief and Bereavement: A Bibliography, 1845–1975* compiled by Robert L. Fulton (New York, Arno, 1977) was prepared at the Center for Death Education and Research at the University of Minnesota. Only scientific research is included, not literary or theological works, and emphasis is on American materials. Arrangement is alphabetical by author, and bibliographic information is given. *Death: A Bibliographic Guide* by Albert J. Miller and Michael J. Acri (Metuchen, N.J., Scarecrow, 1977) lists books, periodical articles, letters, editorials, pamphlets, media information, and audiovisual materials. Arrangement is in broad subject areas of general education, humanities, medicine, religion, science, and social sciences, and bibliographic information is given. There are indexes by author and by subject. *Dying, Death, and Grief: A Critically Annotated Bibliography and Source Book of Thanatology and Terminal Care* by Michael A. Simpson (New York, Plenum, 1979) has as its main part a listing of English language books arranged alphabetically by title and with a brief critical review and evaluation of quality as seen by the author and indicated by a system of stars. There are separate lists of journals, films, and other audiovisual materials, of literature in other languages, and of journal articles on topics not covered by books. Indexes are by author and subject.

Emergencies

The *Handbook of Medical Emergencies* by Jay H. Sanders (New York, Medical Examination, 2d edition 1978) is primarily for health care workers. It is arranged in sections by type of emergency, for example, cardiological, endocrine, gastrointestinal, and so forth. Articles are by different authors, usually several in each section, and each with references. There is an index.

The *People's Emergency Guide* by Jeffrey Weiss (New York, St. Martin's 1980) contains practical information including prevention, first aid, and follow-up. Main sections are yourself, your house, on the road, at sea, your pet, and natural disasters. There is an index. The *Emergency Handbook: First Aid Manual for Home and Travel* by Peter Arnold (Garden City, N.Y., Doubleday, 1980) has these sections: "sudden emergencies, be prepared, care at home, first aid away from home, an ounce of prevention, and fire safety." Procedures are clearly outlined, with illustrations as needed. There is an index.

Mental Health

The International Encyclopedia of Psychiatry, Psychology, Psychoanalysis and Neurology (New York, Van Nostrand Reinhold, 1977) is a twelve-volume set with approximately 2,000 contributors. Arrangement is alphabetical by subject, and articles cover research, theory, and practice. Articles are one page to several pages in length, each with references. There is a name index, and a subject index.

The *Mental Health Almanac* edited by Robert D. Allen and Marsha K. Cartier (New York, Garland, 1978) provides an overview of the field and sources of further information. This volume has three main parts: the population, the concern, and the profession. For each part there are several chapters that discuss various aspects of mental health, for example, marriage and family, adolescence, therapy, crises, licensing, and employment. Each chapter includes a list of references and a list of further readings, audiovisual materials, and "contacts," which are newsletters, bulletins, magazines, pamphlets, speakers, organizations, and so forth. One chapter lists service organizations, with information on purpose and so forth. *Wholistic Dimensions in Healing* compiled and edited by Leslie H. Kaslof (Garden City, N.Y., Doubleday, 1978) is a resource guide. The *Mental Health Yearbook/Directory* (New York, Van Nostrand Reinhold, 1, 1979/80–), published every other year, includes information about various aspects of mental health, lists of education and treatment centers, and information on careers in mental health, including educational and training requirements for various jobs. The largest part of the volume lists mental health facilities alphabetically by state and then by name of center.

The *Handbook of Psychiatric Emergencies* by Andrew E. Slaby and others (New York, Medical Examination, 2d edition 1981) is aimed primarily at mental health care workers. The book begins with a discussion of basic principles of emergency psychiatric care, for example, general principles of emergency room psychiatry, and information on drugs that may be used. This is followed by an alphabetical arrangement of psychiatric emergencies, for example, alcohol use problems, anxiety states, or grief, with information for each including history, symptoms, signs, differential diagnosis, and management. There are also discussions of burn-out of mental health workers, disaster planning, and legal and ethical aspects of emergency care. The book is completed by a bibliography and an index.

Nutrition

The *McGraw-Hill Encyclopedia of Food, Agriculture and Nutrition* (New York, McGraw-Hill, 1977) is international in scope and contains signed articles by many contributors. Articles are arranged alphabetically by subject through the volume, some with bibliographies, and there are also tables of information. *Sourcebook on Food and Nutrition* (Chicago, Marquis, 1978) gathers into one volume a wide variety of information on nutrition and health issues. Main sections cover nutrition in the United States, nutrients, dietary allowances and labeling, nutrition and life cycle, dieting, special diets, health problems, food additives and food–drug interactions, and world food production. Each section contains several articles by different authors, each with references. A list, with addresses, of organizations and agencies interested in food and nutrition is included. There is an index.

Food Values of Portions Commonly Used (Philadephia, Pa., Lippincott, 1, 1937–) is published irregularly, the 13th edition having been issued in 1980. This is a quick reference source for nutrition, arranged alphabetically by categories of foods, for example, beverages, candy, cereals, and so forth. Information is presented in table form, and gives nutrient values for a particular serving portion, including calories, carbohydrates and fat, amino acids, minerals, and vitamins. Tables at the back of the book contain miscellaneous information such as caffeine content. References are included, and there is an index.

Poisoning

The *Handbook of Poisoning: Prevention, Diagnosis and Treatment* by Robert H. Dreisbach (Los Altos, Calif., Lange, 10th edition 1980) is a concise summary of diagnosis and treatment of poisoning. The book begins with general discussion, such as prevention of poisoning and management of poisoning. Then there are sections for types of poisons: agricultural, industrial, household, medicinal, and natural. In each section specific poisons are listed together with clinical findings, treatment, prognosis, and in some cases prevention, as well as references. There is an index. Poisons from insects and animals are covered in *What to Do About Bites and Stings of Venomous Animals* by Robert E. Arnold (New York, Macmillan, 1973).

Sports Medicine

The *Encyclopedia of Sport Sciences and Medicine* (New York, Macmillan, 1971) contains signed articles by many different authors, each with references. Articles are grouped in broad sections on: (1) physical activity in general and in sports, games, and exercise; (2) influence of environment, emotions and intellect, growth, development and aging, and drugs; (3) applications in prevention of disease and injury, the handicapped, and rehabilitation; and (4) safety and protection. Indexing is by subject and author. Another encyclopedia of sports medicine is by George Sheehan, *Encyclopedia of Athletic Medicine* (Mountain View, Calif., World, 1972).

Periodicals

Alabama Journal of Medical Sciences. Birmingham, Ala., University of Alabama, 1964– . (quarterly)

American Corrective Therapy Journal. Houston, Tex., American Corrective Therapy Association, 1947– . (bimonthy)

American Family Physician. Kansas City, Mo., American Academy of Family Physicians, 1950– . (monthly)

American Journal of Clinical Pathology. Philadelphia, Pa., Lippincott, 1931– . (monthly)

American Journal of Medicine. New York, Yorke, 1946– . (monthly)

American Journal of the Medical Sciences. Thorofare, N.J., Slack, 1820– . (bimonthly)

American Medical Women's Association. Journal. New York, American Medical Women's Association, 1915– . (monthly)

Annals of Biomedical Engineering. New York, Pergamon, 1973– . (bimonthly)

Archives of Sexual Behavior. New York, Plenum, 1971– . (6/year)

Arizona Medicine. Phoenix, Ariz., Arizona Medical Association, 1944– . (monthly)

Canadian Medical Association. Journal. Ottawa, Canada, Canadian Medical Association, 1911– . (semimonthly)

Chicago Medicine. Chicago, Chicago Medical Society, 1902– . (semimonthly)

Computers and Medicine. Chicago, American Medical Association, 1972– . (bimonthly)

Diabetes Educator. Pitman, N.J., American Association of Diabetes Educators, 1975– . (quarterly)

Emergency; the Journal of Emergency Services. Carlsbad, Calif., 1969– . (monthly)

Evaluation and the Health Professions. Beverly Hills, Calif., Sage, 1978– . (quarterly)

Family Physician. Oak Brook, Ill., Academy of Family Physicians, 1951– . (bimonthly)

Florida Family Physician. Jacksonville, Fla., Florida Academy of Family Physicians, 1953– . (quarterly)

Health and Society. Cambridge, Mass., Massachusetts Institute of Technology, 1923– . (quarterly)

Health Physics. New York, Pergamon, 1958– . (monthly)

Inquiry; the Journal of Health Care Organization, Provision and Financing. Chicago, Blue Cross Associations, 1963– . (quarterly)

Issues in Health Care of Women. Washington, D.C., Hemisphere, 1979– . (bimonthly)

JAMA: The Journal of the American Medical Association. Chicago, American Medical Associaton, 1848– . (weekly)

Journal of Chronic Diseases; Devoted to the Problems and Manage-

ment of Chronic Illness in All Age Groups. New York, Pergamon, 1955– . (monthly)

Journal of Community Health. New York, Human Sciences Press, 1975– . (quarterly)

Journal of the History of Medicine and Allied Sciences. Minneapolis, Minn., University of Minnesota, 1946– . (quarterly)

Laboratory Medicine, American Society of Clinical Pathologists. Philadelphia, Pa., Lippincott, 1965– . (monthly)

Medical Clinics of North America. Philadelphia, Pa., Saunders, 1916– . (bimonthly)

Medicine and Science in Sports and Exercise. Madison, Wis., American College of Sports and Medicine, 1969– . (5/year)

Origins of Life: An International Journal Devoted to the Scientific Study of the Origins of Life. Dordrecht, Netherlands, Reidel, 1968– . (quarterly)

Perspectives in Biology and Medicine. Chicago, University of Chicago, 1957– . (quarterly)

Rehabilitation Counseling Bulletin. Falls Church, Va., American Personnel and Guidance Association, 1957– . (quarterly)

Southern Medicine. Birmingham, Ala., Southern Medical Association, 1906– . (monthly)

Today's Clinician. New York, Weston, 1977– . (monthly)

PRIMARY LITERATURE MATERIALS

Drug Standards

The *United States Pharmacopeia/National Formulary* (Rockville, Md., U.S. Pharmacopeial Convention, 1979–) is published annually with supplements to keep up to date. Formerly these were separate publications: *Pharmacopeia of the United States* since 1820 and *National Formulary* since 1888, now published together in one volume since 1979. Related current publications also form the United States Pharmacopeial Convention are *USAN and the USP Dictionary of Drug Names* and *United States Pharmacopeia Dispensing Information,* each mentioned earlier. The pharmacopeia section is made up of USP official drug monographs, which act as standards for drugs. The monographs are arranged alphabetically by drug name and give such information as chemical structure, packaging and storage, reference standards, and identification. Other chapters include descriptions of general tests and assays and how to perform them; general information; reagents, indicators, and solutions; and reference tables. The formulary section contains official monographs on pharmaceutic ingredients arranged alphabetically by name. Information given includes chemical structure, packaging and storage, and tests. There is information on antibiotic regulations and other topics, and the volume is completed by a combined index for the USP and NF.

CURRENT AWARENESS MATERIALS

There are two sections of *Current Contents* for medical sciences, *Current Contents: Life Sciences* (Philadelphia, Pa., Institute for Scientific Information, 1958–) and *Current Contents: Clinical Practice* (Philadelphia, Pa., Institute for Scientific Information, 1973–), both published weekly. Each reprints tables of contents of selected relevant journals, international in scope. The contents lists are arranged in broad subject groups, for example, for the life sciences: multidisciplinary, chemistry, experimental biology and medicine, and so forth. There are indexes by subject and author, and the author index includes the author's address. Special features appear at the front of the journal, including contents lists from new books, a condensation of a highly cited article, and editorial materials.

Meetings to be held in the upcoming two-year period are listed in *World Meetings: Medicine* (New York, Macmillan, 1, 1978–). This tool is published quarterly, and is international in coverage. The main entry section is divided into eight subsections for quarters of the coming two-year period. Meetings to be held during that period are listed, with information as to sponsor, content, where to get more informa-

---

MEDLINE

Worldwide professional literature in the biomedical sciences. Corresponds to the printed Index Medicus, but also includes citations from Special Lists. MEDLINE includes several ancillary files: SDILINE--current month of MEDLINE online, replaced each month after Index Medicus is printed; and MEDLINE backfiles--references providing coverage of periods preceding MEDLINE, back to 1966 (output is only available offline through NLM and BRS). BRS has 1966 to 1970 offline, and 1971 to present online. DIALOG has three files: 152 (1966 to 1974), 153 (1975 to 1979), and 154 (1980 to present). See also PRE-MED file.

Prepared by National Library of Medicine.

Coverage: 1966 to present
File size: 3.4 million records
Unit record: citation, abstract
Vendor, Cost/connect hour:
  BRS, $19;
  DIALOG (152, 153, 154), $35;
  NLM, $15-$22

Fig. 12–2. Computer data base: MEDLINE

tion, and so forth. There are indexes by key subject words in the name of the meeting, location of the meeting, date of the meeting, sponsor of the meeting, and deadline date for submission of papers.

QUICK REFERENCE TOOLS

Dictionaries

Melloni's Illustrated Medical Dictionary (Baltimore, Md., Williams and Wilkins, 1979) contains brief definitions with more than 2,000 illustrative drawings. The drawings applicable to each page are placed together at the top of that page, and are simple and specific. Commonly used chemical compounds and drugs are included in addition to medical terms. *Dorland's Illustrated Medical Dictionary* (Philadelphia, Pa., Saunders, 26th edition 1981) also has many illustrations. Plates illustrate anatomical parts, and there are several tables, for example, of anatomic parts. Pronunciation and derivation are included along with definitions of words. *Stedman's Medical Dictionary* (Baltimore, Md., Williams and Wilkins, 24th edition 1982) gives pronunciation for some words, word derivation, and a brief definition. Some drawings are included to illustrate definitons. A separate "word root list" lists the more important Greek and Latin words from which medical terminology comes, with meanings. The appendixes include an alphabetical index of subentries, information on blood groups, weights and measures, laboratory analyses, and abbreviations. *Blakiston's Gould Medical Dictionary* (New York, McGraw-Hill, 3d edition 1972) gives pronunciation, derivation, and a brief definition. The appendix includes anatomic tables of arteries, bones, muscles, nerves, joints and ligaments, and veins.

The following three dictionaries give not only definitions but expanded explanations of terms. *Butterworths Medical Dictionary* (London, Butterworths, 2d edition 1978) also tells word derivation. Drugs are included. An index entitled "anatomical nomenclature" is arranged alphabetically by scientific name and gives the English name and term under which a definition will be found in the main part of the dictionary. *Encyclopedia and Dictionary of Medicine, Nursing, and Allied Health* by Benjamin F. Miller and Claire Keane (Philadelphia, Pa., Saunders, 2d edition 1978) includes a few drawings, tables, and photographs as needed. Anatomical tables, for example, a table of veins, are included in the definitions. Appendixes include tables of weights and measures, conversions, and so forth, and sources for patient education materials. *Taber's Cyclopedic Medical Dictionary* (Philadelphia, Pa., David, 14th edition 1981) includes a few diagrams and drawings, and gives word derivation. Appendixes are extensive, including units of measurement, normal reference laboratory values, tables of anatomical parts, and word equivalents in English, Spanish, Italian, French, and German.

Black's Medical Dictionary (New York, Barnes and Noble, 31st edition 1976) covers medical disorders, telling symptoms, causes, and treatment. It is useful for home emergencies.

Medical Abbreviations and Acronyms by Peter Roody and others (New York, McGraw-Hill, 1977) is arranged alphabetically by abbreviation or acronym, with meanings included. *Abbreviations and Acronyms in Medicine and Nursing* by Solomon Garb and others (New York, Springer, 1976) is similar. This dictionary also includes the Greek alphabet, Greek and Roman symbols, and other symbols that do not fit into an alphabetical order, such as symbols for male and female.

Medical and Health Sciences Word Book compiled by Ann Ehrlich (Boston, Mass., Houghton Mifflin, 1977) is a speller of about 60,000 terms used in medicine, nursing, and other health sciences. Appendixes include trade names of drugs, abbreviations, medical signs and symbols, and more.

There are many dictionaries specialized for a certain subject area. Examples are the *Dictionary of Biochemistry* by J. Stenesh (New York, Wiley, 1975) and the *Dictionary of Nutrition* by Richard Ashley and Heidi Duggal (New York, St. Martin's, 1975).

Some dictionaries of foreign terms in medical sciences are:

Eight-language Dictionary of Medical Technology: English, German, French, Russian, Spanish, Polish, Hungarian, Slovak. New York, Pergamon, 1979.

Elsevier's Dictionary of Public Health: In 6 Languages, English–French–Spanish–Italian–Dutch and German. New York, Elsevier, 1976.

Elsevier's Medical Dictionary in Five Languages. Amsterdam, Elsevier, 2d edition 1975.

Foreign word equivalents are also given in *Taber's Cyclopedic Medical Dictionary,* described earlier.

Compilations

The *Standard Medical Almanac* (Chicago, Marquis, 1, 1977–) is published every two years as an overview of current health care in the United States. Manpower, income and expenditures, education, facilities, diseases, and the role of the federal government are included. There are many tables and graphs. Indexes are by subject, organization, and geographic location. American Hospital Association *Guide to the Health Care Field* (Chicago, American Hospital Association, 1, 1945–) is published annually. Included is information on health care institutions, on the American Hospital Association, on organizations and agencies in health fields, and statistical information and lists, for example, a list of hospitals in the United States arranged by state with information in table form telling number of beds, payroll, personnel, and so forth. There is an index.

Directories and Biographical Tools

Directories are of two general types: lists of people and lists of facilities and organizations. Lists of people, all including address and medical specialities and some including brief biographical information, are:

American Medical Directory. Chicago, American Medical Association, 1, 1906– .
American Psychological Association. *Directory.* Washington, D.C., American Psychological Association, 1, 1916– .
American Psychological Association, *Membership Register.* Washington, D.C., American Psychological Association, 1, 1969– .
Directory of Medical Specialists. Chicago, Marquis, 1, 1940– .
Traveler's Guide to U.S.-Certified Doctors Abroad. Chicago, Marquis, 1976.
American Dental Directory. Chicago, American Dental Association, 1, 1947–

The *Medical and Health Information Directory* (Detroit, Mich., Gale, 1, 1977–) emphasizes the United States although there is some foreign information. The first section lists national and international organizations arranged alphabetically by topic of the organization, telling address and phone, key person, purpose, and publications. Then there are listings of other organizations with health-related interests, state and regional associations, federal government agencies, Veterans Administration centers and hospitals, federal grants, dental care plans, and many more for a total of thirty-six such listings, most just telling address and phone number and director's name. Several sections have an index included with the section; there is no general index. The *National Health Directory* (Rockville, Md., Aspen, 1, 1977–) lists information sources on U.S. health programs and legislation. Its purpose is to enable a person wanting information about national legislation or programs to find out whom to ask. Included are lists of U.S. senators and representatives and other government people and committees in health, and health officials from regions, states, cities, and counties, with names and addresses.

The *Health Services Directory* (Detroit, Mich., Gale, 1, 1981–) lists U.S. programs and agencies that provide treatment, care, and information. Arrangement is in chapters by subject, for example, aged, alcoholism, or cancer. Material varies somewhat in different chapters, but is usually lists of specific centers, clinics, and state programs first, in geographic order; and then federal government agencies and national organizations. For example, in the section on the aged, adult day care centers are listed with address and phone for each. Appendixes list other related medical and social service organizations. Indexing is by organization names and key words. The *U.S. Medical Directory* (Miami, Fla., U.S. Directory Service, 5th edition, 1980) is arranged alphabetically by state and has five listings for each state: medical doctors, hospitals, nursing facilities, laboratories, and medical information sources. Sections are subarranged by city, and usually the only information given for each listing is address. Medical information sources in this case means hospitals that will give information. There is a separate section for Canadian facilities, as well as a geographical list of medical schools with addresses, and a list of poison control centers.

The *National Directory of Mental Health* (New York, Wiley, 1980) has a descriptive subtitle: "guide to adult outpatient mental health facilities and services throughout the United States." The guide is in three sections: (1) a brief discussion on selecting mental health services and practitoners; (2) a directory of facilities and services arranged geographically; and (3) indexes by name of facility and by services and therapies included.

13
Engineering

INTRODUCTORY MATERIALS

A good place to start our reading is in an armchair with Hall C. Roland's *The Armchair Engineer* (Forest Grove, Oreg., Dilithium, 1981). This is a collection of about fifty essays, aimed mainly at laypersons, that were originally written for a newspaper. Essays cover automobiles, boats and aircraft, basic physical and mathematical laws, heat and light, electricity and electronics, nuclear reactors and radiation, and miscellaneous other topics. Drawings are used to illustrate.

Engineering Encyclopedia edited by Franklin D. Jones and Paul B. Schubert (New York, Industrial Press, 3d edition 1963) is a condensed encyclopedia and mechanical dictionary for engineers. Although this encyclopedia is somewhat older, it is still in print and useful. About 4,500 engineering topics are treated, with short articles usually one-third to one-half page in length. Arrangement is alphabetical by topic. Some illustrations are used.

Introduction to Engineering by Leroy S. Fletcher and Terry E. Shoup (Englewood Cliffs, N.J., Prentice-Hall, 1978) is a textbook introduction to engineering, to provide background information and practice in formulation and solution of engineering problems. Three main sections cover (1) overview of engineering disciplines and oportunities open to engineers; (2) problem solving, engineering analysis, and computational tools; and (3) FORTRAN programming fundamentals and use in problem solving. Each chapter also includes references, and there are problems for practice, with answers to selected problems at the back of the book. There is an index.

Engineering: An Introduction to a Creative Profession by George C. Beakley and H. W. Leach (New York, Macmillan, 3d edition 1977) is also a textbook introduction. Material is presented in five parts: a review of the profession of engineering, preparation for engineering careers, preparation for problem solving, engineering analysis, and an introduction to engineering design. Again there are problems with each chapter, with answers to selected ones at the back of the book. Chapter ten is on using electronic hand-held calculators, with hundreds of practice problems. Ideas on creativity and how to make the most of your own creativity are emphasized. The appendixes contain basic mathematical helps and the code of ethics for engineers.

History of Technology and Invention edited by Maurice Daumas was described in the chapter on general science. Charles J. Singer's *History of Technology* (New York, Oxford University Press, 1954–58) is a five-volume set: volume 1 *From Early Times to the Fall of the Ancient Empires,* volume 2 *Mediterranean Civilizations and the Middle Ages,* volume 3 *From Renaissance to the Industrial Revolution,* volume 4 *Industrial Revolution,* volume 5 *The Late 19th Century.* Chapters are by subject experts, and each volume has a bibliography. Many illustrations, tables, and maps are used. *History of Technology* edited by A. Rupert Hall and Norman Smith (London, Mansell and Bridgeport, Conn., Merrimack, 1976–   ) is a series of annual volumes containing papers by different authors aimed at understanding technical problems of different ages and cultures and the means that were used to solve them. Each volume is made up of several essays by different authors.

Bruce Norman's *The Inventing of America* (New York, Taplinger, 1976) provides interesting reading, beginning with the invention of the safety pin in the introduction and going on through American inventions and how they have helped shape the American way of life. The Franklin stove, which enabled people to ''sit with comfort in any part of the room,'' the sewing machine, guns, the telephone and telegraph, the refrigerator, computers, and many more inventions are chronicled. There is a bibliography. David Weitzman's *Traces of the Past; a Field Guide to Industrial Archaeology* (New York, Scribner, 1980) takes us on walks down old railroad beds and such to find evidences of engineering past. Well-illustrated with many photographs and diagrams, this book covers history through railroads, bridges, roof trusses, furnaces, and oil wells. There is a bibliography.

History of the Machine by Sigvard Strandh (New York, A & W, 1979) is a lovely large volume. Necessarily selective, it covers machines from the dawn of history to the present. Arrangement is in chapters by type of tool or machine: ancient, simple machines; machine elements, for example, gearwheel; industrial machines; waterwheels, windmills, water turbines, and so forth; steam and combustion engines; electricity; control systems; computers; and machines in our daily lives. There are many illustrations, mostly drawings showing machines, with description of how they worked. For example, one shows an early vacuum cleaner: the maid with bellows on her feet carries an attached nozzle and bag and walks around to suck up the dust. There is a bibliography. Two books describing historical instruments are *Scientific Instruments* by Harriet Wynter and Anthony Turner (New York, Scribner, 1975) and *Early Scientific Instruments* by Nigel Hawkes (New York, Abbeville, 1980). Both of these volumes cover about the same time period, the sixteenth through nineteenth centuries, and both are illustrated, including many color photographs.

Scientists and Inventors by Anthony Feldman and Peter Ford (New York, Facts on File, 1979) is arranged in chronological order, and contains two-page spreads on each inventor included. There is a description of the person's work, with illustrations and diagrams of the work and a portrait of the person. Indexes are by name and subject. *American Engineers of the Nineteenth Century; a Biographical Index* by Christine Roysdon and Linda A. Khatri (New York, Garland, 1978) is arranged alphabetically by name and tells dates of birth and death and area of specialization. References are given for further information in biographies or obituaries.

Subject Headings and Classification

Agricultural engineering
Bridges
Building materials
Chemical engineering
Civil engineering
Coastal engineering
Earthwork
Electric engineering
Engineering
Engineering design

Engineering ethics
Engineering geology
Engineering graphics
Engineering instruments
Engineering research
Engineers
Environmental engineering
Hydraulic engineering
Industrial engineering
Machinery
Materials
Mechanical engineering
Mechanics, Applied
Mining engineering
Nuclear engineering
Plant engineering
Roads
Sanitary engineering
Strains and stresses
Strength of materials
Structural engineering
Systems engineering
Traffic engineering
Ventilation

Engineering materials will usually be found in libraries shelved in the T to TS section of the Library of Congress classification, or in the 620 to 629 and 660 to 699 sections of the Dewey Decimal Classification.

BIBLIOGRAPHIC MATERIALS

Guides to the Literature

Most of the literature guides described in the chapter on general science include engineering.

How to Find Out About Engineering by Stanley A. J. Parsons (Oxford, Pergamon, 1972) includes chapters on careers and organizations, education in engineering, and reference works, and then has chapters for specific fields of interest such as mechanical engineering, nuclear engineering, and so forth. Information sources in each area are described. *Use of Engineering Literature* edited by K. W. Mildren (London, Butterworths, 1976) is directed to engineers, librarians, and information specialists, with chapters by different authors. Chapters are on engineering literature and communication; classification and indexing; various forms of literature, for example, journals, reports, patents, standards, reference sources; literature searching; personal indexes; and the literature of various areas of engineering, for example, electronics, design, metallurgy, and so forth. For each of these areas there is a discussion of the literature, with selected specific titles mentioned. *Guide to Basic Information Sources in Engineering* by Ellis Mount (New York, Norton, 1976) is a guide for engineering students and researchers. First the technical literature is discussed, and then there are sections for books, periodicals and technical reports, and other sources of information, with specific titles listed for each of these sections.

The American Society for Engineering Education has published a series of guides by different authors on various areas of engineering (Washington, D.C. American Society for Engineering Education, 1970–72) that are now dated but in many cases provide the only literature guide to that area. Information sources are listed, arranged by type; that is, guides, bibliographies, dictionaries, and so forth. Specific titles in this series are:

Guide to the Literature on Aerospace Engineering. 1971.
Guide to the Literature on Agricultural Engineering. 1971.
Guide to the Literature on Chemical Engineering. 1972.
Guide to the Literature on Civil Engineering. 1972.
Guide to the Literature on Computers. 1970
Guide to the Literature on Electrical and Electronics Engineering. 1970.
Guide to the Literature on Environmental Sciences. 1970.
Guide to the Literature on Industrial Engineering. 1970.
Guide to the Literature on Mechanical Engineering. 1970.
Guide to the Literature on Metals and Metallurgical Engineering. 1970.
Guide to the Literature on Mining Engineering. 1972.
Guide to the Literature on Nuclear Engineering. 1972.

Guide to the Literature on Textile Engineering. 1972.
Guide to the Literature on Transportation Engineering. 1970.

The United Nations Industrial Development Organization has also published a series of guides (New York, United Nations, 1, 1972–). These are issued irregularly, each on a different topic, for example, *Information Sources on Woodworking Machinery,* 1978.

Catalogs

The *Classed Subject Catalog of the New York Engineering Societies Library* (Boston, Mass., Hall, 1963 and supplement 1964–73) is made up of reproductions of catalog cards from this library. The basic set consists of twelve volumes, and the supplement of nine volumes. Arrangement is by subject, and books, journals, films, and reports in all areas of engineering are covered. These catalogs are now brought up to date by annual supplements called *Bibliographic Guide to Technology* (Boston, Mass., Hall, 1975–), prepared by the Research Libraries of the New York Public Library and the Library of Congress. Author, title, and subject access are provided in one alphabetical order.

Indexing and Abstracting Services

An index that is well arranged and easy to use is *Applied Science and Technology Index* (New York, Wilson, 1913–). This index is published monthly except July, with a bound cumulation each year. It is an index to selected English language periodicals, currently about 250, in science and technology and has been published since 1913, the 1913–57 issues being called *Industrial Arts Index.* The main part is a listing of periodical articles in groups by subject. Main subject headings are broad but with many subheadings as needed. There is also a listing of citations to book reviews arranged by the author of the book.

The *Current Technology Index* (London, Library Association, 1962–) formerly called *British Technology Index* is published monthly with annual cumulations. Arrangement is alphabetical by subject, with cross-references leading to related subjects. There is no

IONIZATION, Gaseous—Continued
Spatial distribution of ion formation in chemical ionization sources and the ionization ranges of 100-400-eV electrons in nitrogen and the rare gases. G. G. Meisels and A. J. Illies. bibl diag Anal Chem 53:2162-6 D '81

Theoretical model of laser ionization of alkali vapors based on resonance saturation. R. M. Measures and others. bibl diag J App Phys 52: 1269-77 Mr '81; Correction. 52:7459 D '81

IONS
Gas-phase reactions of negative ions with alkyl nitrites. G. K. King and others. bibl diags Am Chem Soc J 103:7133-40 D 2 '81

Measurements of the ion detection efficiencies of Johnston electron multipliers. B. Peart and M. F. A. Harrison. bibl diag Rev Sci Instr 14:1374 D '81

Negative ion states of cyclopentadiene derivatives. S. W. Staley and others. bibl diags Am Chem Soc J 103:7057-61 D 2 '81

Beams
Deep centers introduced by argon ion bombardment in n-type silicon. J. Garrido and others. bibl Solid-State Electron 24:1121-6 D '81

Displacement criterion for amorphization of silicon during ion implantation. L. A. Christel and others. bibl J App Phys 52:7143-6 D '81

High-current D⁻ production by charge exchange in sodium. E. B. Hooper, Jr and others. bibl diags J App Phys 52:7027-38 D '81

Ion beam improves adhesive bonds. Mach Design 53:136 N 12 '81

Optical effects of energetic copper-ion irradiation on copper mirrors. J. S. Hartman. bibl diag App Opt 20:4062-72 D 1 '81

Small electron and ion beams in surface analysis: their optics, interactions and uses. I. W. Drummond. bibl diags Vacuum 31: 579-88 O/D '81

Mobility
Fundamentals of ion motion in electric radio-frequency multipole fields. M. H. Friedman. and others. bibl diags Sci Instr 16:53-61 Ja '82

Pairs
Nuclear spin polarization effects in radical ion pair reactions; a comparison between triplet state and radical ion reactivity. H. D. Roth and M. L. M. Schilling. bibl diags Am Chem Soc J 103:7210-17 D 2 '81

IRON, Powdered
Ferrous powder-metal (PM) parts [properties of materials; tables] Materials Eng 94:C31 D '81

IRON alloys

Chromium alloys
Influence of chromium on the mass transfer limitation of the anodic dissolution of ferritic steels Fe-Cr in molar sulphuric acid. B. Alexandre and others. bibl Corrosion Sci 21 no 11: 765-80 '81

Oxide scale formation on iron-chromium alloys in elevated temperature air environments. P. Fabis and others. bibl il diags Corrosion 37:700-11 D '81

Nickel alloys
Effect of plating parameters on electrode-posited NiFe. J. Horkans. bibl il diags Electrochem Soc J 128:45-9 Ja '81; Discussion. 128:2604-5 D '81

Titanium alloys
Chemical characterization of complex oxide products on titanium-enriched 310SS. A. S. Nagelberg and R. W. Bradshaw. bibl il Electrochem Soc J 128:2655-9 D '81

IRON carbonyls
Reactivity of distorted C₅H₅Fe(CO)₂(olefin) cations toward nucleophilic attack. T. C. T. Chang and others. bibl diags Am Chem Soc J 103:7361-2 D 2 '81

Sonochemistry and sonocatalysis of iron carbonyls. K. S. Suslick and others. bibl Am Chem Soc J 103:7342-4 D 2 '81

IRON compounds
First evidence for the existence of intramolecular C-H-C hydrogen bonds; carbanions of [1.1]ferrocenophane, 1-methyl[1.1]ferrocenophane, and 1,12-dimethyl[1.1]ferrocenophane. U. T. Mueller-Westerhoff and others. bibl Am Chem Soc J 103:7678-81 D 16 '81

IRON in the body
Effects of storage on the bioavailability and chemistry of iron powders in a heat-processed liquid milk-based product. R. A. Clemens. bibl J Food Sci 47:228-30 Ja/F '82

IRON mines and mining

Lake Superior region
Iron ore quality control. D. A. Long. il Eng &

Fig. 13–1. Index to periodical articles: *Applied Science and Technology Index*

author or other index. Journal articles in the fields of general technology, applied science, engineering, chemical technology, manufacturing, and technical services are covered. Bibliographic information is given, but no abstract.

Engineering Index (New York, Engineering Index, Inc., 1884–) is published monthly with annual cumulations, the 1981 annual cumulation requiring five bound volumes. It is arranged alphabetically in subject groups with many subheadings, and for each item cited gives full bibliographic information and an informative abstract. Cross-references lead to related topics, and there is also an author index. Coverage is international, and includes journal articles, books, reports, patents, and conference proceedings. In addition to the author index, the annual cumulation includes an author affiliation index and a list of conferences.

The indexing and abstracting services above cover virtually all areas of engineering. Now we will consider some of those that are specialized for certain areas. In aeronautics and space technology, there is

Scientific and Technical Aerospace Reports (Washington, D.C., U.S. National Aeronautics and Space Administration, 1963–), often abbreviated *STAR*. Issued twice per month, this service covers aeronautics, space, and supporting disciplines including aerospace aspects of earth resources, energy development, conservation, oceanography, environmental protection, and so forth. It is limited to NASA reports and reports of NASA contractors and grantees, other U.S. government reports, translations, and dissertations and theses. Arrangement is in broad subject groups, and reports are listed with bibliographic information and an abstract. There are indexes by subject, author, contract number, corporate source, and report number. Indexes are cumulated semiannually and annually. *International Aerospace Abstracts* (New York, American Institute of Aeronautics and Astronautics, 1, 1961–) is issued twice a month, and gives international coverage of books, periodical articles, conference proceedings, and translations in aeronautics and space science and technology. Arrangement is in broad subject groups, and bibliographic information and an abstract are given. There are indexes by subject, personal author, contract number, meeting paper and report number, and accession number. Indexes are cumulated semiannually and annually.

Electrical and Electronics Abstracts (London, Institution of Electrical Engineers and New York, Institute of Electrical and Electronics Engineers, 1898–) is published monthly. Until recently this was called *Science Abstracts* series B, and in its earliest years, 1898 to 1902, it was issued as part of the physics section of *Science Abstracts*. All aspects of electrical and electronics engineering are covered, as published in journal articles, reports, books, dissertations, patents, and conference papers. Materials are from all countries and in all languages. Arrangement is by subject based on a classification scheme, and bibliographic information and an abstract are given. There are an author index and a subject guide in each issue, and a detailed subject index and cumulated author index twice a year. The twice-yearly indexes also contain a bibliography index, a book index, a corporate author index, and a conference index. *Electronics and Communications Abstracts Journal* (Bethesda, Md., Cambridge Scientific Abstracts, 1967–) is issued ten times per year, the tenth issue being the cumulated indexes. This service gives international coverage of periodical articles, government reports, conference proceedings, books, dissertations, and patents. Arrangement is in broad subject areas: electronic physics, electronic systems and applications, electronic circuits, electronic devices, and communications. Bibliographic information and an abstract are given. Indexes are by subject and author in each issue and cumulated yearly.

Metal Abstracts (Metals Park, Ohio, American Society for Metals and London, Metals Society, 1968–   ) is issued monthly. Arrangement is by numbered subject fields, devised cooperatively by ASM and the Metals Society, for example, constitution, or crystal properties. Bibliographic information and an abstract are given. There is an author index in each issue. Indexing is through separate publications issued monthly by the same publishers: *Metals Abstracts Index* (1968–   ) and *Alloys Index* (1974–   ). *Metals Abstracts Index* provides indexing by subject and author, monthly and cumulated annually. *Alloys Index* lists specific alloys, metallurgical systems, and intermetallic compounds, monthly with annual cumulations. Earlier materials in this subject area are covered by *Metallurgical Abstracts* and *ASM Review of Metal Literature,* which combined to form *Metals Abstracts.*

Applied Mechanics Reviews (New York, American Society of Mechanical Engineers, 1948–   ) is published monthly. Arrangement is in subject area groups, and bibliographic information and an abstract are given for each item. Coverage is international, of books, articles, and reports. There is an index by author, cumulated annually. *ISMEC Bulletin: Information Service in Mechanical Engineering* (Riverdale, Md., Cambridge Scientific Abstracts, 1973–   ) is published monthly. Coverage is international, of journal articles, reports, documents, and patents.

INIS Atomindex (Vienna, Austria, International Atomic Energy Agency, 1, 1970–   ) is published twice a month to give worldwide coverage of publications relating to nuclear science and its peaceful applications. Arrangement is in subject groups with many subdivisions, for example, physics; theoretical physics. Bibliographic information and an abstract are given. There are indexes by personal author, corporate author, subject, report number and names of conferences from which papers came. The indexes are cumulated every six months. The International Nuclear Information System (INIS) makes available many of the items cited, and other information, around the world. Coverage of information on nuclear energy before 1970 is contained in *Nuclear Science Abstracts* (Oak Ridge, Tenn., U.S. Atomic

Energy Commission, Vols. 1–33, 1947–76). This index also gives international coverage, with bibliographic information and an abstract for each item. Indexes are by subject and author, and for reports also by corporate author and report number.

HRIS Abstracts (Washington, D.C., Transportation Research Board of the National Research Council, 1967–) is issued quarterly to cover information on transportation. This service gives international coverage of research reports, conference proceedings, and journal articles. Arrangement is in broad subject areas, for example, vehicle characteristics, or traffic flow. Bibliographic information and an abstract are given for each item cited. Indexes, in each issue and cumulated annually, are by source, author, and subject. The Society of Automotive Engineers' *Transactions and Literature Developed* (Warrendale, Pa., Society of Automotive Engineers, 1965–) is published annually. This volume lists all literature issued by the society during the year, giving author, title, and an abstract for each. All papers are available on microfiche or in photocopy from the society, and those that are part of the *Transactions* are issued in bound volumes. There are indexes by subject and by author.

SECONDARY LITERATURE MATERIALS

Mathematics

Standard Handbook of Engineering Calculations edited by Tyler G. Hicks (New York,, McGraw-Hill, 1972) contains step-by-step calculations. Arrangement is in sections for the various fields of engineering, for example, civil, architectural, mechanical, and so forth. References are included with each section. The *Encyclopaedic Dictionary of Mathematics for Engineers and Applied Scientists* by I. N. Sneddon (New York, Pergamon, 1976) emphasizes the applications of mathematics in engineering. Arrangement is by topic, and for each topic there is a definition and then usually detailed explanation. There is an index by subject. The *Engineering Mathematics Handbook* by Jan J. Tuma (New York, McGraw-Hill, 2d edition 1979) is arranged in parts by area of mathematics, for example, algebra and geometry, calculus, and so forth. The book's graphical presentation facilitates its use, with color added to highlight topics. There is a glossary, and an index.

The International System of Units, abbreviated SI from Système International d'Unités, is presented in John L. Feirer's *SI Metric Handbook* (New York, Scribner, 1977). The first part of this book contains information on the SI measuring system including the history of measurement, and standards. The second part is on applied metrics as used in building construction, machining, and even food preparation. *SI Units in Engineering and Technology* by S. H. Qasim (Oxford, Pergamon, 1977) is a quick reference guide for conversion to SI units of length, area, volume, mass, pressure, stress, and so forth. There are also engineering data tables of information given directly in SI units, for example, physical constants. Information on the SI system and derivations of important units in engineering, are included.

Experimental Methods

Practical Experiment Designs for Engineers and Scientists by William J. Diamond (Belmont, Calif., Lifetime Learning, 1981) is a text for undergraduate students and a guide for practicing engineers. Design of experiments to give useful data, and statistical methods to analyze and interpret results are included, with references for further information. Exercises are included, and answers are provided at the back. *Experimental Methods for Engineers* by J. P. Holman (New York, McGraw-Hill, 3d edition 1978) is a survey of experimental methods, with emphasis on problem solving and importance of accuracy, error, and uncertainty in experimental measurements. Areas covered are statistical data analysis; dimensional and pressure measurements; flow measurement; temperature measurement devices; transport-property measurements; static force, torque, and strain measurements; motivation and vibration measurement devices; thermal and nuclear-radiation measurement; applications of measurements in air pollution control; and electronic data processing. Review questions and problems are included. The appendix contains tabular information, for example, conversion factors.

Theories of Engineering Experimentation by Hilbert Schenck (New York, McGraw-Hill, 3d edition 1979) is intended primarily for undergraduate students in engineering. The order of topics presented in this book is intended to be the same as the order of an engineering experiment. Areas covered are instrument error and its propagation, test planning as related to variable reduction, response and loading of instruments, spacing of test points, and basic methods of data analysis: graphical and mathematical analysis, graphical and statistical analysis, and statistical data analysis. A bibliography and problems are included with each chapter.

Appropriate Technology

Appropriate Technology: Technology with a Human Face by Peter D. Dunn (New York, Schocken, 1979) describes what has been done as appropriate technology projects have been started to bring a complete, integrated, solution to certain problems in underdeveloped countries, and suggests other projects that might be done. References and a bibliography for further reading are included. The *Appropriate Technology Sourcebook* by Ken Darrow and Rick Pam (Stanford, Calif., Volunteers in Asia, 1981) is in two volumes, and contains reviews of publications about tools and techniques that use local skills, local resources, and renewable sources of energy.

Aeronautics, Astronautics

The *International Encyclopedia of Aviation* edited by David Mondey (New York, Crown, 1977) is a large volume prepared by several contributors. Arrangement is in sections: origins and development; military aviation; civil and maritime aviation; lighter-than-air; specialized aircraft; rocketry and space exploration; facts, feats, and records. Articles in each of these sections present a wealth of information, well-illustrated, from historical aspects to modern. A "famous names" section has brief biographical information on several people, with portraits. There is a glossary. A list of air museums arranged alphabetically by country gives address and brief information for each. The *Encyclopedia of Aviation* (New York, Scribner, 1977) is arranged alphabetically by term, with articles by various contributors mostly one or two paragraphs in length. Articles on famous people in aviation are included. There are many illustrative photographs.

The *Complete Illustrated Encyclopedia of the World's Aircraft* edited by David Mondey (New York, A & W, 1978) contains first a history of flight, including early beginnings in balloons, people who pioneered in flight, war uses, and universal transport. Then a section called "A–Z of the World's Aircraft" is arranged alphabetically by name of craft and describes each, many with pictures. *Jane's All The World's Aircraft* (London and New York, Jane's, 1, 1909–   ) is published annually to give international coverage of aircraft. Arrangement is alphabetical by broad topic, usually a type of aircraft: aircraft, homebuilt aircraft, sailplanes, microlight aircraft and hang gliders, airships, balloons, RPV's and targets, air-launched missiles, spacecraft, and aero-engines; and then alphabetical by country. Information on aircraft includes specifications and performance data, with black and white photographs of many. There is a brief glossary at the front.

The *Illustrated Encyclopedia of Space Technology: A Comprehensive Survey of Space Exploration* (New York, Crown, 1981) contains contributions by several author experts from the United States and Europe. Areas covered are manned space flight, moon probes, military satellites, launch complexes, space cities, and more. Many color illustrations are included.

Foundations of Aerodynamics: Bases of Aerodynamic Design by Arnold M. Kuethe and Chun-Yen Chow (New York, Wiley, 3d edition 1976) is a text aimed at the junior or senior level. Some knowledge of calculus and physics is needed for understanding. Topics include fluid medium, flow, waves, wings, dynamics of viscous fluids, boundary layer control, and so forth. The appendixes contain dimensional analysis, tables of information, and problems, some with answers.

Chemical Engineering

Chemical Industries Information Sources by Theodore P. Peck (Detroit, Mich., Gale, 1979) begins with information about organizations and associations, and reference sources. Then other sections are divided by subject area, for example, materials, nuclear engineering, paper and pulp. In each section, materials are listed.

The *Kirk-Othmer Encyclopedia of Chemical Technology* and other sources described in the chapter on chemistry will be useful here.

Introduction to Chemical Engineering by Edward V. Thompson and William H. Ceckler (New York, McGraw-Hill, 1977) is designed to give beginning students in chemical engineering an understanding of the nature and scope of the chemical process industry, and understanding of chemical and physical principles and how they relate to analysis of chemical processes. Arrangement is in six sections, each dealing with a major aspect of material and energy balancing, in different chemical industries, for example, a petroleum refinery, or an ammonia synthesis plant. Chapters in each section build around that industry, with illustrations and problems at the ends of chapters being drawn from the industry. Appendixes of tabular information include properties of elements and compounds. *Basic Practice of Chemical Engineering* by Esbar I. Shaheen (Boston, Mass., Houghton Mifflin, 1975) is an overall introduction to chemical engineering, emphasizing the solution of practical problems in the chemical process industry. Chapters deal with chemical engineering practice; dimensions, units, and definitions; gases, liquids, and humidity; stoichiometry and materials balances; and energy balances in physical and thermochemical processes. References and an extensive set of problems are included with each chapter. Appendixes include a review of mathematics, and tabular information.

Chemical Engineers' Handbook by Robert H. Perry and Cecil H. Chilton (New York, McGraw-Hill, 1934–   ) is issued irregularly. It presents mathematical tables, physical and chemical data, and information on many other topics such as gas absorption, process control, and cost and profitability estimation. There are references with most sections. There is a glossary. *Physical Properties; a Guide to the Physical, Termodynamic and Transport Property Data of Industrially Important Chemical Compounds* by Carl L. Yaws (New York, McGraw-Hill, 1977) was prepared by many contributors. The authors took data on physical properties of chemicals from over 700 literature sources, which are listed at the back of the book, and used this information to compile graphs, tables, and constants presenting physical properties. This book contains those graphs, tables, and constants for the chemicals for which this information is most often needed, with brief explanations. *Computer Aided Data Book of Vapor–Liquid Equilibria* by Mitsuho Hirata and others (Tokyo, Kodansha and Amsterdam, Elsevier, 1975) begins with a discussion of the fundamental aspects of vapor–liquid equilibrium relations. Then vapor–liquid equilibrium data are given for about 1,000 binary systems, in table and graph form.

Construction, Civil Engineering

Guide to Information Sources in the Construction Industry by Jules B. Godel (New York, Construction Publishing, 1975) is made up mostly of lists of organizations and directories of organizations, with some books and periodicals listed also. Arrangement is in sections: owners; design professionals; building managers; standards, codes, testing, inspection, government planning; and other construction interests. In each section items are listed, with annotations. Another guide by the same author, *Sources of Construction Information; an Annotated Guide to Reports, Books, Periodicals, Standards, and Codes* (Metuchen, N.J., Scarecrow, 1977–), is to be made up of several volumes when complete, each volume on a different type of material as listed in the subtitle. Within each volume, entries are listed by subject area, for example, planning, design, materials, and so forth, with bibliographic information and an abstract. There is an index in each volume.

Structures; or Why Things Don't Fall Down by J. E. Gordon (New York, Plenum, 1981) is a witty introduction to the engineering of structures. The *Illustrated Encyclopedic Dictionary of Building and Construction Terms* by Hugh Brooks (Englewood Cliffs, N.J., Prentice-Hall, 1976) gives brief coverage of building and construction. Arrangement is alphabetical by term, and a definition is given; and in many cases a more detailed explanation follows the definition. Many photographs and diagrams are used to illustrate. An index by function lists terms under twenty-three subject areas.

Civil Engineer's Reference Book (London, Newnes-Butterworths, 1, 1951–) is issued irregularly, the third edition being 1975. Coverage includes strength of materials, theory of structures, materials, hydraulics, soil mechanics, loadings, bridges, highways, airports, railways, water supplies, power supply, sewage disposal, insurance, dredging, demolition, and more. *Standard Handbook for Civil Engineers* edited by Frederick Merritt (New York, McGraw-Hill, 1, 1968–) was published in its second edition in 1976. Arrangement is in sections, with many subdivisions for easy reference, and a bibliography in each section. Coverage includes computers in civil engineering; design management; specifications; construction management and materials; structural theory; geotechnical engineering; design and construction in concrete, structural steel, cold-formed steel, and wood; and engineering of buildings, highways, bridges, airports, railways, and tunnels.

The *Building Construction Handbook,* also by Frederick Merritt (New York, McGraw-Hill, 1, 1958–), was issued in its third edition in 1975. Arrangement is in sections by different authors, with many subdivisions. Sections include architecture; building materials; stresses in structures; soil mechanics and foundations; concrete construction; structural-steel construction; lightweight steel construction; wood construction; windows; walls, partitions and doors; brick construction; floor and roof coverings; insulation and fire protection; heating and air-conditioning; water and power supplies; and construction costs. *Structural Engineering Handbook* edited by Edwin H. Gaylord, Jr. and Charles Gaylord (New York, McGraw-Hill, 1, 1968–   ) was issued in its second edition in 1979. This handbook presents concise information on planning, design, and construction of a variety of engineered structures. Arrangement is in sections by different authors, with references in each section. Topics covered include industrial buildings, tall buildings, bridges, arches, suspension roofs, design in reinforced concrete, prestressed concrete, steel, wood, aluminum, masonry, soil mechanics and foundations, and so forth. *Construction Planning, Equipment, and Methods* by R. L. Peurifoy (New York, McGraw-Hill, 3d edition 1979) is a textbook. Areas covered include job planning and management, construction equipment, engineering fundamentals, soil stabilization and compaction, operation analyses, and construction processes such as drilling and blasting rock. Many photographs of construction equipment and methods are included. The *Handbook of Heavy Construction* edited by John A. Havers and Frank W. Stubbs, Jr. (New York, McGraw-Hill, 1, 1959–   ) was issued in its second edition in 1971. It is intended as a reference source for those involved in construction work, and students or others needing such information. There are three main sections: (1) construction management, on construction organization, contracts, supporting services, and job planning and scheduling; (2) construction equipment, mostly on major classes of construction equipment, for example, excavators; and (3) construction applications, which discusses alternative methods for performing tasks in construction, for example, rock excavation, or paving.

Electrical Engineering and Electronics

How to Find Out in Electical Engineering; a Guide to Sources of Information by Jack Burkett and Philip Plumb (Oxford, Pergamon, 1967) is dated but still may be useful for basic sources of information.
Electrical and Electronic Technologies: A Chronology of Events

and Inventors to 1900 by Henry B. O. David (Metuchen, N.J., Scarecrow, 1981) provides an interesting historical view. Arrangement is chronological beginning with the time before Christ and continuing in chapters by century. A short overview of developments in each century is presented, and then year-by-year accomplishments and developments in that century are listed, with brief information on each.

Standard Handbook for Electrical Engineers (New York, McGraw-Hill, 1, 1908–   ) is issued irregularly, the eleventh edition being 1978. This handbook is oriented toward practical applications. Arrangement is in sections by different authors, with many subdivisions. Topics included are circuits, steam generation, generators, alternative power sources, transmission systems, and standards in electrotechnology. Bibliographies are included. *American Electricians' Handbook* (New York, McGraw-Hill, 1, 1913–   ), the tenth edition issued in 1981, consists of tables, circuit diagrams, construction diagrams, how-to-do-it illustrations, units, and conversion. *IEEE Standard Dictionary of Electrical and Electronics Terms* edited by Frank Jay (New York, IEEE, 2d edition 1977) is arranged alphabetically by term, and has brief definitions. At the back is a list of abbreviations and acronyms, with meanings.

Basic Electronics Theory—With Projects and Experiments by Delton T. Horn (Blue Ridge Summit, Pa., TAB, 1981) is an elementary electronics text for the hobbyist and experimenter. Many illustrations are used, including schematics of circuits. Semiconductor devices and circuits are emphasized. The *Art of Electronics* by Paul Horowitz and Winfield Hill (Cambridge and New York, Cambridge University Press, 1980) is a text and reference book on electronic circuit design. By design, no previous exposure to electronics is needed to understand this book. Exercises are included in the chapters. There is a bibliography. Appendixes include mathematics review, a list of electronics journals, and tables and graphs of information. *Electronics: Circuits and Devices* by Ralph J. Smith (New York, Wiley, 2d edition 1980) is an undergraduate text covering circuit principles, cathode ray tubes, transistors and integrated circuits, microprocessors, amplifiers, and more. Exercises are included with chapters, with answers to selected problems at the back of the book. The *Electronic Engineer's Handbook* (New York, McGraw-Hill, 1, 1975–   ) provides reference design data on electronic circuits, systems, and equipment. Arrangement is in sections by different authors, covering principles employed in electronics engineering; components, devices, and assemblies; circuits and functions; and systems and applications.

The *Illustrated Encyclopedic Dictionary of Electronics* by John Douglas-Young (West Nyack, N.Y., Parker, 1981) is aimed at technicians, engineers, and experimenters, and includes formulas, tables, and other essential information for daily work. Arrangement is alphabetical by term, with definitions. Major topics, interspersed with other topics in the alphabetical order, are discussed in longer detailed articles, and these articles are also referred to in the definitions as a place to look for further information. Diagrams, graphs, and drawings are used to illustrate. The *Modern Dictionary of Electronics* by Rudolf F. Graf (Indianapolis, Ind., Sams, 1977) is arranged alphabetically by term and has concise definitions of about 15 to 200 words, with some illustrations and tables included. Appendixes contain information on SI units, schematic symbols, and the Greek alphabet.

The *User's Guide to Selecting Electronic Components* by Gerald L. Ginsberg (New York, Wiley, 1981) is intended for use by engineers to select components to specify for equipment being designed. Arrangement is in parts by type of component: resistors, capacitors, electromagnetic components, power sources, special-function components, and solid-state devices. Each part contains information about the group of components in general, and about different types of specific components within each group. A list of references is included.

The *Encyclopedia of Integrated Circuits: A Practical Handbook of Essential Reference Data* by Walter H. Buchsbaum (Englewood Cliffs, N.J., Prentice-Hall, 1981) is aimed at anyone doing electronics work whether from a kit, or as a technician or an engineer. Articles cover the entire field of integrated circuits, with respect to what they do and how they perform in electronic equipment. Arrangement is in four main groups of integrated circuits: analog, consumer, digital, and interface. Circuits in each group are listed, and for each there is a description, with explanation of key parameters, applications, and comments. The appendix includes a list of manufacturers. *Modern Electronic Circuits Reference Manual* by John Markus (New York, McGraw-Hill, 1980) is a large volume containing over 3,500 circuits, arranged in groups by type, including amplifier circuits, automotive circuits, lamp control circuits, noise circuits, temperature control circuits, and so forth. In each group there are circuit diagrams, with a brief explanation of each and reference to the original published information on the circuit. Indexes are by authors of original sources, and subjects. The *Giant Handbook of Electronic Circuits* edited by Raymond A. Collins (Blue Ridge Summit, Pa., TAB, 1980) is aimed at hobbyists and designers. Schematic diagrams of circuits are given for AM and FM receivers, automotive circuits, computer-related circuits, telephone circuits, television circuits, and more. The *Handbook of Practical Electronic Circuits* by John D. Lenk (Englewood Cliffs, N.J., Prentice-Hall, 1982) is for students, experimenters, technicians, and designers. Approximately 270 commonly used circuits are included, with theory and operation of each circuit and how it is used in electronic equipment. Arrangement is in sections by type of circuit, including audio-frequency circuits, radio-frequency circuits, power-supply circuits, oscillator circuits, electronic control circuits, amplifier circuits, and more. The *D.A.T.A. Book; Electronic Information Series* (San Diego, Calif., Derivation and Tabulation Associates) is issued in several different series, each with a different starting date and frequency of publication. The series treat different types of devices, for example, transistors, digital integrated circuits, linear integrated circuits, and so forth, with the purpose of reporting on which is presently being produced, worldwide, in each type. Characteristics and manufacturer's specification are given.

A few more books that present electronics for the hobbyist, and some that deal with troubleshooting for the hobbyist or the technician, are listed here:

Coffron, James W. *Practical Troubleshooting Techniques for Microprocessor Systems.* Englewood Cliffs, N.J., Prentice-Hall, 1981.
Genn, Robert C. *Practical Handbook of Solid State Troubleshooting.* West Nyack, N.Y., Parker, 1981.
Grolle, Carl G. *Grolle's Complete Guide to Electronic Troubleshooting.* West Nyack, N.Y., Parker, 1980.
Ingram, Dave. *44 Electronics Projects for Hams, SWLs, CBers and Radio Experimenters.* Blue Ridge Summit, Pa., TAB, 1981.
Veley, Victor F. C. *AC/DC Electricity and Electronics Made Easy.* Blue Ridge Summit, Pa., TAB, 1981.

Manufacturing

The *Encyclopedia of How It's Made* edited by Donald Clarke (New York, A & W, 1978) describes the manufacturing processes for many products. Arrangement is alphabetical by product, for example, acid manufacture, antibiotics, aspirin manufacture, beer and brewing, bookbinding, and so forth. Articles are usually several pages long, and well illustrated mostly with color photographs. *Manufacturing Processes* by B. H. Anstead and others (New York, Wiley, 7th edition 1979) is published in two versions, one using SI units and one using both English and SI units. Each chapter begins with a photograph of an ancient wood engraving, a print, a diorama, or a machine that contrasts modern manufacturing processes with earlier ones. Coverage includes basic manufacturing processes, materials, and some particular processes, for example, welding, powder metallurgy, plastics, press work, drilling and boring, threads and thread-cutting, and so forth. Each chapter includes questions, problems, and a case study. References for each chapter are collected at the back of the book.

Materials

Modern Materials Science by Irving Granet (Reston, Va., Reston Publishing, 1980) is a text covering all areas of materials science, and stressing applications. Topics included are mechanical properties of materials; structure of materials; crystal imperfections; phase and equilibrium diagrams; ferrous materials; nonferrous materials; plastics, composites, and ceramics; electrical, magnetic, and thermal properties of materials; and corrosion. A list of references and practice problems are included with each chapter. *Introduction to the Selection of Engineering Materials* by D. P. Hanley (New York, Van Nostrand Reinhold, 1980) aims to introduce the names of most materials of modern technology, with their properties and uses. The book begins with an overview of materials technology that is a discussion of basic properties and classes of materials. Then separate chapters cover ferrous alloys, nonferrous alloys, joinability of materials, electrical and high temperature materials, composite materials, plastics, rubbers and elastomers, other engineering materials, coating, testing, and computerized materials selection. In each chapter, specific materials are named and usually their properties and uses are described, as well as method of production in some cases. The appendixes contain a brief literature guide, and tables of properties of some materials.

The *Encyclopedia/Handbook of Materials, Parts and Finishes* edited by Henry R. Clauser (Westport, Conn., Technomic, 1976) gives concise information on materials, materials forms and parts, and finishes. Arrangement is alphabetical by topic. The *Handbook of Materials Science* edited by Charles T. Lynch (Boca Raton, Fla., 1, 1974–) is made up of separate volumes by different types of materials. For example, volume 1 is on general properties, volume 2 on metals, composites, and refractory materials, volume 3 on nonmetallic materials and applications, and volume 4 on wood. Each volume collects together much information on its area, with many tables used to present information. *Materials Handbook* by George S. Brady and Henry R. Clauser (New York, McGraw-Hill, 1, 1929–) is issued irregularly, the 11th edition being 1977. Part one, the largest section of the book, is arranged alphabetically by names of materials and describes each in articles of about 300 words. Parts two and three contain mostly tables of information, on elements of materials economics and nature and properties of materials. The journal *Materials Engineering* has in its December issue each year a "Materials Selector" that presents up-to-date information on materials and properties. Section A is a directory of products and manufacturers, listing products in groups such as "irons and steels," and giving manufacturers' names for each; section B is a guide to local sources, listing sales offices of manufacturers; section C contains materials selection charts in groups such as irons and steels, plastics, rubber, ceramics, and so forth, and gives properties for each material.

Plastics Engineering Handbook by the Society of the Plastics Industry (New York, Van Nostrand Reinhold, 1, 1947–) appeared in its 4th edition in 1976. This handbook covers plastics materials chemistry, characteristics, and applications; methods of plastics processing such as blow molding; reinforced plastics; foamed or cellular plastics; compounding and materials handling; and performance testing. Coverage begins with a glossary, and then there are chapters by topic, for example, polymer chemistry, or casting. The *Handbook of Plastics and Elastomers* edited by Charles A. Harper (New York, McGraw-Hill, 1975) is a source book of practical data. It covers fundamentals, plastic and elastomeric product forms, specifications and standards, and design and fabrication. Arrangement is in chapters, for example, "properties and end uses for man-made fibers," or "design and fabrication of plastic parts." *Modern Plastics Encyclopedia* (New York, McGraw-Hill, 1925–) is an annual publication giving up-to-date information on properties of plastics. The first part is made up of articles arranged in broad categories by subject and then alphabetically by topic, for example, materials, composites, fabricating and finishing, and so forth. The main part of the volume then presents design and specification data for materials, mostly in table form, a design guide, and a directory of suppliers.

Sources of information on metals are described in Marjorie R. Hyslop's *Brief Guide to Sources of Metals Information* (Washington, D.C., Information Resources Press, 1973). Chapters cover reference tools and other sources of information such as government agencies, searching services, and information centers.

Information on properties of metals may be found in *Metals Handbook* (Metals Park, Ohio, American Society for Metals, 1, 1927–), which has appeared in many editions, the first volume of the 9th edition being published in 1978. This handbook provides data on properties of metals, and practical information to help users select the most suitable metals for specific purposes. Each volume is on a different topic; for example, in the 9th edition volume 1 covers properties and selection of irons and steels, volume 2 properties and selection of nonferrous alloys and pure metals, volume 3 properties and selction of stainless steels, tool materials, and special-purpose metals, and volume 4 heat treating. Each volume contains an index. *Metals Reference Book* edited by Colin J. Smithells (Reading, Mass., Butterworth, 1, 1949–) contains a summary of data relating to metallurgy, mostly in the form of tables and diagrams. Arrangement is in sections, for example, general physical and chemical constants, crystallography, and mechanical properties of metals and alloys. *Woldman's Engineering Alloys* edited by Robert C. Gibbons (Metals Park, Ohio, American Society for Metals, 1, 1936–) is issued irregularly, the sixth edition being 1979. The main section contains alloy data, with alloys listed alphabetically and data given for each on manufacturer, chemical composition, uses, and applications. There are also lists of manufacturers referred to in the data section, alphabetically and in numerical order. An alphabetical list of obsolete alloys and lists of standards of various associations complete this volume.

Mechanical Engineering

Sources of information are listed in Bernard Houghton's *Mechanical Engineering: The Sources of Information* (Hamden, Conn., Shoe String, 1970), which although dated is still useful in some areas.

The *Encyclopedia of How it Works* edited by Donald Clarke (New York, A & W, 1977) describes just how various machines work. Arrangement is alphabetical by topic with articles usually one page or more in length, and well illustrated with photographs of historical and modern machines, many in color. The entry for "cash register," for example, has photographs of historical models from 1879, later models, and modern computer terminals; and discusses mechanical cash registers' keyboard, cash indicator, audit counter and roll printer, cash drawer, and control lock; and electronic cash registers.

Mark's Standard Handbook for Mechanical Engineers (New York, McGraw-Hill, 1, 1916–) was published in its 8th edition in 1978, edited by Theodore Baumeister. This work is arranged in sections by different authors, each with many subdivisions for easy reference. Included are mathematics, mechanics of solids and fluids, heat, strength of materials, materials, fuels, machine elements, power generation, transportation, and instruments and controls. *Machinery's Handbook; a Reference Book for the Mechanical Engineer, Draftsman, Toolmaker, and Machinist* (New York, Industrial Press, 1, 1914–) is a standard reference book on machines or other mechanical products, revised every few years. Information presented includes mathematical tables, mechanics, strength of materials, gears, screws, threads, and so forth.

The *ASHRAE Handbook* (New York, American Society of Heating, Refrigerating and Air-Conditioning Engineers, 1961–) has been published in many editions over the years to provide reference data on air-conditioning, heating, ventilation, and refrigeration. Current editions are made up of four volumes, published on a rotating basis every four years. The fundamentals volume covers theory, general engineering data, basic materials, load calculations, duct and pipe sizing, and general information. The equipment volume includes air-handling equipment, refrigeration equipment, heating equipment, general components, unitary equipment, and general information. The applications volume includes air-conditioning and heating, food refrigeration and freezing, and general information. The systems volume includes air-conditioning and heating systems, industrial ventilation, refrigerating systems, and general information. Arrangement of each volume is in chapters, with a bibliography included for each. A companion volume is the *Product Specification File,* annual, which contains a product directory and other useful information.

Terms are defined in the *Dictionary of Mechanical Engineering* by J. L. Nayler and G. H. Nayler (London, Butterworths, 2d edition 1978).

Nuclear Energy

An overview of nuclear energy that provides a good introduction for the lay reader may be found in Isaac Asimov's *Worlds Within Worlds: The Story of Nuclear Energy* (Seattle, Wash., University Press of the Pacific, 1980). *Nuclear Power* by James J. Dunderstadt (New York, Dekker, 1979) requires, according to the preface, only a "modest" scientific background, and most is suitable for nonscientists. The basic technical aspects of nuclear power generation are coverd, with topics including nuclear energy and the energy crisis, development of nuclear power, basic concepts, nuclear fission reactors, nuclear power generation, thermonuclear fusion, and energy alternatives. There are bibliographic notes with each chapter, and a bibliography for further reading.

Foundations of Nuclear Engineering by Thomas J. Connolly (New York, Wiley, 1978) is an introduction to nuclear engineering intended for students or for others who may be working on problems in nuclear engineering but who have had no formal instruction in the field. Knowledge of basic chemistry, physics, and calculus is needed. Topics covered include energy concepts and analysis; radioactivity, fission, and fusion; interactions of nuclear particles in matter; and effects of radiation on humans. There are references with each chapter. The appendix contains conversion tables, and properties of selected elements and nuclides. *Nuclear Energy Technology; Theory and Practice of Commercial Nuclear Power* by Ronald Allen Knief (New York, McGraw-Hill, 1981) is also an introductory text in nuclear engineering. Materials are presented in six main parts: general overview of commercial nuclear fuel cycle and power reactors; theory needed to understand nuclear energy; reactor safety, including the accident at Three Mile Island, federal regulations, and safeguards; and nuclear fusion as a commercial energy sourse. There is an extensive bibliography. Appendixes include tables of data and information on the use of nuclear power in providing consumer energy. *Nuclear Energy and the Environment* (Oxford and New York, Pergamon, 1980) originated from a review of environmental impacts of nuclear energy for the

United Nations. It is a collection of papers by various international authorities on environmental aspects of the nuclear fuel cycle, with references included as a part of each paper. The book ends with a review of the main elements affecting the future development of nuclear power. *Nuclear Reactor Engineering* by Samuel Glasstone and Alexander Sesonske (New York, Van Nostrand Reinhold, 3d edition 1981) describes fundamental science and engineering principles of nuclear reactor systems, especially those for generation of electric power. Topics include energy from nuclear fission, principles of reactor analysis, nuclear reactor shielding and safety, and so forth. The appendix includes tables such as physical properties of some reactor materials, properties of reactor coolants, and so forth. References are included with chapters.

Samuel Glasstone's *Sourcebook on Atomic Energy* (Melbourne, Fla., Krieger, 3d edition 1979 reprint of 1967 edition) is a basic reference text on atomic energy originally published under the auspices of the U.S. Atomic Energy Commission. It covers the foundations of atomic theory, nuclear reactors, biological effects and radiation protection, elementary particles, and more, with bibliographies included in each chapter. *Nuclear Engineering Handbook* edited by Harold Etherington (New York, McGraw-Hill, 1958) is a compilation of nuclear information and data. Arrangement is in sections by different authors, covering basic mathematical tables and information, and then nuclear physics, experimental techniques, fluid and heat flow, reactor materials, mechanical design of reactors, isotopes, and so forth.

Photography

The *Encyclopedia of Practical Photography* edited at the Eastman Kodak Company (Garden City, N.Y., Amphoto, 1977) is in fourteen volumes. Articles are arranged in alphabetical order by topic, and are often several pages in length. Many diagrams and photographs are used to illustrate, and articles include bibliographies. Emphasis is on practical advice and instruction for individual photographers. Photographic theory and chemistry and biographies of people important in the development of photographic science are also included. *Darkroom Handbook* by Michael Langford (New York, Knopf, 1981) contains practical information to provide basic darkroom methods for beginners and new areas for those who know the basics. Topics covered include darkroom equipment, processing your own film, black and white printing, color printing, basic manipulations, advanced manipulations, workroom techniques, and rediscovering old processes. A glossary of terms is included, and the appendix contains information on chemicals and film.

Radio and Television

The *Radio Amateur's Handbook* (Newton, Conn., American Radio Relay League, 1925–) is a long-standing standard source for radio amateurs. This handbook is published annually to provide practical information for amateurs on such topics as electrical circuits, radio design, solid-state fundamentals, receiving systems, and operating station. Arrangement is in chapters, with many subdivisions for easy reference. Many photographs, diagrams, graphs, and tables are used.

Reference Data for Radio Engineers (Indianapolis, Ind., Sams, 6th edition 1975) is a compilation of equations, graphs, tables, and so forth, needed in radio engineering and design. *Radio, TV and Audio Technical Reference Book* edited by S. W. Amos (London, Newnes-Butterworths, 1977) is a practical account of developments in radio and television, by many contributors. This book covers the fundamentals of sound transmission, electronic circuits, sound transmitters, television receiver installation and servicing, and so forth. *The Television Engineers' Pocket Book* (Rochelle Park, N.J., Hayden, 6th edition 1973) covers basics of television, in sections by several contributors.

Transportation

A bibliography of information sources is Bob J. Davis's *Information Sources in Transportation, Material Management, and Physical Distribution* (Westport, Conn., Greenwood, 1976). Books, government publications, organizations, educational materials, and atlases and maps are listed, with brief annotations.

The *Handbook of Highway Engineering* edited by Robert F. Baker (New York, Van Nostrand Reinhold, 1975) is concerned with principles, processes, and data for application of technology to highway transportation. Covered are policy and planning, location, standards, cost, construction, and maintenance. The *Highway Engineering Handbook* by Kenneth B. Woods (New York, McGraw-Hill, 1960) is a compilation of data on operations, design, and construction of highways. Sections are by different authors, and each includes references. *Transportation and Traffic Engineering Handbook* (Englewood Cliffs, N.J., Prentice-Hall, 1941–) has been issued in various editions over the years, by the Institute of Transportation Engineers. Arrangement is in chapters on such topics as vehicle, highway, and travel facts, vehicle operating characteristics, driver and pedestrian characteristics, traffic characteristics, traffic accidents, computer applications, urban transportation, and parking. Bibliographies are included.

Periodicals

A list of some English language periodicals follows, chosen with an eye to showing the variety that exists in terms of type of publisher, subject matter, frequency, and type of coverage.

American Society of Civil Engineers. Proceedings. New York, American Society of Civil Engineers, 1873– . (monthly) (consists of various journals, e.g., *Journal of the Structural Division; Journal of the Waterway, Port, Coastal and Ocean Division; Journal of the Engineering Mechanics Division*)

British Engineer. Brighton, England, Institution of British Engineers, 1928– . (quarterly)

Chemical and Engineering News. Washington, D.C., American Chemical Society, 1923– . (weekly)

Consulting Engineer: Journal of the Professional Engineer. London, Northwood Publications, Ltd., 1939– . (monthly)

Diesel Engineering. Maidstone, Kent, Whitehall Press, 1905– . (quarterly)

Engineer. London, Morgan-Grampian Ltd., 1856– . (weekly)

Florida Engineering Society. Journal. Orlando, Fla., Society, 1917– . (monthly)

General Engineer. London, Institution of Mechanical and General Technician Engineers, 1891– . (monthly)

Great Britain. Department of the Environment. *Building Research*

Establishment Digest. London, H. M. Stationery Office, n.d. (irregular)

ISA Transactions, Pittsburgh, Pa., Instrument Society of America, 1961– . (quarterly)

Industrial Engineering. Atlanta Ga., American Institute of Industrial Engineers, 1969– . (monthly)

International Journal of Heat and Mass Transfer. London, Pergamon, 1960– . (monthly)

Journal of Quality Technology. Milwaukee, Wis., American Society for Quality Control, 1969– . (quarterly)

Materials Engineering. Cleveland, Ohio, Penton-IPC, 1929– . (monthly)

Newcomen Society for the Study of the History of Engineering and Technology. Transactions. London, Newcomen Society, 1922– . (annual)

Plant Engineering. Barrington, Ill., Technical Publishing Co., 1947– . (fortnightly)

Production Engineer. London, Institution of Production Engineers, 1921– . (monthly)

Society of Engineers Journal and Transactions. London, Society of Engineers, 1854– . (quarterly)

Society of Women Engineers, Newsletter. Boston, Mass., Society of Women Engineers, 1954– . (5 per year)

Technology and Culture: Devoted to the Study of the Development of Technology and Its Relations with Society and Culture, Society for the History of Technology. Chicago, University of Chicago Press, 1960– . (quarterly)

University Engineer. Corvallis, Oreg., Oregon State University, 1965– . (3 per year)

PRIMARY LITERATURE MATERIALS

Standards

Standards collected and made available by the American National Standards Institution and the National Standards Association were described earlier, as were the American Society for Testing and Materials standards. The latter will be described more fully here because they are a part of the engineering literature.

Standard Specification for

GENERAL REQUIREMENTS FOR WROUGHT COPPER AND COPPER-ALLOY PLATE, SHEET, STRIP AND ROLLED BAR [METRIC][1]

This standard is issued under the fixed designation B 248M; the number immediately following the designation indicates the year of original adoption or, in the case of revision, the year of last revision. A number in parentheses indicates the year of last reapproval.

1. Scope

1.1 This specification covers a group of general requirements common to several wrought product specifications. Unless otherwise specified in the purchase order or in an individual specification, these general requirements shall apply to copper and copper-alloy, plate, sheet, strip, and rolled bar supplied under each of the following product specifications issued by the American Society for Testing and Materials: B 36, B 97, B 103, B 121, B 122, B 152, B 169, B 194, B 291, B 422, B 465, B 534, B 591, and B 592.

NOTE 1—This specification is the metric counterpart of Specification B 248.

2. Applicable Documents

2.1 The following documents of the issue in effect on date of material purchase form a part of this specification to the extent referenced herein:

2.1.1 *ASTM Standards*:

Specifications:[2]

B 36 Brass Plate, Sheet, Strip, and Rolled Bar

B 97 Copper-Silicon Alloy Plate, Sheet, Strip, and Rolled Bar for General Purposes

B 103 Phosphor Bronze Plate, Sheet, Strip, and Rolled Bar

B 121 Leaded Brass Plate, Sheet, Strip, and Rolled Bar

B 122 Copper-Nickel-Zinc Alloy (Nickel Silver) and Copper-Nickel Alloy Plate, Sheet, Strip, and Rolled Bar

B 152 Copper Sheet, Strip, Plate, and Rolled Bar

B 169 Aluminum Bronze Plate, Sheet, Strip, and Rolled Bar

B 194 Copper-Beryllium Alloy Plate, Sheet, Strip, and Rolled Bar

B 291 Copper-Zinc-Manganese Alloy (Manganese Brass)

B 422 Copper-Nickel-Silicon Alloy Sheet and Strip

B 465 Copper-Iron Alloy Plate, Sheet, Strip, and Rolled Bar

B 534 Copper-Cobalt-Beryllium Alloy (Copper Alloy UNS No. C17500) Plate, Sheet, Strip, and Rolled Bar

B 591 Copper-Zinc-Tin Alloys, Plate, Sheet, Strip, and Rolled Bar

B 592 Copper-Zinc-Aluminum-Cobalt Alloy, Plate, Sheet, Strip, and Rolled Bar

Test Methods:

B 193 Resistivity of Electrical Conductor Materials[3]

E 8 Tension Testing of Metallic Materials[4]

E 18 Rockwell Hardness and Rockwell Su-

---

[1] This specification is under the jurisdiction of ASTM Committee B-5 on Copper and Copper Alloys, and is the direct responsibility of Subcommittee B05.01 on Plate, Sheet, and Strip.

Current edition approved March 3, 1980. Published May 1980.

[2] *Annual Book of ASTM Standards*, Part 6.
[3] *Annual Book of ASTM Standards*, Parts 6, 7, and 44.
[4] *Annual Book of ASTM Standards*, Parts 6, 7, and 10.

Fig. 13–2. Standards: *Annual Book of ASTM Standards*

The *Annual Book of ASTM Standards* (Philadelphia, Pa., American Society of Testing and Materials, 1939–   ) is published annually, now in approximately fifty volumes per year. Each new edition makes the last obsolete; each standard is printed each year, including those not revised from the year before. Therefore the current edition contains all currently approved ASTM standards and tentative test methods, definitions, recommended practices, classifications, and specifications. Arrangement is in volumes by subject, for example, steel: piping, tubing and fittings; steel: plates, sheet strip, wire; and paper: packaging, business copy products. The standards in each volume are arranged in alphanumeric order. There is a subject index in each volume and a separate index volume for the entire set. The index volume also contains an index of standard numbers, indicating the volume that items appear in.

Standards in Building Codes (Philadelphia, Pa., American Society for Testing and Materials, 1, 1955–   ), published in its 15th edition in 1980, now appears in two volumes. This is a compilation of ASTM standards that have been referenced in national building codes. These standards are included in the *Annual Book of ASTM Standards,* but are scattered through those volumes.

The Society of Automotive Engineers *Handbook* (Warrendale, Pa., Society of Automotive Engineers, 1905–   ) is published annually, now in two volumes. The purpose is to record standards for materials, parts, and equipment and for the vehicles themselves, including cars, trucks, off-road vehicles such as agricultural equipment, and boats. The first volume is arranged in sections: ferrous materials; nonferrous materials; nonmetallic materials; threads, fasteners, and common parts; and electrical equipment and lighting. Volume two is arranged in these sections: powerplant components; emissions; passenger cars, trucks, buses, and motorcycles; off-highway machines and vehicles; and marine equipment. Standards are given in each category. There is a subject index in each volume.

CURRENT AWARENESS MATERIALS

Current Contents: Engineering, Technology, and Applied Sciences (Philadelphia, Pa., Institute for Scientific Information, 1, 1970–   ) is published weekly to reprint tables of contents of selected current journals. Arrangement is in broad subject area groupings, for example, "materials" or "nuclear." There are indexes by subject and by author in each issue, and the author index includes the author's address. Regular features at the front of each issue include an editorial article, table of contents of selected books, and mention of often-cited articles.

Current Papers in Electrical and Electronics Engineering (London, Institution of Electrical Engineers and New York, Institute of Electrical and Electronics Engineers, 1969–   ) is issued monthly as the current awareness service of the same associations that publish *Electrical and Electronics Abstracts,* described earlier in this chapter. Coverage is international, and items are listed in a classified arrangement by broad subjects with subdivisions. Only bibliographic information is given, no abstract, and there are no indexes.

QUICK REFERENCE TOOLS

Dictionaries

Howard H. Gerrish's *Technical Dictionary* (South Holland, Ill., Goodheart-Willcox, 1976) gives brief definitions for general engineering terms. Some specialized dictionaries were mentioned in subject sections of this chapter. Lists of engineering terms with cross-references but without definitions are in the Engineers Joint Council *Thesarus of Engingeering and Scientific Terms* (New York, Engineers Joint Council, 1967) and Engineering Index, Inc., *Engineering Index Thesarus* (New York, CCM Information Corporation, 1972).

A dictionary of graphical symbols is Alvin Arnell's *Standard Graphical Symbols: A Comprehensive Guide for Use in Industry, Engineering and Science* (New York, McGraw-Hill, 1963), which includes only symbols taken from standards approved by technical or engineering societies. It is arranged in sections by subject area, e.g., electrical–electronic symbols, instrumentation symbols, structural symbols.

Foreign language dictionaries for engineering are:

Polyglot:

Bosch, Ten. *Dutch–English–French–German Engineering Dictionary.* New York, Heinman, 11th edition, n.d.

Newmark, Maxim. *Dictionary of Science and Technology in English-French-German-Spanish.* New York, Philsophical Library, 1943.

German:

DeVries, Louis and Theo M. Herrmann. *English-German Technical and Engineering Dictionary.* New York, McGraw-Hill, 2d edition 1967.

Ernst, Richard. *Dictionary of Engineering and Technology: German-English and English-German.* New York, Oxford University Press, 4th edition 1981.

Webel, A. *German-English Dictionary of Technical, Scientific and General Terms.* Boston, Mass., Routledge and Kegan Paul, 3d edition 1969.

French:

Cusset, Francis. *Technical Dictionary: English-French, French-English.* New York, Chemical Publishing Co., 1967.

Kettridge, Julius O. *French-English and English-French Dictionary of Technical Terms and Phrases Used in Civil, Mechanical, Electrical and Mining Engineering, and Allied Sciences and Industries.* London and Boston, Mass., Routledge and Kegan Paul, 1980.

Spanish:

Collazo, Javier L. *English-Spanish, Spanish-English Encyclopedic Dictionary of Technical Terms.* New York, McGraw-Hill, 1980.

Robb, Louis A. *Engineer's Dictionary, Spanish-English and English-Spanish.* New York, Wiley, 2d edition 1949.

Russian:

Callaham, Ludmilla I. *Russian-English Chemical and Polytechnical Dictionary.* New York, Wiley, 3d edition 1975.

Foreign language dictionaries for specific areas of engineering will not be listed here, except for two examples:

Elsevier's Dictionary of Measurement and Control: English/American–French–Spanish–Italian–Dutch and German. Amsterdam, Elsevier, 1977.

Oppermann, Alfred. *Dictionary of Electronics: English–German.* New York, Saur, 1980.

Handbooks

Several handbooks cover engineering in general. Each includes, in one volume, mathematics tables and tables and information on various areas of engineering:

Cheremisinoff, Nicholas and Paul N. Cheremisinoff. *Unit Conversion and Formulas Manual.* Ann Arbor, Mich., Ann Arbor Science, 1980.

Gieck, Kurt. *Engineering Formulas.* New York, McGraw-Hill, 2d edition 1976.

Handbook of Engineering Fundamentals. New York, Wiley, 3d edition 1975. (3d edition edited by Ovid W. Eshback and Mott Souders)

Handbook of Tables for Applied Engineering Science. Cleveland, Ohio, Chemical Rubber Co. Press, 2d edition 1973.

Howatson, A. M., Lund, P. G., and J. D. Todd. *Engineering Tables and Data.* London, Chapman and Hall, 1972.

Perry, Robert H., ed. *Engineering Manual.* New York, McGraw-Hill, 3d edition 1976.

Directory

The *Directory of Engineering Societies and Related Organizations* (New York, American Association for Engineering Societies, 1956–   ), biennial, the 9th edition published in 1979, lists and gives brief information on engineering organizations: national, regional, state, and local.

Biographical Tools

Who's Who in Engineering (New York, Engineers Joint Council, 1970–   ) was published in its fourth edition in 1980. Early editions were called *Engineers of Distinction*. Arrangement is alphabetical by name, and for each person there is brief biographical information including positions held, date of birth, parents, education, and so forth. *Who's Who in Technology Today* (Pittsburgh, Pa., Technology Recognition Corporation, 2d edition 1981) lists more than 11,000 people. Arrangement is in volumes by subject: (1) electrical and related technologies, (2) mechanical and related technologies, (3) chemical and related technologies, (4) civil and earth sciences, (5) physics and related technologies, (6) biomedical energy technologies. A seventh volume contains technical and scientific cross-references.

ENERGY

INTRODUCTORY MATERIALS

Survival 2001: Scenario from the Future by Henry E. Voegeli and John J. Tarrant (New York, Van Nostrand Reinhold, 1975) states in its title what many energy professionals and environmentalists believe to be the issue at hand: survival of our society and our environment as they are now. This book provides interesting browsing through its many drawings and its text. It is written from a twenty-first century perspective, as if solutions to today's problems had been found, and so is really presenting possible solutions. It discusses air-conditioning, insulation, and reclamation of wastes for houses; wind power; solar energy; energy from water and waves; and transportation. Drawings or diagrams of most things described are well labeled. *Energy Basis for Man and Nature* by Howard T. Odum and Elizabeth C. Odum (New York, McGraw-Hill, 1976) aims to provide a short, concise statement of the principles of energy and their effect on society historically, now, and in the future. There are three main parts, each consisting of several chapters: (1) energy principles and the flows of energy in our environment; (2) the energy basis for humanity, for example, the energy basis for preindustrial societies, processing energy sources for humanity, and energy and the individual; and (3) possibilities for the future, for example, energy crisis and inflation, a steady-state economy, and a hopeful future. Exercises and activities are included in each chapter, and there is a glossary, and a list of references.

Future Energy Alternatives; Long-Range Energy Prospects for America and the World (Ann Arbor, Mich., Ann Arbor Science,

1978) is concerned with possible alternatives for energy sources in the future. Information on each alternative is presented in a clear, concise fashion. Included are fusion energy, solar energy, coal and hydrogen, nuclear fission, energy from wind, geothermal energy, and water power. The book ends with a discussion of the future, and four possible scenarios of how our energy problems may be solved or not solved. References are included for each topic.

The *United States Energy Atlas* by David Cuff and William J. Young (New York, Free Press, 1980) provides an overview of available resources. Resources are presented in two main parts: nonrenewable resources, including coal, oil and gas, nuclear, and geothermal; and renewable resources, including solar, wind, hydroelectric, ocean thermal, and biomass. Part three is an overview and conclusions. The text is well illustrated with photographs, and many graphs, diagrams, and tables are used. A glossary, a bibliography of references and of further suggested readings, and brief tables of information complete the book. *World Energy: The Facts and the Future* by Don Hedley (New York, Facts on File, 1981) covers energy production and consumption worldwide. The first part is an explanation and discussion of future energy alternatives, whereas the second part consists of information presented in tables and charts. *Renewable Energy* by B. Sorenson (New York, Academic, 1979) is an overview of renewable energy resources, including technology and the effect on our daily life of switching from oil to renewable resources. References are included.

Consumer's Energy Handbook by Peter Norback and Craig Norback (New York, Van Nostrand Reinhold, 1981) contains background and practical information for the consumer. There is information on the legal aspects of solar and nuclear energy, how to conserve energy through such means as weatherizing and insulation, where to get information, and manufacturers of solar equipment. A glossary is included. The *Homeowner's Energy Investment Handbook* by Michael McClintock (Andover, Mass., Brick House, 1981) is designed to tell the homeowner how to make the best economic choice of energy-saving improvements. It takes into account different climates and different type of houses. *Home Energy Management; Principles and Practices* by Stephen J. Mecca and Joseph E. Robertshaw (New York, Van Nostrand Reinhold, 1981) is a practical guide to energy production, use, and conservation for homeowners and others. Topics included are space heating, mechanical energy, heat energy, electrical energy, and chemical energy. The U.S. government issues much energy-related information, which may be found through the *Monthly Catalog of United States Government Publications* or through bibliographies. An example of these publications is *The Energy-Wise Home Buyer: A Guide to Selecting an Energy Efficient Home* prepared by the United States Department of Housing and Urban Development (Washington, D.C., U.S. Government Printing Office, 1979).

Energybook: Natural Sources and Backyard Applications (Philadelphia, Pa., Running, 1, 1975–   ) is a series of large but slim volumes, issued irregularly, that aim to give an overview of possible alternative sources of energy, primarily for laypeople and "backyard experimenters." Each volume is made up of a collection of articles by different authors, presenting ideas that are practical now plus some other approaches that may become important in the future. There is some theory and some application. A selected bibliography with annotations is included, as is a list of other sources of information.

Subject Headings and Classification

Bioenergetics
Biomass energy
Direct energy conversion
Electric power
Energy conservation
Energy consumption
Energy facilities
Energy policy
Energy storage
Power resources
    (also subdivision of Power resources)
    —Research
Renewable energy sources
Solar air conditioning
Solar collection
Solar engines
Solar heating
Solar power plants
Solar energy
Solar wind

Materials in libraries on energy will usually be found shelved in the HD 9502, TH 7413, TJ 163 and TJ 810 to TJ 827, and TK 2896 to TK 2960 sections of the Library of Congress classification, or in the 333.7 to 333.9, 621.4 to 621.49, and 697 to 697.9 sections of the Dewey Decimal Classification.

BIBLIOGRAPHIC MATERIALS

Guides to the Literature

Energy Guide: A Directory of Information Resources by Virginia Bemis (New York, Garland, 1977) includes a wide range of materials, for teachers, librarians, students, energy professionals, and interested laypeople. Arrangement is in chapters by type of material, for example, instructional aids, reference materials, periodicals; or in the case of materials from organizations and government agencies, by who issues the material. Each chapter has a brief introduction, and then items are listed with brief annotations. There is an index. *Information Sources in Power Engineering: A Guide to Energy and Technology* by Karren Metz (Westport, Conn., Greenwood, 1975) lists periodicals, books, conference proceedings, and reference tools, on energy resource development and power conversion, transmission, and distribution. The first three chapters cover periodicals and conference publications, and indexing and abstracting services, with annotations; then there are lists of organizations and federal agencies with address, phone number, and brief information, followed by information centers and libraries, also with address, phone number, and brief information, and then lists of textbooks, and lists of bibliographies and other reference sources, with annotations. There is an index.

Bibliographies

The *Energy Bibliography and Index* (Houston, Tex., Gulf Publishing, 1, 1978–   ) is a six-volume set, the sixth volume being an index for the entire set. This bibliography covers all kinds of literature of the 1900s on energy and related subjects, in books, periodicals, documents, and reports, about 25,000 items in all. Bibliographic information and an abstract of about seventy-five words are given for each item. There are indexes by subject, key word in title, personal author, and coprorate author. This set, compiled by the Texas A and M University Library, is partly published and partly in preparation at the time of this writing.

Two other similar bibliographies have also been prepared by Texas A and M University. *Coal Bibliography and Index* (Houston, Tex., Gulf Publishing, 1981–82) provides retrospective and current coverage, including literature from the 1800s. Items listed have complete bibliographic information and a brief abstract. Indexing is by key word in title, author, corporate author, and subject. *Synfuels Bibliography and Index* (Houston, Tex., Gulf Publishing, 1981–82) is in two volumes, covering current and retrospective literature in books, conference proceedings, reports, and government publications. Topics covered include biomass, bioconversion, in situ processes, hydrogenation, and coal conversion.

Reviews of the Literature

The *Annual Review of Energy* (Palo Alto, Calif., Annual Reviews, 1, 1976–   ) is published yearly. Each volume contains long articles on current topics, with extensive lists of literature cited. There are indexes by subject and author. Most articles deal with developments in a particular area of energy research or technology, such as in volume 6, 1981, "Solar Energy Technology—A Five-Year Update," and "Implications for Reactor Safety of the Accident at Three Mile Island." There is an article (in volume 6, pages 445–482) on energy information, listing several sources of information, mostly government agencies and other non-print sources.

Indexing and Abstracting Services

Many of the indexing and abstracting services described in other chapters would be useful for energy information as it is related to the various scientific disciplines. In particular these services contain extensive energy-related references:

Applied Science and Technology Index
Bibliography of Agriculture
Electrical and Electronics Abstracts
Engineering Index
Environment Abstracts

Government Reports Announcements and Index
INIS Atomindex
Monthly Catalog of Unived States Government Publications
Nuclear Science Abstracts
Physics Abstracts
Scientific and Technical Aerospace Reports

Energy Information Abstracts (New York, Environment Information Center, 1976–) is published monthly except May/June and November/December double issues, to give international coverage of journal articles, special reports, government documents, and conference proceedings. The main part, called the review section, is arranged in twenty-one broad subject categories. Items are listed with bibliographic information and an abstract. Indexes in each issue are by subject, industry, source, and author. There is a list of new books. Full copies of articles cited are available from the publisher. *Energy Index* (New York, Environment Information Center, 1971–) provides annual indexing for *Energy Information Abstracts*. Indexes are by subject, personal and corporate author, and industry and geographic area. Each index gives complete bibliographic information and refers to the abstract number in *Energy Information Abstracts*. In addition to the indexes, *Energy Index* contains a review of major events in the field in the past year. For example, energy statistics occupied over 100 pages of the 1980 edition; other topics were energy legislation, a synopsis of major bills, concressional committee hearings and status of pending legislation; a list of major energy meetings in the past year with names and addresses to contact for proceedings and papers; and a list of new books and films on energy.

Energy Abstracts for Policy Analysis (Oak Ridge, Tenn., U.S. Department of Energy Technical Information Center, 1, 1975–) is published monthly to index nontechnical information from U.S. government reports, state and local reports, and periodical articles. This service includes materials on all areas of energy analysis, for example, research and development progress, economics, social aspects, legislation, and environmental effects. The technical counterpart of this service is *Energy Research Abstracts* (Oak Ridge, Tenn., U.S. Department of Energy Technical Information Center, 1, 1976–), published twice a month to abstract and index all scientific and technical reports, journal articles, conference papers and proceedings, books, patents,

much longer time of order $a^2/D_{\perp}$ parallel/, denoted by tau/sub eta/. (This occurs because there is not cylindrically symmetric resistive steady state with a reversal in $B_{z(r)}$.) The cross field particle diffusion takes place on a still longer time scale of order $\beta^{-1}a^2/D$ parallel/. (These estimates are valid provided β eta/ sub perpendicular to/ << eta/sub parallel/.)

31579 (LA—8944-C, pp 34-38) **Plasma power balance of a pulsed RFP reactor.** Christiansen, J.P.; Roberts, K.V. Jan 1982. NTIS, PC A14/MF A01.

From Reversed field pinch theory workshop; Los Alamos, NM, USA (28 Apr 1980).

A preliminary study was made of the power balance of a reactor plasma with variable plasma parameters. Some of the conditions for ignition by Ohmic heating and plasma stability are examined. The reactor configuration corresponds to the design by Lawson of an RFP reactor which will be referred to as the PRFPR (pulsed RFP reactor).

31580 (LA—8944-C, pp 75-78) **Progress on RFP stability problems** ince the **Padua workshop.** Robinson, D.C. (Culham Lab., Abingdon, England). Jan 1982. NTIS, PC A14/MF A01.

From Reversed field pinch theory workshop; Los Alamos, NM, USA (28 Apr 1980).

Both linear and non-linear stability problems associated with cylindrical RFP equilibria have been investigated.

order and is not assumed to be small. This solution of the Vlasov equation is a generalization of the method used by Cayton and Lewis for studying stability and RF heating of a sharp-boundary screw pinch. In the present work, in addition to not restricting the size of ω/ω sub ci/ and the parallel streaming derivative, the equilibrium profiles are allowed to be diffuse. The dispersion differential equation is obtained by substituting the approximate solution of the ion Vlasov equation into the perpendicular component of the Maxwell del x B equation (the pressure balance equation) without further approximation. The final form of the dispersion differential equation is an equation for the Laplace transform of the electron fluid displacement.

31584 (LA—8944-C, pp 93-96) **Low-frequency microinstabilities in cylindrically symmetric systems with arbitrary β and strong magnetic shear.** Linsker, R. (Princeton Univ., NJ). Jan 1982. NTIS, PC A14/MF A01.

From Reversed field pinch theory workshop; Los Alamos, NM, USA (28 Apr 1980).

The microstability analysis of low-frequency modes ($\omega << \Omega$/sub ci/) in magnetically sheared systems with arbitrary β is of particular relevance to reversed-field pinch theory. A method is described for the practical calculation of such modes in cylindrical geometry, with particular attention to the strongly sheared case. It is also shown that in the electrostatic sheared-slab limit, some recent integral-equation analyses gives incorrect results for the drift eigenmode when the shear and density gradient scale lengths are comparable (L/sub s/ ~ L/sub n/).

Fig. 13-3. Indexing and abstracting service: U.S. DOE, *Energy Research Abstracts*

COMPENDEX | The Computerized Engineering Index data base covers international engineering literature from over 3,000 publications, including all fields and disciplines of engineering.

Prepared by Engineering Information, Inc.

Coverage: Jan 1970 to present
File size: 1,015,881 records
Unit record: citation, abstract
Vendor, Cost/connect hour:
  BRS, $54-$68;
  CAN/OLE, $40 plus royalty;
  DIALOG (8), $80;
  SDC, $95

Fig. 13-4. Computer data base: COMPENDEX

theses, and monographs originated by the United States Department of Energy, its laboratories, energy centers, and contractors. Also included are reports from federal and state government organizations, foreign governments, domestic and foreign universities, and research organizations. Emphasis is on nonnuclear energy, as nuclear energy is the primary emphasis of *INIS Atomindex.* Arrangement is in broad subjects by a classified scheme, for example, coal and coal products, petroleum, and materials, and items are listed with full bibliographic information and an abstract. Indexes in each issue and cumulated semiannually and annually are by corporate author, personal author, subject, DOE contract number, and report number.

Energy Abstracts (New York, Engineering Index, 1974–   ) is published monthly. Information is taken from the data base for *Engineering Index,* with energy-related materials from several external data base sources added, to form a multidisciplinary service covering such areas as energy sources, production, transmission, distribution, utilization, conservation, and conversion. Full bibliographic information and an abstract are given for each item.

Some indexing and abstracting services cover specialized areas of the energy field. One of these is *Solar Energy Index; the Arizona State University Solar Energy Collection* (New York, Pergamon, 1980–   ), which is a printed index to the library collection, with annual additional volumes planned. Over 10,000 items dating from the late 1800s to 1979 are included in the first, basic, volume, including books, jour-

DOE ENERGY DATA BASE | DOE ENERGY DATA BASE provides comprehensive coverage of the field of energy from 1974 to date, relatively comprehensive coverage from 1965 to 1974, and some coverage from 1940. Emphasis is on coal and alternative energy sources, with lighter coverage of petroleum. Includes government reports, journal articles, books, special studies, and some patents. This file is expected to be online on DIALOG by March 1982.

Prepared by U.S. Department of Energy, Technical Information Center (TIC). Direct questions on file content to TIC.

Coverage: 1974 to present
File size: 775,000 records
Unit record: citation, abstract
Vendor, Cost/connect hour:
  BRS, $22-$36;
  DIALOG (103), $35;
  SDC, $45

Fig. 13-5. Computer data base: DOE ENERGY DATA BASE

nals articles, government documents, patents, and other materials dealing with energy. Arrangement is alphabetical by author and by subject in one alphabetical sequence. Information given is brief, and one must consult a key at the front of the volume to decipher the "call number" into bibliographic information. Examples of other specialized services are *Petroleum Abstracts* (Tulsa, Okla., University of Tulsa, 1961–), published weekly, and *Coal Abstracts* (London, International Energy Agency, IEA Coal Reasearch, n.d.–).

SECONDARY LITERATURE MATERIALS

Encyclopedias

The *McGraw-Hill Encyclopedia of Energy* edited by Sybil P. Parker (New York, McGraw-Hill, 2d edition 1981) is a one-volume encyclopedia. The first section is on energy perspectives, and includes overviews of about ten pages each by a different author, on energy conservation, exploring energy choices, risk of energy production, energy consumption, outlook for fuel reserves, and protecting the environment. The second part is on energy technology, arranged alphabetically by topic, with brief articles usually of one to three pages. Appendixes include measurement systems, conversion factors, and energy-related publications. References are included with each article, and there are many illustrations throughout.

World Energy Book: An A–Z Atlas and Statistical Source Book (New York, Nichols, 1978) is a reference guide to energy sources, terminology, economics, and factors related to the search for, extraction, production, and utilization of sources of energy, both major and alternative. The main section is arranged alphabetically by topic, with brief articles of about 100 words. Many diagrams and tables are used. An energy resources atlas section consists of thirty-four maps that provide detailed information on such things as location of oil and gas, and so forth. The statistical appendixes include tables of information and conversion charts.

Resources

Summaries of energy resources for the world from the World Energy Conference appear in *World Energy Resources, 1985–2020; Executive*

Summaries of Reports to the Conservation Commission (Guildford, England, and New York, IPC Science and Technology Press, 1978). Topics covered are worldwide petroleum supply limits, future for world natural gas supply, appraisal of world coal resources and their future availability, hydraulic resources, contribution of nuclear power to world energy supply, unconventional energy resources, energy conservation, and world energy demand. Each article includes discussion, as well as data presented in tables and graphs. The full text of these reports is published in several volumes: *World Energy Resources 1985–2020; Full Reports to the Conservation Commission* (Guildford, England, and New York, IPC Science and Technology Press, 1978). The first volume of this set deals with renewable energy resources, including unconventional energy sources and hydraulic resources; volume 2 with oil and gas resources, including worldwide petroleum supply limits, and the future for world natural gas supply; volume 3 with nuclear resources; volume 4 with coal resources; and volume 5 with world energy demand to 2020. Each paper is made up of discussion and statistics.

Technology

The *Handbook of Energy Technology* by V. Daniel Hunt (New York, Van Nostrand Reinhold, 1982) is based on reports by the United States Department of Energy. It contains an overview of energy technology, and then has sections on fossil energy; solar, geothermal, electrical, and storage systems; fission energy; nuclear waste management; and magnetic fusion. Federal energy policy and planning data are discussed, as well as energy technology program trends and perspectives, regional and environmental effects of certain energy programs, and international efforts. Many photographs, drawings, charts, and tables are used to illustrate and present data. A reference information section at the back of the book contains a glossary of terms and of abbreviations and acronyms, an extensive bibiography, and units, symbols, and conversion factors.

The Intersociety Energy Conversion Engineering Conference *Proceedings* is published annually by various sponsoring societies, for example, the American Chemical Society or the American Society of Mechanical Engineers. Each of these annual conferences is on a theme, for example, 1980: "Energy to the 21st Century"; 1981:

"Technologies for the Transition." Papers are by different authors, most with references, and usually make up several large volumes. The Energy Technology Series of the Ann Arbor Science Publishers is made up of volumes on individual sources of energy. These volumes provide clear, concise information on technology for solar, gasohol, wood, biogas, wind, coal, hydrogen, hydroelectric, geothermal, and ocean thermal energy.

The *Handbook of Energy Audits* by Albert Thumann (Atlanta, Ga., Fairmont, 1979) defines and describes energy audits, which are designed to determine where a building or plant facility uses energy to identify energy conservation opportunities. There are guidelines of how to perform an audit. Several case studies are included, each by a different author and on a different type of audit: educational facilities, hospitals, government buildings, and food service facilities.

There are many books on each type of energy. We next discuss a selection of those on solar energy and wind energy, areas chosen because they seem to be areas of widespread interest, about which concerned laypersons may especially want information to put to practical use in their homes.

Solar Energy

Solar Energy by Donald Rapp (Englewood Cliffs, N.J., Prentice-Hall, 1981) is intended as a textbook for undergraduate engineers, or a book for others including do-it-yourselfers who want to learn about solar energy applications. The book begins with a review of patterns of energy use and resources in the United States and the place of solar energy. It then presents basic background information on solar geometry, solar intensities, flat plate collectors, and economics; information on applications of solar energy in a domestic hot water system and in heating; heat pumps; solar air cooling; storage techniques; and solar total energy system. Many examples are used throughout, and diagrams, tables, and graphs help make the presentation clear. Appendixes include tables of climatic data and thermodynamic properties of moist air. There is an index. *Principles and Applications of Solar Energy* by Paul N. Cheremisinoff and Thomas C. Regino (Ann Arbor, Mich., Ann Arbor Science, 1979) aims to present an overview of major aspects of solar energy technology in an easy-to-read form. Areas covered are the history of solar energy, solar energy availability, thermal collection devices, thermal solar energy applications, photovoltaic generation of electricity, energy from wind, ocean thermal gradient power, chemical conversion of solar energy, biological conversion of solar energy, and a look at the future. Appendixes include a glossary, tables showing insolation on inclined surfaces, mean daily insolation maps, and conversion factors. There is a bibliography.

The *Solar Energy Handbook* by Jan F. Kreider and Frank Kreith (New York, McGraw-Hill, 1981) attempts to collect into one volume data and procedures for solar system assessment and design, current as of the preparation date of the handbook. Arrangement is in sections, with several chapters by different authors in each section, each with a list of references. The main sections are perspective and basic principles, solar-thermal collection and conversion methods, low-temperature solar conversion systems, solar high temperature and process heat systems, and advanced and indirect solar conversion systems, the book ending with a section covering architecture, economics, the law, and solar energy. Appendixes include a glossary of abbreviations and symbols.

Solar Energy in America by William D. Metz and Allen L. Hammond (Washington, D.C., American Association for the Advancement of Science, 1978) deals with strategies of research, capturing sunlight, collector systems, wind power, energy storage, and ocean thermal energy. There are tables of solar supply projections, and a bibliography. A directory of available solar collectors, with manufacturers, is included.

Solar Energy; Fundamentals in Building Design by Bruce Anderson (New York, McGraw-Hill, 1977) covers fundamentals of solar energy in buildings. Topics included are an introduction to solar energy and how it has been used; designing buildings for solar use; heat collection and storage and retrofitting buildings; solar hot water; systems for indirect use of solar energy, for example, solar cooling, solar collectors, auxiliary heating, and so forth; and energy and solar energy phenomena. Many photographs and diagrams are used to illustrate. The appendixes contain design information, including conversion factors, degree days and design temperatures, and insulating values of materials. There is a bibliography several pages in length. *Solar Engineering for Domestic Buildings* by William A. Himmelman (New York, Dekker, 1980) covers basic concepts, emphasizing the practical aspects of solar energy. Topics included are space heaters, domestic hot water units, pool heaters, cooling systems, greenhouses, windmills, biogas generators, and wood-burning alternatives. There is also information on how to select an appropriate lot or how to retrofit existing buildings. The appendix contains a glossary of solar terms, climatic information, radiation and other data, and directory of solar suppliers.

Author John H. Keyes has written the *Consumer Handbook of Solar Energy for the United States and Canada* (Dobbs Ferry, N.Y., Morgan and Morgan, 1979) to enable the potential consumer of solar equipment to make educated judgments in this area. The book includes an introduction to solar energy equipment and information on making a home an energy-efficient passive solar heating system, selecting a dealer, determining the size of solar equipment needed, and how to determine potential fuel saving. There is also a ranking of how efficient and practical the use of solar energy would be in different locations in the United States and Canada. For this ranking, the author assumes the same house is placed in each of 342 cities. Appendixes include tables of information for making determinations of needs and so forth, a list of deceptive practices in the solar energy industry, and rules to follow when shopping for solar equipment.

Daniel J. O'Connor's *101 Patented Solar Energy Uses* (New York, Van Nostrand Reinhold, 1981) represents only about 5% of all patented solar energy inventions, chosen to give a broad overview of solar uses. Each invention is illustrated by a drawing with a brief description and name of invention, inventor, and patent number. *How to Make Your Own Solar Electricity* by John W. Stewart (Blue Ridge Summit, Pa., TAB, 1979) is a survey of existing technology. *Your Solar Energy Home; Including Wind and Methane Applications* by Derek Howell (Oxford and New York, Pergamon, 1979) is clearly written and practical. *Practical Solar Heating Manual with Blueprints for Air and Water Systems* by DeWayne Coxon (Ann Arbor, Mich., Ann Arbor Science, 1981) includes an introduction to solar energy, passive and active solar systems, and Jordan systems. *Fundamentals of Solar Heating* by Richard Schubert and L. D. Ryan (Englewood Cliffs, N.J., Prentice-Hall, 1981) is a textbook that includes the economics of solar heating, solar insolation, calculating heating loads, solar storage, distribution systems, applications, swimming pool heating, and more. *Passive Solar Retrofit; How to Add Natural*

Heating and Cooling to Your Home by Darryl J. Strickler (New York, Van Nostrand Reinhold, 1982) is a practical guide intended for homeowners.

Sources of further information may be found in *Sun Power; a Bibliography of United States Government Documents on Solar Energy* compiled by Sandra McAninch (Westport, Conn., Greenwood, 1981); *Solar Energy for Domestic Heating and Cooling* by A. Eggers-Lura (New York, Pergamon, 1979), which is an international bibliography of current and retrospective literature; and *Solar Energy in Developing Countries* by A. Eggers-Lura (New York, Pergamon, 1979), which includes general information on solar energy activities of interest for developing countries, state of the art, and sources of literature and information, with an extensive bibliography with abstracts.

Wind Energy

In *Windpower* (New York, Van Nostrand Reinhold, 1981) author V. Daniel Hunt aims to present an overview of wind energy in one comprehensive reference book. The book begins with a discussion of wind energy use in the United States, and its historical development. Then topics covered are wind characteristics and their impact; fundamental operation of wind energy conversion systems; aerodynamics in wind power; towers and systems installation; energy conversion and storage; the federal wind energy program; commercialization on small and large scales; environmental, institutional, and legal barriers; international development; and the future of wind power. References are included with each chapter, and there is a bibliography. This handbook ends with a glossary of terms and of abbreviations and acronyms, a directory of manufacturers, and reference information including monthly kilowatt-hour usage chart for various home appliances, conversion factors, and monthly average windpower in U.S. and Canadian locations. *Wind Power: Recent Developments* (Park Ridge, N.J., Noyes, 1979) aims to present most of the important developments in wind power technology in the United States in recent years. After an overview and history, topics covered include a synthesis of national wind energy assessments; developments since 1975 in rotors, turbines, and applications in electric utilities, and farm use; and legal, social, and environmental issues. References are included. The appendix contains a list of manufacturers and distributors. *Wind*

Machines by Frank R. Eldridge (New York, Van Nostrand Reinhold, 2d edition 1980) is a survey of the present status of wind machines that might be used to meet future energy needs in the United States. Also included are possible applications of wind machines, siting problems, performance characteristics, system designs, and future utilization. Appendixes include a glossary and a list of manufacturers or suppliers. There are references and an extensive bibliography.

Wind Energy by Tom Kovarik and others (Chicago, Domus, 1979) gives background, theory, and many practical do-it-yourself ideas. Included are a history of wind power, wind characteristics in general and in some specific countries of the world, site selection, generation of electricity by wind power, and energy storage. The book has a bibliography and a list of other sources of information through organizations and government agencies, a directory of suppliers, and a section on equipment that gives information on some specific components. *The Wind Power Book* by Jack Park (New York, Van Nostrand Reinhold, 1981) is for do-it-yourselfers building their own wind power system or buying it. Topics covered include wind-generated electricity, and the use of windmills for water pumping, mechanical power, water heating, and home heating. Many photographs and diagrams are used to illustrate. Some reference information is included, such as average wind speeds at selected locations through the United States. Another practical guide is *Putnam's Power From the Wind* by Gerald W. Koeppl (New York, Van Nostrand Reinhold, 1981).

Periodicals

Applied Energy. Essex, England, Applied Science, 1975– . (bimonthly)

Energy Action Weekly. Washington, D.C., Capital Services, 1976– . (weekly)

Energy Conversion and Management. New York, Pergamon, 1961– . (quarterly)

Energy Digest. Washington, D.C., Resources News Service, 9, 1970– . (semimonthly)

Energy Engineering, Association of Energy Engineers. New York, Fairmont, 1904– . (bimonthly)

Energy Insider. Washington, D.C., U.S. Department of Energy, 1977– . (semimonthly) (free)

Energy Management. Cleveland, Ohio, Penton-IPC, n.d.– . (6/ year)

Energy News. Dallas, Tex., Energy Publications, 1970– . (biweekly)

Energy Sources; an International Interdisciplinary Journal of Science and Technology. New York, Crane, Russak, 1973– . (quarterly)

Energy Systems and Policy; an International Interdisciplinary Journal. New York, Crane, Russak, 1973– . (quarterly)

Geothermal Energy. Camarillo, Calif., Geothermal World, 1973– . (monthly)

Home Energy Digest and Wood Burning Quarterly. Minneapolis, Minn., Investment Rarities, 1976– . (quarterly)

Institute of Energy Journal. London, Institute of Energy, 1927– . (quarterly)

Journal of Energy Resources Technology. New York, American Society of Mechanical Engineers, 1979– . (quarterly)

Monthly Energy Review. Washington, D.C., U.S. Energy Information Administration, 1974– . (monthly)

Solar Age: A Magazine of the Sun. Harrisville, N.H., Solar Vision, 1976– . (monthly)

Solar Energy: The Journal of Solar Energy Science and Engineering. New York, Pergamon, 1957– . (monthly)

Solar Engineering Magazine. Dallas, Tex., Solar Engineering Publications, 1976– . (monthly)

Weekly Coal Report. Washington, D.C., U.S. Energy Information Administration, n.d.– . (weekly)

Wind Power Digest. Bristol, Ind., Jester Press, 1974– . (quarterly)

Wind Technology Journal. Washington, D.C., American Wind Energy Association, 1977– . (quarterly)

Wood 'N Energy. Concord, N.H., New Hampshire Times, 1980– . (monthly)

CURRENT AWARENESS MATERIALS

Weekly Government Abstracts: Energy (Springfield, Va., National Technical Information Service, 1973–) is published weekly to announce publications produced as part of completed or ongoing government contract research in the area of energy. A complete bibliographic citation is given for each item, and an abstract.

Several current awareness services sponsored by the U.S. Department of Energy are published by the National Technical Information Service, Springfield, Virginia. Each is issued monthly, and each contains indexing and abstracts of current literature in the subject area of its title. These are:

Current Energy Patents
Energy and the Environment
Fossil Energy Update
Fusion Energy Update
Geothermal Energy Update
Solar Energy Update

The *Monthly Energy Review* (Washington, D.C., Energy Information Administration, 1974–   ) is published monthly to provide current data and statistics on energy. Information is given on current data and trends for U.S. energy production, consumption, stocks, imports, exports, and prices; international production of crude oil and production of electricity from nuclear energy; and consumption of petroleum products. Information is given mostly in tables and graphs, very clearly presented and labeled, with sources of information cited. Some issues include a feature article, for example, "Interstate and Intrastate Natural Gas Markets."

QUICK REFERENCE TOOLS

Dictionaries

The *Energy Dictionary* by V. Daniel Hunt (New York, Van Nostrand Reinhold, 1979) contains brief definitions of about 4,000 terms on all aspects of energy, including acronyms. There is also a bibliography.

Foreign equivalents are given in *Standard Terms of the Energy Economy; a Glossary for Engineers, Research Workers, Industrialists, and Economists* edited by E. Ruttley for the World Energy Conference (New York, Pergamon, 1978). Languages are English, French, German, and Spanish.

Handbooks

The *Energy Factbook* by Richard C. Dorf (New York, McGraw-Hill, 1981) is made up mostly of graphs and tables of information with some explanation and photographs and diagrams. Aimed at the lay-person, information covers fossil fuels, alternate sources of energy, and policy matters. Arrangement is in sections by general topic, for example, energy and society, projections of energy consumption, coal, transportation, and so forth. There is a glossary. The *Energy Handbook* by Robert L. Loftness (New York, Van Nostrand Rein-hold, 1978) is made up mostly of data in table and graph form, with explanations. Areas covered include energy and man, fossil and min-eral energy resources, renewable energy resources, energy consump-tion trends and projections, recovery of fossil fuels, nuclear power, geothermal energy, solar energy, energy conversion and storage, energy efficiency and conservation, energy transport, environmental aspects and control, energy costs, and energy futures. The appendixes include a glossary and a table of energy conversion factors.

Energy Technology Handbook edited by Douglas Considine (New York, McGraw-Hill, 1977) contains concise information with many tables and graphs. Sections, written by many different contributors, cover coal, gas, petroleum, chemical fuels, nuclear energy, solar energy, geothermal energy, hydropower, and general power technol-ogy trends. References are included with each section.

Directories

The *Energy Directory* (New York, Environment Information Center, 1974) lists U.S. organizations and agencies concerned with energy: federal bureaus, congressional committees, state government agen-cies, trade associations, professional associations, and citizens' associations. Organizations and agencies are listed with brief informa-tion as to energy interests, address and phone number, and key per-sonnel. Indexing is alphabetical by names of organizations and agen-cies, and by subject, standard industrial classification code, and geographic location. This directory is kept up to date by *EIC Energy Directory Update* (New York, Environment Information Center, 1974–   ), issued bimonthly. The same brief information is given in these directories, including address and phone number, purpose, pub-lications, and key personnel. *Energy: Sources of Print and Nonprint Materials* edited by Maureen Crowley (New York, Neal-Schuman, 1980) lists professional and trade associations, educational organiza-tions, consumer groups, businessess, research centers, and government agencies. Information for each includes purpose or activity, publications, and services.

Federal Energy Information Sources and Data Bases by Carolyn Bloch (Park Ridge, N.J., Noyes, 1979) is a directory of where to locate energy data in the U.S. government structure. It includes cabinet departments, administrative agencies, congressional offices, and related centers and agencies. Information given for each describes libraries and information centers, data bases, and special services and publications.

World Energy Directory (London, Longman, distributed by Detroit, Mich., Gale, 1, 1981–) is a worldwide guide to nonatomic energy research. Institutes, companies, and so forth are listed.

Appendix

LIBRARIES

Following is a list of libraries in the United States that have major collections in science and technology, in most cases approximately 500,000 volumes or more. Sources used in compiling this list were *Directory of Special Libraries and Information Centers,* (Detroit, Mich., Gale, 6th edition 1981), *Subject Directory of Special Libraries and Information Centers* (Detroit, Mich., Gale, 4th edition 1977), and *Brief Guide to Sources of Scientific and Technical Information* by Saul Herner (Arlington, Va., Information Resources, 2d edition 1980).

Battelle-Columbus Laboratories
505 King St.
Columbus, Ohio 43201

Carnegie Library of Pittsburgh
4400 Forbes Ave.
Pittsburgh, Pa. 15213

Cleveland Public Library, Science and Technology Department
325 Superior Ave., N.E.
Cleveland, Ohio 44114

Cornell University Libraries
Ithaca, N.Y. 14853

Engineering Societies Library
345 E. 47th St.
New York, N.Y. 10017

Georgia Institute of Technology, Library
225 North Ave., N.W.
Atlanta, Ga. 30332

Harvard University Libraries
Cambridge, Mass. 02138

Iowa State University Library
Ames, Iowa 50011

John Crerar Library
35 W. 33rd St.
Chicago, Ill. 60616

Library of Congress Science and Technology Division
John Adams Building Room 5116
Washington, D.C. 20540

Linda Hall Library
5109 Cherry St.
Kansas City, Mo. 64110

National Agricultural Library
see U.S. Department of Agriculture

National Library of Medicine
Bethesda, Md. 20209

Naval Observatory, Matthew Fontaine Maury Memorial Library
34th Street and Massachusetts Ave., N.W.
Washington, D.C. 20390

New York Public Library, Science and Technology Research Center
Fifth Ave. and 42nd St.
New York, N.Y. 10018

Ohio State University Libraries
Columbus, Ohio 43210

U.S. Department of Agriculture, Technical Information Systems Library
10301 Baltimore Blvd.
Beltsville, Md. 20705

U.S. Department of the Interior Natural Resources Library
18th and C Sts., N.W.
Washington, D.C. 20240

U.S. Geological Survey Library
National Center
Reston, Va. 22092

University of California, Berkeley, Libraries
Berkeley, Calif. 94720

University of California, Los Angeles, Libraries
Los Angeles, Calif. 90024

University of Illinois Libraries
Urbana, Ill. 61801

University of Michigan Libraries
Ann Arbor, Mich. 48109

University of Minnesota Libraries
Minneapolis, Minn. 55455

University of Texas at Austin Libraries
Austin, Tex. 78712

Yale University Libraries
New Haven, Conn. 06520

Regional Medical Libraries:

Kentucky-Ohio-Michigan Regional Medical Library Program
Wayne State University Medical Library
4325 Brush St.
Detroit, Mich. 48201

Mid-Atlantic Regional Medical Library
National Library of Medicine
8600 Rockville Pike
Bethesda, Md. 20014

Midcontinental Regional Medical Library Program
University of Nebraska Medical Center
42nd St. and Dewey Ave.
Omaha, Nebr. 68105

Mid-Eastern Regional Medical Library Service
College of Physicians of Philadelphia
19 S. 22nd St.
Philadelphia, Pa. 19103

Midwest Health Science Library Network
John Crerar Library
35 W. 33rd St.
Chicago, Ill. 60616

New England Regional Medical Library Service
Francis A. Countway Library of Medicine
Harvard University
10 Shattuck St.
Boston, Mass. 02115

New York and New Jersey Regional Medical Library
New York Academy of Medicine Library
2 E. 103rd St.
New York, N.Y. 10029

Pacific Northwest Regional Health Sciences Library
Health Sciences Library
University of Washington
Seattle, Wash. 98195

Pacific Southwest Regional Medical Library Service
Center for the Health Sciences
University of California
Los Angeles, Calif. 90024

South Central Regional Medical Library Program
University of Texas Health Science Center
5323 Harry Hines Blvd.
Dallas, Tex. 75235

Southeastern Regional Medical Library Program
A. W. Calhoun Medical Library
Emory University
Atlanta, Ga. 30322

UNITED STATES GOVERNMENT DEPOSITORY LIBRARIES

Auburn University at Montgomery Library
Documents Department
Montgomery, Ala 36193
(205) 279-9110

University of Alabama Library
Documents Dept., Box S
University, Ala. 35486
(205) 348-6046

Department of Library, Archives and Public
Records
Third Floor, State Cap.
Phoenix, Ariz. 86007
(602) 255-4035

University of Arizona Library
Government Documents Dept.
Tucson, Ariz. 85721
(602) 626-4871

California State Library
Government Pub. Section
P.O. Box 2037
Sacramento, Calif. 95809
(916) 322-4572

University of Colorado Library
Government Pub. Division
Boulder, Colo. 80309
(303) 492-8834

Denver Public Library
Government Pub. Department
1357 Broadway
Denver, Colo. 80203
(303) 573-5152

Connecticut State Library
Government Documents Unit
231 Capitol Avenue
Hartford, Conn. 06115
(203) 566-4971

University of Florida Libraries
Library West
Documents Department
Gainesville, Fla 32601
(904) 392-0367

University of Georgia Libraries
Government Reference Dept.
Athens, Ga 30602
(404) 542-8949

University of Hawaii Library
Government Documents Collection
2550 The Mall
Honolulu, Hawaii 96822
(808) 948-8230

University of Idaho Library
Documents Section
Moscow, Idaho 83843
(208) 885-6344

Illinois State Library
Information Services Branch
Centennial Building
Springfield, Ill. 62756
(217) 782-7597

Indiana State Library
Serials and Documents Section
140 North Senate Avenue
Indianapolis, Ind. 46204
(317) 232-3678

University of Iowa Libraries
Government Pub. Department
Iowa City, Iowa 52242
(319) 353-3318

University of Kansas
Document Collection, Spencer Library
Lawrence, Kans. 66045
(913) 864-4662

University of Kentucky Libraries
Government Pub. Department
Lexington, Ky. 40506
(606) 257-2639

Louisiana State University Library
BA/Documents Department
Middleton Library
Baton Rouge, La. 70803

Louisiana Technical University Library
Documents Department
Ruston, La. 71272
(318) 257-4962

University of Maine
Raymond H. Fogler Library
Documents Depository
Orono, Maine 04469
(207) 581-7178

University of Maryland
McKeldin Library, Documents Division
College Park, Md. 20742
(301) 454-3034

Boston Public Library
Government Documents Department
Boston, Mass. 02117
(617) 536-5400, Ext. 295

Detroit Public Library
Sociology Department
5201 Woodward Avenue
Detroit, Mich. 48202
(313) 833-1000

Michigan State Library
P.O. Box 30007
735 E. Michigan Avenue
Lansing, Mich 48909
(517) 373-0640

University of Minnesota
Government Pub. Division
409 Wilson Library
Minneapolis, Minn. 55455
(612) 373-7813

University of Mississippi Library
Documents Department
University, Miss. 38677
(601) 232-7091, Ext. 7

University of Montana
Mansfield Library
Documents Division
Missoula, Mont. 59812
(406) 243-6700

Nebraska Library Comm.
Federal Documents
1420 P Street
Lincoln, Nebr. 68508
(402) 471-2045

University of Nebraska–Lincoln
D. L. Love Memorial Library
Documents Division LL201N
Lincoln, Nebr. 68508
(402) 472-2562

University of Nevada Library
Government Pub. Department
Reno, Nev. 89557
(702) 784-6579

Newark Public Library
Social Services Division
5 Washington Street
Newark, N.J. 07102
(201) 733-7812

University of New Mexico
Zimmerman Library
Government Pub. Department
Albuquerque, N.Mex. 87131
(505) 277-5441

New Mexico State Library
Reference Department
P.O. Box 1629
Santa Fe, N.Mex 87503
(505) 827-2033

New York State Library
Empire State Plaza
Albany, N.Y. 12230
(518) 474-5563

University of North Carolina
   at Chapel Hill Library
BA/SS Division Documents
Chapel Hill, N.C. 27514
(919) 933-1151

North Dakota State University Library
Government Documents Department
Fargo, N.Dak. 58105
(701) 237-8886

(in cooperation with)

University of North Dakota
Chester Fritz Library
Documents Department
Grand Forks, N.Dak. 58202
(701) 777-4646

State Library of Ohio
Documents Department
65 South Front Street
Columbus, Ohio 43215
(614) 466-9511

Oklahoma Department of Libraries
Government Documents
200 N.E. 18th Street
Oklahoma City, Okla. 73105
(405) 521-2502

Oklahoma State University Library
Documents Department
Stillwater, Okla. 74078
(405) 624-6546

Portland State University Library
Documents Department
P.O. Box 1151
Portland, Oreg. 97207
(503) 229-3673

State Library of Pennsylvania
Government Pub. Section
P.O. Box 1601
Harrisburg, Pa. 17105
(717) 787-3752

Texas State Library
Public Service Department
P.O. Box 12927
Austin, Tex. 78711
(512) 475-2996

Texas Tech. University Library
Government Documents Department
Lubbock, Tex. 79409
(802) 742-2268

Utah State University
Merril Library, U.M.C. 30
Logan, Utah 84321
(801) 750-2682

University of Virginia
Alderman Library, Public Documents
Charlottesville, Va. 22901
(804) 924-3133

Washington State Library
Documents Section
Olympia, Wash. 98504
(206) 753-4027

West Virginia University Library
Documents Department
Morgantown, W.Va. 26506
(304) 293-3640

Milwaukee Public Library
814 West Wisconsin Avenue
Milwaukee, Wis. 53233
(414) 278-3000

State Historical Library of Wisconsin
Government Pub. Section
816 State Street
Madison, Wis. 53706
(608) 262-4347

Wyoming State Library
Supreme Court and Library Building
Cheyenne, Wyo. 82002
(307) 777-7281

NASA INFORMATION CENTERS

Aerospace Research Applications Center
1201 East 38th Street
Indianapolis, Ind. 46205

Kerr Industrial Applications Center
Southeastern Oklahoma State University
Durant, Okla. 74701

NASA Industrial Applications Center
701 LIS Building
University of Pittsburgh
Pittsburgh, Pa. 15260

NASA Industrial Applications Center
University of Southern California
Denney Research Building
University Park
Los Angeles, Calif. 90007

NASA/Florida State Technology Application Center
State University System of Florida
500 Weil Hall
Gainesville, Fla. 32611

NASA/UK Technology Applications
 Program
University of Kentucky
109 Kinkead Hall
Lexington, Ky. 40506

New England Research Applications Center
Mansfield Professional Park
Storrs, Conn. 06268

North Carolina Science and Technology
 Research Center
Post Office Box 12235
Research Triangle Park, N.C. 27709

Technology Applications Center
University of New Mexico
2500 Central Avenue, S.E.
Albuquerque, N.Mex. 87131

U.S. PATENT DEPOSITORY LIBRARIES

Because of variations in scope of patent collections and in their hours of service to the public, it is advisable to call the library before using the patent collection.

State	Name of Library	Telephone Contact
Alabama	Birmingham Public Library	(205) 254-2555
Arizona	Tempe: Science Library, Arizona State University	(602) 965-7607
California	Los Angeles Public Library	(213) 626-7555 Ext. 273
	Sacramento: California State Library	(916) 323-4572
	Sunnyvale Patent Library	(408) 736-0795
Colorado	Denver Public Library	(303) 573-5152 Ext. 222
Delaware	Newark: University of Delaware	(302) 738-2238
Georgia	Atlanta: Price Gilbert Memorial Library, Georgia Institute of Technology	(404) 894-4519
Illinois	Chicago Public Library	(312) 269-2814
Louisiana	Baton Rouge: Troy H. Middleton Library Louisiana State University	(504) 388-2570
Massachusetts	Boston Public Library	(617) 536-5400 Ext. 265
Michigan	Detroit Public Library	(313) 833-1450
Minnesota	Minneapolis Public Library & Information Center	(612) 372-6552
Missouri	Kansas City: Linda Hall Library	(816) 363-4600
	St. Louis Public Library	(314) 241-2288 Ext. 214, 215
Nebraska	Lincoln: University of Nebraska-Lincoln, Engineering Library	(404) 472-3411
New Hampshire	Durham: University of New Hampshire Library	(603) 862-1777
New Jersey	Newark Public Library	(201) 733-7814
New York	Albany: New York State Library	(518) 474-5125
	Buffalo and Erie County Public Library	(716) 856-7525 Ext. 267
	New York Public Library (The Research Libraries)	(212) 790-6291
North Carolina	Raleigh: D. H. Hill Library, N.C. State University	(919) 737-3280
Ohio	Cincinnati & Hamilton County Public Library	(513) 369-6969
	Cleveland Public Library	(216) 623-2870
	Columbus: Ohio State University Libraries	(614) 422-6286
	Toledo/Lucas County Public Library	(419) 242-7361 Ext. 258

Oklahoma	Stillwater: Oklahoma State University Library	(405) 624-6546
Pennsylvania	Philadelphia: Franklin Institute Library	(215) 448-1321
	Pittsburgh: Carnegie Library of Pittsburgh	(412) 622-3128
	University Park: The Pennsylvania State Libraries	(814) 865-4861
Rhode Island	Providence Public Library	(401) 521-7722 Ext. 224
Tennessee	Memphis & Shelby County Public Library and Information Center	(901) 528-1957
Texas	Dallas Public Library	(214) 748-9071
	Houston: The Fondren Library, Rice University	(713) 527-8101 Ext. 2587
Washington	Seattle: Engineering Library, University of Washington	(206) 543-0740
Wisconsin	Madison: Kurt F. Wendt Engineering Library, University of Wisconsin	(608) 262-6845
	Milwaukee Public Library	(414) 278-3043

PERMISSIONS

Sewell quote on p. vii: Reprinted with permission from page 2 from
Guide to Drug Information by Winifred Sewell published by Drug Intelligence Publications, Inc., 1241 Hamilton, IL 62341.

Figures 2-1 and 2-3: Photo courtesy of DIALOG Information Services,
Inc. Databases taken from Database Catalog, August 1982, courtesy of
DIALOG Information Services, Inc.

Figure 3-1: Reprinted from ULRICH'S INTERNATIONAL PERIODICALS
DIRECTORY with permission of the R.R. Bowker Company, 1180 Avenue
of the Americas, New York, New York 10036. Copyright 1981 by
Xerox Corporation.

Figure 3-2: General Science Index copyright © 1982 by the H.W. Wilson
Company. Material reproduced by permission of the publisher.

Figure 3-3: Reprinted from American Men and Women of Science, Physical
and Biological, 15th edition, with permission of R.R. Bowker. Copyright
© 1982 by Xerox Corporation.

Figure 4-2: Reprinted with permission from CRC Handbook of Tables for
Mathematics, 4th edition. Copyright The Chemical Rubber Co., CRC Press,
Inc.

Figure 6-1: Reprinted with permission of INSPEC, The Institution of
Electrical Engineers. Copyrighted 1982. All rights reserved.

Figure 7-1: Reprinted with permission from Current Contents®/Physical,
Chemical and Earth Sciences, 22(23):119, 7 June 1982. Copyright 1982
by the Institute for Scientific Information®, Philadelphia, PA, USA.

Figure 7-2: Reprinted with permission from CRC Handbook of Chemistry
and Physics, 61st edition. Copyright The Chemical Rubber Co., CRC Press,
Inc.

Figure 10-1: Reprinted with permission from Dictionary of Plants Used
by Man by George Usher published by Hafner Press, New York.

Figure 10-2: Reprinted from The Complete Trees of North America with
permission from Book Division, Times Mirror Magazines, Inc., 380 Madison
Avenue, New York, NY 10017

Figure 12-1: Copyright © 1982 Physicians' Desk Reference, published by
Medical Economics Co., Inc., Oradell, NJ 07649.

Figure 13-1: Applied Science and Technology Index copyright 1982 by the
H.W. Wilson Company. Material reproduced by permission of the publisher.

Figure 13-2: Copyright, American Society for Testing and Materials,
1916 Race Street, Philadelphia, PA 19103. Reprinted, with permission.

Index